Madonna: Like an Icon

Also by Lucy O'Brien

Dusty

Annie Lennox

She Bop I

She Bop II

MADONNA
Like an Icon

Lucy O'Brien

HarperEntertainment
An Imprint of HarperCollins*Publishers*

HarperCollins books may be purchased for educational, business, or sales promotional use. For information please write: Special Markets Department, HarperCollins Publishers, 10 East 53rd Street, New York, NY 10022.

FIRST EDITION

B
MADO

Designed by Lovedog Studio

Library of Congress Cataloging-in-Publication Data has been applied for.

ISBN: 978-0-06-089896-0
ISBN-10: 0-06-089896-8

07 08 09 10 11 OT/RRD 10 9 8 7 6 5 4 3 2 1

To Malcolm, Erran, and Maya

and

Dorothy O'Brien

(1906–1951)

CONTENTS

INTRODUCTION

I FIRST BECAME A FAN OF MADONNA IN 1985. I REMEMBER one evening going into my friend's bedroom, where she was watching TV. "What's on?" I asked, plonking myself next to her. "It's Madonna doing her show," she replied. "Oh no." I nearly walked out again. For me, Madonna was that cheesy pop bimbo in Lycra, writhing on a Venetian gondola for the "Like a Virgin" video. "No, wait a minute," my friend said. "She's actually quite good. Quite funny. There's something about her that's really attractive."

I carried on watching. And within minutes, I got it. The woman who came across as a desperate starlet on *Top of the Pops* had a whole other dimension. In fact, the video of her Like a Virgin tour was the first time that many people understood what was so engaging about her. She had a warm, ebullient energy. She spoke directly to her female audience. She had a pudgy midriff and she didn't care. She smiled a lot, winked at the crowd, and invited you to share in the joke. And her music—beats-driven, danceable, and fused with melodic sass—was very appealing.

She sparked my interest with the Like a Virgin tour, and when the film *Desperately Seeking Susan* came out, she won me over. Here she played a cheerful, street-smart, devil-may-care woman. She wasn't just another manufactured icon; she was herself. Madonna then went through many changes of image—from the peroxide vamp of the mid-80s *True Blue* era, to the smells, bells, and dark-haired mysticism of *Like a Prayer*. To a former Catholic girl, the latter was inspiring. Seeing the Blond Ambition tour, with its enormous cathedral nave and a penitent Madonna, stopped my heart.

Then there was the commercial glitz of the *Dick Tracy* movie, and the decadent elegance of 1990s "Justify My Love" video, directed in black-and-white in an anonymous Parisian hotel by Jean-Baptiste Mondino. There was the sheer joy of "Vogue," the soundtrack to a summer of dancing, before the revelations of her *Sex* book and the *Truth or Dare* documentary. She once said, "I'd rather be on people's minds than off," but by 1992, this became a challenge even for her most devoted fans.

Yet I still admired her adventurousness, her fearlessness, and the way she championed in her work alternative cultures and ways of being—whether it was the S&M lesbians of the *Sex* book, her convincing pastiche of gay disco in *Confessions on a Dance Floor*, or kissing a black Christ full on the lips in the "Like a Prayer" video. Madonna has always done this with an eye on mainstream appeal—with her starring role in the film *Evita*, for instance, she turned herself into a more conventional Hollywood-style icon. After she became a mother, it seemed like the rebellious days were over and she had settled down, but then she came up with the boldly experimental textures of the 1998 *Ray of Light* album and *Music*, released in 2001. With these records she won her first Grammy Awards, and was finally accepted by the rock crowd as a serious artist.

SINCE THE 1988 Who's That Girl tour, I have seen Madonna's every live show, and watched her develop as an artist. I've also followed her personal life with interest, seeing many parallels with my own. We are from the same generation. Like her, I was a lapsed Catholic girl fired up by feminism. I played in an all-girl band and knew the thrill of performing. Like her, I was drawn to punk and the underground club scene. Like her, I focused on my career until I met and married my partner later in life. Like her, I had two children (a boy and a girl) after I turned forty. In many ways, her story is typical of my generation—feminism made us brave, yet, despite the freedom we fought for, there was still intense conflict between work and motherhood.

In her music and art, Madonna says a lot about what it means to be a woman in today's world. She puts it in popular terms and packages it to the hilt, but it strikes a chord every time. As a music writer who has focused on female artists, I have always found her fascinating. Her singularity resonates with me. She doesn't have the vocal greatness of Billie Holiday and Ella Fitzgerald, and she hasn't seared a generation with raw rock 'n' roll, like Janis Joplin or Patti Smith, but she is a towering presence in popular music because of her breathtaking range. Like a cultural magpie, she has picked her influences from thousands of sources and funneled them into one vision. That, in itself, is a work of art.

"I am the work of art. I am the art. *Je suis l'art,*" Madonna once said to Sebastien Foucan, hero of the French *parkour* (the physical art of overcoming obstacles) movement, and a key dancer on her Confessions tour. In the focus on her provocative media image, what truly motivates Madonna as an artist and musician has been overlooked. "There are very talented singers who hire a producer, expect them to do all the work, sing the songs three times in the studio, and go home. Madonna is *not* one of those artists," says Guy Sigsworth, a producer on her futuristic, millennial album *Music.* "She's very intimately involved in the whole creative process, as a collaborator and producer. That side is ignored by people so fixated on her image. With all those hit songs, it can't just be twenty years of great hair."

That music—combined with an odd, luminous beauty, compelling energy, and highly theatrical shows—has made Madonna a quasi-religious icon. Dubbed the "Immaculate Conception" by actor friend Rupert Everett, she commands a kind of mass worship. "Her [eyes] were the palest blue, strangely wide-set; any further and she would look insane or inbred. When they looked in your direction, you froze," he said about the first time they met in the 1980s. "In no way was she conventionally beautiful. She was a bit like a Picasso . . . there was an energy field around her, like a wave, that swept everyone up as it crashed into the room."

Madonna the pop star appeared as a challenging twentieth-century image of an ancient icon. Where the traditional Virgin symbolized modesty and purity, this Madonna preached sexual empowerment *and* spirituality. To writer Camille Paglia, she "has rejoined and healed the split halves of women: Mary, the Blessed Virgin and Holy Mother, and Mary Magdalene, the harlot." Songwriter Tori Amos agrees, saying: "I believe that the joining of the themes 'Madonna' and 'Virgin' and sex was the rebooting of the historical Madonna computer. It represented a major sexual awakening for Christian girls—Catholic girls, Protestant girls, Mormon girls, Baptist girls—bring 'em on. The significance of a female called Madonna singing the words 'Like a Virgin' could not be downplayed, nor could the effect of little girls around the world singing along with her."

IT HAS often been asked, who is the "real" Madonna? The popular negative stereotype is that of a publicity-hungry, manipulative ball-breaker, while for many women, she is a beacon of feminism. I have always found her work clear and autobiographical, but her personality complex and disarmingly changeable. Having written biographies of the artists Dusty Springfield and Annie Lennox, and a history of women in popular music, I have always wanted to get to the heart of Madonna's motivations. She is, after all, the best-selling female artist of all time, with over 200 million albums sold throughout the world and fifty-eight top ten U.K. hit singles.

Ever since her "Like a Virgin" days, I had been building up my own personal Madonna archive, and in 2005 I started writing a book about her. I wanted to look at her life and work as she was approaching fifty—what kind of issues would this bring up? How had she managed thus far to create and maintain an aesthetic that people of all generations responded to? What *was* she really about? Perplexed by the contradictory personae—vamp, lady of the manor, Kabbalah crusader, female shaman—I was searching for a way to understand her. Madonna was more than a postmodern collection of symbols. She was a flesh-and-blood woman, but her shifting identity made her a puzzle.

Whenever I have been faced with this conundrum, I always go back to the songs. Music leaves a psychic imprint. In recorded sound there is the artist's world and the artist's mind. Using that as my starting point, I listened to Madonna's music and found a compelling story. Whether it was the layers of Catholic liturgy in *Like a Prayer*, or the dark depths of *Erotica*, or the shimmering trance of *Confessions on a Dance Floor*, where Madonna's voice has just become a texture in the music, she was on a personal journey. Sometimes she was in denial, or she was living a melodrama, but often through music she was confronting pain and searching for joy.

I wanted to find out more about how she constructed this journey, and, in so doing, went on one of my own. I went from state-of-the-art recording studios to an apartment in Hornsey, North London, where Doug Wimbish and the post-punk Tackhead crew still hang out. I drove around old haunts in Michigan with a woman who went to school with Madonna, and wandered the windy streets of Detroit. I interviewed directors by swimming pools in L.A., and traveled to New York to meet former friends and collaborators. I walked in Wiltshire fields and trod the plush interior of the Kabbalah HQ in London. I talked to dancers, choreographers, musicians, and producers—people who had all worked with Madonna. Along the way, I thought about my own Catholic background and my grandmother, who died young after having six children. I thought about what it means to be a woman of a particular generation, born into the first decade of feminism and punk and gay liberation. And what it means to come to motherhood late, and how having a girl makes you militant about wanting to get it right this time.

My search for Madonna became maddening. I kept getting two stark pictures of her: there was the woman who was ruthless in moving on and rude to the competition. And there was a woman that I'd never seen before—sweet, childlike, and captivating. "When she's in a public place and anywhere she's being looked at, she's very steely and kind of puts up a wall. She seems imperious, like she's acting the star," Madonna's friend, the director James Foley told me. "But when she gets home and takes off her coat, it's as if she takes off her personality. Her accent even changes from fake Brit to native Detroit." If it was simply a case of public versus private, that would be understandable. But Madonna shifts between the two in a more complex way. It took me a long time to figure it out, right to the end of writing the book.

In interviews Madonna comes across as guarded and studied, as if, as Norman Mailer once remarked, "she is playing secretary to herself." The famous sense of humor that so many collaborators mention is not much in evidence. She can be this way with friends, and even dances around husbands and lovers with an intricate push-pull game. But many people who have worked with Madonna talk about her warmth and easy, earthy manner. Is she two different people? It wasn't until I saw footage of her in rehearsals for the Confessions tour that the penny dropped. She looked relaxed and happy. Her face was devoid of makeup, and her clothes casual, but you could tell that every cell of her body was alive and consumed by the process of performance.

The only place where she seems truly herself is when she is doing her work. Away from that she can be self-conscious, status-conscious, everything-conscious. Only in performance are those layers stripped away and it's just her. For the moment that she is caught up in the creative process, she forgets herself. Madonna is the sum of all her influences in a given moment. She pulls those influences in—whether it's from cinema, club culture, literature, or visual art—and lets them move through her body. She reacts to the world, first and foremost, as a dancer, processing and expressing all the information that comes her way. And when it comes out, it isn't haphazard, chaotic, or open-ended. In Madonna's world, it is tied to an aesthetic that she has kept near and clear all her life.

Like all the significant divas, Madonna feeds her life into her work. From the childhood Catholicism to her mother's death to that terrible sexual attack in New York to the white-hot anger of the *Sex* years to the salvation she found as a mother, Madonna's life *is* her work, her reason for existence. In 2006 she was at the center of headlines worldwide when she adopted the thirteen-month-old baby, David Banda, from an orphanage in Malawi. Her action sparked off an intense debate—whether she was motivated by a social conscience or her own selfish desires. Stung by the hailstorm of criticism, Madonna said privately: "I haven't been this hated since I brought out my *Sex* book in the early 90s. What have I done to deserve this?"

Her style is confrontational, her ambition unbound, yet she constantly, compulsively turns her life into fascinating pop art. As her old boyfriend producer Steve Bray said: "Her most effective trait was to have her completely dominate you and for you to somehow enjoy the experience." Madonna has become a goddess of our age, and an icon that we have all created. This is her story.

Lucy O'Brien
London, 2007

Book One
BAPTISM

THE DEATH OF
MADONNA

JUST NORTH OF DETROIT IS THE SUBURB OF PONTIAC. Now a depressed area, back in Madonna's day it was a thriving manufacturing town servicing Detroit's huge automobile industry. Rising up by the highway is a cavernous bubble-shaped structure called the Silverdome. It was built in 1970s for Detroit's football team, but since the Lions moved downtown in 2002, it's been more or less abandoned. In its heyday, it hosted the NBA All-Star games and welcomed such rock bands as Led Zeppelin and The Who. In January 1987, Pope John Paul II celebrated a mass there.

Just across the road from the Silverdome is a small working-class neighborhood. Here Madonna spent her early childhood, at 443 Thors Street, in a modest, pale green single-story house. When I arrived there in 2006, it had a worn, dilapidated air, as if the ghosts hadn't quite left the building. Back in the early 1960s it would have been filled with children. It was Madonna's parents' first house, the place where they started their married life and where their eldest daughter first hatched her adventurous dreams.

"My grandparents came from Italy on the boat . . . [they] spoke no English at all. They weren't very educated, and I think in a way they represented an old lifestyle that my father really didn't want to have anything to do with," Madonna once said. Her grandfather Gaetano Ciccone came from Pacentro, a small village in the Abruzzo region of Italy. He came from a family of peasant farmers, but was encouraged to go to school and broaden his opportunities. In 1920, there was no work for this ambitious teenager, so he left for America, and made his way to Aliquippa, a steel town just outside Pittsburgh. After finding a job working on the blast furnace floor, he brought from Italy his young wife, Michelina di Ulio. They lived in a rented one-bedroom house near the steel mill, and raised six sons, five of whom worked at the mill. The youngest, Madonna's father, Silvio (also known as Tony), was the only one fortunate enough to go to college.

The Ciccones found being an immigrant family tough: there was considerable prejudice against the new wave of European immigrants, particularly Italians, who often came from impoverished backgrounds and were vulnerable to exploitation in the non-unionized mills.

Gaetano worked hard and got into politics. Spurred on by the historic National Labor Relations Act of 1935, which recognized unions, he helped organize a brief but crippling strike at the Aliquippa mill in the summer of 1937, which led to an improvement in the lives of the workers. Madonna later inherited that sense of justice with her inclusive politics and her open support of the Democratic Party. In the early 1990s, for instance, she filmed a public service announcement for the U.S. Rock the Vote campaign, a movement cofounded by MTV, which led to a 20 percent increase in youth turnout in the 1992 election that ushered in President Clinton. And in the wake of the 2003 Iraq War, Madonna was vocal in her opposition to George Bush, urging her fans to go and see Michael Moore's controversial documentary Fahrenheit 9/11. In 2004 she endorsed Wesley Clark's Democratic nomination for the U.S. presidential election with the impassioned statement: "The future I wish for my children is at risk." Then, two years later, she expressed support for Hillary Clinton's campaign for the presidency.

Though she hasn't been as politically active as other major artists, such as Bono or Peter Gabriel, Madonna has campaigned for years on issues like safe sex and AIDS awareness, and has always opposed discrimination, whether on the grounds of race or sex. As a daughter of second-generation immigrants, she was keenly aware of social marginalization.

Her grandfather Gaetano was a strong disciplinarian, who managed to provide for his large family, but daily life was a struggle. The strain showed in his addiction to drink, a habit that took hold after he began making his own homemade wine. Madonna has said that both her paternal grandparents were alcoholics, a factor that played a part in her more abstemious attitude toward drink and drugs. Although the Italian community in Aliquippa was close-knit, it was also restrictive, with women expected to be little more than mothers and homemakers. And higher education, with its threat to traditional values, was treated with a degree of suspicion.

Studious and devout, Tony decided to break free from the restraints of his background. "He wanted to be upwardly mobile and go into the educated, prosperous America," Madonna once told *Time* magazine writer Denise Worrell. "I think he wanted us to have a better life than he did when he was growing up." After a stint of military service in Texas in the U.S. Air Force, in 1952, he returned home to Pennsylvania to get a degree in engineering at Geneva College, a Catholic institution in Beaver Falls. He had a long-term plan. The previous year he had met Madonna Fortin, the younger sister of his air force friend Dale Fortin. Tony was invited to Dale's wedding at a small chapel on the Goodfellow Air Force Base in Texas, where they worked. The seventeen-year-old Madonna was maid of honor. A quiet beauty with wry wit and a gentle smile, she descended from pioneering French-Canadian stock—generations of farmers and lumberjacks who worked the land with a pragmatic, determined outlook. Her father, Willard Fortin, was a top manager in a Bay City construction company, and together with her mother, Elsie, raised their eight children to be pious Catholics. "She was very beautiful," remembered Madonna. "I look like her. I have my father's eyes but I have my mother's smile and a lot of her facial structure."

It wasn't just Madonna Sr.'s beauty that attracted Tony to her, but the fact that she came from a similar hardworking ethnic Catholic background. Both had high ideals and a strong attachment to family. They began courting almost immediately, Tony making the lengthy round trip from Pennsylvania to Bay City as often as he could. A windy town on Lake Huron, near the border with Canada, Bay City was once a center of the logging industry. By the time Madonna Fortin was born, the lumber barons had moved on and the sawmills were nearly gone, to be replaced by the fishing industry. Life there was slow and quiet, like Tony and Madonna's three-year long-distance relationship. They got married after Tony's graduation on July 1, 1955, at the Visitation Church in Bay City. After starting a job as a defense engineer with Chrysler, he moved with his new wife to Pontiac, near Detroit.

Very soon after their wedding, Madonna Sr. became pregnant, and their first child, Anthony, was born on May 3, 1956. Martin arrived a year later on August 9, and the following year, on August 16, 1958, their first daughter, Madonna Louise, was born while the parents were vacationing in Bay City. This little triumvirate was at the center of Ciccone family life: Madonna Jr. had a competitive relationship with her two elder brothers, and together they vied for their parents' attention, a factor that is present in the combative, mocking way that Madonna sometimes treats her men. "I was considered the sissy of the family, because I relied on feminine wiles to get my way," Madonna said. "My older brothers . . . picked on me, and I always tattled on them to my father." It has taken years for these sibling rivalries to be resolved, and even now there is an uneasy truce. Had Madonna Sr. lived longer, maybe the family dynamics would have been less polarized. By 1959, Madonna lost her status as the only girl, when her sister Paula was born. Christopher arrived in 1960 and Melanie in 1962. By then a shadow hung over the family. Although the Fortins and the Ciccones put on a brave face, pretending that it was business as usual, Madonna Sr. was dying.

WHILE PREGNANT with her youngest daughter, Melanie, Madonna Sr. was diagnosed with breast cancer. Many blamed it on her work as an X-ray technician. The protective lead-lined apron that is now obligatory was then rarely used. Treatment had to be delayed until after Melanie was born, but by then it was too late. Madonna Sr. struggled on for another year, spending more and more time in a hospital. The children were farmed out to relatives, and the times when their mother was at home, she was too exhausted to give them the nurturing they needed.

For five-year-old Madonna Jr., just becoming aware of herself and her place in the world, this was an intensely bewildering experience. As the eldest daughter, she had a strong sense of independence, yet also a deep need to be noticed. She was always challenging her parents, even as a child. Madonna remembers her mother cleaning compulsively, kneeling in the kitchen, scrubbing the floor. "She was always picking up after us. We were really messy, awful kids. I remember having these mixed feelings," said Madonna. She spoke of loving her mother but being confused at the lack of boundaries. "I think I tortured her. I think little kids do that to people who are really good to them. They can't believe they're not getting yelled at . . . so they taunt you. I really taunted my mother."

The more her mother's energy ebbed away, the more the little Madonna tried to physically summon it back. There was one oft-quoted memory of her ailing mother trying to rest on the sofa and Madonna beating her on the back, desperate to get a response. Her anger faded when she realized her mother was crying. "I remember feeling stronger than she was. I was so little and I put my arms around her and I could feel her body underneath me sobbing and I felt like she was the child." This was a critical moment. Scared by her mother's frailty, Madonna would develop a lifelong aversion to weakness. "I knew I could be either sad and weak and not in control, or I could just take control and say it's going to get better."

Despite her lax discipline with the children, Madonna Sr. was a trooper. She was remembered as "forgiving and angelic." A former dancer and lover of classical music, she had grace, poise, and considerable quiet inner strength. She laughed and joked with her children whenever possible, tried to keep up with the housework, and pretended nothing was wrong; but the strain showed. She spent a year going in and out of the hospital. Then, on December 1, 1963, nine days after the assassination of President Kennedy, she slipped away. She was only thirty years old.

In her teenage years Madonna read Anne Sexton, and discussed with her sisters how much the Pulitzer Prize–winning poet looked like Madonna Sr. Sexton's poetry resonated with her, no doubt because of its intense exploration of life, art, and death. Like many of the women Madonna admires, from Sylvia Plath to Virginia Woolf and Frida Kahlo, Sexton had a troubled life, fighting depression and inner torment. And, like the work of these women, her work was highly personal, often autobiographical, and laced at times with gallows humor. Sexton committed suicide in 1974, after publishing eight collections of poetry that combined beat style with high-art Romanticism and a graphic sense of the emerging feminism. Her economy of language and unflinching look at death in poems such as "Madonna," which was about the death of Sexton's mother from cancer, would surface later as an influence on Madonna's later albums. But in the early 1970s, to a teenage girl missing her mother and looking for answers, Sexton's poetry just offered a strange kind of solace.

Madonna Sr.'s funeral was held in 1963 at the Visitation Church in Bay City, the same church where she had gotten married eight years previously. She was laid in an open casket, decked out like an angel. Only one thing was askew. Her mouth, as Madonna remarked many years later, "looked funny." When she got closer and peered at her mother's face, she saw that Madonna Sr.'s lips had been sewn together. This nightmarish image was to haunt her for years to come, and it was one she appeared to have later captured on the somber black-and-white video for "Oh Father." After her death, Madonna Sr. was symbolically silenced. The angel of the house, the humble martyr, could never again speak her truth, could never tell her daughters what her life was really like, could never grow old with them, could never mature and in that maturing show her fallibility, her doubts and insecurities as well as her wisdom. Instead all that was preserved were a few precious photographs, some enigmatic Super 8 film of family occasions, and a pristine memory of perfection that could never be tarnished. For Madonna Jr., her mother's perceived purity was a standard that was also impossible for her to live up to.

No wonder Madonna's work is littered with allusions to secrecy and the need for disclosure, with urgent exhortations to speak out and express oneself. "I hardly said a word, I couldn't stop her talking," remembers Pet Shop Boys vocalist Neil Tennant, who interviewed her as a *Smash Hits* journalist in the early 1980s. Many friends remark on her garrulousness, her need to verbalize what she is wrestling with at any given moment. In interviews she is articulate, wordy, sometimes using words as a shield to protect herself from people she accuses of trying to "rape [her] soul."

Madonna's journey through songwriting started here. First, as a former boyfriend and DJ Mark Kamins says, through "nursery rhymes" that projected the artful innocence of her five-year-old self, a Dionysian celebration of loving and dancing, a world populated by angels and heroes. Then there was the searching, rebellious phase, the questions about religion, sex, and erotica; and then there was the movement toward spiritual transformation, political doubt, and a new kind of transcendence. The restlessness, however, would never be resolved.

Madonna's life has been set up in opposition to her mother's. If her mother's silence meant death, then she would speak out. If her mother's illness meant sleep was dangerous, because one could die in her sleep, well, then, she would stay awake. If her mother's body failed her, Madonna would make sure she was in peak physical condition. She chose dance, not just as her primary means of expression but also as a way of exhibiting physical strength and stamina, feeling alive and rooted in the present. "Sometimes I just assume I'm going to live forever," she once declared. "I don't want to die. It's the ultimate unknown. I don't want to go to the dark beyond." She avoided drugs and alcohol, because anything that tranquilized the spirit was a mini-death, a threat to her being focused and "knowing where everything is." A friend suggests that Madonna doesn't reflect. "She just doesn't do it. She has no interest in what she did last week, let alone ten years ago. It's accomplish one thing, then on to the next."

Madonna has talked about "growing up fast" after her mother's death, and learning to rely on no one but herself. According to the groundbreaking psychologist John Bowlby, "the most frightening characteristic of a dead animal or a dead person is their immobility. What more natural, therefore, for a child who is afraid he may die than for him to keep moving." He also identified "overactivity and . . . compulsive self-reliance" as a disorder that often develops after childhood bereavement.

At odds with this picture, though, was the grief-stricken five-year-old who became agoraphobic, who couldn't leave the house without being physically sick, who stayed close to her father, almost clinging to him for comfort. "For five years after she died, I dreamed every night of people jumping on me and trying to strangle me," she once said. Madonna also became what Bowlby termed a "compulsive caregiver," looking after her younger siblings and replacing her mother as the next little mother of the household. For as long as her father remained a widower, grieving and single, she could continue under the illusion that she now fulfilled that crucial role. In later years, she acted that part with her dancers, proclaiming that she was mother to them all, a common instinct with choreographers keen to keep their company intact and working as a team.

A succession of housekeepers were employed to keep the Ciccone tribe in check. But like the governesses dispatched by the Von Trapp family in *The Sound of Music*, or those repelled by the children in *Nanny McPhee*, they never lasted more than a few months. That was until the disciplined but devoted Joan Gustafson arrived. Until then, a bereaved Tony Ciccone had retreated and buried himself in his work, struggling to keep his young family together. Like the traditional Victorian patriarch, he couldn't do it on his own—he needed a woman to nurture his six motherless children. Joan coaxed him out of his shell, and within six months the two were married. At the age of eight, Madonna was usurped. On top of losing her mother, she was abandoned by her father, the person with whom she felt she had a special relationship.

From that point, she began to develop a tough emotional edge. You can see it in the family pictures: a prepubescent Madonna, long brown hair cascading to her waist, one hand placed possessively on her father's arm, looking uncertain, haunted, into the camera. Uncertainty dogged her, but anger replaced the earlier sadness. She rebelled against her stepmother, Joan, refusing to call her "Mom" and flouting her rules. In her mother's death, Madonna found a curious kind of liberation. "I think the biggest reason I was able to express myself and not be intimidated was by not having a mother. Women are traditionally raised to be subservient, passive . . . the man is supposed to be the pioneer. He makes the money, he makes the rules. I know that . . . my lack of inhibition comes from my mother's death," she once said. "For example, mothers teach you manners. And I absolutely did not learn any of those rules and regulations."

Madonna did not grow up with a constant model of motherhood, but in the end, that gave her an alternative way of looking at the world. In 1976, the feminist poet Adrienne Rich wrote: "Mother stands for the victim in ourselves, the unfree woman, the martyr." In her flawless devotion to her religion and her family, Madonna Sr. provided a model of selflessness. "Catholicism is a very masochistic religion. And I saw my mother doing things that really affected me. She was passionately religious, swooning with it," Madonna remembered.

Madonna Sr. had been influenced by Jansenism, an interpretation of Catholic doctrine formulated in the seventeenth century by the Dutch theologian Cornelius Jansen. A product of the Reformation, it was Catholicism with a Puritan streak, marked by an austere, pessimistic view of life. According to theologian Richard McBrien: "It promoted the theory of predestination and a morally rigorous style of Christian life . . . Since Original Sin has so radically corrupted human nature, everything purely natural is evil. Grace is given only to the few." It was popular in France, becoming a key part of the training of many priests, and was transplanted with the immigrant population to French-speaking Canada. "Much of pre–Vatican II U.S. Catholicism's obsession with sexual morality," continues McBrien, "and its relatively narrow eucharistic piety (e.g., infrequent reception of Communion and then only after 'going to Confession') has been linked . . . to this Jansenist influence."

Much has been made of Madonna's Italian Catholic background, but her mother's French side is just as strong. French Catholicism is a defining force, a source of energy for worldwide Catholicism. Her mother's faith was about living a life of holiness, with a daily examination of conscience. The theory of Original Sin is that one is born with alienation from God, and a believer has to work his or her way back to God through daily prayer. For Madonna Sr., every day was, in a sense, working toward her death, as the quality of her passing was dependent on how she lived her life. Her devotional practice—whether it was stringent fasting, kneeling on rice, or sleeping on coat hangers—involved pain and perseverance. Though Madonna Sr. nurtured her young family with kindness and compassion, she also did so with a stringent sense of self-discipline, assuming her mothering role with the seriousness of a vocation.

"My mother was a religious zealot," Madonna said later. "There were always nuns and priests in my house growing up. I don't know how curious my mother was, how much she pushed to know what was going on behind the curtain, and that's my personality—I want to know what's going on behind what I can see . . . my mother was certain she was doing the right thing, so maybe we have that in common." As a small girl, Madonna imbibed this holy atmosphere. On the Good Friday before Easter her mother would cover up all the religious pictures and statues in the house with purple cloth. "Until Christ rose from the dead. I thought it a bizarre ritual but quite beautiful," Madonna said. She was also aware of her mother covering up the Sacred Heart statues when a woman once came in wearing jeans. Much later Madonna referenced this image with a close-up of the crotch of her denim jeans on the cover of her 1989 *Like a Prayer* album. The jeans also appeared with a working zipper on a limited edition of the single "Express Yourself." In her mother's day, jeans amounted to sacrilege. According to the doctrine of Enthronement, having a Sacred Heart image was like having a priest in your home. As religious writer Joseph P. Chinnici suggests, "It's a central act, the placement of the picture of the Sacred Heart in a prominent place, accompanied by the family's commitment to pray . . . for society's apostasy, was consciously directed against the forces of divorce, ir-religious education, the violation of the sanctity of marriage, and the 'campaign against Christian standards of modesty in dress, in the press and in the movies.'"

GIRLS USUALLY begin a gradual separation from their mothers at puberty, but Madonna had to make that separation much earlier. With her mother's death, she felt psychologically free in a way that was unusual for a girl of her generation. As therapists Luise Eichenbaum and Susie Orbach argue, "When a woman gives birth to a daughter she is in a sense reproducing herself . . . Mother must prepare her for a life spent, like hers, in taking care of others. Mother, whether she is consciously aware of it or not, must also prepare her daughter to take her place in society as a second-class citizen."

A woman learns from her mother how to suppress her own needs, and passes this on to her daughter. Instead of absorbing this ambiva-lent message, the young Madonna shifted identification to her father. According to Eichenbaum and Orbach, the father is "the link to the world outside the family, and the daughter must use him as access to that world . . . Father encourages his daughter to charm him and a male audience, to attract and hold his attention in specifically defined feminine ways, as she will later need to do." Teenage girls often iden-tify with Daddy as a way of gaining independence, but for Madonna, this process started early. The "showing panties" stories are legion: At any given opportunity she would do gymnastics, show off, or flip up her skirt at the boys. She was acting out teenage anxiety before she was even a preteen. She was preparing her way in the world from the age of five, and her model—proactive, self-determining, goal-centered—was male.

ONE OF Madonna's first, primary relationships was with her audi-ence. It has been remarked that although they were very volatile, the Ciccone family "didn't seem that close." Consciously ignoring stepmother Joan, competitive with her siblings, and craving attention from her hardworking father, Madonna grew up with a deep longing to be touched. Physicality has always been important to her, not just through sex and the dynamics of relationship but also in the connection she experiences with an audience. While she performs, the audience feeds back her own pulsating energy.

She has always had an awareness of dress, of costume, of disguise. The nuns at Saint Andrew's, her Catholic elementary school, fascinated her, because they wore long, dark habits. Curious about what lay beneath these mysterious clothes, she and a friend would climb up to convent windows to spy on them undressing.

She recognized their power.

The nuns' habits were symbolic of their status as brides in mourning. When a nun took her vows, it was as if she were marrying Christ. She would lie prostrate before the altar (an image that Madonna has replicated in both her *Sex* book and her Confessions tour), as a declaration of love for the Holy Spirit. Because priests and nuns remain celibate, there is a seam of repressed sexuality in Catholicism. As a result of that repression, sexuality becomes the focus.

Early on, Madonna felt compelled to acknowledge the sexual undertow she felt in Catholic teaching. Chafing against Joan's insistence on dressing all the Ciccone girls in clothes cut from identical patterns, Madonna found ways to assert her own style—whether it was wearing tight sweaters, short skirts, and red lipstick, à la 1950s floozy, or going to church in a coat and nothing on underneath. She made it her mission to solder that connection between sex and spirituality and this was the link that she was to make in her work, over and over, for years to come.

A MAGICAL PLACE

IN 1968, MADONNA'S FAMILY MOVED FROM PONTIAC TO A bigger house in the more affluent suburb of Rochester. Her father was doing well in his career, working as an optics and defense engineer for General Dynamics. The house where she spent her teenage years was at 2036 Oklahoma Street, Rochester Hills, a colonial-style building with a generous garden surrounded by pine trees and poplars.

"Even though people thought our parents were crazy for living in Rochester, saying 'How could you live out there? All the way out there?', it was a real comfortable place to grow up," Kim Drayton told me. A woman who was at school with Madonna, she has warm memories of their hometown. "You could ride your bike three miles into town, and there was a big forest behind our subdivision that we could explore. In the summertime you'd leave in the morning and not come back till dinner. You'd have lunch at a friend's house or pack and go somewhere, ride your bike through the woods or by the fields." When Madonna was young, Rochester was a new suburb on the edge of the countryside, near dirt roads, farms, and open fields. Kim paints an idyllic picture of a close-knit community of young families: "It was a huge mixture of families. Just about everybody worked for the car companies. All the dads, I should say, as back then moms didn't work outside the home. And just about everybody went to church, and you knew everybody in the church."

Madonna's family went to Saint Andrew's church, a large concrete 1960s affair decorated with iron sculptures of Christ and vivid stained-glass windows. The car park is spacious—Drayton asserts that in its heyday, on a Sunday it would be full. The Ciccone family were regulars there, and made an impact in the neighborhood. "They were a big Catholic family. I remember her dad looking old, kind of weathered. And her stepmom, very attractive," says Kim. Her mother, Maree Cooper, worked with Joan as a teacher's aid at the elementary school. "Joan was a wonderful, wonderful girl. She had two younger ones—Jennifer, a sweet girl, and Mario, a little guy who was great with video equipment. Every time we had a problem we went to him, he was so mechanical. Joan was very concerned about her children, particularly those two," she recalls. "Whenever we needed her we could call on her. You couldn't say that for everyone." As for Madonna's father, Maree met him only once or twice. "He was a very quiet little man. Not at all like his daughter!"

The Ciccone children were a mixed bunch. According to a former classmate, Martin was "flamboyant, loud, and kind of obnoxious. He was quite over the top, and later he did try and take advantage of his relationship with Madonna." Anthony was "very smart and quiet and kept himself to himself," while Christopher, an agile dancer with a strong artistic flair, turned out to have the most in common with his famous sister. However, he was always more guarded. "I'm a very private person and not terribly gregarious. I cherish the privacy that I have and I'm sorry that she doesn't have as much," he once said. "But that's what she wanted—I don't need to be a star."

As for the girls, Paula is fiercely independent and a little more angular than her sister. "She was really nice, not as eccentric as Madonna," remembers Kim. "Madonna had the looks, she was very attractive, even way back then, but Paula was always very plain, not a lot of makeup, not being a cheerleader or anything like that." Melanie, too, had some of that Ciccone quirkiness. "She was half blonde and half brunette, and I remember her being different . . . being, you know, just different," Kim laughs. Then there was Madonna's half brother and sister, Mario and Jennifer. As the eldest girl, Madonna was required to change nappies and help with household chores. She doesn't recall this period as being much fun. "I resented it, because when all my friends were out playing, I felt like I had all these adult responsibilities. . . . I saw myself as the quintessential Cinderella."

The children went to the same schools, moving from Saint Andrew's elementary to West Junior High, a squat, square building on Old Perch Road in Rochester. The move marked a transition in Madonna's development as a performer—she took tap and jazz lessons, and began to act in school productions. The turning point came at the age of twelve, when she shocked the audience at the school talent show by dancing to The Who's "Baba O'Reilly" wearing little more than a fluorescent body stocking. Her father was not impressed. A disciplinarian at home, he felt uneasy with his daughter appearing so publicly "out of control." Madonna's eldest brother, Martin, remembered a home life where certain values held sway. "I wouldn't call it strict, I'd call it conservative. My father was a strong believer in leadership, maintaining a competitive edge, pray, do well at school, and you will reap the rewards of your investment."

Yet although Madonna rebelled against sartorial rules and criticized the double standards that meant her brothers could get away with behavior she couldn't, she has always had a deeply conventional streak. A straight-A student (spurred on by the extra pocket money Tony Ciccone gave if one of his children had a good report card), she knew how to play the system from the start. "Bitch never had to study, man. Never. Got straight As," recalled Martin. "I studied all the time but my mind wasn't on it. I did it because I was supposed to. Madonna did it 'cause she knew it would get her on to the next phase." And maybe Tony's financial reward for achievement planted in Madonna's psyche the need to always make her art a commercial success.

In 1972 she transferred to Adams High, a large, brand-new school on the corner of Tienken and Adams, next to open fields and golf courses. It attracted higher-income families. "Kids nicknamed it the Country Club," says Drayton. "Those of us who had gone to West

Junior High divided into those who went to Adams High, and those who went to Rochester. We became rivals in all of our games. Rochester was downtown, and because of the way the boundary lines were split, the Adams area was more high-income." Here, the aspiring Madonna gained the ultimate marker of social status and acceptance by joining the cheerleading squad. It seems strange that, with her nonconformist streak, Madonna opted for such a conventional role in high school. But this combination of athletics and choreography was a physical outlet for her. It also gave her a degree of power among her peers.

"High school campuses are like little villages, and being a cheerleader is the apex of female status in that hierarchy," suggests Dr. Wendy Fonarow, writer and anthropologist at UCLA. "You can wear cute, sexy skirts that are very appealing. It's provocative dress that's socially sanctioned. Cheerleading is the high school ideal; you can use it to solidify your queen bee status. And there's prestige for guys going out with cheerleaders; it's a great way for a girl to get noticed. For the cheerleaders and football players, high school is often the best time of their lives. They're the kings and queens of their universe."

Adams High has a well-equipped mini-stadium. You walk down a slope at the side of the concrete school building to the football field at the end. Though windy and exposed, this is an atmospheric place. It feels carefully tended and well-loved, and it is easy to imagine the young teenage Madonna executing her choreographed moves here, getting her first taste of crowd adulation. "In her junior year, she looked very mainstream. She was part of the 'Kids Lend a Hand' program, where older students helped out the younger ones," recalls Kim. "A lot of those girls were cheerleaders; most of them were very smart. Now it's about the show-offs, but back then it was those who were smart, pretty, and popular. If you weren't all those things, you never tried out for cheerleading. You didn't fit, so to speak."

Madonna took part in the teenage party scene. Although she wasn't a big drinker, the social whirl revolved around alcohol. "We used to go out drinking all the time," says Kim. "Then there were still a lot of dirt roads in the area, so we'd meet at the gravel pit and bring liquor and there'd be big parties until the cops came. People would have live bands and kegs of beer at their parties. We'd pay five bucks and it was all-you-could-drink. I remember we'd rent out rooms at the Spartan Motel, and have parties there." Madonna's father observed a fairly strict curfew, however, so sometimes she had to sneak out under cover of darkness to go to a party.

Popular, sexually curious, and never short of boyfriends, Madonna lost her virginity at the age of fifteen, to a high school heartthrob, Russell Long. After a spell of long trysts in the back of his light blue 1966 Cadillac, Madonna shifted her attention to a school football player, Nick Twomey (now a reverend in Traverse City, Michigan). Both have described her as a sensitive, confused person, troubled by her family relationships. Although her outward persona was the alpha-female loudmouth, that was misleading. Because she was upfront and flirtatious, she was branded by some of her peers as a slut, but Madonna has protested that she was never promiscuous; she slept only with her steady boyfriends. Here we have a misreading that set the tone for the rest of her life's choices. On one level, she has been perceived as a shameless, publicity-hungry harlot who makes run-of-the-mill pop music. On another level, there is the thoughtful artist who turned herself into a vivid spectacle. Achievement and approval were clearly important to her, but she also cultivated a rich inner life—one that was questing and nonconformist from the start.

Like the anti-cheerleaders dressed in somber black in the Nirvana video for "Smells Like Teen Spirit," with their limp pompoms and blood-red anarchy signs on their vests, Madonna took a sudden left turn. She drifted away from the jocks to ballet, bohemianism, and existentialism. "There was a real transformation," recalls Kim. "In the sophomore year, she was a cheerleader, with smiles on her face and long hair and very attractive, then by her senior year she had short hair. She was in the thespian society, and she didn't shave her legs anymore, you know, like all of us did, and she didn't shave her armpits. Everyone was like, 'Oh, what happened to *her*?' She was popular as a cheerleader, then became very individual, so different from everybody else. She didn't smile so much and was kind of standoffish."

Wyn Cooper, a former date and close friend, remembers Madonna as one of the few students who moved between groups. "Adams High was a school that was divided between the jocks, those into sports, and the freaks, who were into smoking pot and cigarettes and not going to class. Madonna was a cheerleader, so that put her into the jock category, but she was also a free spirit and thinker, so that put her more in the freak category."

Cooper met Madonna when she was fourteen and had just transferred to Adams High. He was a year ahead of her, and quite struck by her. "She wandered around our neighborhood with a couple of other young girls, and one day came over to my house. I remember thinking, There's an interesting, pretty girl. She seemed kind of shy. We developed a friendship and hung out." He remembers their high school as being predominantly middle-class. "The school had money, so it got high-quality teachers. There was also rampant drug abuse—mainly pot, also acid and mushrooms and a lot of drinking. I had a Mercury Capri with an eight-track tape player and giant cassettes. Madonna and I would hop in the car, drive around, and listen to Ziggy Stardust and the Spiders from Mars while enjoying a little marijuana." Though Madonna said later that she wasn't interested in drugs, it seems she wasn't averse to a little teenage experimentation.

The picture he paints is at odds with the received notion of Madonna the teenager as endless feisty party girl. "She was a little bit aloof. She took herself more seriously than most of us did at that age. She kept to herself more than most, she didn't run around in cliques. She read more than your average high school student," says Cooper. "I read a book a day. School was good but it wasn't challenging for me. She'd ask me what I was reading, and I'd pass books on to her. She loved *Lady Chatterley's Lover*, and Aldous Huxley." Now an established poet and songwriter (his poem "Fun" was turned into Sheryl Crow's 1993 Grammy Award–winning song "All I Wanna Do"), Cooper impressed Madonna with his pithy poetry. "She used to say, 'When you grow up you're going to be my favorite poet.'"

Cooper saw another side to her one day. "It was really hot, so I said, 'D'you want to go skinny-dipping?' I ripped my clothes off and dove into a pond. She slowly stripped off her clothes. I was stunned. She usually wore loose-fitting clothes and didn't stand out as extraordinarily beautiful, but underneath she had a *perfect* body." Cooper dated her a few times, but their romance didn't take off, as they had more in common as friends. Once he made a short 8-mm film with her, as part of a high school project. It featured Madonna and her best friend, Carol Belanger, in bikinis by a swimming pool.

"It's a silly little film with eggs at the center of it," recalls Cooper. Madonna stands facing the camera, takes a raw egg, cracks it above her head, and lets it drip into her mouth. The camera watches as it drips down her chin between her breasts. She then lies down on the deck and Carol cracks a raw egg onto Madonna's stomach. With a quick, surreal twist, the egg is fried on the stomach. "For that shot Carol went into the house and fried an egg. I spliced the film together with Scotch tape. Suddenly a fried egg is sitting there. Carol puts salt and pepper on it and eats the egg off Madonna's stomach. I painted the closing credits across a urinal and got a friend to stand to the side and slowly piss it off. I'm very proud of it. I got an A for it in film class!"

With its subliminal hint of lesbian erotica, the film was Madonna's first foray into acting. "It was the first time she appeared in a film. It was also a film that focused on her navel—which became her logo." With Cooper, Madonna started exploring an interest in the arts that was to blossom later when she went to New York. Although she had an ease and charm popular with the "jock" section of the school, there was a side to Madonna that had yet to be expressed.

"She wasn't an overly charismatic personality. You'd *never* have guessed she'd become a world-famous pop star. That's why it was so surprising to many of us when she became big. I remember going to the store and seeing her face on an album. I thought, 'Oh my God, that's *her*. I don't believe it!' Everyone was very shocked. How did she get to be there? It seemed like such a big change," says Cooper.

Madonna the stage persona was an invention, a powerful projection fed by a childhood diet of Hollywood films, Broadway musicals, and offbeat poetry. It was as if this fermented inside her for years until she found the right outlet for her talent. "The only thing that stood out was how well she could dance," recalls Cooper. "Everyone would get out of the way and watch her. She combined The Temptations with little syncopated routines, a cross between that and modern dance and Broadway musical. Her thing was a real mishmash, but it worked." Kim Drayton, too, remembers how Madonna's true self seemed to shine on the dance floor. "She danced incredibly and so different from everyone else. It was a kind of showstopper. I remember thinking, 'Oh wow, she can dance!'"

What spurred Madonna's move from cheerleader to bohemian was ballet. By the age of fifteen, she had outgrown high school politics and popularity contests, and reached the limits of local jazz and tap classes. Looking for something more rigorous and demanding, Madonna joined an evening ballet class in a second-floor studio on Main Street in Rochester. This was where she met Christopher Flynn, thirty years her senior. He was her dance teacher, mentor, and the most important man in her life after her father.

AS SOON AS she met Christopher Flynn, her life took off. Not only did he demand from Madonna complete dedication to her craft, but he also broadened her influences, encouraged her reading and her interest in fine art. He took her to concerts and art galleries in Detroit, and they went dancing in gay clubs. "Madonna was a blank page, believe me, and she wanted desperately to be filled in," he once said. "She had a thirst for learning . . . that would not be denied."

Madonna's escapades in Detroit separated her from her schoolmates. The race riots of 1967 had left the area in turmoil. Car-manufacturing industries were beginning to pull out of the city, and there were marked social divisions. "Detroit was a no-go area in the 70s," recalls Kim. "Back then, it was, 'Black people live in Detroit' and you don't go there, you don't mix with those kind of people. My grandparents lived on Woodward Avenue, at Nine Mile, and you were never allowed to go to Eight Mile. You know, Eminem's Eight

Mile. That was the dividing line between white and black, between right and wrong."

Despite the racial prejudice that divided the city and its suburbs, there was a rich musical cross-pollination that Madonna grew up with, and which later influenced her sound. Right back to her early childhood in Pontiac, she had a strong interest in black style. She remembered dancing in backyards to Motown 45s with her black girlfriends. "None of the white kids I knew would ever do that," she said. "I wanted to be a part of the dancing . . . I had to be beaten up so many times by these little black girls before they would accept me, and finally one day they whipped me with a rubber hose till I was, like, lying on the ground crying. And then they just stopped doing it all of a sudden and let me be their friend, part of their group." Madonna's backyard dancing gave her the edge over her white schoolmates, an understanding of what was musically hip.

"Like everything else in Detroit, it goes back to the automobile, and specifically the black Southerners who migrated here in the early twentieth century and brought music traditions with them," says Brian McCollum, music critic for the *Detroit Free Press*. "It's one of the ironies of Detroit that it's considered to be one of the most segregated cities in the United States, but in the cultural sphere there has always been a mingling of black and white. You saw it with Motown, which was basically a group of black musicians and entrepreneurs catering not just to a black audience but, in a big way, to a white audience for the first time."

The automobile industry created a new, more prosperous blue-collar class, which allowed a vigorous nightlife to flourish. There was a collision of R&B and rock with white 60s and 70s artists like Mitch Ryder, Ted Nugent, and Bob Seger. "They were literally just imitating black singers. Today, Eminem and Kid Rock are obvious examples of white stars who've latched onto black music forms," McCollum adds. Because of the lack of a public transit system, people in Detroit drove everywhere in their cars, and by the 1950s radio became very important. There were numerous stations playing an eclectic range of music. "Madonna would have been exposed to that simply by being a typical Detroit-area teenager, turning on her radio after school. She would've been hearing stuff on WGLB, the big black station. It was a really vibrant place. You could kind of soak it up like a sponge."

On her trips to downtown Detroit, Madonna also became aware of gay culture, which in the early 1970s was totally taboo. "Just leaving Rochester, our safe little haven, and seeing the world in Detroit's eyes would be so different," says Kim. "And back then homosexuality wasn't even discussed." Just as Madonna's adult self was emerging at the age of sixteen, she found a gay man to make sense of her world. For a young woman raised in stultifying suburbia, negotiating her way around the straight binary gender politics of high school, the gay underground represented freedom and release. "In school I felt like such a misfit . . . I kept seeing myself through macho heterosexual eyes. Because I was a really aggressive woman, guys thought of me as a really strange girl. I know I frightened them. I didn't add up for them. They didn't want to ask me out. I felt inadequate," she said later. "And suddenly when I went to the gay club, I didn't feel that way anymore. I just felt at home. I had a whole new sense of myself."

In the mid-1970s, pre-AIDS, this subculture was buoyed up by the exuberant campaigns of the gay liberation movement. In its hedonistic pursuit of pleasure there was a theatricality and creativity that captivated her and became one of her key reference points.

The main club that Flynn took Madonna to was Menjo's. Originally a ritzy supper club where Al Capone used to take his mistress, it opened as one of Detroit's premier gay night spots in December 1974.

"It was the hottest dance club in the city. We were open seven days a week from noon to two a.m., and there were always people waiting in line," recalls one of the cofounders, Randy Frank. "Madonna used to come here and act all crazy and giddy and dance around. She was the center of attention. She didn't drink, she was just the life of the party. She was a cool chick, really outgoing. She had beautiful eyes. I remember her eyes—God, they were beautiful."

Then a classic 70s nightclub with mirrors on the wall, carpeting on the floor, and an expansive dance floor dominated by a huge mirror ball, Menjo's was a hot venue in a new era of freedom for gay men. Until the Stonewall riots in 1969, when crowds of gay and transsexual people clashed with New York City police and created a watershed moment for gay rights worldwide, homosexuals going to bars were regularly harassed and victimized. "In the 60s there was a Detroit bar called Woodward that was constantly being raided. My uncle was bailed out once a month. He'd get busted and beaten up going in and out of the bars. Young gays don't realize how good they got it now," says Frank. "When Menjo's opened in the 70s, it was still technically illegal in Michigan to promote 'sexual deviancy.' Luckily the guy next door was friendly with the police department, and so, they left us alone." Frank remembers how the disco scene "brought us out of the closet." He paints a vivid picture of a Sunday tea dance at three-thirty, packed to the gills with eight hundred people. Co-owner with Frank was a charismatic man named Michael Crawford, who ran the place "like Michigan's Studio 54, but without the promiscuity and the drugs. This bar put gayness on the map. We were legendary."

Madonna drew on its energy and danced to hundreds of disco classics there, from KC & The Sunshine Band's "That's The Way I Like It" to Earth Wind & Fire's "Twelfth of Never." She continued going there even after she left Detroit. There are mixed memories of the early Madonna. Richard Hojna, a barman at the club since 1975, says: "She was just a little girl from Rochester. That was before she was 'Madonna.' She liked to party, but none of us thought she'd be anyone special. She was just one of the crowd." To Crawford (who passed away in 1988), though, Madonna had a dynamic quality. "He was flamboyant in a classy, dignified way," remembers Frank. "'Nothing but the best for my customers,' he'd say. He'd go crazy to put on a party and make people happy. He had this energy about him. Madonna got his attention, and he got hers."

Madonna has described herself as a "gay man trapped in a woman's body," motivated by the Hollywood sirens of high camp. She once asked Christopher Flynn why he was attracted to men, saying "I wish I understood it." Even in her early student days, she was keen to tap into the gay sensibility. "Look at women like Judy Garland and Marilyn Monroe," she said. "I wish I knew what it is about them. Is it the glamour? Is it their behavior?" When Flynn suggested that it was because of their air of tragedy, something gay men as an oppressed group could identify with, Madonna scoffed: "Forget it, I could never be tragic." What she did pick up on, however, was these divas' love of extravagant artifice and heightened sense of irony.

To the teenage Madonna, Flynn was a love object, an older man who was a guide to the theatrical world she craved, safe because he was gay. "He was my mentor, my father, my imaginative lover, my everything," she has said. It made her less vulnerable to exploitation, it gave her psychic space. He created the perfect dynamic for her: career opportunities and artistic passion. She responded well to his strict regime of ballet lessons, and lapped up the freewheeling "street" education he gave her in the fine arts. It was also in the gay clubs that she discovered her own bisexual identity and yen for sexual experimentation.

DESPITE HER confident, A-student persona, Madonna felt like a misfit. Flynn was the first person who made her feel beautiful. "I knew I was voluptuous for my age, but I'd never had a sense of myself being beautiful until he told me," she said. Thanks to his attention to discipline and fine, expressive lines of ballet, she was able to find herself. "I feel superior. I feel a warrior," she declared. A dedicated teacher of dance, Flynn had a slightly sadistic edge, making his students dance until their feet bled, or pinching their thighs to make them stretch higher, or holding a sharp pencil between a dancer's throat and chin to make sure she kept her head straight. Madonna was undeterred by this—maybe her desire to create the ideal physical shape echoed her mother's own strenuous efforts at perfection.

As her artistic world opened up, Madonna withdrew from her classmates in the senior class and changed her appearance. She wore dungarees, combat boots, and no makeup. Friends were shocked at the transformation. "The wisecracks were out," remembered one. "She became almost like a gypsy," said another. Much has been made of Madonna as a postmodern icon, yet all her reference points have been resolutely modernist—from Steinbeck and Fitzgerald to Virginia Woolf and Sylvia Plath, to her predilection for narrative, psycho-analysis, and personal exploration. In the same way that she later created a succession of images, Madonna adopted the look of beat-poet bohemian, and the aloof attitude to go with it.

By 1976, she was already "outta there." As her friend Wyn Cooper says, "She, like many of us, got the hell out as soon as we could. We knew there was a bigger, more interesting world out there." Madonna was to take the work ethic of Detroit and apply it to her show-business career. "She was a product of her environment," says Brian McCollum. "I've heard people say here, 'I knew a Madonna in high school. I knew somebody who had that personality and that attitude and that vibe.'" Detroit turned out many self-motivators because, according to song-writer Gardner Cole, a native from the area, "There was nothing to do. The winters are so brutally long there, unless you're into snowmo-biling or ice-fishing there's nothing to do but stay indoors. We called it 'wood-shedding.' Like if you were into music, you'd go into a room and keep playing and playing. It's not like L.A. We didn't have a beach to hang out on. So, later on, when some of us went out West, we'd run circles around everybody, because we were much more driven."

COMBINING THAT driving energy with judicious application, Ma-donna graduated from Adams High a semester early. Backed up by Flynn, she won a dance scholarship to the University of Michigan in Ann Arbor. It was here that her horizons truly broadened. By the time she arrived at the University of Michigan, Christopher Flynn had taken up a professorship in the dance department, so he was able to continue tutoring his young protégée. A laid-back, pleasant col-lege town half an hour west of Detroit, with "dreaming spires" and alternative cafés, it was a comfortable place for her to be. One of the top colleges in the United States, it has been dubbed "the Harvard of Michigan." The dance department is part of the Performing Arts faculty, with spacious, airy dance studios. "Michigan's long tradition of academic excellence and strong technique training is sure to put its dancers on the edge of the evolution of dance," asserts Bill DeYoung, chair of the department. "It's about using your discipline of dance as your creative voice, and then finding your own way, finding your vocabulary. I mean, we want rebels. Modern dance is an art form of constant rebels."

Madonna was a typical dance student in that she had an intellectual curiosity, good time management, and was very driven. At seventeen, she cut a coltish, sassy figure. Determined to be different and follow her own rules, she would come to ballet class chewing gum and wearing a cut-up leotard held together with safety pins. "It was a punk look but really it was childish, a little girl desperate for attention," recalls one of her fellow students, Linda Alaniz. Competitive with other dancers, Madonna was disappointed if she wasn't always the best.

Madonna lived at the stately Stockbridge Hall dorm on campus, and her roommate there, Whitley Setrakian, remembered her as "brilliant, articulate, and very, very thin." Rebellious in a lighthearted way, Madonna was happy to give herself over to the discipline of dance, with two ninety-minute technique classes a day and two hours of rehearsal for college performances. Desperate to have the approval of Professor Flynn, she lived on a diet of popcorn to achieve the sylph-like body image he desired. At the start of every class, he would make students weigh in, and if they were over 115 pounds, he'd exhort them to shed the extra weight. "I'm sure at the time (Madonna) was borderline anorexic," said Alaniz. Flynn was exacting, but laced his lessons with a dry humor. "He always had a cigarette in his mouth, even when he was teaching," recalls DeYoung. "He was puckish, but wise. He had a wicked sense of humor, and those students with a more worldly sense were drawn to him and hooked into his sensibility. He'd play a character to a certain extent to shake up people's thinking."

Madonna absorbed a great deal from Flynn, but she was also inspired by the charismatic Gay Delanghe, who taught at the faculty from 1974 until shortly before her death from cancer in August 2006.

"She was a real card," remembers DeYoung. "She was a feminist who battled with the male hierarchy. She stood up for what she believed in. There was a good chemistry between her and Madonna. I've heard that Madonna appreciated her honesty, and being herself. Certainly Madonna has no trouble being herself. There's not a sense of looking for propriety. Propriety is a trap or a funnel for our consciousness."

Delanghe went to Cass Technical High School in Detroit and was classmates with Lily Tomlin and Aretha Franklin. She worked as a dancer in New York City before coming to Ann Arbor. "If there was ever an example of *indelible*," recalls another colleague, Peter Sparling, "it was the impression burned into my memory of a creature with a shock of red hair, infinitely long legs, and dagger feet as she bounded across the stage and hovered in midair." To him, Delanghe was a potent role model for young women who wanted to emulate her "strength, persistence, and defiance in the face of all odds."

Madonna responded well to her teachers, even though she found the classes "draining and demanding." She still had energy to go clubbing at night with her girlfriends Whitley (now an Ann Arbor singer called Whit Hill), Linda, and another student, Janice Galloway. They would take over the floor at such Ann Arbor clubs as the Ruvia and the Blue Frogge. It was at the latter that she met Steve Bray, a local musician who played drums on the Detroit lounge circuit. He would become a key collaborator a few years later, but then she was just hanging out and dating him, along with a few other boyfriends. Bray found Madonna, whom he once described as "a force of nature . . . not completely human," hard to pin down from the start. She liked to turn up at his gigs and dance. "I played drums in the Cost of Living band, and Madonna was one of two or three people at the venues dancing up a storm. In fact, I wondered if people came to the shows because they knew she'd be there dancing," recalled Bray.

While Madonna enjoyed her flings with men, at college she began what would become a major pattern in her life—the need to have a significant female by her side. "She embarked on what seemed to be a calculated campaign to be my friend," Whitley told writer Randy Taraborrelli. Though she enjoyed Madonna's company, Whitley found her, underneath the bravado, to be needy and emotionally fragile. Madonna relied on her a great deal, and was physically very demonstrative. They would have long talks about Madonna's dead mother, and Whitley felt her roommate was still mourning. Madonna was not simply looking for a mother substitute; it was as if she needed to envelop herself in female energy, at some level to be taken care of by a woman.

Not surprisingly, one of her key frames of reference was the woman-centered artist Martha Graham. Born in 1893 in Pennsylvania, Graham "was to modern dance what Pablo Picasso was to modern art." She was the heroine of a movement that originated in the early 1900s, when dancers like Isadora Duncan and Ruth St. Denis rebelled against the rigid constraints of classical ballet with their own expressionistic interpretation of dance. Peter Sparling, who danced with Martha Graham in the early 70s, recalls how "she saw a challenge in herself to break me so that I didn't dance to the music but that I assumed her mythic dimensions and personas that she created in her works . . . There was an eloquence and a poeticism about the way she spoke and the way she used images. Later on she could still generate this fierce visceral heat even as she was sitting in her director's chair all shriveled up and arthritic."

DESCRIBING DANCE as "the hidden language of the soul," Graham looked for new ways of expressing emotion, and incorporated natural human actions, such as walking, running, and skipping. Ballet moves were seen as fossilized and unreal. As dance writer Deborah Jowitt says, "It was not natural to live on tiptoe and turn out 180 degrees." Inspired by psychoanalysis, Freud, and Jungian theories of the unconscious, Graham drew on rich literary metaphor for her pieces—the poems of Emily Dickinson, for instance, or the writings of the Brontë sisters. She delved into her Puritan ancestry and American history, Greek myth and twentieth-century cinematography, to express something essential about American womanhood. For Madonna, this form of dance had an immediate, instinctive appeal. To a Catholic girl from the suburbs, it was exhilarating, female-centered, and free.

Her other main influence was Alvin Ailey, a black choreographer from a small town in Texas, who combined modern dance with ballet and African tribal dance. From the 1950s to his death in 1989, Ailey's repertory company toured the world, acting as a kind of repository for black American choreography. His most famous work, *Revelations*, features gospel and rock 'n' roll, and movements that are athletic, assured, and "as broad as California." He saw dance as a democratizing force: "I don't believe in the elitist philosophy where [people] believe that classical dance is beyond them. I always wanted to have the kind of company that my family in Texas could relate to; people on farms or the ghettos," he once said. "We're still building audiences in the United States. We're trying to convince people that dance is for everybody. It should always be given back to the people."

Ailey influenced a new generation of black choreographers, from the dark, expressive pieces of Pearl Lang to Twyla Tharp, whose work spanned Broadway musicals, movies, and modern dance. When Madonna went on to tear up those dance floors in New York, she wasn't doing the latest disco shuffle. She was a whirling dervish of all her influences: "In the nightclub I was all over the place, I combined everything. Street dance, modern dance, a bit of jazz and ballet. I was Twyla Tharp, I was Alvin Ailey, I was Michael Jackson. I didn't care, I was free," she said. In her stage shows, she was to return again and again to those influences, using Graham's style as her lodestone, and assembling her dancers with the same multicultural awareness as Ailey. "The dance floor was quite a magical place for me," she said later. "The freedom that I always feel when I'm dancing, that feeling of inhabiting your body, letting yourself go, expressing yourself through music. I always have thought of it as a magical place."

The 1970s was a prolific, experimental time for contemporary dance, and Madonna was eager to place herself right into its center. In 1977 she won a scholarship to dance with the Alvin Ailey American Dance Theater at their six-week summer workshop in New York. It

was the first time Madonna, then nineteen years old, found herself
surrounded by dancers as good and ambitious as she was. "Everybody
wanted to be a star," she recalled. Although she was slightly overwhelmed by the experience, it renewed her determination to become
a leading dancer.

A year into her course, she got the opportunity to work with Pearl
Lang when the choreographer visited Ann Arbor as an artist in residence. Lang created a work for the students with music by Vivaldi,
and Madonna distinguished herself as one of the dancers for the
piece, performed at the local Power Arts Center. Lang's recognition
of Madonna's budding talent was the spur she needed to move to the
epicenter of dance—New York. Though only halfway through her
four-year degree, she decided to leave. Christopher Flynn was her ally,
encouraging her to "take [her] little behind" to the city. His colleague
Delanghe was disappointed, however, feeling that Madonna "didn't
get good advice." She would have preferred for Madonna to finish her
degree and fulfill her potential.

Madonna, however, had bigger fish to fry. She was concerned she
would lose momentum within the careful, slow-moving world of academic dance; she felt she had already squeezed as much as she could
from the Michigan course. Her father was deeply opposed, seeing
this as a waste of her scholarship—coming from a working-class immigrant background, he had unswerving faith in the power of education, believing that her degree would lead to more solid opportunities.
"Stop trying to run my life for me!" she screamed at him one night,
throwing a plate of spaghetti at the wall in a fit of rage. Tony was
mortified. Although she rushed to apologize, that row would be the
beginning of a rift that took years to heal.

For now, she was hell-bent on making a name for herself. "Madonna had to get out of Detroit to make it. There was no Internet
then, and there weren't those sorts of conduits for someone to succeed in Detroit. She needed the machinery of New York or L.A.,"
says Brian McCollum of the *Detroit Free Press*. While she was at college, Madonna worked behind the bar at a gritty rock club on Liberty
Street, called Second Chance, which is now called Necto's. As bands

passed through, she was getting a taste for a rock 'n' roll lifestyle—at odds with the sometimes rarefied world of contemporary dance. She didn't know exactly what she was going to do, but somehow she was going to express all the different parts of herself. She had an internal "fame" clock, and needed to be noticed *now*. In the late 70s, New York was the only place to be.

THE ARROGANCE AND
THE NERVE!

Madonna used to go to shows by The Slits, the anarchic U.K. all-girl punk band who fused dub reggae and scratchy rhythms to create a new female sound. She would stand in the front row, studying the lead singer, Ari Up, and guitarist Viv Albertine. "I'm pissed off she's never worn a T-shirt with THE SLITS written in sequins. She owes us. She ripped off all her early fashion ideas from Viv," Ari said in 2005. Viv would wind rags in her hair and don lingerie as outerwear. "We'd be dressed half in bondage fetish gear, half in Doc Martens, with our hair all out there, scowling at everybody," Albertine told me in 1997. "People didn't know if we were a pin-up or what. It freaked middle-aged men particularly, that mixture of rubber stockings, DMs, and fuck-off-you-wanker-what-are-you-staring-at. They didn't know if they were coming or going."

Whether Madonna customized their look or created one of her own, she was inspired by the sartorial dash of punk—its flirtation with ugliness and the everyday, its way of turning the codes upside down and imbuing them with an assertive femininity. To dress the way she did was a radical act in late 70s America. It wasn't just the way that women were supposed to look: fluffy hair tamed by hairspray, soft blue eye shadow, and flowery skirts, but the way women were supposed to behave. To gain male approval, women had to tone themselves down. Madonna touched on it years later with her song "What It Feels Like for a Girl." If a woman was upfront, sexually assertive, and loud, she was marginalized as "weird" and seen as fair game for physical attack.

To be twenty years old in the late 70s was to be at a cultural shifting point, when a binary world of black/white, male/female, good/bad, virgin/whore was beginning to break down. With her unfailing instinct, Madonna tuned in to this change and embodied it, turning herself into a cultural force. She combined elements of punk style with underground dance and Europop disco to come up with the concept of Madonna. But it took several wrong turns and identity shifts before she reached that point.

IN THE SUMMER of 1978, Madonna arrived in New York, eager to be the center of everything. But it was to be four long years before she got her first record deal, let alone the kind of fame she desired. Like any young suburbanite, she needed to break the big city to make it hers, and that would take time. She stayed with a college friend near Columbia University before moving into an apartment in Hell's Kitchen on the west side of New York. She continued with her dance studies and after she got settled in New York that July, attended the annual American Festival of Dance in Durham, North Carolina. During this session, she encountered Lang once again, and introduced herself. "The arrogance and the nerve!" Lang recalls. "Madonna asked me outright, 'D'you think you need a dancer in your company?' I'd never have dreamed of doing that when I was young. I told her, 'We always need an understudy.' And she said, 'I'd like to do that.' I said, 'Wait a minute, you live in Michigan. I'm in New York City.' 'I'll manage.' Anyway, I forgot about her and went home."

Back in New York, Lang was busy at the American Dance Center, which she'd formed with Alvin Ailey. They each ran their own company there. "In November, the door opened to the class and there was

Madonna," continues Lang. "I used her for about two years." Lang was an astute choice, a key figure in modern dance and formerly one of Martha Graham's principal dancers. When I interviewed her in New York in 2006, she was eighty-five, and had retired only two years earlier. She lived and breathed dance from a young age. "When I was three or four, I came from Chicago with my mother to see the Isadora Duncan student company at Symphony Hall. My mother was a fan of Isadora's, she was a heroine of the women's movement at the time. I saw these girls dancing—one came skipping from back to front of stage, opened her arms wide, and the audience gasped. 'I'm going to do that,' I vowed." Lang ended up dancing with Martha Graham's company during the 1940s, when the choreographer was at her peak. "Martha had a remarkable mix of music and poetry. It wasn't just kicking your legs up and doing top-drawer nonsense like Balanchine. She was one of the great artists of our day. She stops your heart. She's been compared to Picasso."

Lang set up her own company in 1953, evolving a powerful woman-centered style. Her approach was flexible, working on complex moves with dancers until they got it, or getting them to perform another way. Madonna, luckily, was able to cope with what was thrown at her. "She did what she was asked. The work itself was technically very difficult, but she made it."

Soon after joining the company, Madonna was rewarded with a dancing part in *I Never Saw Another Butterfly*, a piece about the Holocaust. Young and thin, she made a graceful Jewish ghetto child. She also brought out Lang's motherly instincts. "I got her a job at the Russian Tea Room, checking hats and coats, because I thought she was losing weight and needed one decent meal a day," Lang remembered. "I'm sorry to say but I'm pretty sure that was the one decent meal she was getting."

Madonna could also be "kinda funky" with the way she dressed. "It was that period when they wanted to be as unusual and messy as they could," said Lang. But despite the torn leotard and safety pins, she was impressed with the dedicated way Madonna threw herself into dance.

"She was very aggressive in her approach. But in a good way, that's necessary. If dancers hide they don't come across so well."

Madonna danced in about six of Lang's productions, including *Shorebourne*, a bright beach piece set to Vivaldi's strings, and *Piece for Brass*, with an American jazz influence. Lang remembers that for the latter, the set featured "metal pipes that you see on top of buildings. I used them in the choreography, with people falling out of them and being sucked into them. It was very strong, modern, and hard." Much later this influence could be seen in the set for Madonna's 2006 *Confessions* tour, on the stage set for the song "Jump." She also danced for Lang in a suite of Spanish folk songs. "I remember her upstage left," says Lang. "She did it very well."

Though prestigious, dancing was work with very little financial reward. Struggling to make ends meet, Madonna took various short-lived jobs at Dunkin' Donuts and Burger King, before returning to the slightly more lucrative work of nude modeling for artists. Although she was posing naked, she saw this as art photography and therefore "legit." According to writer Michael Mackenzie, "The other way a dancer could make money was topless dancing, which a lot of the dancers, even some of the bigger dancers, did. They'd go to New Jersey and do it on the side. It was sorta out of sight, out of mind. Madonna never did that, she saw it as too compromising."

Madonna's youth made her a fearless risk-taker. But, like any young woman on her own, she was vulnerable. One day, not long after she joined Lang's company, she was in a run-down part of town. She was grabbed on the street by, as she described to a friend, a heavyset black man, who led her at knifepoint up the steps of a tenement block to the roof. There he forced her to perform oral sex. When he was finished, he left her crying and shaking on the roof. For a long time she stayed there, too afraid to leave in case he was on the stairs. Eventually she made her way down and went home, profoundly shocked by the experience. It seems that rather than reporting the assault to the police, Madonna internalized it, burying deep her sense of shame and isolation. Years later she talked about it with a therapist, and then said in an interview: "I have been raped, and it's not an experience I would ever glamorize." Memories of the attack surfaced again in 1992, during the filming of the movie *Dangerous Game*. In character, Madonna related the story of her rape exactly as it had happened. "It was a very heavy sequence," said the director, Abel Ferrara. "I didn't know she was going to tell that story."

Although Madonna didn't talk about it much at the time, the trauma went deep. It can be argued that her anger at the attack came out afterward in a need for complete sexual control. Many friends have suggested that she used sex to get attention, get dinner, get a bed for the night, and one of her preferred methods was fellatio. For a young woman who felt powerless, it was one way to show men that she was the dominant one and she didn't care. Sex became a mask, a way of psychologically turning the tables on her attacker.

Even though Madonna played street-smart, shrugging off the assault when she confided to a few friends, it led to the dissolution of her dream. Before long, she was losing concentration in classes, complaining to Lang that dancing gave her back pain and that some of the moves were too difficult. It was as if the attack made her self-esteem crumble, and she abandoned her pursuit of contemporary dance. Besides, it would have meant years of backbreaking work before she could become a principal dancer or establish herself as a successful choreographer. "Dancing is physically hard. There are no tears and whining. You work hard and there's plenty of people better than you," says British choreographer Jane Turner. "The choreographer is the auteur in modern dance. You devote yourself to your company and you earn very little. You're a dedicated disciple. There's no income. It's impossibly uncommercial. No fame."

Maybe Madonna felt unsupported and isolated. Maybe she doubted her expertise as an avant-garde dancer. Maybe she needed to do something fun after her dark experience, to use dance in a different way. Whatever it was, she needed a quick hit. She fell out with Lang. Although she had been content to submit to Christopher Flynn's dance regime, she bristled under the older woman's discipline. "You're supposed to take a class every day, most dancers do, but Madonna was becoming listless," recalls Lang. "She said one day, 'I'm going to an audition, I'm going tomorrow, so I won't be in class.' She lasted one more week, and then I never saw her again."

Lang admired Madonna's strength but not her manners. She is also skeptical about Madonna's technique. "I put her on the stage, that's for sure. It's how you attack a movement. Someone will sail into it, others will attack it. Madonna had that kind of energy, she was able to keep up with them. She was all right. But she wasn't as good as my good dancers, because she had this other thing on her mind, the pop stuff." She scoffs at the suggestion that Madonna was influenced by Graham. "No way, no where. There's nothing of mine or Martha's in what she's doing. She's now pop culture."

Traumatized by her attack, tired of scraping together a living as a dancer, Madonna moved on to far more glamorous territory. Although deep down the sexual assault was a devastating experience, it acted like a trigger, propelling her forward. For now, the club scene was the most exciting place to be—and the best place to forget her fears.

Madonna found the next few months a challenge. She remained in dancer mentality, going to classes in Manhattan and practicing at home, but felt a little lost without the security of Lang's company. She met graffiti artist Norris Burroughs at a party, and they had a brief relationship. Her time with him was a short hiatus, a sort of calm before the storm. They would spend long, sunny afternoons making love or wandering through peaceful uptown parks. Burroughs loved her elemental spirit. He described her as "sensual and sexual," but said there was something elusive about her, as if she were "made of light."

In 1979 she transferred her affections to an aspiring musician, Dan Gilroy, who, with his brother Ed, had formed The Breakfast Club, a band specializing in ska-influenced punk pop. Gilroy's account of their first date is symbolic of many of her future relationships. They met in a bar on the Upper West Side on a weeknight, when the place was virtually empty. "I'm a beats-oriented dancer. She was whirling around with a leg around her neck and spinning and all that. It was frightening being in the middle of a dance floor with no one else there, and she's working the floor very nicely and I'm . . . in my place."

Madonna's affair with Gilroy was put on hold when, soon after they met, she got a job performing with the Patrick Hernandez disco revue in Paris. According to Burroughs, Dan and Ed had an act that was part of an alternative vaudeville show called *Voidville*. This came to the attention of Hernandez's Belgian producers Jean van Lieu and Jean-Claude Pellerin. They met Madonna through Dan and encouraged her to audition for the disco star.

When she got to France, she was looked after by van Lieu and Pellerin, two smooth operators who wanted to mold her into a funky Piaf-style showgirl. There was a lot of talk and expensive dinners, but nothing much materialized. Accustomed to a fierce workload, Madonna chafed at the lack of activity. Though she has been very dismissive of this period in her life, she went there at a formative time, when she was changing from being "just a dancer" to becoming a dancer who sang. In Paris in 1979, she couldn't help absorbing the showgirl style of venues like the Moulin Rouge and the influence of Eurodisco. With his hit "Born to Be Alive," Patrick Hernandez was a master of the latter. It's no coincidence that her first records had a Europop feel.

Paris then may have been a backwater in terms of music industry, but its café culture was very much alive. Madonna made sure she went to the right parties, establishing contacts and a love for the city that was to feed into later collaborations with artists like Mirwais, Mondino, and Jean-Paul Gaultier. "In the 70s, Paris was a good place for café society," recalls Californian socialite Melinda Patton, who lived there at the same time as Madonna. "Anybody could meet anybody. You'd sit in a café and meet the whole social gamut from top to bottom. Everybody goes out all the time. You met one person, you'd meet a thousand."

Although Madonna enjoyed the social life, she saw her career stagnating. Feeling cosseted but at the same time misunderstood, a disappointed Madonna decided to head home. There, desperate for any avenue of success, she answered an ad for a movie role in *Back Stage* magazine, asking for "a dark, fiery young woman, dominant . . . who can dance and is willing to work for no pay." She sent a two-page résumé to the director Stephen Jon Lewicki, and got the job. Her first foray into film was the rather unprepossessing *A Certain Sacrifice*, a low-budget movie in which she plays the part of Bruna, a New Wave dominatrix who hangs around listlessly with her S&M tribe until she meets a nice boy from the suburbs, who's just waiting to be corrupted. They become a couple and she moans rather unconvincingly to him about how she is caught up with her "slaves" in a trap of domination and submission.

Bruna ends up being raped in a restroom. For Madonna, filming this scene not long after her real-life attack must have been difficult, and for a moment on-screen she seems genuinely distressed. In the film, Bruna's abuser is ambushed by the gang and there follows an orgy of blood sacrifice set to a dirge-like Goth rock soundtrack. Madonna exudes a callow sensuality and strenuously emotes, but cannot save the movie. Although its grainy footage of early 80s New York has curio value, the script is clumsy and the acting unconvincing. Lewicki went for a low-budget *Mean Streets* feel, but ended up with an amateurish art film. He ran out of money toward the end of shooting, and didn't finish it until after Madonna was famous. He released it in 1985, much against her wishes. What's interesting about the Bruna role, though, is how it foreshadows the virgin/whore dichotomy that she later explores. In *A Certain Sacrifice*, she plays a woman punished for her active sexuality—a theme that would come up time and again in her work.

Back in 1980, Madonna was hitting her stride as a musician. She moved in with Gilroy and his brother in an old boarded-up synagogue in Queens, and joined their band. Her dancer's rhythm meant that she had a knack for drums, so for the first few months she played drums, occasionally darting out front to sing. They spent hours rehearsing, and she worked hard, picking up chords on guitar and learning enough to piece together songs. Excited about this new direction, she felt that rock music was the ideal place to express her individuality. Her dancer friend Angie Smit was recruited on bass. The foursome played a few gigs, but the chemistry wasn't working, partly because Madonna felt ill at ease sharing the spotlight with another attractive female. Plus Smit was more of a dancer than a committed musician, and soon began to lose interest in the band.

She was replaced by bassist Mike Monahan, and when drummer Gary Burke took over, Madonna was promoted to what she now felt was her rightful place as lead singer. It was inevitable that the band couldn't contain her—not with the Gilroy brothers writing all the songs and choreographing the moves. After some heated discussions, during which an exasperated Dan Gilroy shouted, "You're all naked ambition and no talent!" (an accusation that went deep), Madonna left with Monahan and Burke to form the short-lived Madonna & The Sky. Tired out by his day job and frustrated by Madonna's impatient criticism, Burke dropped out. Luckily for Madonna, her old friend from Michigan, Steve Bray, had just moved to New York and was looking for work. "She had a set of songs ready to go and at the same time needed a drummer. Naturally we started working together," he said. When the musically confident Bray joined the band, Madonna swiftly moved into her next incarnation as part of The Millionaires, and then Emmy, evolving into a ska-meets-early-Pretenders sound.

She and Bray rekindled their romance, but he realized early on that being Madonna's boyfriend was a difficult job. "Some people are very upfront and some are, like, you'll find out eventually you're not my boyfriend and that I'm seeing twelve other people. That was more her approach," he said. "I learned . . . not to count on her in that area." Although disappointed, the modest, self-effacing Bray sensibly decided to concentrate on the music he could make with her. It was a challenge, though, when she announced after a few months that the band would now be called Madonna. Bray protested that it sounded too Catholic. "And is everything about you? I realized far too late that, yes, it is all about you."

Despite her bold move in the naming department, Madonna was floundering around. Though desperate to make it, she hadn't evolved a distinctive style. She was yet to come into her own as a songwriter. And she didn't really have a clue about the business. She sensed that she needed a strong professional eye, someone to help her focus, to bring out that emerging sound. And that person was Camille Barbone.

IN THE SPRING of 1981, Emmy were rehearsing on the tenth floor of the Music Building, a scruffy conglomeration of rehearsal rooms on West 39th Street. The only recording studio in the building, Gotham Records, was owned by a thirty-year-old Italian-American, Camille Barbone. She was a dark-haired, energetic self-starter, qualities that Madonna recognized in herself. At the same time, Madonna was a little afraid of the older woman, and wanted to impress her.

On their first meeting in the elevator, Madonna turned to Camille and said with a conspiratorial smile: "Did you do it yet?" Camille was amused. "She did that a lot—used non sequiturs to get people's attention. Was she alluding to sex? I don't know. She was always very flirtatious with me," recalls Camille. "She knew I was a gay woman. She'd work it." Madonna invited Camille to a gig she was playing at Max's Kansas City, and after Camille didn't show up, Madonna stormed into her office, haranguing her. Camille made sure she went to Emmy's next concert, and was "blown away. She sparkled, in a very street way. Not fairy nymphet. It was hard and guttural and in-your-face. She very much typified the New York music scene."

Camille offered to be her manager, but on one condition: that she ditch the band. Madonna was overjoyed. Although she felt loyal to Mike Monahan and Steve Bray, her career was more important. They were less than impressed with the news, but within a few months, she managed to win them back, and the musicians remained on friendly terms, even giving her advice.

The next thing Camille did was to move Madonna into a new apartment and give her a $100-a-week salary. "Madonna had a lot of peripheral trash going on just to get what she needed to do her job," recalls Camille. "And she had a very hard time letting go of all the peripheral stuff. She was a street-savvy kid who'd pick up someone to go home with if she was hungry and needed a meal. That's how she survived. She was very upfront about it. She justified her behavior, saying she wasn't being victimized because 'I *let* them take advantage of me.' That's a contradiction in itself. She was living in a hovel in a dangerous part of town. I wanted to give her a safe haven, because in a lot of ways she seemed wounded."

After Madonna's apartment on West 70th Street was broken into, Camille found her a new place, off Riverside Drive, and from this point, the two became inseparable, a kind of double act. It is interesting that it took a woman to see Madonna's real potential. "I was one of the few female managers in a totally male industry. Men looked at Madonna as someone they wanted to bed as opposed to sign. That was a difficult situation to overcome—my whole vibe in managing her was, you don't have to do that anymore. Let's do it based on the fact that you have a unique personality, you're an artist, and you have a lot to offer," says Camille. "I brought her into the mainstream music business in a way that she didn't have to fuck for. I brought her credibility. Word got around that someone was investing money in her, someone with a studio and contacts. As a result, within the industry, they began to take her seriously too."

Like Madonna, Camille had worked hard to establish herself despite the old-boy network. The daughter of a New York City policeman and a housewife, Camille began her career at major labels before starting up her own Gotham management company and studio in the late 1970s. She remembers going to the monthly meeting of the East Coast Managers' Conference in the New York theater district. "I walk in and there's seven old men with pot bellies, smoking cigars. They were all managers for killer acts. It wasn't just the old-boy network, it was *old.* I must have been twenty-four years old and 110 pounds. I didn't wear a bra. No one looked at my face, just my chest. That was the first and last meeting I went to."

Together, she and Madonna made a formidable team. In the early 80s there were very few successful mainstream female artists. Women were still seen as a novelty, and not taken seriously as long-term investments. This presented a considerable obstacle, but Madonna was the first of a new breed, fusing punk attitude with a high-glam sexuality and taking it one step further into the pop mainstream. "My role models were people like Debbie Harry and Chrissie Hynde, you know, strong, independent women who wrote their own music and evolved on their own," Madonna said. "They essentially weren't marketed, produced, or put together. They weren't the brainstorm of a record company executive . . . Debbie Harry gave me courage."

She took many of her early cues from Harry, a fact that clearly irked the Blondie frontwoman. "It should have been me!" she exclaimed years later, when Madonna was at the peak of her stardom. But in a sense, Harry had paved the way for Madonna. In the mid-70s, when Blondie were starting out, they were subject to an unofficial radio boycott in the United States. "An aggressive female frontperson had never really been done in pop," she said. "It was very difficult to be in that position at the time—it's hard to be a groundbreaker."

With her bee-stung lips and cartoon peroxide style, Harry's image was an ironic comment that celebrated the tradition of glamorous blonde while sending it up. She was the first Warhol-style pop-art blonde in pop music. Madonna said later: "I was hugely influenced by Debbie Harry when I started out as a singer and songwriter. I thought she was the coolest chick in the universe." Harry's response was: "Hmmm. I haven't thought of myself as a 'chick' in some time, but the universe is a good reference." Madonna was to take that 50s Hollywood-blonde schlock one step further by welding it to a self-driven 80s global marketing. Dan Gilroy recalled how Madonna once heard someone say that the camera loved Debbie Harry. "That made a huge impression on her. She thought, 'Yeah, the camera loves me too.' Something clicked there," he said. When she met Camille, though, that camera-friendly image was still a long way off.

"Most of the obstacles were broken down because Madonna was so unique. But you couldn't tell that from her demos, only if I marched her into a meeting," recalls Camille. "I realized early on that was the way to do it. She understood that. We made a deal. We always made a good impact." Camille knew it was important to surround Madonna with strong musical collaborators. Was she a gifted musician? Camilla pauses. "Gifted? No. She was a meat-and-potatoes musician. She had just enough skill to write a song or play guitar. She had a wonderful sense of lyrics, however. She read pretty impressive books and that helped her lyrics-writing. But more than anything it was her personality and that she was a great performer."

Madonna was given the opportunity to jam with session musicians like Jeff Gottlieb and David Frank, until the new lineup gelled around keyboard-player John Bonamassa, bassist John Kaye, drummer Bob Riley, and Jon Gordon on lead guitar. Madonna responded well to being given professional musicians with sturdy equipment. "If you gave this one the tools, she used 'em. As a manager you can spend a lot of money on someone and nothing happens. But she used it all. She'd pick their brains. They'd rehearse four times a week, and they went on stage tighter than hell. She didn't have to worry about a thing musically. We took that stupid little guitar away from her. She had a mike in her hand and the freedom to improvise with her dancing."

ONCE THE group was up and running, Camille stipulated that there were to be no affairs between band members. Riley fell victim to Madonna's manipulativeness when he had an affair with her, got fired, and the preferred candidate, Steve Bray, was installed in his place. Having the talented Bray in the band undoubtedly added resonance to Madonna's music, but it also meant there was constant tension, an irreconcilable pull between the genres of rock and dance.

This became apparent that summer, when she recorded her first Gotham demo at Media Sound, an old converted church on 57th Street that had once been home to the Hungarian composer Béla Bartók. It was also a favorite with many pop artists, from Frank Sinatra to The Beatles. Now twenty-three years old, Madonna felt she was finally on the way to realizing her dream. To Jon Gordon, a young aspiring producer and musical director of the session, committing her ambitions to tape was a challenge. "It was not the most organized session I've been involved with," he remembers. "There was a certain amount of pushing and pulling between Madonna and Camille, regarding the stylistic direction of the music. Camille saw her more in the mold of Blondie downtown New Wave rock, while Madonna was at that point becoming very influenced by club and rap music. She and Camille didn't see eye to eye, and there was a lot of back and forth."

Camille disputes this, saying, "I often get the blame for the rock thing. But that's what Madonna was doing when I signed her up. She didn't want to change that, because she wanted to be Chrissie Hynde. The dance thing came by accident, and Steve Bray had a lot to do with that."

In preparing for the session, Madonna gave Gordon tapes of songs she had been writing, and they would work on preliminary arrangements. She spent hours in Camille's rehearsal studio, where she had access to the instruments. Gordon recalls that Madonna wrote most of the melody, lyrics, and chords herself. "She'd bang around on guitars, the organ, and the drum machine to get a structure, and then she'd put lyrics on top. She used all her personal resources. The tapes were good. They conveyed the essence of the song. She had a sound— and it was my job to translate that into the bones of an arrangement for the band. I didn't have to invent something out of thin air."

Over the next few weeks they recorded four songs, with Gordon acting as a kind of musical referee. At one end, there was David Frank—"a frighteningly talented individual who'd come up with amazing sounds"—and at the other, pared-down funky groove-merchant Steve Bray. "I wish I'd been better able to utilize that," sighs Gordon. "I was more a rock 'n' roll traditionalist at the time. I was trying to hold it all together."

Of the songs, which make up the Gotham tape, each inhabit, as Gordon puts it, "their own domain." There was the ska-influenced pop of "Love on the Run," and "High Society," which is more meditative and orchestral. "I was trying to model it on the T. Rex song 'Get It On (Bang a Gong).' It had a lot of odd sounds. We rented an electronic sitar for the occasion. And Madonna's scratch vocal take ended up being the one we went with. It captured the energy of the moment." Over the years many have criticized Madonna's vocal ability, saying she is a weak singer. Gordon disagrees: "Technically, of course, there're people who can sing rings around her. But she could grasp a song and present it in a catchy and intelligible way. She was very good at making her vocal limitations work for her. She's a strong interpreter and she doesn't over-embellish things."

Another song they recorded was "Get Up," a dance-oriented track that at one point included a rap by Bray. "There was a battle over how this one was going to sound—it represents where Madonna was trying to go," says Gordon. The closing track, "I Want You," sounded like Phil Spector on acid. "I was trying to make it sound like a big hit single and failed miserably," he laughs. Despite the artistic disputes, Madonna had a clear idea of what she wanted, even if she wasn't sure how to get it. "We were all taking direction from her," he continues. "She was open to suggestion, but she'd speak up very quickly if she didn't like the way things were going. I was a means to an end. 'Gordie,' she called me at the time. 'This part isn't working, I want it to be more like this.'"

Madonna's band began to play regular gigs, from club venues like Cartoon Alley and The Underground to Max's Kansas City and U.S. Blues on Long Island, as well as the college circuit. Slowly she was building up a following. "There was a group of fourteen-year-old girls who started following us around. I'd say it was a core group of four or five girls—they were the original wannabes," remarks Gordon.

Madonna's appeal lay in her earthiness, the sense that she was a normal pretty girl. Even though she had her hip New York devotees, when she started out, Madonna attracted a mainly teenybop crowd of enthusiastic girls. The early 80s fans were responding to "honest-to-goodness blood, sweat, and lip gloss" rather than some remote goddess. "Her hair was brown, all spiked up, and she wore the crucifix and accessories. She was a little plump, she wasn't slender or chiseled in the way she became later," says Gordon.

Camille remembers that the female fans were the key to Madonna's initial breakthrough. "An element that was so important to her success was that women didn't resent her. Normally, when women see their boyfriends riveted on a girl, there's resentment, but the girls were riveted too. She emitted a kind of bisexual vibe. She was open and honest in her songwriting. No frills. They're not mind-boggling concepts—they're ones that every woman can relate to easily. That was why it was so easy to get the girls to dress like her—they were watching every move she made." Girls started to imitate her, wearing a scarf in the same way, fishnet stockings with pumps, errant costume jewelry, or paint-splattered chinos. "They wanted to be like her because she was the free spirit in their minds. They admired what she was possessed by."

The other factor that had everyone stunned was the way she turned the crowd into voyeurs. "She had absolutely no self-consciousness at all," asserts Camille. "It was like what people do when they're in a bedroom by themselves singing in front of a mirror. But she wasn't in her bedroom, she'd do it in front of a whole audience. We talked about it a lot. She pretended her audience was a Peeping Tom. They weren't there, they were sneaking a look. That's a very unique way of thinking about performing!"

Early on, Madonna set up the subtext of pleasuring herself, planting the seed in people's minds that what she was doing was somehow illicit and forbidden. Relatively innocuous sexual moves would be reinterpreted as lustful and daring, because of what was going on in her psyche. She exhibited a kind of narcissism that drew people in, because it was about relishing the self, and self-pleasure. This approach spilled over into her everyday life and her drive for stardom. Ken Compton, her boyfriend at the time, was a little bemused when she once asked frankly: "So what d'you like best about me?" Gordon remembers Madonna as being "clearly obsessed with herself and her career."

But, despite her egotistical approach, Madonna could be overwhelmingly charming. "If it's possible to be fearless and vulnerable at the same time, she was," says Camille. "It was the thing that made her unstoppable. And very disarming." There was a strong attraction between the two women, and Camille felt that Madonna would have made the relationship sexual to exert greater control. "I resisted it because it would've been my doom . . . and it was my doom anyway, because the relationship we had wasn't physical but in every other way it was completely sexual." Madonna would openly flirt with her, and the two had passionate arguments that were fueled by unexpressed sexual tension. It was all Camille could do to concentrate on the job.

She circulated the Gotham tapes around various record companies, but despite a few talent scouts coming to gigs, no one was biting. Madonna became impatient. "When the Gotham tapes didn't do well, it put a permanent strain on my relationship with Madonna and Camille," says Gordon. Camille remembers it differently. "She had a great musical collaboration with Jon, but then he got a bad crush on her and that was the end of that. They had a huge fight onstage one night and she kinda shoved him, he shoved her back, but a bit too hard, and she fell. She came offstage and said: 'He's gone.' All right. He's gone."

Madonna was never one to linger when a situation wasn't working for her. "She's fast. She gets it. She can look at a room and know who the power button is, as well as the person she has to steer clear of," says Camille. But her ruthlessness was tempered by an intense neediness. Camille felt that the young star "drew out every maternal instinct in my body." She wasn't sure if Madonna got the kind of support and protection she needed from her family. "She didn't care about her dad's approval, and she had no strong woman figure. Her stepmom never did that for her." Camille thought that Joan brought her own children up well, but was "less focused on Madonna and her siblings." As for Tony, "He mourned a long time. She had him wrapped around her little finger. He was a typical Italian dad—hardworking, loved his daughter, would shake his head a lot and pray for her safety."

As a result, the band became her surrogate family. They would joke and call her "the kid." "Did somebody feed the kid today? She gets real grouchy if she doesn't eat." Although Madonna likes to imply that she's always been a woman in control of her career, much of her life in those early days was chaotic. Camille found herself taking charge of Madonna's dental appointments, cleaning up after her, and being on call during the night. "She'd call me at four in the morning: 'I can't sleep.' She'd show up at my door: 'Take me to a movie.' If she was hungry, I'd get her something to eat." At times, she behaved like a hyperactive child: "I had to drive her around after a gig just to get her tired. She'd get overtired, like a cranky baby, but wouldn't sleep. She didn't want to miss something. Very often I'd drop her off after a gig at three a.m. and she'd go back out."

When she got bored, Madonna would delight in mischievous practical jokes, like the afternoon she spray-painted in block letters on Camille's prize poodles the words "FUCK" and "SEX." "In her mind, it rinsed off. What was the big deal? It wasn't anything permanent." She also specialized in belching at all the wrong occasions—like in a lunch meeting with talent scouts from a top agency. "She'd belch and cackle hysterically. She'd try to get your attention by misbehaving. She wanted you to chuckle and relish it. That stuff didn't bother me," says Camille. "It was the sexually exploitative stuff that did. I'd say, 'Don't add to the misogyny of this business.' She was her own worst enemy. I had to convince her that she was entitled to her success, she didn't need to denigrate herself."

They understood that playing the bimbo got attention, but no one in the industry was ready yet to take a gamble and sign her. Madonna began to get impatient; she felt her career wasn't moving fast enough. When it came to renewing her contract in September 1981, Madonna stalled, complaining to Camille that her promise of a record deal wasn't yet fulfilled. A prestigious gig at the Underground Club had been scheduled for November; Camille threatened to pull it if Madonna didn't sign. The latter renewed her contract and went on to have a successful gig, plus opening on New Year's Eve for David Johansen, formerly of the New York Dolls. He escorted her that night to a party for the then-fledgling MTV cable channel, introducing her to many influential figures. Things seemed to be looking up, but behind Camille's back, promoters and record executives were trying to lure away her young charge with better offers. Sensing betrayal, Camille tried to hold on even harder, and the two became locked into heated rows. This was exacerbated by the fact that Camille started drinking heavily.

"I didn't have enough juice to get her to the next level. I was falling apart from it. I'd invested so much money. I basically had a meltdown. Because I was losing it, and I knew she was going to go all the way

to the top. And it blew my mind." In retrospect, Camille believes she
should have gone to a major manager and cut a deal—"let them carry
the ball and go in on the back end. It was my own pride that got in the
way. I was young and as headstrong as she was."

In February 1982, Madonna called Camille and her business partner Bill Lomuscio to a meeting with a high-powered music attorney,
Jay Kramer, ostensibly to discuss her future. During the meeting,
Kramer told Camille that they were terminating her contract with
Madonna, and the singer no longer required her services. Camille and
Bill left the room, stunned yet determined to take legal action. This
led to years of wrangling that left copyright issues over the Gotham
tapes unresolved. It wasn't until 1992 that Camille secured a modest
settlement.

Camille felt hugely betrayed. The years after the split were particularly painful, as Camille struggled financially while watching Madonna's star rise. She went through an emotional crisis, finding it almost
unbearable to hear Madonna's music on the radio, or see her face in a
magazine. She dropped out of the industry for a while, but then came
back in the 90s. She now runs her own successful Winedark record
label and lives on a ranch in New Jersey. Hindsight has made her
wise and forgiving. "I was totally ill-equipped to have that kind of a
hit. My philosophy now is, it wasn't meant to be. I drank a lot then. I
needed to mellow out the way she needed to mellow out."

She is even amused at how Madonna has managed to keep her
ever-widening audience throughout the years with that mischievous,
debunking sense of irony. "Madonna has never turned into a cartoon
character, like Cher. The Gaultier bras never clouded the fact that it
was just Madonna, burping at lunch. In a way, she's replicated that
burp over and over again."

JAM HOT

In the 1970s, New York was a city on the brink of collapse. There were two eras of recession, 1973–75 and 1980–82, which produced some of the most creative genres of music—disco and hip-hop.

In the pre-AIDS world of the 70s, disco was the pulsating heart of gay culture, a phenomenon that spread rapidly after the film *Saturday Night Fever*, until at one point there were over a thousand discos in Midtown Manhattan. Alongside this sprang up the downtown punk scene, drawing lifeblood from disco, if only to satirize its commercialism and inject its bpm energy into the mores of white rock. Bands like The New York Dolls, Television, Blondie, and The Ramones expressed the tension of the time while celebrating the antihero. Rents in Manhattan were dirt-cheap, which attracted a new generation of musicians and artists. Both disco and punk scenes revolved around sexual experimentation, artistic flamboyance, and lavish drug use.

"It was a run-down city, it was like a war zone," recalls Maripol Fauque, the stylist and fashion expert who helped to customize much of Madonna's early look. "The parks were taken over by drug dealers. Look at Martin Scorsese's film *Mean Streets*—it was just like that.

But New York was also a magnet. Once you come here it's hard to get out. You cannot find anywhere with this creative energy. I ran away from France in 1976, came here for three months, and never left. Manhattan is like a weird magnet, because you feel kind of trapped." There is also a more prosaic evaluation of that time and Madonna's place in it. "There was a downtown bar that everyone would go to, a real dive," recalls an artist from that period. "There was a chef in the kitchen who also dealt cocaine. Everybody would hang out there, including Madonna. She was really annoying, and constantly in that kitchen." While it is rumored that she wasn't averse to experimenting, friends suggest that she was careful to give the appearance of being high while never, in fact, being high. "I saw her like she was drunk out of her mind when she was only drinking ginger ale with a cherry in it," said photographer Michael Mackenzie. "She understood those people would see her as an outsider if she was 'straight.'"

TO MANY of the "in-crowd," though, Madonna was déclassé. "She seemed like this girl from out-of-state who wasn't totally in-the-know yet," said artist Futura 500, while another Danceteria regular claimed, "She was hideous. No one liked her. She'd do outrageously stupid things. Like there was a girl who worked at the Danceteria who had a really striking style and she wore her hair a certain way. One day Madonna came in with her hair cut and dyed the same way, an exact copy. We'd say, 'Is she nuts?' She says she ate out of trash cans, that she felt lonely—there was no reason to feel lonely, it was such a supportive scene, it was a community. But Madonna was so competitive."

Madonna wasn't totally accepted by the downtown scene ("She wasn't underground, she wasn't at the alternative art galleries," says a local musician), but she didn't care. She was happy to just to soak up the ambience and energy.

It was an environment unaffected by corporate branding, where the DIY ethic was at its most pronounced. "There was a new generation searching on their own," recalls Maripol. "There was Pere Ubu at one extreme, The Lounge Lizards did their thing, and Jean-Michel

Basquiat had a band called Gray. I remember going to the Mudd Club and seeing The B-52's the first time they ever played. I saw Devo live, I saw Blondie live, I saw David Byrne . . . Nico playing the piano in a really small venue. Nothing was concrete, nothing was corporate yet, nothing was institutionalized and like 'Oh let me call my PR please.' It was much more natural."

New York was an appropriate place for Madonna, because any-body could wind up being somebody. "I knew Debbie Harry when she was a mousey drug addict. She went away one day and came back as part of Blondie," recalls a former scenester. "Madonna, too, was just one of many. Like a lot of people on the Lower East Side, she was jockeying for position, aware of it as a scene. Then she went away one day and came back as Madonna."

AFTER SHE left Camille Barbone, Madonna was still "jockeying for position." Negotiations she began at this time with the William Morris Agency failed to materialize into anything, and she was back to decrepit rehearsal studios and hustling for a deal. By this time, though, she had gained valuable live experience and had established for herself a vibrant network of club-going friends and industry contacts. Now she began to move to the center of alternative New York nightlife, which was focused first on the Mudd Club, and then on the Dance-teria, a four-story club that had just relocated from West 37th to West 21st Street. By 1981, disco music was being superseded by "freestyle" dance music, hip-hop, and sounds from the United Kingdom. "The disco scene was dying. The whole glitter, getting into Studio 54, all that feeling-special shit was over. All the hip people got tired of the glitz, and the Mudd Club became the cool place because it was way downtown, at the bottom of Manhattan," recalls Mark Kamins, the DJ who "discovered" Madonna.

Back then, Kamins was party DJ for the nuevo-punk band Talking Heads, and a roving A&R man for Chris Blackwell's Island Records. When the Danceteria opened, he was there, with cult British DJ Shaun Cassette, mixing up the playlist with everything from The Pop

Group to James Brown, Grace Jones, and Kraftwerk. The beautiful people migrated to the Danceteria, which featured live bands on the first floor and a third-floor video lounge. Kamins saw this as a pivotal time in the city's history, a reaction to the grimness of the 1970s. "New York was so musically creative at that point," he says. "The late 70s was a very bad time. The Bronx was burning. There was no work. We were political, but there was nothing to motivate us other than music. There were no rules for a while. Musically, everybody experimented and everyone wanted to try something new."

For him, this was encapsulated in an act like James Blood Ulmer, who collided jazz with rock and punk. First-floor bands included the cream of alternative acts, from The Buzzcocks and Magazine to The Cramps, Birthday Party, and the B-52's. "The Danceteria ran from eight p.m. to eight a.m. It was a very special place, like Warhol's Factory," recalls Kamins. Sade worked behind the bar, Keith Haring and The Beastie Boys were busboys, LL Cool J was the elevator operator. "It was one of those places where we lived. When the club closed, Keith went to the subway and painted his little figures until we opened the club at noon and started cleaning. He lived at the Danceteria, we all lived there. It was more than a club. Everybody there was doin' something."

Madonna, he remembers, was "just one of the personalities. She had a very unique fashion style. She was always on the dance floor, and when she danced, everyone would stand around her." For Madonna, this club symbolized the freedom she'd been waiting for after the rigorous world of contemporary dance, and the time spent playing lackluster venues in marginal rock bands. It was the dance floor that suited her best. "You can dance for six hours and nobody will bother you and you don't have to drink. I felt an incredible sense of liberation, and I felt happier," she said. "There was nothing fun or glamorous about my life and I needed some excitement."

One night she approached Kamins's DJ booth with a demo of the song "Everybody" she'd been working on with Steve Bray. "She came without asking," says Kamins. "But I'm a very spontaneous DJ and when promo guys I respected came to the booth, I knew they'd be giving me a really good record to play. It's not like I had to take it home to listen to it first. I love spontaneity, I believe it's the magic of life. Madonna had a cassette, I threw it on, and it worked." He shrugs. "I'm not sayin' the place went mad crazy, but it worked."

Madonna became his girlfriend, and they moved into a small railroad apartment on the Upper East Side. "We had no money and we were sleeping on egg crates. She wasn't a homemaker," he remembered. There was only one thing on her mind. "I bought some lingerie for her one night and she wasn't interested. To Madonna, a boyfriend was secondary. She knew how to use her sexuality to manipulate men, everyone from promotion guys to radio programmers."

But Chris Blackwell, the head of Island Records, wasn't easily swayed. A demo was sent and a meeting was arranged, but the record mogul passed on it. "He didn't want to sign his A&R's girlfriend, and she'd had a rough night, she hadn't taken a shower, so Chris said she didn't smell too good that day." After Blackwell turned her down, Kamins brought Madonna to Seymour Stein at Sire. "He said, OK, I'll give her a deal, not because he believed in her but 'cause he believed in me," claims Kamins. Madonna was offered a $15,000 two-singles deal—nothing spectacular—but it gave her the opportunity she had dreamed of. She was so eager to get the ink dry on the contract that she visited Stein in a hospital after a heart surgery. "I think if I was lying in a coffin but had my hand out ready to sign, that would've suited her," Stein said later, laughing. "She was very anxious to get her career going, she believed in herself that much."

The recording session for "Everybody" and "Ain't No Big Deal" took place in the summer of 1982 in Blank Tape studios. As a result of the deal, Bray was edged to the sidelines, while Kamins took on his first role as a producer, feeling his way into the job. Although Madonna could be brash, for this session she was almost humble. "This was the first time she was in the studio with real, real musicians. I'd hired top New York studio players, with Leslie Mink on drums and Fred Zarr on keyboards," says Kamins. "She let me do my thing musically and when it was time for her to do the vocals, she just went off and did them. She was innocent. You lose that: after you have your first hit, you're not innocent anymore. That was her only record where you can hear innocence in her voice."

Kamins worked hard in the studio but was aware of his limitations as a producer. "I'm a DJ. For me it's all about the vibe, the music. I can't tell an A-minor from a C-minor, I'm not a musician. But I can tell you if it's good or bad. If I'm not standing up and dancing, it ain't happening, that's my criteria. For 'Everybody' it was, yo, fuck the demo, let's rock the house. Give me your bass." Madonna did her vocals in one take. "She was pretty confident about her vocal. She'd been on tour with Patrick Hernandez, been onstage. She was also a little awed by being surrounded by the best musicians, four guys who'd played on every record in the top twenty. But she went out there and did it. She didn't drink or do drugs, so it always came from the heart," Kamins recalls.

"Everybody" has a youthful exuberance, combining Madonna's ir- repressible treble with simplistic but locked-down bass and drums. It was a song that Fab Five Freddy from Grandmaster Flash said he heard on a boom box hauled down the street by two Puerto Rican teenagers. It was hip. The track sets the blueprint for future Madonna songs, with its lyrics about sensing the rhythm and being guided by the music. Her voice is cajoling, directing, demanding. It's as if she is on the dance floor, aware of everyone in the room—who wants to dance, who doesn't, who's about to, who's shy and who's not. She is the leader, taking everyone by the hand, drawing them to the floor where they can lose themselves. She *invites* people to play. She gives them permission.

At the time, another act produced by Mark Kamins—Johnny Dynell and New York 88—had a hit with the experimental hip-hop song "Jam Hot." Dynell remembers: "Madonna and I were both East Village downtown people suddenly on the radio. It was a big deal. She didn't have a lot of friends, she was very focused. She wasn't really about hanging out with the rest of the kids. I remember being on the roof of some building talking with her about the future. She thought my record 'Jam Hot' was very weird, she didn't really like it. It was about prostitutes, very street, very arty. When I first heard 'Everybody,' I thought it was catchy and hooky but the words were too sim-plistic. I offered to help her with the lyrics, but she said, 'I know what I'm doin'. And twenty-five years later, they're still dancing to it.'"

Initially the song was marketed by Warner—with a failure of nerve, to the dance charts. With no picture of Madonna on the cover, it was assumed she was black. Though it was niche marketing, it successfully established her as a credible dance artist. To Wendy Fonarow, author of *Empire of Dirt*, an anthropological study of indie music, Madonna was "totally dance culture." Fonarow remembers going to an underage dance club in L.A. called The Odyssey, which attracted mainly gay men and avant-garde teens. "We liked dancing until it closed at four a.m. The DJ knew what the current singles were at the Danceteria, and he'd test them out on us. When we heard 'Everybody,' we loved it. We thought it was just another throwaway black dance diva, but when we saw her—unwashed, stringy dyed blond hair, lacy fingerless gloves, lots of bangles and scraps of clothing—we were totally hooked on the way she looked. She was dressed in the same way we were. We weren't Madonna wannabes; it was a reflection of what was going on in our club culture in L.A."

Although it failed to make a dent on *Billboard*, in November 1982 the record went to number one in the dance charts. Madonna was then moved to write one of her best-known songs, "Lucky Star," about Mark Kamins. Along with Steve Bray, Kamins had set her on the road and helped create the musical identity she needed. Although Madonna's face wasn't on the cover of her first single, she made sure that after the next one she was no longer anonymous. She would do her homework, tagging along with Warner plugger Bobby Shaw, ac-companying him at meetings with radio and club promoters to soak up information and contacts. "She wanted to be a star. She'd do any-thing to be a star. She wasn't difficult to be around—she just didn't stick around," says Kamin. "Music is like a horse race. Madonna had timing on her side, fashion on her side, and her get-up-and-go. She was on a mission. She never stopped."

At the same time as "Everybody" was setting New York alight, Madonna became a lover of a young, up-and-coming black artist,

Jean-Michel Basquiat. Like her, he was ambitious, claiming: "Since I was seventeen, I thought I might be a star." The difference between them lay in his urge to self-destruct. A self-confessed "party animal," he took copious amounts of drugs and was prone to depressive moods. But when he worked, he was brilliant. "I don't think about art while I work. I try to think about life," he said. His naive expressionist paintings were influenced by graffiti art and imagery from popular culture. His alter ego was called SAMO, an entity that was given to such messages as SAMO AS A NEO ART FORM. SAMO AS AN END TO PLAYING ART.

He became contemptuous of the high-art echelons that courted him—satirizing capitalist culture while at the same time enjoying its money and celebrity. Madonna met him in the early 80s, while he was still establishing himself and not yet affected by the fame that derailed him. His depictions of marginal black urban culture, his use of found objects and old furniture, the sheer inventiveness with which he turned popular culture inside out, all this influenced her. And she impressed him with her feisty professionalism. "Jean was this male chauvinist, and Madonna was into sexual energy. The relationship was kind of like an act for both of them," said Nick Taylor, an artist and close friend of Basquiat's. "It was before these two people were so famous, but it was like a regal, arranged marriage."

She was her own tag line. She was the BOY TOY scrawled on countless subway stations. Her style, an amalgam of thrift store and punk, was about wearing found objects—that old pair of tights, that clumsy wooden crucifix, those rubber typewriter bands as bracelets. Basquiat made his identity—ethnic and street-aware—a core feature of his art. In the same way, Madonna began to build her persona of the good Catholic girl gone bad. She understood early on how to make an impact. Once she threw a party filled with graffiti kids. As Taylor said to writer Phoebe Hoban: "Madonna turned on the tape machine and everybody jammed. I remember around that time [she] lived on 4th Street between A and B. It was a really sleazy neighborhood, filled with street gangsters. She had these two little Hispanic kids that were kind of her bodyguards. She'd bring them everywhere."

By the spring of 1983, Madonna had grown tired of Basquiat's negativity. Her disciplined lifestyle contrasted with his penchant for getting stoned and sleeping till the afternoon. She mingled easily with his friends but didn't take part in the rituals. While everybody was doing drugs, she would munch carrot chips. According to Basquiat's assistant, Steve Torton, Madonna bailed out because Basquiat "never saw the sun. She said she couldn't take it. I saw her at Bond's and I said, 'How's Jean?' and she said, 'He's on dope. I went over there tonight and he was nodding out on heroin. I'm not having anything to do with that.' She moved out, just like that, totally emotionless."

As they drifted apart, she focused her attention on her second single, "Burning Up." It was crucial to make the follow-up to a number one dance single just as powerful. Mark Kamins assumed he would be producing the song, but Warner drafted in the heavy-hitter of R&B, Reggie Lucas. "When it came to working with vocals, I didn't have the experience," says Kamins. "If you listen to 'Everybody,' it's a very thin voice. If you listen to the stuff Reggie did, he worked more, took her voice up to another level. That's what Madonna needed." She said at the time: "I wanted Mark Kamins to *direct* me, but 'Everybody' was the first record he'd ever done." She referred to a version of the song Steve Bray had recorded as "really full and lush-sounding, which is how it should have been." Although disappointed at not being able to take his protégée further, Kamins (who'd been savvy enough to sign her to his own production company) cut a deal with Warner that granted him a percentage of future royalties. This was a considerable sweetener. "I didn't mind 'cause I had my little piece of the rock. I had no problems with that, I wasn't jealous or upset," Kamins asserts.

On "Burning Up," Madonna has better vocal control, singing with more restraint and a sense of authority. The song itself, however, is not as dynamic as "Everybody." Over a New-Order-meets-gay-disco dance beat there squalls a corny rock-guitar riff. In the song she plays a woman frustrated by unrequited lust. She'll do anything, she declares with cheerful self-abasement. She's down on her knees panting like a dog, but her reluctant suitor is not impressed—a factor no doubt influenced by the dated early 80s synth sound.

Sire financed a video for "Burning Up," which received heavy rotation on the fledgling MTV cable station. It was a rudimentary early 80s affair, complete with campy surrealism—her eye, a flower, a car, a Grecian head. She plays a hot chick writhing in the road, waiting to be run over by her boyfriend (Ken Compton) in a pale blue convertible. The only shot that saves it from being standard exploitative fare is that at the end of the video *she* is the one driving the car—a neat twist that showed right from the start Madonna was aware of subverting the female-as-victim role. It was the first time many people saw the girl behind "Everybody," and with that, her wider audience began to bite.

Madonna then went on an aggressive promotional tour with her dancers Erica Bell, Bags Riley, and Martin Burgoyne. "I told her there were asses she had to kiss and she did that, no problem," said her A&R man Michael Rosenblatt. "Saturday nights, we'd get in my car and do three discos. A coupla songs, a coupla grand." From the beginning, Madonna has always had a strong rapport with her dancers, a symbiotic energy she learned from doing contemporary dance. Erica and the crew weren't just her backup, they were close clubbing friends. When they were off-duty, Madonna and Erica would go to the Mudd Club and terrorize all the attractive men. Madonna would say: "Rica, I'm the best-looking white girl here, and you are the best-looking black girl here, so let's do it." They'd target cute boys, boldly kiss them on the mouth, take their phone numbers, and while the boys were still watching, crumple up the numbers and throw them away. That spoiled defiance spilled over into their live performances, making them compelling to watch. "You couldn't take your eyes off her," recalls Ginger Canzeroni, former manager of The Go-Go's, who saw Madonna perform at a downtown club. "She was very attractive, she was street. There was something different about her."

With a club tour and two successful singles in the bag, Sire took up their modest album option, and Madonna went into Sigma Sound studio with Reggie Lucas. This is where their differences really became apparent. A former guitarist for Miles Davis and producer for sophisticated soul singers like Stephanie Mills and Phyllis Hyman,

Lucas was used to coaxing subtle sounds out of his musicians, adding texture and complexity to the mix. Madonna sang well within a certain range, but knew her voice would get lost amid complicated arrangements. "Reggie, I thought, might be able to push me, having worked with Phyllis Hyman and Roberta Flack. The only problem was that he wanted to make me sound like them," Madonna said later.

Not long after the sessions started, they began to clash. Madonna complained that Lucas wanted to put "too much stuff" in, as opposed to the minimalist demos she favored. She said that the track "Borderline," for instance, was much too subtle, but ironically it has become a key favorite with Madonna fans. Notable for its sweet melody line and sense of yearning, "Borderline" is about trying to secure love that is just out of reach. The music mirrors the sentiment of the song, with a slowly evolving keyboard motif and no clear-cut chorus—so with each line there is tension but no release. In a study about what makes "commercial song a global object of desire," musicologist Luiz Tatit suggests that hit songs have clear "identity markers," that they are "concentrated around the refrain." A typical example of this would be "Lucky Star," with its simple structure and upfront vocal. This was the template for Madonna's early sound—clear, direct, and unambiguous. She instinctively understood what made a Top Ten hit.

By contrast, "Borderline" is about thematic exploration, "a search," as Tatit states, "for completion in the area of melody," with the tune echoing the lyrical lovers' misunderstandings and separations. It wasn't where Madonna wanted to go just yet, and although it reached a respectable number ten in the *Billboard* charts, it wasn't the smash she needed. If Madonna had gone in Reggie Lucas's direction, it would have taken her longer to imprint herself on national consciousness, but maybe she would have won that elusive artistic credibility sooner.

Anthony Jackson, a top session player for everyone from Paul Simon to George Benson and Steely Dan, played bass on "Borderline." "It was a catchy song: that type of writing is musically unique. Reggie [Lucas] always had a very good harmonic and melodic sense—his approach resembles that of Philadelphia producer Thom Bell. It requires a depth of knowledge, training, and sophistication to pull it off," he recalls. An old high school friend of Reggie Lucas, Jackson ended up playing on "Borderline" by accident. "I was doing a session, and Reggie was in one of the other rooms. He came to me and said, 'When you're done with your session, there's something you might like to play on. She's a new artist. Her name's Madonna.'"

Jackson went in and doubled the synth bass line, underpinning the track with a rich, laid-back, funky groove. "She was completely unknown at the time. I have to give Madonna a lot of credit. She knows she's not the greatest singer, but she knows how to get the music down. She's got *style*, and a way of choosing songs and guiding the way they go," says Jackson.

Madonna has dismissed her self-titled debut as little more than an "aerobics album." It's true that some of the tracks exude the air of a gym workout. "Physical Attraction," for instance, is a song that breathless 70s pop act Olivia Newton-John would have been proud of, while "Think of Me" laces its full-tilt disco energy with some perfunctory jazz-funk saxophone. "Lucky Star," though, stands out for its shimmering keyboards, synth claps, and the earthy backing vocals of soul sister Gwen Guthrie. Madonna's backup singers have always provided a strong counterpoint to her straightforward girlish mid-range vocal—while she delivers the melody and the message of the song, they weave around her, embellishing the lower registers and filling out her sound. In the same way that her dancers act as a foil for Madonna the star, so her singers, from Guthrie to Siedah Garratt, Niki Haris, and Donna DeLory, give her songs a rich texture with their call-and-response and harmonizing.

Keyboards, too, form a major part of her sound, though this album was a little heavy on the baroque, almost progressive rock chords of the song "I Know It," a strange piece about the end of a relationship. It is an uneven album, very much a beginner's one, with some of Madonna's motifs in place. Struggling to break out of early-80s disco pop to find her own style, she sometimes hits it bang-on, while in other places she sounds like a cross between pop rocker Pat Benatar and white "chocolate soul" artist Teena Marie.

Lyrical themes emerged that became typical of Madonna's oeuvre—romance songs of unrequited love, songs of female bravado and the search for men and meaning. Mingled in with that was a rudimentary sense of spiritual exploration. In "Lucky Star," she sings for the first time about the angel as her spirit guide and protector. But early Madonna is mostly about the power of the dance. This is best expressed in "Holiday," a song that cemented her style. With its bubbling Latin undertow, crunchy bass and strings, and Fred Zarr's elegant closing piano riff, it's one of her most persuasive numbers. There's tension, release, resolution, and celebration, complete with Madonna's playful commands and exhortations. Written by Curtis Hudson and Lisa Stevens, the song was recorded for the album at the last minute and produced by a new hotshot DJ, John "Jellybean" Benitez. In the same way that Mark Kamins steered her to the starting block, the honey-eyed Benitez helped to take Madonna to the next phase.

Benitez was a hip young dude from the South Bronx, who had been deejaying since his teens in the early 70s. "Most of my friends aspired to be drug dealers, pimps, or bouncers, and we had a hangout in the basement of the apartment building—the clubhouse. We had a turntable there and I would bring my record collection and sit . . . and play records—never leaving the turntable, for fear that they would be stolen or scratched or broken somehow," he told Bouncefm.com in 2006. People began to refer to him as "the DJ," but to the young Benitez, "a DJ was someone that was on the radio—did weather and commercials and things like that." It wasn't until he saw a club DJ in action working two turntables at once that he discovered his calling.

"The music never stopped . . . Both songs playing at the same time. When I saw it happening, I was like, 'Wow, this is cool!'" Benitez's enthusiasm was infectious. He perfected his skills at sweet-sixteen parties and local clubs before doing gigs in Manhattan. By 1981 he was a DJ at the Funhouse. Located in a Manhattan warehouse district on West 26th Street, the club attracted Hispanic and

Italian-American teenagers from Brooklyn and the Bronx. Known as "buggas," the crowd would wear cut-off T-shirts, sweatpants, and bandanas. They were passionate devotees of Benitez. As writer Peter Shapiro documents: "The vibe was a combination of hip-hop and disco: the crowd would bark if they liked a song that Jellybean was playing and boo if they didn't; the boys would be prowling the dance floor looking for people to battle with (both with dance moves and with fists) while the girls would be singing along to the cathartic songs of heartbreak."

Into this melee came Madonna with Warner promo guy Bobby Shaw at her side. "It was quite common for record companies to bring new artists to meet DJs at that time," recalled Benitez. "I had a very high profile, very credible, underground crowd . . . Madonna came in the DJ booth. We hit it off and she asked me to remix some of the songs on her record." The two became lovers and quickly moved in together. The ideal partner for Madonna at that time, Benitez found himself remixing a large portion of her debut album. Just before it was in the bag, Madonna dropped "Ain't No Big Deal," a track she'd cowritten with Steve Bray that the latter had already produced for a group called Barracuda. That left space for another song.

"So she decided that she wanted a new song and I had a demo of 'Holiday.' She loved it and we went to the record company and they said, 'Fine, you have to have it ready by Friday,'" Benitez recalled. "I had never produced a record at that point . . . I didn't know that much about making records! Although I knew how to take a track apart and restructure it, I'd never produced a record from scratch before." Never one to back down from a challenge, Benitez thought up the sound in his head, assembled some musicians, and hummed the parts to them. Combining that with Madonna's "very soulful approach to singing a pop song," he created what was to be one of her most enduring hits. He has said since: "That launched my career and hers simultaneously."

Madonna noted that her best results thus far had been with rooky producers. These hungry DJs and remixers were open to suggestion, and vital for keeping her music one step ahead. With her next album, she was determined to nail a pop sound that was uniquely hers. "I now know what I want on my next record. The production won't be so slick, because where Reggie . . . comes from is a whole different school," she said shortly before *Madonna* was released. "There will be a more crossover approach to it this time . . . In America, Warner doesn't know how to push me, whether to push me as a disco artist or as New Wave because of the way I look. I'd rather just start another category."

Madonna's goal was to bring dance music to the people—and, crucially, to the elusive programmers of daytime U.S. radio. "She was a spunky little white girl coming on like a black chick," recalls New Musical Express writer Barney Hoskyns. "We've seen that a lot since with hip-hop; ambitious white kids appropriating black gestures." For Madonna, it was just a matter of inventing a new category of her own. The cover for her debut album said it all. The original artwork featured Madonna in bleached-out gold soft focus. She could have been anybody. The final version featured her with short peroxided hair and dark roots, looking straight into the camera, grabbing at a dog collar around her neck. She wore heavy black eyeliner, strong lipstick, and dozens of silver bracelets, chains, and leather wristbands. Her eyes were shining out with tremendous will, her image one of stylized rebellion. Shot in plain black-and-white, it seemed to say, I'm here, with chains and keys. Unlock me, unlock my power, I'm ready to be unleashed.

It was a stark image, styled by Maripol. A former art student from Nantes in northern France, Maripol was a jewelry designer who ended up becoming art director for Fiorucci in New York. She has a chic yet flamboyant style, captured on dozens of Polaroids that she snapped on the club scene. "Maripol was to fashion and art what occultists call a 'secret chief.' Certain people make things happen," said writer and scenester Glenn O'Brien. Maripol developed her style from an early age. "Since I was a little girl, I loved to get in my mom's closet and pick up everything and put on her high heels. I grew up with three brothers and a father who was very rough and macho. It was hard for me to find my feminine side, and the only way I was doing it was through fashion."

She found a muse and kindred spirit in Madonna. The two first met at the Roxy, dancing to hip-hop acts like Afrika Bambaataa and Fab Five Freddy. "She was this little girl with blue eyes, so funny, cute, and charming, high energy, simple, and deeply, deeply spiritual," she says. Martin Burgoyne, who had been working on record sleeve ideas, then brought Madonna to Maripol's loft to do her look. "She needed a direction. Erica was doing some clothes for her, and she had her own sense because she was a dancer. There were a lot of 'cutouts' [cropped tops]," Maripol recalls, pointing to her midriff, "but it was always inspired by the street. My source of inspiration was the street, materials that I found outside the ordinary circuit. That's why I did the industrial rubber jewelry. The cross earrings were already part of my collection—they were a form of rebellion against my own education. Why wear crosses around your neck? We were in the middle of punk, and they looked great with chains and safety pins. They were also a symbol of peace for me. Israel and Lebanon were at war, there were so many problems in the world. What with her name and her naturalness, the crosses hooked up so perfectly with what Madonna was doing."

With Maripol's direction, Madonna honed that seismic Boy Toy look that, with the cropped tops, bangles, and lace, focused on her curvy stomach and belly button. She exuded the sensuality of a young, modern Aphrodite. By November 1983, when her debut album began its slow climb up the U.S. charts, people were beginning to take notice. Buoyed up by three hit singles—"Holiday," which went to number sixteen, "Borderline" at number ten, and "Lucky Star," which in 1984 made it to number four—the album eventually reached sales of nine million worldwide. At that point, however, Madonna was itching to move on to her breakthrough second album—the one that would imprint her name on public consciousness forever.

Book Two
CONFESSION

SICK AND
PERVERTED

I'm going to rule the world.
—Madonna

FLAUNTING HER NAKED AMBITION LIKE A PREFIGHT
boxer, Madonna announced on Dick Clark's popular *American Band-
stand*: "I'm going to rule the world." She also claimed, like John Lennon did two decades earlier, that she would be "bigger than Jesus."
It was January 1984, and she knew the pressure was on to make her
second album work. Her debut was doing very nicely, thank you, but
if she was to vault over the heads of other acts to superstardom, she
needed to nail a new sound.

The critical person in this equation was Nile Rodgers. The architect of futuristic disco and the man behind Chic, he was also
the man who reshaped David Bowie's sound with the hugely commercial *Let's Dance*. A fan of Bowie's androgynous image and authori-
tative pop skills, Madonna took notice. Rodgers was invited by Jellybean Benitez and an enthusiastic Warner executive to a gig she
was playing, opening for the Sony artist Jenny Burton. "Not everyone in the room got it, but boy, I got it! There was this girl singing and dancing at a time when nobody was doing it. That was

black music's heritage and here was this white girl bringing it back," Rodgers recalled.

He invited Madonna over to his apartment to listen to her demos for the next album. He wasn't sold on all the songs, but she made it clear that if he didn't learn to love them, they wouldn't be working together. Her experience with Lucas had made her defensive and anxious. She still had only a two-album deal with Warner at this stage, and she was determined to get it right. Rodgers thought the main problem was in the execution of the demos—too much sequencing, not enough live band. "I told her, if you sequence this stuff, all you'll end up with is really cute pop songs, but if we play the songs and get the interpretation of great musicians, then we can really take this to a higher level. I told her being able to perform in front of a band would establish her as a real artist."

The key song for Madonna was "Like a Virgin," which at the time Rodgers felt was one of the weakest. "She was convinced it was the one. I was like, 'Are you nuts?'" The chorus was catchy, but it had a corny, novelty air. Madonna knew instinctively, however, that it was her signature tune. It worked on two levels: both as a passionate look at personal transformation and also as a ditty dripping with irony. It was written by the then relatively unknown songwriting duo of Tom Kelly and Billy Steinberg. The latter had had a hit with Linda Ronstadt's "How Do I Make You" and a couple of tracks with Pat Benatar, but had yet to establish himself. In 1983, he was driving around in his pickup truck, musing on his love life. "I'd survived a very traumatic divorce. Then I met somebody and felt very elated about it. It seemed a miracle to me—I'd made it through the wilderness, I felt brand-new," Steinberg told me. "When people suffer a disturbing breakup, they feel a bit shell-shocked, that they'll never be able to open their heart again."

Steinberg wrote a song about his new love. He kept the verses sincere, with a sense of longing and life experience, but decided to do something "cutting edge, risqué, and playful" for the chorus. "Believe me, I wasn't a weirdo thinking that 'like a virgin' would be a normal, sincere statement. I knew it would be provocative. I wasn't writing my diary, I wanted to write a hit song." Inspired by Smokey Robinson's song "Virgin Man," Steinberg wrote the chorus with a tongue-in-cheek 50s twist. When Tom Kelly added the music, he approached the song as a ballad. "But the chorus sounded ridiculous as a ballad. He tried numerous approaches, then in his frustration began bashing the piano and singing falsetto. 'That's it! Right there!' I said." Though delighted with the result, the duo found it a difficult song to "place," and were turned down by numerous artists and labels. "They laughed, saying 'No one will ever sing that song.' In a way, it was written for one person. Thinking of the word 'virgin' and the name Madonna—how perfect can you get?" says Steinberg.

Warner Bros. executive Michael Ostin finally snapped it up, saying it was perfect for his artist Madonna. When she first heard it, she deemed it "sick and perverted," but that wasn't a problem. "Sick and perverted always appeals to me," she said, ". . . there were so many innuendoes in it, I thought, 'This is great. This will really screw with people.'" For a post-Catholic girl steeped in Vatican II dogma, she knew it would work well with the cheery virgin/whore dichotomy she was developing. And for the first time she could see the look, the music, and the personal philosophy coming together. When she argued with Nile Rodgers to keep the song on the album, she declared: "Losing your virginity is the most important thing that ever happens to a girl. It's all girls talk about and girls will all relate to it."

In Steinberg's opinion the finished song is "an absolute blueprint" of his original. In his view, they didn't do anything else apart from bringing in a live drummer. And, with an approach that would later get her into trouble, "Madonna sang every note exactly the way Tom Kelly did, right down to the word 'hey!'"

THE *Like a Virgin* sessions took place that spring at the Power Station studios in Midtown Manhattan. The record boasted the powerhouse Chic lineup of the bassist Bernard Edwards, drummer Tony Thompson, and Rodgers on guitar. It also featured Jimmy Bralower, a drummer who had worked with Kurtis Blow, Chic, and Hall & Oates, and who was making a name for himself as a whiz kid with fledgling electronic drum technology. Responsible for the album's pop sheen and snappy drum programming, he pulled the live instrumentation and electronics together. "The album is very landscaped, tight, and precise—a little different for the time," he says. "We had the earliest computerized drums—what hip-hop has become—those were the tools. Twenty years later, this music is part of history, but at the time there was no other music to take a cue from. It was like driving without directions, purely on instinct."

For Bralower, this was an exciting record to make. "When Nile brought me in, I thought, I dig 'Borderline' and 'Holiday'—oh yeah, I guess I'm going to be making one of those. Then I was handed 'Like a Virgin' and 'Material Girl' and I thought, What is going on?" He quickly realized that this would be a departure from Madonna's disco roots. "She and Nile had in mind something bigger than anyone else envisioned for her."

The record kicks off with "Material Girl," the song that would become Madonna's personal anthem for the 1980s. It's notable that now she rarely performs that song live, and doesn't identify with the sentiment, however ironic. But back in the early 80s, when the "Greed Is Good" yuppie dystopia was emerging, this was a clarion call. Ronald Reagan was in the White House, shoulder pads and power-dressing were high fashion, and the sense of a hippie alternative had been pushed so far to the margins it was about to disappear. As one of her former backup vocalists, Gwen Guthrie, once sang to an idle boyfriend, "Ain't Nuthin' Going on but the Rent." Money had become the big motivator in the 80s culture. Although the video accompanying "Material Girl" clearly shows an antimaterialist backstory, the main thrust is one of credit, interest, and cold hard cash. Mr. Right is to be someone of equal financial status, a well-dressed peacock who can stand beside her in the power pop firmament.

An upbeat radio song, its very conventionality is undercut by the camp male chorus and Madonna's asides; those yelps and girlish vocals that have become her trademark. It's the complement to "Like a Virgin," her second most enduring hit from these years. Here her voice sounds sweet and adolescent, a mock-up of the girl-group style. She sings of the renewing force of love with total self-belief, comfortable with the pitching and phrasing, delivering it like the anthem it becomes. With its lascivious swing, Four Tops–style bass line, and suggestive lyrics, she knows it is "her" song, and puts her stamp on it. Jimmy Bralower remembers laying down the "sonic landscape" for the rhythms. "If you listen to the drums on 'Like a Virgin,' they're big, fat, and wide. They take up a lot of space. If it had been done any other way, the song would've lacked authority. We were clear about how the sounds would move listeners subliminally." And much of this song's attraction is in the persistent way it hooks into the subconscious.

Continuing the theme of lushness and excess set by "Material Girl," the song "Dress You Up" uses fashion as a metaphor. Sung by a woman clearly addicted to clothes, this is a love tune that rocks. With its heady groove and carefree vocal, it accentuates Madonna's physical, sensual world. As a dancer, she is moved by touch and texture, and it's all here in the lyrics and kinetic delivery. "With 'Dress You Up,' I was going for a popping, closer, more immediate sound," explains Bralower. Similarly, with the track "Angel," he helped create a sense of intimacy, propelled by driving rhythm. "If we'd given 'Angel' the same wide sound as 'Like a Virgin,' it would've been lumbering, there would have been no snap to it. For the whole record we were consciously creating extreme sounds—backbeats, snare drums very high-pitched, bass drums fat, wide, and long. It was not a normal set of sounds. We were pushing the envelope on the cartoon-like quality."

Back at Warner Bros., people were getting worried. This was clearly not going to be a reprise of her debut. "Phone calls would come in from various places. 'What are you doing? What is this record you're making?' People were scared out of their minds, fearful of change. When you have three hits in a certain vein, you do the same thing again. If it ain't broke, don't fix it. Madonna was bucking all normal trends, she was *fighting* trends," recalls Bralower.

Nile Rodgers resolutely stuck by his artist. His approach was efficient. As Bralower says, "He kept the record rooted in dance rhythms and he'd break past the obvious. His recording style was organized;

clean, tight, a little bit aggressive. We made the record in six weeks from top to bottom. Procedurally it was like a well-oiled machine." That suited Madonna, who liked to work at a similar pace. "The thing between us, man, it was sexual, it was passionate, it was creative," recalled Rodgers. Even though he admits the songs were "rudimentary Chic exercises . . . one-take stuff," there was liberation in their simplicity.

Madonna varied the tone with mid-tempo ballads like "Pretender" and "Stay," but these were less successful—the former marked by a limp arrangement, and the latter weighed down by that dated 80s synth sound. Ironically, at this stage, Madonna was more powerful singing about abstract love of the dance or a lust for life rather than the day-to-day mundanity of breaking up and making up. With its driving, clattering beats, the survivalist anthem "Over and Over" was more her style. This reflected her attitude at the time—that love was fine but her real focus was personal ambition and the energy it needed to take her higher. The standout *Like a Virgin* songs were the backdrop for Madonna the star. "She was saying, 'I wanna be a movie star,'" says Bralower. "She knew something." As her East Village friend Johnny Dynell says: "She saw music as a way to get into the movies. 'I wanna be Jessica Lange,' she told me. I don't think she ever thought she'd be doing music thirty years later."

Although Madonna wasn't yet a full-blown star ("She wasn't particularly comfortable in her lifestyle, she hadn't seen royalties yet," Bralower says diplomatically), she was acting like one. "She could be headstrong and—I'm being very kind—rambunctious. But she was smart, she made her playground extreme," he adds. She was the restless boy-toy girl with the colorful bracelets, focused on every minute of the session. "Very often artists show up to sing and then go shopping, but she was there the whole time. This was a very important record to her."

She was careful with the album artwork, introducing her virgin/whore persona with proud transparency. The cover was shot by a cool new name in fashion—Steven Meisel. Here Madonna props herself up on silk cushions, looking straight to camera, all curves and seductive temptress. She wears a huge drop earring, a silver crucifix, diamond choker, and an exquisite lace bustier. Her extravagant tulle skirt and dainty fingerless gloves are offset by the hip-hop BOY TOY belt. It's a picture of ironic innocence, the virginal bride with fake 80s blush. On the reverse she appears stripped down in a black negligee, wearing minimal jewelry and sheer stockings. She sits on a threadbare, beaten-up bed, with plain sheets, an existential cup of coffee placed on top, and her hair is mussed with that look of all-night wanton sex—a Cindy Sherman–esque picture in its sense of a backstory, a continuing narrative. She is the star in her own B-movie.

BY NOW, Madonna was moving on and up, and had left her Michigan roots far behind. She was contacted out of the blue by her old boyfriend from high school, Wyn Cooper. "I called her up, her name was in the phone book, believe it or not. I didn't recognize her voice. I said, 'Is that Madonna Ciccone?' pronounced *Si*-ccone. And, using the more Italian pronunciation, she answered, 'No, it's *Chi*-ccone.' Oh God, I thought, you get to New York and change the pronunciation of your name. She didn't seem interested. 'I don't have time to talk to you,' she said. 'I'm on my way to Fire Island.'"

She felt ambivalent about old school friends, uncertain about where they fitted in her new life. On one level, she yearned for the security of home, while on another level, she had to keep in step with the superstar persona she was creating. She would call her former best friend Carol Belanger in the middle of the night, crying and saying: "I feel so lonely. I've got no one to talk to." Then, when she'd come to Detroit to do a gig, she would leave tickets for Carol for an after-show party. "But when Carol turned up, Madonna would be surrounded by other people and wouldn't speak to her," says Cooper. "Carol was very hurt by that."

Madonna was socializing in different circles. No longer sleeping on egg crates, she moved into a spacious apartment with Jellybean on Broome Street in SoHo. They were entranced with one another ("She was my girl," he said), and both were moving fast in their careers. "We spent hundreds of hours necking in the studio between takes," he recalled. "We had a very open relationship. It was part of my lifestyle, her lifestyle. I believe we were meant to meet and work together. A lot of great things came out of that relationship."

WITH *Like a Virgin* in the bag, Madonna was anxious for it to be released. Seeing this as her ticket to a film career, she was not pleased when Warner sat on it. Her debut album was doing so well, they wanted to wait until it had played itself out before unleashing *Like a Virgin*. When it was eventually released in November 1984, the record stood out amid stiff competition. Despite her impatience, the timing was just right. "Music is the main vector of celebrity. When it's a success its impact is just as strong as a bullet hitting the target," she has said.

In the pop world, she was competing with Michael Jackson (at the peak of his career with the 25 million–selling *Thriller* album), and Prince (who had just reached critical mass with *Purple Rain*). The record industry was changing. As Gil Friesen, former president of U.S. A&M Records, said: "It was no longer a free-for-all expanding market. It was, going into the 1980s, an industry where there was tough competition for market share, with business principles that governed."

The teenage audience that had kept the business buoyant in the 1960s and 1970s grew smaller, leading to the 1979 "crash." Singles sales slumped to 10 percent of record sales, and major record company CBS lost 46 percent of annual profits, having to sell stock to survive. The 1980s was about the rise of the corporate artist. Stars like Jackson, Prince, Bruce Springsteen, and Lionel Ritchie were pulling the industry out of its slump. According to CBS Records' Al Teller, "The superstar is the giant bonanza. The big hit is to develop superstar careers. That is the biggest win you can have."

Madonna needed to establish herself as a priority act for Warner. Major labels were not going to take risks and were heavily reliant on saleable images, particularly for female artists, who have long been considered more difficult to "sell." Madonna was lucky in that MTV had become second in importance to the music industry as a promotional vehicle. She was to use this medium with devastating aplomb, but at the time of *Like a Virgin*'s release, she was yet to make her mark as the video queen. In 1984, the big female sellers were black artists like the Pointer Sisters, Tina Turner, Sade, and Chaka Khan—women with big soul voices and lived experience to match. They exuded glamour and dignity, but (with the exception of the anarchic Chaka Khan) not an offbeat quirkiness.

Madonna was a different proposition: white (and therefore easier to market), thoroughly sexual, and provocative. Her only major rival in mass pop terms was Cyndi Lauper, a powerhouse pop talent from Queens, New York, who in 1984 had a major hit with the sparkly girly anthem to female solidarity "Girls Just Wanna Have Fun." Like Madonna, she came, on her mother's side, from an Italian-American lower-middle-class background. Like Madonna, she had a subversive, cartoon image, dying her hair green and wearing vivid thrift-store clothes. She had a peculiar voice and impressive range—from the soulful balladry of "Time After Time" to the tongue-in-cheek delights of "She Bop," a top-three hit song about female masturbation. And she also had a huge audience of screaming wannabes.

Used to being the gawky misfit from a single-parent background, Lauper wanted success "out of anger. People would give me grief about the way I dressed, then Boy George's success opened the door for me," she told me in the early 90s. "I was shocked at the reaction. I'd go out onstage and the audience would be filled with girls screaming, ripping at my clothes. I'd never heard girls screaming over a woman before, and at first I thought, They think I'm gay. The only bad thing is I wasn't!"

Both Madonna and Lauper had tapped into that rich seam of adolescent female desire. The longing expressed by the screaming was a longing to *be* the desired object, to have her as your metaphorical best friend, to literally walk in her shoes. That way led to self-determination, glamour, and happiness. Add a degree of sexual confusion, and you have a potent mix.

At first, Lauper stole the march, with four top-ten singles and a 4.5 million–selling debut album, *She's So Unusual*. "If you were to take Cyndi's first album and compare it with Madonna's first album, my God, Cyndi's is so much better. Just out of the starting gate, she took the lead real fast," says Billy Steinberg, who went on to write for Lauper such hit songs as "True Colors" and "I Drove All Night." But while Madonna thrived on adulation and success, Lauper found it an unwelcome pressure. "You can't live in that sort of atmosphere as a meteoric phenomenon, it doesn't go with being creative. It's always been a struggle for me to sell myself," she says. Steinberg believes that Lauper also made a mistake by ditching her producers. "Her first record was such a success, she got a bit headstrong, saying, 'I'm taking over the reins.' With that she sort of sabotaged her career. Madonna was much more shrewd about who she chose to collaborate with."

By the early 90s, Lauper had retreated more into the background as a songwriter. At one point, she suggested that Madonna "seemed kind of alone, with all her bodyguards," that she was "a terrific businesswoman and entertainer, but I don't know if moving people is important to her." She later modified that view, telling me: "We like a lot of the same things but are very different. When she approaches the rhythm, she comes from that dancer place. It's almost like Eartha Kitt. She certainly pushes everybody's buttons. I think every woman has a sexuality and shouldn't be castrated. They always compare us— but they do that to women. It's like, no matter what I said or she said, it would always come out like a cat fight. It's silly."

The main difference between Madonna and Lauper lay in the former's urge for immortality, for becoming an icon. And there is no better place to realize that than on celluloid.

Madonna on her 1985 Like a Virgin tour, performing at Madison Square Garden, New York.

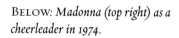

Below: Madonna (top right) as a cheerleader in 1974.

Madonna as a girl in her first holy communion dress.

Right: Clockwise from top left, Madonna's half-sister Jennifer, half-brother Mario, father Tony and stepmother Joan in 1987.

Photos from Madonna's high school yearbook in 1975 and 1976.

BELOW: Madonna doing the hokey-pokey with the school Thespian Society in 1975.

LEFT: *Madonna on the roof of Gramercy Park Hotel, New York, in 1981, and* (RIGHT) *another early photo, from sessions commissioned by Camille Barbone.*

LEFT: *An early '80s portrait of Madonna, from the private collection of Camille Barbone.*

ABOVE RIGHT: *On the UK TV show The Tube, at Manchester's Hacienda Club in 1984.*

RIGHT: *Age twenty-four, the young star inspired by the New York club scene.*

BELOW RIGHT: *With her boyfriend Jellybean Benitez in 1983, photographed by Andy Warhol.*

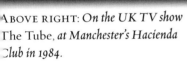

Madonna with Erika Belle and Christopher Ciccone, the two backing dancers in her "Lucky Star" video.

BELOW: *The 1984* Time *magazine cover that put Madonna on the map as a global star.*

ABOVE: *Arriving at the Hollywood premiere of* Desperately Seeking Susan *in 1985.*

BELOW: *Madonna as Susan, with her costar Robert Joy, who played Jim.*

ABOVE: *Performing at Live Aid in Philadelphia, 1985.*

LEFT: *The flip side of her breakthrough album,* Like a Virgin.

BELOW LEFT: *Madonna with her* Desperately Seeking Susan *costar Rosanna Arquette.*

BELOW RIGHT: *On her Like a Virgin tour.*

Madonna at the first annual MTV
Video Music Awards in 1984, just
after she had shocked the nation
with her simulated sexual display.

How I Stopped Worrying and Learned to Love Madonna

"I've been working my ass off for years . . . I've worked for everything that I've got and I worked long and hard, so when I got it I thought I deserved it. I always knew it would happen," Madonna once said. But in September 1984, she took a risk that could have easily backfired. At the first MTV Awards Ceremony, broadcast live from the Radio City Music Hall in New York, she sang "Like a Virgin," dressed in her white bustier, tulle skirt, and veil, writhing and simulating sex atop a giant white wedding cake. The audience, including host Bette Midler, were bemused. "Tom and I were shocked. There was this amateurish camerawork as Madonna rolled around the stage, exposing her voluptuous, slightly pudgy body," recalls Billy Steinberg, cowriter of the song. "I thought, oh no, now our song is doomed, it'll never be a hit."

Many felt uneasy at her display of hyped-up, over-stylized sexuality, but TV viewers jammed the switchboards. "If something that spontaneous, strong, and true comes along, people love it," Steinberg says with hindsight. Maripol remembers the press and photographers clamoring to get a picture after the show. "Cyndi Lauper was there, and it was like, 'Move out, baby!'" she says. "I remember kids at the window and Madonna was looking at them in the limo, like in awe, you know? She knew that she was going to be big, but not that fast and not that big."

Amid the controversy, the fact that Madonna was celebrating the nomination of "Borderline" for Best New Video got overlooked. In this video, she plays a graffiti girl torn between a rich uptown photographer and her break-dancing Hispanic boyfriend. Her first collaboration with director Mary Lambert, it was a step away from the rudimentary gyrations of "Burning Up" and "Lucky Star." With one eye on movie stardom, as soon as she could afford it, Madonna made videos with mini-narratives and high production values, raising the standard for women on MTV. In a way that would happen time and again, though, her aesthetic achievement was swallowed up in the provocative hype that surrounded it.

Before the awards show, Madonna had been determined to do something that would challenge the TV audience, so she consulted Maripol. "At first she wanted to appear inside a cage, with a wild animal. So I told her it was pointless, as Grace Jones had just done it for Jean-Paul Goude," said Maripol. "I insisted that when you sing a song called 'Like a Virgin' and you look nothing like a virgin, it's better to turn the whole thing upside down." The previous year, Maripol had done an event for Fiorucci, where Madonna jumped out of a huge rubber cake with a zipper. "So we decided to make a giant wedding cake."

SUCCESS SOON went to Madonna's head. "I remember Warner threw a big party for her in West Hollywood just before the MTV Awards," recalls songwriter Gardner Cole. "She had to get up and speak. She was a little inebriated. She was boisterous, loud, and obnoxious, and the Warner executives were cringing. But somehow she managed to turn it around. By the end everyone was cheering. It's not easy to get jaded Hollywood people in the palm of your hand. I thought, She's definitely going to go places."

Who was this cocky new artist? Was she a plastic bimbo or was she for real? To many feminists, she seemed tacky, selling sex and little else. This was borne out by the "Like a Virgin" video, where she vamps up the virgin/whore imagery, gliding through a boudoir in full wedding outfit and dancing suggestively in black and blue Lurex on a Venetian gondola. Shot by Mary Lambert like a twentieth-century fairy tale, the video also features a lioness stalking around the pillars (Madonna's alter ego, the wild woman within), and a mystery man in a mask. It's a modern tale of transformation, complete with beauty and the beast. Madonna's energy leaped off the screen, but people were still undecided about her. She had an ever-growing tribe of wannabes, but women weren't sure if she was truly supportive of other women.

"Like a Virgin" arrived at a time of high anxiety for feminism. There had been the heady revolutionary rhetoric of the 1960s, when Gloria Steinem, the "Wages for Housework" campaign, and Valerie Solanas's *SCUM Manifesto* galvanized a new generation to fight for women's liberation. This was followed by the Equal Opportunities legislation of the 1970s and a gradual recognition of gay rights. But by the early 1980s, the backlash had begun, with Reagan's administration in the United States and Margaret Thatcher in Britain ushering in a new era of conservatism. Civil rights were under attack, including women's abortion rights.

Many saw a continuum between advertising, music videos, and soft porn, with women constantly depicted as submissive beings, there for the pleasure of men. This is why Madonna's exploration of the virgin/whore stereotype was so incendiary—not just to the Christian right wing of the "moral majority," but also to feminists who saw it as disempowering. Where Madonna fitted in the continuum was a matter for debate. Was she part of the problem or of a solution? Was she a competitive female, just there to grab male attention—or did she have something original to say? Women continued to be ambivalent until the seismic eruption of *Desperately Seeking Susan*. This was when Madonna's true strength, Madonna as a three-dimensional human being, fully emerged. "How I Stopped Worrying and Learned to

Love Madonna," read the cover of the U.K. feminist magazine *Women's Review* in 1985. With her most acclaimed movie role and her first world tour, Madonna began to convince the nonbelievers, becoming a figurehead for popular feminism.

IN 1984, an up-and-coming director, Susan Seidelman, was looking for a supporting actress in her movie *Desperately Seeking Susan*, a comedy about bored housewife Roberta Glass, who, out of curiosity, trails Susan, a feisty, punky girl from the personal ads. After getting involved in murder and mayhem, Roberta ends up transforming her life so she is more like Susan. It was an unusual film for the time, revolving, as it did, around two women in a positive, upbeat way. Back then, Hollywood females were usually the wives or girlfriends of male heroes, and there was little representation of women's everyday emotional reality.

"Going to film school in the 1970s, I was growing up in a new feminist environment. I've always had female protagonists. To me it was a natural decision," says Susan Seidelman, with whom I spoke in New York. "There weren't many female directors at that time, and I didn't want to work on territory that guys had already mined. *Desperately Seeking Susan* was not just for a female audience—it was one of the first female-driven films able to get a commercial hold on the marketplace."

After starting out as a fashion student from Philadelphia, Seidelman went on to graduate from NYU Film School in the late 70s. She studied film at an exciting time. "I lived downtown, in the East Village, under Philimore East rock club. It was very funky. New York was going through a recession. It had a bankruptcy crisis that was bad for the city but great for the arts scene. Everything was cheap, and there were a lot of abandoned buildings. The punk independent film scene rose out of that. It was very atmospheric." Here she made her first low-budget feature film, *Smithereens*. Costarring Richard Hell of the Voidoids, it was a "blank generation" hit about the adventures of a groupie in downtown Manhattan. Selected to be shown at the

Cannes Film Festival in 1982, it put Seidelman on the map as an up-and-coming director.

As a result, she was sent dozens of scripts, but only one stood out: *Desperately Seeking Susan*, written by Leora Barish. "It dealt with two worlds that I knew," explains Seidelman. "I grew up in the suburbs of Philadelphia, I know what being a bored suburban girl was like. I could've been Roberta Glass. I also moved to New York and knew what was funky and appealing about the world of downtown Manhattan. The film was a fantasy about crossing over from one world into another . . . about who we are on the outside and who we want to be on the inside."

The script also chimed with the preoccupations of young 80s women. "The character of Roberta was a stereotypical female figure taking control of her destiny, and not fitting in with her husband and family. It fitted in with feminist ideas of the time. Feminists of the 70s were passing on those ideas, and in the early 80s we were redefining ourselves."

When it came to casting, Rosanna Arquette was chosen for the role of Roberta. She was a starlet who had made a name for herself playing the girlfriend of murderer Gary Gilmore in the 1982 TV film *The Executioner's Song*. "There was a big buzz about her," recalls Seidelman. Finding Susan was a trickier proposition. Many new young promising actresses were auditioned, including Ellen Barkin, Melanie Griffith, Kelly McGillis, and Jennifer Jason Leigh. Despite their credentials, none were right for the part. Seidelman then looked to the New York music scene, and Madonna, who was living down the street from her at the time. This was before "Like a Virgin," when the singer was still relatively unknown.

"Although she wasn't an experienced actress, there was something about her attitude. She was so self-confident and right for the character," says Seidelman. "I thought, If we can bring this quality to the part, that will be amazing. The studio were more cautious. They were used to actors with previous experience. But the *Smithereens* stars weren't regular actors. I felt confident I could get that quality onto film; I didn't mind about the film résumé."

Ellen Barkin was Orion Pictures' first choice, but Seidelman talked them into doing a screen test for Madonna. The studio wanted to keep the film at a modest $6 million budget, but what really swung it for Madonna was the fact that the son of the studio boss had seen her "Lucky Star" video on MTV and declared her "hot."

Shooting began in September 1984, and, from the beginning, the mood was buoyant. The film is memorable because of the attention to detail. There's the opening shot of Roberta in a beauty parlor, with pampering pedicures, hair-styling, and The Chiffons singing "One Fine Day." Shot through cameraman Ed Lachman's pinky gel (a technique that was groundbreaking at the time), all this captured a retro, girlish world. Then we move to Susan blowing bubble gum and taking Polaroids of herself in a hotel room. The camera dwells on her fishnet gloves, customized jacket, bangles, and round hatbox packed with the trinkets of an urban-drifter lifestyle. It's that eye for detail that gives the film its authenticity, that speaks so accurately to its female audience. There's that first shot where Roberta sees Susan, the latter nonchalantly striking a match on her boot and lighting a cigarette. There's Susan, putting on a stolen Nefertiti earring, a multimillion-dollar Egyptian artifact, as if it's a thrift-store find. And Susan, wearing big old trousers and drying her underarms in a train-station ladies' room, her black bra showing under a pink top. This is *her* version of girly grooming.

"That's one of my favorite moments," recalls Seidelman. "It tells you everything you need to know about the character without relying on stereotypical shots or poses. Maybe guys would resort to more femme fatale visual clichés." As the artist Andy Warhol later noted appreciatively in his diary: "Madonna . . . does some good things, she sleeps in the bathtub and dresses up and shoplifts."

Susan's wardrobe was based on what was in Madonna's closet at home. According to Seidelman, stylist Santo Loquasto brought out what was vivid about the way she already dressed, without imposing a style on her. Maripol remembers it differently. "Madonna was always complaining over the phone: 'It's horrible, they want me to wear retro clothes,' and I said, 'Don't do that, take advantage of the movie to simply stay Madonna . . . use this opportunity.' She was coming over to my house every night and we changed the look they had created for her. She really insisted on keeping her own style and they agreed."

The film also features Madonna's pumping, worldwide number one "Into the Groove." Cowritten and coproduced by Steve Bray, the song captured Madonna's irresistible ebullience. It's the soundtrack to the film's underground club scene, shot with regulars at the Danceteria. Here, on the dance floor, Madonna is queen of all she surveys, this is her territory.

Seidelman drew out of Madonna what's been widely acknowledged as her best film performance yet. She has often worked well with female directors. "Maybe it's a more down-to-earth relationship because there isn't the kind of sexual politics and games that men and women play. There's less of the sexual bullshit," Seidelman says. She was also fortunate in that she worked with the star before the latter became famous. "I found Madonna easy to work with. It was a relatively low-key set. In the beginning, there's a scene with her walking down St. Mark's Place, going to sell her jacket at a vintage store. Because she wasn't well known at the time, we didn't have bodyguards, agents, managers—it was very organic. But by the time we finished filming, her *Like a Virgin* album had just hit and we could no longer just film on the street without crowd control. Things changed considerably within two months."

Seidelman bridles at the oft-repeated truism that Madonna was successful in the movie because she was playing herself. "I've heard that it was 'Madonna just being Madonna.' In all fairness, acting isn't easy. You're saying lines you have to learn, there are marks on the floor where you have to stand, the camera is just two feet away. Anyone knows that making a fictional movie with a crew of a hundred people is not a documentary. I felt Madonna was a very self-disciplined person, who was able to learn those skills that make you an actress. Because she was a dancer, her sense of timing was good. She'd done videos, she used the camera, she knew how to project herself. She was able to deliver scripted lines in a way that was believable, not wooden or posy."

Seidelman suggests that later movies didn't work so well for Madonna because of the "layers of bullshit" that accompany celebrity. "In subsequent films, I don't know if there were a lot more agents, managers, and hangers-on. As a performer becomes an icon, it makes it harder for people to see beyond the icon 'baggage.'"

Although she was a newcomer to Hollywood filmmaking, Madonna handled the situation with aplomb. "I've never seen her nervous," says Seidelman. She showed unusual self-control, pursuing a strenuous exercise regime. "First call for the actors would be around six thirty in the morning. Madonna was picked up even earlier. Before she showed up on set, she'd get up about four a.m. to swim laps at the YMCA. She had amazing self-discipline."

By the time the film was released eight months later, the Madonna circus was in full swing. For Rosanna Arquette, this was a little galling. When the project was initiated, she was the star element that got the film green-lighted. By the time filming was finished, the press were speaking of "the Madonna movie." Arquette complained later: "I thought I was going to be making this small, charming film, not some rock video." Seidelman concurs: "It must have been disorienting. Circumstances had changed. And Madonna's character got to wear the funkier clothes, do the fun stuff, while Rosanna's character was a frumpy housewife in pink chiffon. It had to be hard." Seidelman could see the film reflecting real life. "Ironically, the subtext of the Roberta character strangely paralleled the whole Madonna phenomenon that was to follow. There'd be all these Madonna dress-alikes, wanting to be like her."

Madonna's free-spirited energy pulsated from the screen. The release of the film coincided with her Like a Virgin world tour, where many people would see her live for the first time. It was at this point that many "got" her. In the tour video, she is a study of pure exuberance. Warm, engaging, funny, she speaks directly to her predominantly female audience. "I couldn't believe it," says Dan Kleinman, director of the video. "The crowd was made up almost totally of girls dressed like her." He shot the film on the last date of the tour in Detroit. "We were given a very tight budget," he remembers, "so we had to be as inventive as we could with just a few cameras. It wasn't easy. Live videos weren't a big priority in the music business then—the full concert film with backstage shots and arty angles; that didn't come till later."

Although it is a basic, no-frills production, the film captures Madonna's earthy appeal. Wearing a turquoise miniskirt, purple leggings, and booties, she wiggles her wide butt and round belly, yelling out, "Are you ready? Tonight you're mine!" with unfettered delight. The show is no more complicated than two backup dancers, a band, and a few costume changes, but it's definitive. Madonna sings slightly flat and out of breath, while dancing strict, choreographed routines. She changes into black leggings and crucifix for her chic, pop, biker-chick look, and then wears her white wedding outfit for the "Material Girl" finale. At the end of the song, she shouts to the girls in the front row: "I'm not a material girl, ain't that right ladies?" Throwing off her fake mink stole and diamonds, she yells, "I don't need money; I need love!"

It's an emotional night for her. She gazes out over the crowd, jubilant through her tears. "I was never elected the homecoming queen or anything, but I sure feel like one now," she says, trembling. For many women, this was the moment we realized she was one of us. She was eager to reach her female fans, and though the sexuality projected in her videos seemed to be aimed at men, there was a mischievous subtext that we could find if we looked hard enough. The joy was that in the live show this subtext became totally transparent. Here we got the Madonna who loves life and other girls, because she seemed so comfortable in her own skin. She was a celebrant and conduit for female energy. This was an explosive message for young 80s women finding it hard to express their sexual desires at the same time as they were fighting for equality. With a glorious disregard for male approval, Madonna expressed the urges that many of us felt compelled to hide: her obvious libido and lack of inhibition were powerful tools.

"I like to combine things but in a humorous way, like a uniform skirt and fishnets," she said at the time. "I love dresses like Marilyn Monroe wore, those 50s dresses that were really tailored to fit a voluptuous body. A lot of stuff made now is for an androgynous figure, and it doesn't look good on me." She dismissed her critics by saying that her fans came from a wide age range and all kinds of backgrounds. "If they're happy, I'm happy—so much for all the goofs who want to decide if my show deserves an R or an X rating." Maripol did a merchandising line with Madonna for the tour, and sold truckloads of bracelets and crucifixes. Her New York shop, Maripolitan, was doing big business. "It was great—I refilled, refilled, refilled, you know? There was such a craze with my rubber bracelets."

The Virgin tour was different from the stadium spectacles Madonna went on to produce. Running across the United States from April to June, it was essentially a rock gig that grew and grew as more people responded to the Madonna phenomenon. 1985 was her year. "We started in Seattle playing to two thousand people, and then all hell broke loose. We ended up playing Madison Square Garden in New York with a capacity of twenty-two thousand," recalls Bill Meyers, the keyboardist in her live band.

He remembers being contacted by Pat Leonard, who had been hired as musical director after his work on Michael Jackson's Victory tour. "There was a band tryout and all but one of the members were accepted. The one who didn't get it was a great guitar player, but he was losing his hair. Madonna wasn't too happy about that. After I was chosen, she came up to me and said: 'You're the most like a man, you're the most mature.' I thought that was pretty forward, but kinda nice." The band, including drummer Jonathan Moffet and James Harrah on guitar, were forced into shiny Nehru-collar suits with Beatle boots. "They were godawful," laughs Meyers. Like the gangsters in the Quentin Tarantino film *Reservoir Dogs*, each musician had to pick his color. "Pat Leonard was working on his synthesizer when the tailor came, so the only thing left for him was silver. He was fighting a weight problem at the time, so he ended up with his gut hanging out, looking like the Tin Man from *The Wizard of Oz*. We laughed uproariously, and he disappeared. Five minutes later, Madonna stormed out to me, yelling, 'You asshole. He's demanding another suit, and it's all your fault!' I tweaked the tail of the dragon there,"

Meyers adds mischievously. Leonard had to wear the silver suit all the way through the tour, with Madonna encouraging him to work out when it was over.

Madonna's relationship with Leonard was intense from the start. A respected musical director and keyboardist who went on to play with Pink Floyd, he had more of a rock sensibility. When he was initially approached to musically direct her tour, he declined, saying she was "too poppy." Madonna then called him personally and persuaded him to change his mind. "I've never known anyone so direct in all my life," he said. "She knew exactly what she wanted and what she expected. . . . It typified Madonna." Once on board, he threw himself wholeheartedly into the project, smoothly translating her sound on record to a live format.

There was a sense of camaraderie on this tour, and a democratic dynamic. "Madonna was young and new and inexperienced. She relied on the musicians a lot more than other tours did. We were up on stage with her," says Meyers. As ever, she worked hard. "She always impressed me as someone who did the absolute most with what she had. At one point, she asked to do some vocal takedowns with me, her and the vocal coach. Some singers feel they don't have to do much, but she did." A trainer was brought on tour with her, and she would run five miles a day. "She and her dancers invited me to play basketball, so I joined them and they had me dying after five minutes of strenuous workout!"

Morale was good. Madonna had seven U.S. top-five singles throughout 1985, including four number ones, so as the hits racked up, Madonna-mania spread from city to city. Although she loved her fame, the constant pressure and lack of privacy was a challenge. "I saw her grow up as the tour went on," observes Meyers. "She had fears and insecurities, but she had the courage to stand up and face those things. She didn't run away from the challenge."

He met her father, Tony Ciccone, when they played Detroit. "Madonna had talked about him, the conflict they had. So I was surprised, when I met him, at how soft-spoken and caring he was. He was in a no-win situation. She wasn't real comfortable with showing insecurity . . . and people who showed insecurity—she'd have a hard time with that. I would talk back to her and she liked that. She liked other people to be strong."

While they were on tour, something happened that indicated how much the phenomenon was escalating out of control. "We played a bizarre, standing-room-only venue in San Francisco. The promoters didn't realize what a force she was becoming. The place was absolutely jam-packed. Even Prince had come, and was standing with his bodyguards, a hooded figure in the middle. Madonna was working the crowd, getting close to the edge of the stage. I could see people reaching out to grab her and pull her down, so I shouted as loud as I could, 'Stay away from the front of the stage!'" recalls Meyers. "Afterward she came to me and said, 'Thanks.' She could see it was getting out of control. She didn't do any more gigs like that. She was getting too big."

Meyers and his fellow musicians took their direct access to her for granted. On later tours, musicians were less the visual focus. They were seen as more of a "pit band," there to accompany the stage show. "I heard she would get mad if musicians didn't address her through the proper channels. After the film *Truth or Dare* came out, people asked me: 'Was she really like that?' It wasn't always like that. Ultimate power corrupts," he says.

While the *Like a Virgin* album and tour transformed her career, Madonna's personal life, too, was changing. Gradually, she would bring that more and more into her work, creating a story that was as disturbing as it was compelling. With the entrance of Sean Penn, she shifted to another gear, and the footloose Aphrodite got hitched.

MAKEUP IN THAT GREAT HOLLYWOOD WAY

It was the end of 1984. Sean had broken up with his previous girlfriend [Elizabeth McGovern], and he was living on my couch. We were watching MTV and "Like a Virgin" came on. Sean mentioned that a friend's sister was working as assistant director on a new music video called "Material Girl." I lived in Hollywood quite close by, so we decided to go down and check out this chick.
—Film director James Foley,
on the first time he and best friend
Sean Penn talked about Madonna

AT THIS POINT, SEAN PENN HAD ALREADY MADE A NAME for himself as one of the emerging Hollywood "Brat Pack" actors, a group that included Emilio Estevez, Charlie Sheen, Demi Moore, Rob Lowe, and Molly Ringwald. Sean was devoted to acting, having done repertory theater as a teenager. While he was in high school, he made a sixty-minute Super-8 film with his brother Christopher (who also became a Hollywood actor), called *Looking for Someone.* "We were out all night in Westwood, shooting in parking lots and doing stunts that nobody would ask a stuntman to do," he said. This fearlessness became a strong element in his acting. He could take emotional risks and improvise much like, as the late film critic Pauline Kael suggested, a young Marlon Brando or James Dean. By the time he met Madonna, he had already received acclaim for such film roles as the rebellious military cadet in *Taps* and the surfer stoner in *Fast Times at Ridgemont High*.

Though gifted, Sean was building up a reputation as a young hothead, on- and offscreen—which increased his desirability to women. He had been engaged to rocker Bruce Springsteen's sister Pamela, and Elizabeth McGovern was one of his costars. The twenty-four-year-old liked to appear cool, however, and despite the fact that it was his suggestion to go to the "Material Girl" video shoot, Sean seemed unmoved by the early Madonna. "When we were sitting around talking about who's hot, he never expressed any particular notice of her," maintains Foley.

Neither, it seems, did she. Although she said later that she saw Penn on the set and thought, There's my future husband, when they approached her, the reception was lukewarm. "Madonna was getting made up between shots. She was correct, polite, and no more. By that time Sean was famous. He'd been on the cover of *Rolling Stone*. She knew who he was, but made no indication that she did. She reminded me of how somebody acts when they're the queen of England. It wasn't unattractive, there was no social awkwardness. Just very straight-ahead," recalls Foley.

At that point, Madonna had other things on her mind. Her career was blossoming, but her personal life was fraught. For the previous two years, her boyfriend Jellybean had been her rock and her ally. He had helped her steer a path through the business, but because he was equally ambitious, they often ended up competing with one another. While their relationship was falling apart, she found herself pregnant with his child. She decided not to keep the baby, but it was an agonizing decision for her. While she cavorted on a soundstage in pink satin, à la Marilyn Monroe, she was feeling torn inside. Foley sensed that discrepancy between her private and public self. "The way she acts when she's dancing around in costume and being Marilyn Monroe is a totally different person from the one sitting in the chair getting made up. As I got to know her, I saw that difference between her onstage and offstage personality again and again."

As Madonna extricated herself from her relationship with Jelly-bean, she began spending time with Sean. "At first, she was a minor interest for him. They did old-fashioned dating for a while. It wasn't passionate love at first sight in the beginning, but it slowly became that for both of them. It was kinda unexpected. Marriage wasn't on either of their minds," says Foley. But within a few months, something clicked. "Suddenly they were madly in love and inseparable and couldn't wait to get married. She became the center of Sean's life."

Meeting Sean caused a huge shift in Madonna's life. He became her protector and a jealous, domineering force. But he was also her artistic alter ego—moody, troubled, prone to violence, but passionately dedicated to his craft. His aesthetic was one informed by writers like Raymond Carver and Charles Bukowski, the rugged, disaffected American individualist. His single-minded vision was the opposite of hers. Brought up in pampered Hollywood, he was cynical about celebrity, unimpressed by names and fame. His brattish air of privilege was tempered by strong political convictions and an alienation from the star system that spawned him.

Madonna left behind her world in New York and settled on the West Coast with Sean. This caused a little consternation among her old clubbing friends, many of whom had their reservations about Sean. Danceteria DJ and musician Johnny Dynell recalls: "Sean would say things like 'your faggot friends.' He was kinda stupid back then." With Sean, however, Madonna could cement her dream of becoming a movie star. She found someone as rebellious and ambitious as she was, with the sense of artistic confidence she sometimes doubted in herself. He, meanwhile, thought he'd found a soul mate who understood his needs. "The only thing I'm certain about is the choices I've made in relation to acting," he said at the time. "The other stuff is just part of the experience. I've met someone whom I always want to be with, she takes care of me. She knows what I'm doing without me having to say anything." When they decided to get married, he didn't fully appreciate how much of the press attention, which he loathed, would be focused on him. "She was in the process of becoming the biggest star in the world. I just wanted to make my films and hide," he said later. "I was an angry young man. I had a lot of demons and don't really know who could've lived with me at the time."

His demons were severely challenged when shortly after they set a wedding date, nude pictures of Madonna taken when she was penniless and modeling in New York were featured in both *Playboy* and *Penthouse* magazines. Although she was secretly excited by the publicity this generated, she scorned the use of the pictures, appearing at Live Aid in several layers of frumpy clothing on a sweltering July day. Live Aid for her was a momentous event.

A marathon fund-raising trans-global benefit for the starving millions in Ethiopia, Live Aid took place in London and in Philadelphia on July 13, 1985, featuring every chart act at the time, from Phil Collins to Tina Turner and Queen. Bill Meyers was part of Madonna's live band for the show. "It was a pretty wild experience. No one really knew what it was about until everyone in the world came to the hotel in one day! There was so much money dropped on cars, rooms, flowers, and so on. There was a really good vibe. It felt special," he says.

Although Live Aid was a supposedly egalitarian event for an important cause, that didn't stop backstage assertion of the pop hierarchy. Meyers noted the graciousness of old-school Hollywood stars like Jack Nicholson and Timothy Hutton, and "Phil Collins couldn't have been nicer." But Duran Duran's Simon Le Bon "was there with a couple of model girlfriends and wouldn't give you the time of day. We were dirt on the linoleum. The Thompson Twins lavished Le Bon with praise, and looked at me like, 'Who are you?'" Bolstered by her relationship with Penn, Madonna was also anxious to assert her celebrity A-list status.

She felt snubbed when a backstage organizer told her that she would have to vacate her trailer after a couple of hours. "He was some guy from Philly, with a real Philly accent, saying, 'Just to let you know you can stay in your trailer from one thirty till three p.m., and then Tina Turner gets it. There's only so many trailers . . . ,'" laughs Meyers. When Madonna protested, the organizer turned to someone and said: "Hey, I don't even like the broad. If Madonna don't want to split, I don't care." Eventually Madonna and Penn were moved to a different trailer that they could keep for the rest of the day.

Despite her haughtiness behind the scenes, onstage she won over the global audience with a warm, wry performance. "I remember the sun burning on my face . . . and I was really hot and it was right at the time when the *Playboy* magazine had come out and people were screaming, 'Take it off, take it off!' And I said, 'I ain't taking *shit* off!'" Madonna said later. "Before I went on, I really thought, I can't do this. I just can't. I was so unsure of what was going to happen . . . So I decided to be a warrior, and it worked, and that was the first time that I really understood my power." Afterward she was the one woman photographed amid a lineup featuring all the "great and good," from Mick Jagger and Keith Richards to Bob Dylan. This publicity shot showed how far she had broken down the barriers of the "old-boy network." Finally she was making a global impact.

The next major event on Madonna's calendar was her wedding to Sean Penn, which took place on her twenty-seventh birthday on the grounds of a cliff-top house in Point Durne, near Malibu Beach. The A-list gathered, a glittering throng that included Cher, Diane Keaton, Carrie Fisher, Andy Warhol, Martin Sheen, and Christopher Walken. While many famous acquaintances were there, some of her old friends from New York weren't invited. Andy Warhol was surprised that Johnny Dynell did not get an invitation. "'But you're her friend!' Andy said to me," Dynell recalls. "'That doesn't make any difference. I'm not in a movie.' Then Andy said: 'You should just ride her coattails, she's going to be so famous.' 'She is already.' 'No, but even more!'"

On her wedding day, Madonna wore white taffeta and a bowler hat that was buffeted by the wind. Despite tight security, news of the venue had been leaked to the press, and in their determination to get a shot, photographers disrupted the ceremony by hovering over the site in helicopters. "It was very bonkers," recalls James Foley, who was Penn's best man. "Suddenly the sky was full of helicopters and you couldn't hear a word the preacher was saying. It's common now to have paparazzi shooting pictures from the air, but then helicopters were only used like that by police tracking down criminals. Madonna and I thought it was amusing, but Sean was not amused at all."

Bill Meyers also recalls the craziness. "I was standing next to Martin Sheen as the helicopters came in. He was flinching and jerking involuntarily because it reminded him of his experience in filming *Apocalypse Now*. Madonna was going ballistic, giving them the finger, while Sean was running in the house for his shotgun. The funniest thing about it was they were serious. It wasn't staged." Despite the gravity with which she took her vows, Madonna ended up laughing at the spectacle. "It turned into a circus," she said. "You couldn't have written it in a movie. No one would have believed it." An hour after the ceremony, in an attack that was to be the first of many, a drunken Penn grappled with Kip Rano, a U.K. photographer, who had crashed the wedding with a hidden camera.

Andy Warhol considered it the most thrilling weekend of his life. It was "the perfect mixture of nobodies and celebrities," and the hovering helicopters were "the most exciting thing ever." He painted a vivid portrait in his diary, saying, "I looked really close at Madonna and she is beautiful. And she and Sean are just so in love. She wore white and a black bowler hat, I don't know what that was supposed to mean." Nightclub owner Steve Rubell was "really out of it on I guess Quaaludes. And I think I saw Madonna kick him away from her and later he threw up in the car. She was dancing with the only little boy there. . . . And those young actors seemed like they were in their fathers' suits, like Emilio Estevez and Tom Cruise. All those movie-star boys with the strong legs who're 5'10" or so. I guess that's the new Hollywood look."

The next day Sean celebrated his twenty-fifth birthday as the couple jetted off to Antigua for their honeymoon. After their return, they settled in Beverly Hills and took the obvious next step of starring in a film together. When they got the script for *Shanghai Surprise*, a romantic adventure set in 1930s China, they envisioned a modern classic along the lines of *The African Queen*, the 1951 John Huston film starring Humphrey Bogart and Katharine Hepburn. *Shanghai Surprise*, however, was an altogether more prosaic affair. Produced by ex-Beatle George Harrison's Handmade Films, it was a messy amalgam of textbook action adventure and arch romance. Madonna stars as Gloria Tatlock, a prim missionary who hires an adventurer (played by Sean) to track down a stash of opium for wounded soldiers before it falls into criminal hands. It was a challenging role for Madonna to play. Gloria Tatlock was "someone very removed from how I actually am . . . I still needed a role where I could prove to people that I could really act."

This was a risky decision for her. *Desperately Seeking Susan* had worked well for Madonna because it revolved around a world she knew. She had also worked with Susan Seidelman, a sympathetic director skilled at motivating non-actors. In *Shanghai Surprise*, Madonna was playing in a period piece, totally removed from her daily experience. This would have been challenging even for a seasoned actress. No wonder her performance seems stilted, self-conscious, and inconsistent. In one scene she plays prim and proper, while in the next she is handling cash like a hustler and seducing Penn's character with admirable ease for a moral-bound missionary. Madonna complained afterward that the director, Jim Goddard, "had no knowledge of what he was doing . . . [he] didn't have an eye for the big screen and it seemed as if he was in a bit over his head." Though he was an accomplished TV director, this was his first major feature. As Seidelman pointed out, Madonna liked a lot of direction, and maybe this wasn't Goddard's style.

They were also filming in difficult circumstances, in a run-down, dangerous area of Hong Kong, where gangs daily demanded protection money just so the crew could keep filming. They were at one location for eighteen hours, for instance, because a man had blocked the exit and demanded $50,000 to move. It was a freezing cold January, rats ran under the trailers, and cast and crew were down with food poisoning. To top it all off, they were hounded by the international press eager to get an intimate shot of the star couple. Penn lashed out at a photographer caught in their hotel room. His overt hostility to the press and her exasperation with the whole filming process led to their being dubbed "the poison Penns," a nickname that stuck. "I kept saying, 'I can't wait till I can look back on this thing, I can't wait,'" said Madonna. "It was a survival test. I know I can get through anything now."

George Harrison flew out to see the stricken crew, and when they returned to England to shoot indoor scenes at Shepperton Studios, he called a press conference in an effort to smooth over the situation. By then, little could be redeemed, especially when the couple's limousine accidentally ran over a photographer's foot. Madonna lashed out at Harrison, saying, "He has given me more advice on how to deal with the press than how to work on a movie."

The ex-Beatle later commented that on-screen Sean looked "pissed off" rather than professional, while Madonna had fallen into the trap of being a "famous pop star . . . They get surrounded by people saying how fab they are, all these sycophants. You have to see it from the other side, too—it sometimes does get you crazy when you can't do anything because everybody's bugging you and shooting cameras in your face. So I can sympathize from that point of view, too. But all Madonna needs is five hundred milligrams of some good LSD."

When it was released in August 1986, the film was universally panned. *Variety* dismissed it as "a phony . . . concoction," while esteemed critic Leslie Halliwell called it "astonishingly abysmal."

Andy Warhol was slightly more impressed: "I was the only one awake in the theater but the movie isn't bad," he wrote in his diary. "Madonna was beautiful, the clothes were great." For Madonna, the experience was bitterly disappointing. And for Sean, who'd been carefully building up his reputation as a serious actor, it was galling. "As a friend, please don't watch it," he once said to Chrissie Hynde. It's notable that he and Madonna never worked on a movie together again.

Madonna was on safer ground with her music career. In the autumn of the previous year, she had began recording her third album, *True Blue*. For this she teamed up in the studio for the first time with

producer Pat Leonard. He helped her create the quintessential commercial Madonna sound. Her debut album had been disparate songs
in search of an artist, while the quirky *Like a Virgin* was a sound in
development. With certain tracks on *True Blue* she nailed her signature style—rhythmic, dramatic, danceable, and distinctively melodic.
Leonard drew melodies out of her as if he was excavating a pit. He
looked beyond the dance diva and the ironic pop princess to find
something more personal.

It took a while before she trusted him in the studio. A musical director on Madonna's Like a Virgin tour, Leonard had been eager for
her to notice him as a songwriter. "They had a tumultuous relationship," recalls Bill Meyers. "Pat was as relentless as Madonna—a hard
worker and a fine musician. He knew that with Madonna the smart
move would be to push her to write with him. He'd leave tapes at her
hotel door and be dismayed at her ignoring them. I would have given
up, but he kept offering them to her. Then, through the course of the
tour, he made friends with Sean, and Sean invited Pat to have a go at
the soundtrack for *At Close Range*. If you don't get in with Madonna,
you go to the one closest to her!"

The result was "Live to Tell," a mood-driven song that appealed to
Madonna's sense of drama. With her unerring instinct for successful
collaborators, she decided to make Leonard the main producer on
her new album. "She needed someone with strong ideas. They fought
continuously. Pat's a proud, incredibly creative person, and so's she.
They worked really hard together," says guitarist Bruce Gaitsch, who
played on many of the *True Blue* sessions.

Though the album has been her biggest seller, the initial recording
was in a tiny studio in Leonard's basement. "The studio was so small
that, besides tape and recording equipment, there was only room for
two people," Gaitsch recalls. "You don't need big rooms to make big
records." Madonna was in a giddy mood. "She'd just learned to drive.
She rented a car and on the first day drove it through Pat's fence. He
wasn't too happy about that!" The accident didn't dent her optimism,
however. "She was having a blast. She'd just show up, stick her gum
on the mike, and sing. And she was totally in love with a sexy, fun,

nice guy. Sean would come to the studio sometimes, jingling his car keys. He wanted to get her outta there as fast as he could. They were so into each other."

Madonna was also feeling elated because it was the first record she coproduced. "She didn't have to hire expensive people anymore. Although *True Blue* turned out to be her biggest album, the previous record she recorded (*Like a Virgin*) was four times more expensive, because it was with a famous producer," says Gaitsch.

The first song she and Leonard laid down was the declarative "Open Your Heart," which was written by Gardner Cole, songwriter for a host of 80s chart acts including Cher, Michael MacDonald, and Tina Turner. "I composed it with Peter Rafelson (son of the famous director Bob Rafelson). It took a long time to get it together—we worked on it, on and off, for about a year," he says. A demanding song to sing, with a wide octave range and long notes, Madonna simplified it before recording. "She dropped a few lines out of the bridge and took out the second half," Cole recalls. He was pleased with her delivery. "It's a powerful song with a high range for her. She wasn't used to belting stuff out, and this opened up a whole new range for her. It's one of the first songs where she used a hard voice—most of the others were pretty light, but with 'Open Your Heart' she had to dig in. It's not easy to sing, it took her a long time to get it right." The labor paid off, because it went straight to number one in the United States when it was later released. "I was so thrilled," remembers Cole, "my publishers framed a *Billboard* for me."

Madonna's songs had always been easy on the ear, leading to the assumption by many critics that her sound was routine, formulaic pop—what cultural theorist Theodor Adorno would have called "standardization" and rapper Vanilla Ice "friendly-ass corny shit." In 1941, Adorno sealed a "high art/low art" divide in pop music criticism when he wrote: "In popular music, position is absolute. Every detail is substitutable; it serves its function only as a cog in the machine." For years, Madonna was underestimated as a musician, because of the deceptive simplicity of her songs. Some album tracks were mere "cogs in the machine," but her singles always had rich melody lines and lyrical twists. "Open Your Heart" marked a step up for her to a sound that was popular and radio-friendly, but still ambitious. As she grew more confident with her voice, her songs gained depth.

With its sophisticated sheen, *True Blue* took Madonna firmly out of the dance-diva category into a global pop market. It wove the teen appeal of the 60s girl-group sound into chunkier dance textures, with a mood that was up and unassailable. Madonna was newly married and supremely optimistic. Never again would she sound as pristine and sure. As well as the percussive, joyful air of "Open Your Heart," there was the jubilant title track, where she revisited the Motown girl-group sound she had grown up with. A song that echoed the call-and-response simplicity of The Dixie Cups' 1964 hit "Chapel of Love," it featured Siedah Garratt and Edie Lehman on back vocals, and had the clarity of a convent-school-choir-meets-the-projects. It was a ditty that verged on schmaltzy nostalgia but for the fact that Madonna's voice rang out with such conviction.

This sense of romantic thrill reverberates through the busy, good-time dance track "Where's the Party." It also flows into "La Isla Bonita," a song with music that Gaitsch and Leonard originally wrote for Michael Jackson. "He didn't want it, thank God. I didn't like him. I always thought he was a freak, just creepy. He gave me the willies, like meeting a ghost of a person," says Gaitsch. Leonard then suggested they give it to Madonna, who was in Hong Kong at the time, filming *Shanghai Surprise*. "I was so glad it went to her. She's the most present person there is, a force to be reckoned with."

Unhappy and pining in Hong Kong, Madonna wrote lyrics about her ideal place, a far-off tropical island in the sun. When she told them what the title was, Gaitsch was shocked. "I thought, oh great, that'll never be a hit. It was so simple. But then I was wrong. It's hugely popular, and it has become the national anthem for the island of San Pedro." It's Gaitsch's Latin-flavored guitar part that really makes the song distinctive. "This one evolved naturally. I try to do the best for the song and I like strong melodies. I don't like lots of notes, just notes that matter."

With its vivid Latin influence, the song was later seen as an attempt to reach the massive Hispanic demographic in the United States. It became a major hit, going to number one in the United Kingdom and number three in the United States, and was accompanied by a striking video featuring Madonna in a rich red dress dancing flamenco. Madonna dedicated it to the "beauty and mystery of the Latin-American people." Not everyone was entranced with this, however. Miami-based star Gloria Estefan wryly told me at the time: "It's only Anglos who see her as having popularized Spanish. Madonna's a bit confused about her Spanish. She mentions a tropical island in the sun—that's Puerto Rico, then samba—that's Latino, and then flamenco guitar—that's Spain. There's a mishmash of everything in the song. But hey, every little bit helps!"

For this album, Madonna's love for Sean seeped into every song. "White Heat," one of the less successful tracks she wrote with Leonard, is a slightly plodding tribute to actor James Cagney, whose unhinged gangster in the 1949 movie is driven to notoriety by the death of his mother. There were some parallels with her life here, not just in Madonna's loss of her mother but also the romanticizing of Sean as a violent bad boy. He pops up again as a lovable wild card on the tune "Jimmy Jimmy." She just can't get him out of her head. "She was very much in love. It was obvious if she's in love she'll write love songs," said a sage Steve Bray, who produced four tracks on the album (including a coproduction of "Where's the Party" with Leonard).

While Leonard set the tone for much of this album, Bray also contributed to its high pop alchemy. The opening track, "Papa Don't Preach," is one of his triumphs. Written by Brian Elliot with additional lyrics by Madonna, it is an 80s take on girl-group pop opera, described by her as "a message song that everyone is going to take the wrong way." Beginning with a dramatic string intro—"That was the first time she worked with a large live string section," says Bill Meyers, who arranged the intro, "it led to a prosperous career for me as an arranger, a lot of success came out of that"—and underscored by Bray's clipped, assured drumming, this is an adolescent girl's plea to be taken seriously. She's pregnant, she's struggling, and she tells her disciplinarian dad she wants to keep the baby. Madonna's voice is rougher than on previous records. Here she sings in a grainy, deeper register, as if constantly on the verge of tears. It's a compelling song with a problematic message. Anti-abortion groups heartily approved of the song, while many others criticized it for condoning teenage pregnancy.

As is often the case with Madonna, the song became inextricably linked to the video. Against a decaying New York skyline, Madonna plays a gamine teenager with cropped blond hair and a heart-stoppingly pretty car-mechanic boyfriend. Her estranged, heavyset Italian father (Danny Aiello) is doing his best to bring up his daughter alone, yet feeling inadequate to the task. These scenes of social realism are intercut with Madonna in a body-hugging black leotard, with bleached hair and glamorous red lips, doing a spotlighted *Flashdance*-style dance routine.

James Foley directed the video with his trademark attention to gritty detail. "Madonna said she wanted to play a character. Narrative videos at that time, with a little story, were new. We filmed it in Staten Island, New York, where I grew up. I wanted people I went to high school with to read about it and be jealous!" he says. Unlike some of her wooden movie appearances, Madonna is comfortable with video. She projects an image, and uses her body like a dancer, aware of the subtle shapes she can create through posture or expression. "The indigenously glamorous Catholic working-class girl—Madonna pushes that button very well," says Foley. "It was her idea to cut to her dancing on a black stage; very much the 'hot-fudge sundae' concept (that is, contrasting shots) of the heat of the dancing and the coldness of the other scenes. Something bothered me, which shows how Catholic I am. I asked her, 'Can a pregnant woman dance around in this skintight black thing?' She just laughed as if it was the most ridiculous thing she'd heard in her life."

One of the most memorable aspects of the video is Madonna's T-shirt, emblazoned with the slogan ITALIANS DO IT BETTER. "That was a masterstroke," recalls Foley. "She had someone send it to me on set, asking if it was all right to wear. 'Yeah! That's great!' I said. I wouldn't be surprised if she'd seen it on someone in the street and

bought it from her. It made me laugh when people said she was calculating. She's not at all. She could be very spontaneous." The video
marked a new direction for Madonna, and a more streamlined look. It
was less stylized and arch, reflecting her slowly growing stature as an
artist. "I'm proud of that video. It caught the essential elements of her
in a correct way and put them side by side. It showed two very different
individuals in the same body. That's real acting," declares Foley.

Madonna also conveyed passion and sense of theater on "Live to
Tell," a *True Blue* track that took her away from the bubblegum image
and presaged the dark tones of *Like a Prayer*. With its oblique lyrics and
dense strings, this is a forceful morality ballad. She sings of the burning power of past secrets and shame. Secrecy, initiation, and the gaining of knowledge were to become key themes in her work—here she
sings of it for the first time. It was also featured on the soundtrack to
At Close Range. Directed by James Foley, the movie was a brutal father-
son drama about a criminal who returns home to kill those he feels
know too much about his past. Starring Sean Penn and Christopher
Walken, it received mixed reviews when it first came out in 1986, but
has since achieved a major cult status.

Although "Live to Tell" was an obvious hit, there was opposition
from Warner about putting the song on the film soundtrack. "I remember having lunch with Madonna and a big-cheese record executive. She got up to go to the bathroom, and he held my wrist, looked
directly at me, and said, 'If you're her friend, tell her you don't want
that in the movie. It'll ruin her career,'" says Foley. *True Blue* wasn't
ready yet, and releasing a single without an album would disrupt their
careful marketing plans. Having had two hit albums, Warner Bros.
were keen to keep up the momentum on their terms. When Madonna
came back to the table, Foley's head was spinning. "Being selfish, I
convinced her to do it, but then asked if she was sure. I brought up
what the Warner guy had said—'Your album's not ready yet'—and she
said, 'I don't give a shit.'"

"Live to Tell" went on to become one of her most enduring hits,
and a live favorite. It resurfaced twenty years later as the key number
on her 2006 Confessions tour, where she was presented on a giant

mirrored cross with a crown of thorns. Far from ruining the impact of her new album's release, it provided the perfect advertisement for it.

TRUE BLUE came out in June 1986. The cover showed Madonna in profile, with head thrown back and eyes closed, her bleached-out skin and platinum-blond crop against a background of sky-blue. Taken by Herb Ritts, it was a moment of Warholian pop art. A mixture of innocence, idealism, and hand-tinted 50s-style Technicolor and hand-tinted color like a 60s Warhol silkscreen print, this was our first glimpse of Madonna as a classic icon. "She was already highly aware of the value of her image and was in control of it," said Jeri Heiden, the album's cover designer. Gone was the mussed hair and the belly button of the boy-toy era. This album ushered in a newer, sleeker Madonna, while drawing on the enduring appeal of celluloid icons like Marilyn Monroe. "It was like she was floating—her clothing was not visible. She took on the appearance of a marble statue—goddess-like," recalled Heiden. With this picture Madonna made explicit the connection between Warhol and herself; the vivid nexus between pop art and commerce. The late 1980s marked a new era of the pop artist as a brand, and Madonna was one of the first to exploit this.

Madonna and Warhol always had a guarded appreciation of one another. "I asked Madonna if she would be interested in doing a movie, and she was smart, she said that she wanted more specifics, that she just didn't want to talk and have her ideas taken," Warhol wrote in 1984. "She's very sharp. She's really hot right now." Then, in 1985, when her Like a Virgin tour was in full swing, he sighed: "Gee, Madonna was just a waitress at the Lucky Strike a year ago." He is there at her wedding, clothed in black, the negative to her white dress. He responds to her surface glamour, seeing her with the detailed eye of the painter: "Madonna really knows how to do her makeup in that great Hollywood way," he wrote. "Somebody must have showed her or always does it for her—everything painted just perfectly."

There are points where Madonna and Warhol meet: they shared gay friends in New York. They were both awestruck by the power of celebrity, while at the same time undercutting it with a camp sense of irony. They both came from hardworking immigrant Catholic backgrounds in the Midwest to realize their dream in New York City, and they both had a zeal for money. Reflecting the rootless nature of twentieth-century America, they were accused of being vampiric in their art, drawing ruthlessly on popular culture. They were unafraid of blurring the lines between fine art and "business art." Writer Wayne Koestenbaum described Warhol as wanting to "ease—to lubricate—the wheels of production, to make fabrication a more accessible, democratic, and openhearted realm of conduct." The same could be said of Madonna. Both loved candy and popcorn. But that is where the similarity ends.

While she was restless and constantly reconfiguring her style, he loved repetition. He was patient, liked dull things, found boredom inspiring, and was resolutely passive. Warhol suffered from chorea and endured pain most of his life. He portrayed bodies as ruptured while his own body was falling apart. Like Madonna, he wore corsets, but his were for medical reasons. In 1968, he survived a near-fatal assassination attempt when he was shot by the unhinged radical feminist Valerie Solanas. After the shooting he couldn't quite believe he was still alive. According to Koestenbaum, "Profoundly disembodied already, he became, after the assassination attempt, more radically severed from his body, now a canvas of wounds and scars—the apparatus of his torn and flayed flesh held in place, for the rest of his life, by tightly bound abdominal belts, corsets that Brigid Berlin dyed for him in optimistic pastels like the colors of his silkscreens."

By contrast, Madonna is profoundly *embodied*. Her portrayal of the body is as whole, healthy, and beautiful. What place was there in her work for illness and death? For bad skin? The *True Blue* cover echoed the bright outdoors light of a world that was alive and alert. Warhol filmed his subjects sleeping, whereas Madonna was in constant motion. Staying still was an anathema to her, and therefore to be avoided at all costs. Warhol was fascinated with the gripping banality of life, what a slow study of "nothingness" revealed, whereas Madonna felt compelled to fill her world with "something." He invariably dressed in stark black with his trademark platinum wig, while her image was colorful and ever-changing.

By now, Madonna had reached the level of fame that Warhol once predicted. Her New York friend Johnny Dynell remembers going to the supermarket one day and seeing her on the cover of *Life* magazine. "Then it hit me like a ton of bricks. It almost knocked me out," he says. "Oh my God, I thought, the bitch did it. It's not the *Village Voice*, it's the cover of *Life*. For a long time I thought of her as the same as us, but then I realized, Oh my God, she's a millionaire. She's rich. She's done it." And for Madonna, there was no turning back.

ME IN
THE PICTURE

IN 1987, WE HAD YET TO "READ" MADONNA. HINDSIGHT and a body of work spanning decades has put her early "oeuvre" into a more sophisticated perspective. But that doesn't invalidate the reactions at the time. We'd had the pleasant shock of *Desperately Seeking Susan* and the Like a Virgin tour, but back then, her commercial tunes and dancing in her underwear meant one thing: mainstream capitulation. She wanted it both ways, it seemed—intellectual respect and huge commercial success. That is a tricky balance to achieve, particularly if the images one toys with are hackneyed and conventional. With the "Open Your Heart" video, she was feeling her way into a more interrogative pose.

It's a good example of her artistic psyche at the time, demonstrating irony and vanity in equal measure. Directed by Jean-Baptiste Mondino, it shines with the same primary colors as the *True Blue* cover. As extrovert as Warhol was introvert, Madonna put her new body on display in a black bodice and tasseled bra. She had been working out, working to eradicate the generous belly with its famous navel, and her copious hair was cropped short. In the video, she plays a peep-show queen, teasing the men who have come for titillation. She makes explicit her interest in modern art, with a Tamara de Lempicka–style nude gracing the entrance of the establishment where she "works." Her unprepossessing customers show one emotional tone: some look dumb, some cynical, some bored. There is even a slavering bull dyke. Madonna dances in a precise, disengaged way, from one window to the next, offering and withdrawing herself by turns. She is always at one remove. The punch line is that she runs off with a little boy, reasserting her girlish innocence.

Aspiring to be pop art, the video is too arch in its sensibilities. But it paved the way for a more conceptual approach. "Madonna was the first woman to take on David Bowie's mantle," cultural writer Peter York told me. "With her self-actualizing and reinventing, she did in the 1980s what he did in the 1970s." Madonna's new, sleek look left her former stylist Maripol high and dry in New York, with boxloads of boy-toy bracelets and crucifixes which she could not shift. "I was clearly put at a disadvantage. But I understand she couldn't sport the look forever," she says. Maripol's company went bankrupt, and she stopped making jewelry for the next ten years. Feeling lost, she went to an ashram to learn yoga and met a female Indian guru who taught her not to fret about material things. "So when the Material Girl got released . . . I actually un-materialized," laughs Maripol.

Madonna, meanwhile, had set her sights on movie stardom. A few months after the release of *True Blue*, Madonna decided to try another film role. This time it was a part closer to her heart. In *Who's That Girl* she played Nikki Finn, a good-time girl walking the streets of New York, on parole for murder, determined to clear her name. Louden Trott (played by Griffin Dunne) is a hapless lawyer ordered by his boss to get her on a bus to Philadelphia. The two end up having a series of adventures in a film that featured a live cougar, fights, car chases, and the inevitable denouement: a wedding. "I was really excited about doing a physical, screwball comedy," Madonna said at the time. She also identified with the character of Nikki. "I had a lot in common with [her]. She's courageous and sweet and funny and misjudged. But she clears her name in the end, and that's always good to do. I'm continuously doing that with the public." Nikki has a street-smart simplicity. "The toughness is only a mask for the vulnerability she feels."

With her fire-engine-red lipstick, leather jacket, and Betty Boop–style voice, Madonna invented a cartoon character that was an amplification of her showgirl self. She took on a role she was comfortable with—Madonna against the straight world—but the result was only partly convincing. As in *Desperately Seeking Susan,* her best scenes were those in which she was "off duty" and unself-conscious: when she says good-bye to her girlfriends in prison, for example, or the spirited way she handles a gun, or the assertiveness with which she deals with the cougar (reprising the lion-taming theme in her "Like a Virgin" video). The rest of the film is a star vehicle for mid-80s Madonna. She is in nearly every scene, talking a lot of dialogue, much of it affected and cute.

The director James Foley found making this movie a chastening experience. Having shot the low-budget *At Close Range,* he was excited at the chance of making a major feature. "I was young, I was twenty-eight. So, being given the opportunity to work on a Warner Bros. film with a huge star was attractive to me for all the wrong reasons. Everyone has a bit of Hollywood lust in them," he recalls. He was approached by Warner Bros. because they "knew I knew Madonna and could convince her to do it. *At Close Range* was a dark film, and going to comedy was totally the wrong direction. But I didn't care." By the summer of 1987, preproduction was well underway. There was only one problem.

"Madonna was in a hurry. She had a tour planned. The night before we started shooting I sat in the writer's bedroom in New Jersey thinking, This script stinks. But I had no choice. The train was on the track, I couldn't pull out. I tried to make the script better but it was lousy. So I take responsibility, I fault myself and the script, not her," says Foley. Madonna plowed gamely on, saying: "All Warner's executives were real positive about the project. It was a process—with the writers—of honing the script, making it better."

When it came to the shoot, she was ready to take direction, relying on Foley to give her all the cues. He'd been looking forward to working with her, but found the process oddly elusive. "In person, Madonna actually seems to morph into a whole different body and self. That works most dramatically in her videos. You think that'd be the perfect attribute to have for screen acting. But although she 'acts' very well sometimes, she doesn't push the right buttons at the right times over the course of a film." The failure of *Shanghai Surprise* had left its mark.

"She was very uptight and into every detail, determined to get it right this time. She's extremely competitive with herself," says Foley. "That's probably why it wasn't so good. In *Desperately Seeking Susan*, when she didn't know what she was doing, she was being natural and at her best." When it came to cutting the film, Foley was happy with what he had. "Now I look back and see the stupid bits and how to fix 'em. But before a movie opens, you don't know it's a bomb because you've a built-in survivor mechanism, your mind keeps you in love with it."

When the film opened in the summer of 1987, it received mixed reviews. Some were condescending: "What's lacking is pure and simple good humor," said *Variety*, while others, like the *New York Times*, were downright scathing. "My father rang me and said, 'the *New York Times* put down your movie as the worst of the year.' I took it very personally," recalls Foley. "Boy, when it bombed it took me two years to get over the physical pain every time I thought of that movie. It was my first taste of failure, and it was a very public failure. I felt very bad it didn't work, because Madonna so believed what I was having her do. She gave me her trust and I squandered it."

Madonna's response was sanguine. With classic toughness, she chalked it up to experience and moved on. "I remember the first time I saw her after it flopped. I was in the lobby of a hotel in Paris and saw her with her movie agent. She was about to walk in the elevator when she said: 'So it's a flop, right? . . . Hmm.' That's the only time she ever mentioned it. She never referred to it again. It was as if we both unconsciously agreed it didn't exist. Sean reacted the same way. He never brought it up, and I never bring up *Shanghai Surprise*. That's the thing you do when you have a failure, if you're still friends."

Later, Sean said, "When she and Jamie Foley made the movie they made—I saw another version that I think would have been more encouraging to her as an actress at that time. But . . . she's been wildly discouraged, externally. . . . There's a lot to be said for people having encouragement and rewards for their risks. I don't know if there's anybody who doesn't require that."

Madonna got her rewards in another arena, a fact that impressed itself on Foley when he went to see her Who's That Girl show. "She was playing a half hour out of Paris in a giant meadow behind a castle. The place was packed beyond belief, a spectacular concert. I was standing backstage watching her, seeing a hundred thousand people scream and clap. I felt worse than she did about the film, because she had this other career, a place where people really loved her. Her ego went through a lot of different experiences that day." Madonna's assessment of the situation was simple. "There are people who don't want me to do well in both fields," she said.

Now Foley jokes that he would like to do a director's cut of Who's That Girl, only it would be thirty minutes instead of ninety. "In that I could show her as an excellent actress, an extreme turn, a cartoon version of herself. Despite the reviews though, it's a film that still does well. I get more residuals from that movie than any other I've made."

THE FAILURE of the film was eclipsed for Madonna by her worldwide Who's That Girl tour, a Broadway-revue-meets-post-disco spectacular that competed with the fellow travelers Prince and Michael Jackson in its sheer size and scale. It was in a different league from the Like a Virgin show; here, she moved away from the rock-concert format to a multimedia production. "The first tour was just some choreography and lights, whereas with Who's That Girl Madonna became more theatrical and focused, and she used projections," says Peter Morse, who was the tour lighting designer. He went on to work with her on every show up to the 2006 Confessions tour. Though they had a very fruitful relationship, it didn't get off to an auspicious start.

Morse first met Madonna in 1985, when she was preparing for her Virgin tour and had hired him for the lighting job. Morse had already worked for top acts like Dolly Parton, Lionel Ritchie, and Tina Turner, but he was nervous. "Madonna was younger and more explosive back then," he says. He went to where she was working in a studio. "I was sitting patiently in the control room waiting for my moment, and saw a little dish of nuts on the table. I ate a handful. They were the worst thing ever, they tasted like dirt. Then she comes in and starts talking. She has a little dog. It eats from the dish—it turns out the nuts are dog food. This is not a good start."

Madonna wanted to see ideas, but not being an artist, Morse got someone else to draw a design. "She was an early MTV artist—visually oriented and used to seeing storyboards. I showed her the design. She looked at it, frowned, and said, 'Where's *me* in the picture?' I said I'd get someone to draw her in. 'Do it now,' she snapped, 'I don't have time.'" Morse then drew a little childish stick figure in the middle of the picture. "Madonna wasn't happy about that. She doesn't like it if you get funny with her!" recalls Morse, who was unceremoniously fired.

For the next tour, however, she was back on the phone. "They were in the last week of rehearsals of the Who's That Girl tour. Things hadn't worked out with their lighting designer, so they brought me in. I had a week to save it." Morse's dramatic flair and confident use of color were perfect for the show, so by the time it started that June in Japan, he was back in Madonna's good books.

She had a much bigger cast for this show, including two new backup singers—Niki Haris and Donna DeLory—who would become her close friends. Together they would become a triumvirate, a force to be reckoned with onstage and in the studio. Donna was the daughter of famous L.A. producer/arranger Al DeLory, who'd played with The Beach Boys and Glenn Campbell. She started dancing and singing at an early age, doing backup vocals for a range of artists, including Carly Simon and Santana. In 1986, she was Gardner Cole's girlfriend, and she actually sang the original demo of "Open Your Heart." Cole remembers Madonna calling him soon after she got the song, asking, "Who sang the demo?" Donna met Pat Leonard, and was swiftly recruited for the tour. "She and Madonna have similar qualities in their voices, they sound very alike," says Cole. "And Donna is really sweet as well."

Niki Haris was a Michigan girl, like Madonna. Though her father, Gene Harris, was a Grammy Award–winning jazz artist (and former pianist with Count Basie), Niki had no plans for show business, wanting instead to be a history teacher. She fell into singing as a struggling student in L.A. "I went out with musicians, and before I knew it, one gig turned into four. I saw the music business as work, a way to make a living," says Niki. She had been working with Anita Baker and Whitney Houston, and was singing with The Righteous Brothers in Las Vegas when Madonna's manager Freddy DeMann called her, saying, "Can you learn seventeen songs and seventeen dance moves in five days?" Niki went to an audition feeling decidedly underwhelmed.

"I was more into jazz and R&B than pop, and I didn't know who Madonna was," Niki recalls. "There were two hundred girls at the audition, and I was thinking I'll never get the gig, please let me go on the first flight back to Vegas. Wham bam, before you know it, I was in the back of Madonna's limo, looking for a phone to call the Righteous Brothers' people. 'You can't go back, don't you know who I am!' she screamed at me. I said, 'I'm grateful for the gig, and the money's cute, but let me be polite!'" Niki then joined the tour, and quickly mastered the songs and dance routines. "Luckily enough I fit the costumes, and the music wasn't that hard. I'm a quick study. It wasn't brain surgery, it wasn't like learning *Porgy & Bess* or *Carmen.*" At first it was just another gig for Niki, "but then we started to become friends and hang out more outside the tour. It was fun."

There was plenty of showboating in the Who's That Girl tour—the gold lamé jackets, gangster hats, and guns shtick; the moving walkway; the Busby Berkeley–style stairs. But undercutting this were ironic moments like the "Dress You Up" medley, where Madonna popped up as a clownish trickster figure, dressed in a pantomime-meets-Carmen-Miranda costume with the word KISS on her behind. There were songs delivered with moving passion; when she sang "La Isla

Bonita" to an audience of thousands, for instance, the song tran-
scended its coyness, gaining the resonance of a popular folk tune. The
image of her in the red flamenco dress has become as iconic as the boy
toy or the black-corseted siren.

This was the first glimpse of Madonna's circus. Onstage she was
MC and ringmaster, and as agile and muscular as the girl on the flying trapeze. She was the young boy, the acrobat, the clown—she was
them all. The beefy backup dancers were her animus, the female
singers—Niki, Donna, and Debrah Parson—were her anima. They
danced around her and with her, they were her tribe. The stage was
big enough, it seemed, to encompass her talents. It was here that all
her interests were drawn into focus. This is why so many fans point
to the live experience as the "real" Madonna.

The show was Madonna's psyche writ large. For the song "Open
Your Heart," she amplified the video, dancing in black corset and tas-
sels, a giant Tamara de Lempicka portrait projected behind her. The
Polish artist was an apt choice—her distinctive style was known as
"soft cubism," epitomizing the cool modernism of Art Deco. Born in
1898, de Lempicka fled to the United States at the start of World War
II. Actively and scandalously bisexual, she explored themes of desire
and seduction in her work. One of her best-known paintings is *The
Musician* (1929), featuring a woman in a flowing blue dress playing the
lyre. She's heavily made up, with copper-red hair and long fingernails,
and behind her is the jumbled, jazzy New York skyline. Displayed
in the Who's That Girl show, it was a summation of Madonna's approach, mixing high art with glamour, vulgarity, and the urbane. It's
woman as a muse, creator, and sexual being. No wonder it held such
power for Madonna.

As a presage of ideas she would explore later, the backdrop to the
song "Papa Don't Preach" featured a church nave and a succession of
images, including the Moon landing, 1960s civil rights riots, John F.
Kennedy, Richard Nixon, Black Power, and Ronald Reagan. Here
she positioned herself as a child of the 60s, turning "Papa Don't
Preach" into a message song against racism and censorship. As musical director, Pat Leonard had an acute understanding of music as

drama. A master at creating tension, he also brought out the dark side of the song "Live to Tell," making it long, slow, and loaded. Madonna's rendition emphasized a sense of isolation, being cut off from the crowd. In one part she knelt low on the stage, her head down. When she performed this in London, someone decided to disrupt the private intensity of the moment and lobbed an empty drink carton onto the stage. They succeeded in riling her. "Don't throw shit at me," she barked, after the song was over. It was as if she had been pulled away from an extended meditation.

Much of the show was about celebration, the spinning energy of life. But within that was expression of some gnawing doubts. At the end of "Who's That Girl," a song jubilant in its evocation of the female spirit, she sang the words over and over till they echoed around the auditorium in ghostly form. "Who's that girl?" she sang, as if trying to decide herself.

This show and the *True Blue* album were her stab at immortality. The record sold 19 million copies worldwide—no studio album by Madonna has sold more. And the Who's That Girl tour went on to establish her as a global phenomenon. As writer Danny Eccleston said: "In a funny way, it's been downhill from here." The previous winter, her beloved friend Martin Burgoyne passed away of an AIDS-related illness. Four months before Madonna's tour started, Andy Warhol died of a heart attack after a routine gall-bladder operation, and in 1988, her former lover Jean-Michel Basquiat died of a heroin overdose. Sean, meanwhile, began to show more and more of his violent side. The sunny skies of *True Blue* were beginning to darken. Through this, Madonna began to feel her way to a different style of songwriting—to a deeper reflection of her own psyche.

By 1987, it was apparent that the man Madonna had married was becoming a liability. From the moment they got engaged, they found themselves prime fodder for tabloid stories. For Madonna, who had striven for fame all her life, this attention was annoying but bearable. For Penn, however, it was torture. Paparazzi were a permanent irritant, to the extent that his period with Madonna was littered with incidents of assault and ensuing criminal charges.

In 1986, for instance, while they were filming *Shanghai Surprise*, he was arrested after hanging an intruding photographer by his ankles from their ninth-floor balcony. He broke out of jail and escaped the country by jetfoil. In 1987, while Madonna was on her Who's That Girl tour, he served thirty-three days of a sixty-day sentence in the Los Angeles County jail for skipping probation. The sentence was for assaulting songwriter David Wolinski, who had kissed Madonna on the cheek. Sean had a predilection for punching photographers, and an attachment to guns. Seemingly uncomfortable with her gay friends, jealous of her ex-lovers, and fond of whiskey, he wasn't an easy person to be around. "It was internal combustion," Sean said later. "There wasn't anything that resembled peace in my spirit."

As a child, he was troubled and shy, and didn't really speak outside his home until he was five. His father, Leo Penn, was an ex-actor and Communist sympathizer, who in the 1950s was blacklisted by the House Un-American Activities Committee. Unable to find work, Leo moved into directing for television, making high-profile shows like *Columbo*. When asked by his son how work was going, Leo would joke wryly: "Trying to make a better piece of shit out of a worse piece of shit." This led to what musician friend David Baerwald described as a life "much diminished." Both Leo and Sean's mother, the actress Eileen Ryan, had a drinking problem.

Every night they would drink heavily. "She never started drinking till we were in bed," recalled Sean. "They could both get up early the next morning and function." There was an underlying tension at the heart of his childhood, and somehow Sean shouldered the burden of his father's failure—trying to make up for the family's collective disappointment by establishing himself as an A-list actor, fighting injustice, and, later in his career, becoming an outspoken political activist. He wanted to be a hero, but as a young man he confused that with Ernest Hemingway–style macho posturing and antisocial behavior. It was that volatile nature, though, that drove his acting and made his parts memorable. "It's hard to get through to him, and you feel that at any minute he could blow up at you," said Woody Allen. "It makes it so interesting."

It is intriguing that Madonna, so controlled and savvy in her public life, saw Sean's fractious temperament as strength. She once said
that he reminded her of her brothers. "They were wild and rebellious,
starting fires in the basement, throwing rocks at the windows . . .
I've always been attracted to people [who're] rebels and irresponsible
and challenge the norm. I'm attracted to bums!" Her friends were
bemused by Sean. Niki Haris liked him: "He was smart and tough,
but gentle at the same time. Kinda shy and quirky." Others were less
convinced. "He was a bit awkward. She'd hold court at dinner while
Sean just sat there silent, not saying anything," recalls musician Billy
Meyers. "Once I was talking to the bodyguard about the Dodgers,
when Sean piped up: 'The Dodgers. I hate the Dodgers. They're the
worst team!' 'Are you a baseball fan?' I asked. 'No, not particularly.'
Everyone was looking at him. But then he put his head back down.
Wow, we thought, that was a strange interruption."

In her own way, Madonna mirrored Sean's social awkwardness
with her need to be direct to the point of rudeness. "She could be
very trying. When she took an obstinate stance during an argument
you'd give up, thinking, Screw it," says Meyers. "Well, Sean would go
the final mile. She found it endearing. She *wanted* that. If you gave up
too quickly, she didn't like it."

A year into their marriage, the volatile energy between them started
to get out of control. She became worried about his attachment to
guns. She once told Dennis Fanning, the L.A. policeman whom Penn
shadowed for research on the film *Colors*, "Sean is very impressionable
so I want you to *please* be very careful with what you're teaching my
husband." There were reports of heated brawls, with Sean pushing
and shoving her in public. In December 1987, she filed for divorce,
and while estranged from him, had a three-month dalliance with the
late John F. Kennedy Jr. The son of President John F. Kennedy, "John-
John" was extremely well-heeled and well-connected. "In grabbing
[him], Madonna hit the jackpot," said his biographer Wendy Leigh.
Madonna enjoyed the fact that her Hollywood idol Marilyn Monroe
had had an affair with the father, but like Monroe, she was persona
non grata in the regal Kennedy clan. Despite Madonna's best efforts

to meet John-John's mother, the elegantly glacial Jackie Onassis, she was rebuffed. "The mother hates me," she confided to Niki Haris. The affair soon cooled, not just because of Jackie O's hostility. Madonna was less than impressed with John-John's lovemaking technique. "It's like going to bed with a nine-year-old," she said later.

She went back to Sean, but by the summer of 1988, when Madonna was acting on Broadway in David Mamet's play *Speed-the-Plow*, her marriage was in trouble again. When she sought escape and solace with lesbian comedienne Sandra Bernhard, Sean was furious. Pithy, abrasive, and on her way up, Bernhard was a more serious rival for his wife's affections. Like Madonna, she was a Michigan girl with a knack for defying social conventions. Proud of her Jewish features, Bernhard once said, "I'm the only actress in Hollywood who didn't pay to have these lips." Once a performer at the L.A. Comedy Store, she first appeared on TV on the *Richard Pryor Show* in the late 1970s. By the time she met Madonna, her stand-up act was evolving into performance art, culminating in the iconoclastic 1988 Broadway hit *Without You I Am Nothing*.

It irked Sean that Bernhard (whom he had introduced to his wife) was now Madonna's new best friend, accompanying the couple wherever they went. There were rumors that Bernhard and Madonna were having an affair, after they appeared on the *Late Show with David Letterman* wearing the dyke uniform of knee-length jeans, white T-shirts, and black shoes, and talked about going to lesbian watering holes like the Canal Bar and the Cubby Hole. "She's one of the only girls that can take me. She's a really ballsy girl," Madonna said triumphantly. Although Bernhard and Madonna spent a lot of time making mischief, it wasn't just a surface flirtation. Bernhard was a strong source of support while Madonna's marriage was falling apart, and their attachment went deep.

Sean, meanwhile, tried to blot his problems out by drinking heavily. By the end of the year, he had reached a point of psychological crisis. On December 29, he allegedly held Madonna prisoner in their Malibu home. Some claim he pinned her down and sat on her for hours. "She is never still for a minute, so to do that was like death to her," said a friend. Sean later alluded to the incident by saying: "She developed a concern that if she were to return to the house, she would get a very severe haircut." Madonna called a SWAT team to the house, but didn't press charges, and never spoke publicly about the incident. That fight symbolized the broader power struggle between them. He wanted her to settle down, have children, and lead a quiet life with him (not unlike his second, and enduring, marriage in the 90s to Robin Wright Penn), but Madonna had no intention of retiring from the limelight. Since he was unable to deal with her defiant independence, the only thing left to him was to try to break her spirit.

After their disastrous Christmas, Madonna filed again for divorce, only this time her decision was final. The failure of her marriage was devastating. Here she was, thirty years old, with a glittering, global career, and her emotional life was in tatters. She told friends that she still loved Sean. The heartache forced her to dig deep within herself as she tried to make sense of what was happening. During that troubled year of 1988, she began to reflect on her family background and what had brought her to this point. Steadily, she fed that back into her songwriting, recording what was to become her artistic breakthrough—*Like a Prayer.*

THE SIN IS
WITHIN YOU

March 1989. I am the music editor of London listings magazine City
Limits. *An avalanche of brown cardboard record envelopes lands on my
desk. I slowly sift through the overwhelming pile. I open one at random
and pull out a record. The smell of patchouli hits me in the face. The
scent has been rubbed into the vinyl grooves. And there's a picture of
Madonna's bejeaned midriff, festooned with beads. She's also on the cover
of* Rolling Stone *with long, dark hair, looking like a hippie. Atta-
girl! The record yields more treasures: dark, more complex songs, more
autobiographical than ever before. The woman has become an Artist. It
cheers up my morning.*

"I didn't try to candycoat anything or make it
more palatable for mass consumption . . . I wrote what I felt," Madonna said of *Like a Prayer*. With this album, she moved in a rockier
direction, leaving some vocals ragged and raw, keeping arrangements
simple, and eschewing the high-pop gloss of previous records, like
True Blue. She was in tune with the times, as the pop mainstream
was gradually being infiltrated by such alternative rock bands as Faith
No More, Jane's Addiction, Throwing Muses, and The Pixies—

precursors to the explosion of early 90s Seattle grunge. The rise of these bands, plus intense rap acts, like Run DMC and Public Enemy, signaled a change in public mood. The glitz of the "greed is good" 80s was tarnishing as the long-term impact of Reaganomics made itself felt. In October 1987, the Black Monday stock collapse saw 25 percent lopped off the Dow Jones index. This was larger than the 1929 crisis that had triggered the Great Depression.

In the late 80s, the world was sliding into recession, and it would have been imprudent for Madonna to sing of glamour and parties. The commercial gloss that adorned *True Blue* now seemed dated. She was growing up, her fans were getting older, and it was time for her to move away from teen appeal to fresh audiences and the longevity of the album market. It was the beginning of the "downsizing" era, when bright primary colors were replaced with hues of black and blue; when fashion spreads and movies lost their sheen in favor of the gritty and the grainy. Madonna's new sound was instinctive rather than calculating. She needed to change. She was thirty years old, caught in an unhappy marriage. She wanted to sing about her emotional reality. She reached inside and ended up traveling back to the influences that formed her: the Catholic faith, God the Father, and the mother she had lost.

"She was upset and in tears a lot of the time. Normally she's a very fast worker, but it took maybe three or four times as long to make the record because she kept breaking down," recalled Pat Leonard. "We called it her divorce album." Madonna was in a tense mood. "She and Pat fought even more on this record [than *True Blue*]. They were fighting tooth and nail. It was her second time producing, and she had to prove to everyone it wasn't a fluke," says Bruce Gaitsch, a guitarist on the album. "Madonna was in a determined mood. Things were falling apart with Sean and she was on her way to becoming single, so she was concentrating on the music. She'd make very detailed notes on our playing. A lot of the time I was sweating."

Bass player Guy Pratt, a London musician who came up through the punk mod scene before playing for Bryan Ferry and Pink Floyd in the '80s, remembers her getting very irate when the drummer he had chosen for the sessions pulled out at the last minute. "That initially got me sacked," Pratt told me. "Before I arrived in L.A., she was shouting to Pat, 'If this fucking guy can't get a fucking drummer to turn up he isn't fucking playing on my record!' Fair point. Pat had already had to sell me to her. I called him up. 'Pat please, I gotta have this gig.' Two days before I was meant to fly out, I was woken by the phone at four o'clock in the morning. I picked it up. 'I hear you're funny. Make me laugh,' shouted this voice. I told her a joke, I did make her laugh, and that got me reinstated."

The ordeal wasn't over with, however. When he touched down at LAX, he rang Leonard and was told, "Can you come down to the studio? She wants you now." Pratt got into his rented car feeling "absolutely knackered" after the flight from London. "I walk in, Madonna's having dinner. 'Thanks for coming.' Very clipped, really horrible. Like, not thanks at all. And that was it. That's all she wanted. 'You can go home now.'"

The next day in the studio, Pratt was terrified. "She's a formidable, frightening woman," he recalls. "It stayed like that for a bit. Then I realized, you have to keep your wits about you. There were all these top L.A. session guys being very quiet and deferential, whereas Chester [Kamen, a guitarist] and I were the punk rockers. I thought, you've got to be fucking cheeky, or you're not going to get anything on the record. I ended up getting into great arguments with her about Catholicism. She responded to it so well. She likes a bit of *metal*."

Leonard's choice of a few English players was deliberate. A fan of British rock, he wanted some of that attitude and quirkiness on the album. "Because *True Blue* had been so huge, he pretty much had free rein," says Pratt. "We were recording it at Johnny Yuma, a fabulous new studio he'd built from the *True Blue* money."

Not only was Madonna delving deep for lyrical content, she was also a new woman in the studio. Gone was the girl on the *Like a Virgin* sessions, just working on a hunch and instinct. With *Like a Prayer*, she had clear knowledge, not just of what different instruments were capable of but how to articulate and achieve the sounds she heard in her head. Guy Pratt recalls: "I remember the first take of my first session with all the band. We played the song 'Oh Father' once through with Madonna singing. As soon as we finished, she said: 'OK, Jon [drummer Jonathan Moffet], do less of the high hat in the middle eight and more of a fill toward the end. Guy, I want duck's eggs [semibreves] on the end, and Chester, bring in your guitar on the second verse . . .' While singing this song for the first time with us, she noted what each of us had done, and could convey what she wanted in clear, concise English. We ran through it once again, did one take with vocals, once more with the strings, and that was it. I was amazed."

Bruce Gaitsch was impressed with her decisiveness. "She'd say to Pat, 'That's as good as it's gonna get.' He'd raise an eyebrow. She'd say, 'I'm serious. It's done.'" Perhaps Madonna's growing musical confidence led to a more personal album. She had to be more *inside* the music this time, because the album was more about her. "The whole record has a concept," says Gaitsch. "She was getting in touch with her Catholic upbringing." The Holy Trinity of the songs "Like a Prayer," "Oh Father," and "Promise to Try," for instance, are a deep evocation of the effect that religion had on her life.

WHEN I was a young girl, my brother and sisters had this game of cards that, for want of a better name, was called Catholic snap. We had to pair together images of Church objects, like cruets (communion goblets), surplices (white linen vestments worn by the altar boys), and hosts (the wafers put on our tongue at communion). This was our catechism, a way of learning the liturgy. Those objects of Catholicism are indelibly imprinted on our minds. Catholics believe in transubstantiation: that the wine and wafer don't just symbolize the body of Christ, they *are* the body of Christ. During the Mass they *become* the thing. It isn't just a ritual; these objects are laden with transformative power. And every word in prayer has a precise meaning, over and above its everyday use.

This is the culture that Madonna grew up with. She collected crucifixes and rosary beads; for her, they weren't just a prop, they were talismans. The crucifix is her central theme. "I don't think that wearing the crucifix was an attempt to seek out controversy," says Mary Lambert, director of the "Like a Virgin" and "Like a Prayer" videos. "I think it had meaning for her—religious significance, mystic significance. Madonna is a very religious person in her own way." Madonna imbued her songs with concrete memories of her childhood faith. "Sometimes I'm wracked with guilt when I needn't be. And that, to me, is left over from my Catholic upbringing," she told the *Rolling Stone* writer Bill Zehme. "Because in Catholicism you are born a sinner and you are a sinner all your life. No matter how you try to get away from it, the sin is within you all the time . . . Catholicism is not a soothing religion. It's a painful religion."

What is remarkable about the songwriting on *Like a Prayer* is her use of liturgical words. On the title track, for instance, there is the surface meaning: forging sexuality and religion with fluent pop lyrics that sound easy on the ear. But underlying that is a rigorous meditation on prayer. "It's a song that explores the word 'prayer,'" says Andrae Crouch, leader of the Los Angeles Church of God choir that sang on the record. He told me that they researched the lyrics beforehand "to find out what the intention of the song might be. We're very particular in choosing what we work with, and we liked what we heard." The choir was well established in the L.A. community, and had sung for such artists as Quincy Jones and Chaka Khan, and on such Hollywood film soundtracks as *The Color Purple*. Their flamboyance matched Madonna's conviction.

In this song, Madonna is unashamedly her mother's daughter—kneeling alone in private devotion, contemplating God's mystery. She sings of being chosen, of having a calling. Traditionally, a vocation is a summons by God. For her mother, a life of holiness meant looking after her children, being a good wife, and bearing her suffering with grace. A vocation that Madonna herself takes no less seriously is the fusing of female power in her music with spirituality and sexuality. Some Christians consider this blasphemous and see her as the fallen angel. Thinking she is lost, Madonna beseeches God in the song to help her. She has to surrender herself, like a child, before she can be rescued.

Feeling joy at being chosen, she is filled with an ecstatic sense of the Holy Spirit. This is emphasized by the full-blown gospel choir and church organ. Throughout the song, Madonna lurches from doubt to confirmation, and the music mirrors this, moving from the innocence of her voice and the choral harmonies to the segments where the drums kick in and the tempo swings. "Madonna wanted something churchy, a very full sound, so I tried to blow up what she did and make it as powerful as I could," recalls Crouch. What makes it such a dynamic track is the sense of people possessed.

"That's the best bass performance I've ever done on a record. The fact that I could do what I did on 'Like a Prayer' still startles me. It's just nuts," says Guy Pratt. "By the end, Madonna was going, 'Guy, more! More!' By the end of the fade I'd run out of licks and I had to go back to the beginning again." He was so wrapped up in the moment that when he was later invited to hear a mix of the record, he couldn't believe it was him. "There was this insane bass part, I thought, but no musician is allowed to perform on a record like that, this is meant to be a star vehicle for her. I asked Madonna: 'The bass is amazing. Who's that?' 'You, you dummy!' she said."

The song was a triumph and a number-one favorite with fans. As Pratt says, "Everyone from Johnny Marr to Dave Gilmour said, 'Unarguably brilliant record.'" For Madonna, the song was something that emerged spontaneously between her and Pat Leonard. "I really wanted to do something gospel-oriented and a cappella, with virtually no instrumentation, just my voice and an organ," she said. "So we started fooling around with the song, and we'd take away all the instrumentation so that my voice was naked. Then we came up with the bridge together, and we had the idea to have a choir."

Madonna was so immersed in the recording process that she didn't have time to think about clothes and makeup. "You'd think she would look glamorous, but she didn't come to the studio with diamond rings and glitter. I was expecting all the hoopla, I didn't recognize her at first," says Andrae Crouch. "She looked so normal—she wasn't highbrow or nothin' like that. She hugged us and made us feel comfortable."

Crouch was struck by her dedication to the music. His sister Sandra was playing tambourine on the track, and for the recording they tried out different rhythms. After a while, Madonna stopped and said, "Sandra, will you go back to that bar thirty-two and do that," and she tapped out the rhythm. Years of dancer training had given Madonna perfect timing. Crouch was shocked. "Madonna knew what bar it was and we'd gone through it just one time. I wouldn't expect her to remember that in a thousand years—I can't do that! She knows her music," says Crouch.

Madonna's focus meant that she went further than ever before into difficult feelings, and she wanted to keep the results clear and unadorned. Her decision to experiment with her voice "naked" works particularly well on the track "Promise to Try." On this short, piano-led ballad, Madonna has an imaginary conversation with her mother, her voice husky with emotion. There's the sadness of trying to keep her elusive, fading memory alive. Madonna knows she must let her mother go, but to do that means feeling utterly abandoned. It is not surprising that since her mother's death, Madonna has tried to make the whole world love her, but the emptiness can never be filled. As an expression of grief, this song is notable for its restraint. "We did it with a double quartet and piano," remembers string arranger Bill Meyers. "We pared it down. We could've put the whole thirty-five-piece orchestra on it, but we resisted that temptation."

Instead, the orchestra ended up on "Oh Father," the third song in her "Trinity." This dramatic, slightly portentous ballad isn't just about the disciplinarian father who, she thought, didn't care. "It's me dealing with all authority figures in life," she said. Emphasizing each word, Madonna sings of her bewilderment at his disapproval and anger. Her delivery in places has a Courtney Love–style rasp, and she attacks the song with a personal passion. She says she recorded the song in "a very, very dark state of mind" while she was doing her Broadway stint with *Speed-the-Plow.*

The play was a bleak, cynical piece written by David Mamet. Madonna played the role of Karen, a secretary to a movie producer who bedded her on a bet. Karen later gets her own back, but is depicted as being just as seedy and conniving as the men who exploit her. In an attempt to exorcise the demons brought up by the part, Madonna found herself letting go in the recording of "Oh Father."

She worked on the song with Pat Leonard in "this really dingy, awful little studio in the Garment District in New York. It was grotesquely dirty and cramped, and that's what came out of it," Bill Meyers recalls. "It was a brilliant piece of work. She seemed very moved. The song suggested incest, and controversial themes like closet beatings and being afraid of him. I don't know if it was autobiographical. Imagination is a powerful thing with artists; she could put herself in another person's shoes."

Madonna has never mentioned physical abuse in her family, though she has said that her father was a disciplinarian and that her stepmother was hard on her. It was probably more a case of emotional neglect: with her father locked up in grief, the children's basic needs were taken care of, but there were no frills. When he married again, his new wife was wrapped up with the two babies, so the older children were often left to their own devices. Madonna's girlhood was at times troubled and without much joy. "Maybe I wasn't the greatest father in the world," Tony Ciccone said later, "but life wasn't easy for any of us." Madonna used her imagination to escape. "Oh Father" is a potent example of the pictures she could create to express that bleak inner landscape.

Because of her difficult childhood, Madonna had insecurities, and this showed up in anxieties about her vocal performance. "She's consistent," says Meyers. "If she bends the note or sings something flat in a certain spot, she'll do that each time. Some people need to do warm-up vocals, then hit their stride. Others burn out after a while, and some do it different every time. With Madonna, what she sang was what you were going to get. She didn't vary it a whole lot. After we recorded 'Oh Father,' I said to her: 'I think this is the strongest vocal performance you've ever given.' She started to say thank you, then she looked confused. She's so bright. She'd picked up what I meant. I realized I had to be careful, because she was very sensitive to her limitations."

Besides religion, the other major theme that Madonna explored on *Like a Prayer* is family. There's the percussive drama of "Till Death Us Do Part," a song about domestic violence. "It's very much drawn from my life, factually speaking . . . about a relationship that is powerful and painful," Madonna said, obviously alluding to Sean. "It's about a dysfunctional relationship, a sadomasochistic relationship that can't end." She drew the line at sacrificing herself, however, saying she would never want to stay in a violent relationship until death. Rapid-fire and moving, with a soaring melody, this is one of the strongest tracks on the album, an aching swan song to her marriage.

Also dedicated to family is the Sly Stone–influenced track "Keep It Together," an upbeat meditation on sibling power. Produced by Steve Bray, it is robust and packed with harmonies. There is the sense that Madonna, isolated by fame and shaken by the failure of her marriage, is reaching back to the stability of family roots. Presenting a homey image of brothers and sisters joshing together, she felt a need to restore bonds that had become fraught or distant. Likewise with "Dear Jessie," a slightly sugary lullaby to Pat Leonard's young daughter, she harks back to a childlike innocence, summoning up a psychedelic fairy-tale landscape where pink elephants roam with dancing moons and mermaids. Madonna was to return to the lullaby more successfully on such later albums as *Bedtime Stories* and *American Life*—on this first attempt, she overdid the elaborate imagery.

Mining the same fairy-tale vein, she came up with a feel-good doo-wop style for "Cherish," a plea to Cupid to provide her with a good match. The fanciful video, shot in the ocean spray by Herb Ritts, has Madonna looking delirious and cavorting with mermen. A song more typical for the old Madonna, this one would have fit more comfortably onto the more "candycoated" *True Blue* album, while other oddball tracks, like "Love Song" and "Express Yourself," point to where she was going next.

Coproduced with Prince, "Love Song" is experimental, flawed, and rambling. Long-term admirers of each other's work (and roughly equal in their superstardom), Prince and Madonna got together in the late 80s at his Paisley Park studio to write a musical. The process was haphazard, as the two of them had such different personalities. She liked things organized, quick, and simple, while his method was mercurial and improvisational. "[We] didn't really finish anything," Madonna said. "We started a bunch of stuff, then we would go on to the next thing." Although they finished "Love Song" for her album, it has the feel of a work in progress—probably a reflection of how it was written. "We sent tapes to each other back and forth between L.A. and Minnesota. Then we would talk on the phone, and he would play stuff for me over the line." This was a new direction for her. Spare and intimate, with a lot of compression, dirty drum beats, and snare. Her voice was held in, clipped, and there in the mix as a mere texture. Each line of the song was like a long lick, and very Prince-ish in approach. A curious exercise for her, this was a flexing of musical muscles that lay the groundwork for future albums, like *Erotica*.

Then, bestriding the album like a colossus alongside "Like a Prayer," is "Express Yourself." Produced by Steve Bray, it is a feminist call to arms, complete with muscular brass-playing and soulful voice. Here Madonna is the anti-materialism girl, exhorting her female audience to respect themselves. That means having a man who loves your head *and* your heart. If he doesn't treat you right (and here's the revolutionary rhetoric), you're better off on your own. Like a female preacher, Madonna emphasizes each word of the chorus, invoking God and the power of orgasm. In parts *Cosmo*-woman, girl-talk, and swinging dance track, it presages the deliciously declarative stance of "Vogue" and shows Madonna moving from introspective to survivalist mode.

With its evocation of German expressionism and Fritz Lang's *Metropolis*, the video for the song has become one of her best-known and most talked about. Directed by David Fincher, it depicts a cross-dressing Madonna holding sway over a factory of glistening muscle-men in chains. She is the queen bee lording it over her workers. In this fantasy of sex and power, she wears an iron collar and chain, but she is in control. She summons a man into her boss's boudoir, wrapping him in satin sheets. Not surprisingly, it became one of the most popular videos with her female audience.

To CONCLUDE her album, Madonna returned to the religious theme with "Act of Contrition." Beginning with whispered invocation, it features distorted guitar and backward-tracking of the gospel choir. Jubilant and anarchic, it is anything but contrite. When Madonna was born, a central tenet of the Catholic Church was confession. As historian James M. O'Toole writes, up to the mid-1960s, "confession had been central to American Catholic practice . . . it was something that Catholics did but Protestants and others did not. Often, Catholics did not like doing it, but they did it anyway. . . . Confession seemed to them to express something fundamental about human nature and about their own, individual relationship to God."

The sacrament has three stages: contrition—an examination of conscience; then confession of one's sins to the priest, followed by penance and "satisfaction." Penances were tailored according to the nature of the sin. Seminary professors would advise their newly ordained, for instance: "For sins of the flesh, some mortification; for stinginess, alms according to means; for pride, prayer." The penitent would then absolve him- or herself with a short prayer known as the Act of Contrition.

Madonna mocked this process, aware that her relaxed attitude toward sex would have cost her more than a few Our Fathers and Hail Marys outside the confessional box. For her, it was important that personal freedom shouldn't be curtailed. But on a deeper level, she wanted to acknowledge sexuality as a positive force. According to Saint Augustine, "The sexual impulse is a sin and a shame . . . the genital organs are indecent and dishonorable. . . . They are the bodily instruments for the transmission of Original Sin." That medieval viewpoint remained pretty much intact until Madonna's girlhood. Although many attitudes were breaking down by the late 1980s, she still felt there was a fundamental split between the "virginal and holy" and "low-down and dirty." She told writer Paul Zollo: "You have to put the two together with people. You have to let both of them surface. And it has so much to do with being honest with yourself and the people you're with."

She fused the two ideas in the most provocative way possible in the video for "Like a Prayer." Initially, she had signed a $1 million deal to star in a commercial for Pepsi Cola. An innocuous commercial was made and aired just before the release of her "Like a Prayer" single in March 1989. But before it could be fully exploited, Madonna's video came out. Featuring a racially motivated murder, Madonna kissing a black Christ, Madonna with stigmata and tears of blood, and Madonna dancing in front of a field of burning crosses, this was a bold, blaring statement about sex, race, and religion. The gospel choir that appears on the video is not the one she recorded with. "We didn't want to be a part of that," recalls Andrae Crouch. "It's like an architect building rooms in a hotel. He would build the lobby and the dining room, but he wouldn't want to have a part in the back room where they're gambling. With the video, the intimacy between a boy and girl on the altar—that was way over the line for us. The altar of God is a sacred place. The House of God is there for us to have contact with God rather than our flesh desires. We didn't want people to think we were endorsing that."

The video was banished to late-night MTV, and there was a storm of protest from religious groups condemning Madonna's "blasphemy." When church leaders urged their followers to boycott Pepsi, the commercial was swiftly pulled. Madonna's contract was terminated, but she kept the $1 million.

Many praised her marketing acumen, seeing the video as a publicity stunt. But to Madonna, this was more than just commerce—she was interested in the nexus between art and commerce, in projecting a progressive message into millions of homes. "The 'Like a Prayer' video was about overcoming racism and overcoming the fear of telling the truth. I had my own ideas about God and then I had the ideas that I thought were imposed on me," said Madonna. Maybe, underneath her business demeanor, Madonna was ambivalent about the

THE SIN IS WITHIN YOU 135

association with Pepsi, and her video was a way of distancing herself from such an obviously corporate deal.

LIKE A PRAYER proved to be a turning point artistically for Madonna, and she gained a whole new audience. Personally, though, she was in a lonely place. Guy Pratt remembers one day during recording sessions she came in and asked if anyone wanted to go with her to see George Michael. "This was George Michael playing the L.A. Sports Arena on the Faith tour at the absolute fucking peak of his powers. Everyone went, 'Er . . . mmm.' So I put my hand up and said, 'I wouldn't mind.' There was no one else, just me and her. It was like a date."

She picked him up at eight in her limousine. "It was fantastic to have the time with her on her own. She was a completely different person. It was incredibly poignant. I said, 'How're you finding living in L.A., because you strike me as such a New York person?' She said, 'I have to be here now. I can't live in New York, because all my friends are dead.' It was the height of the AIDS thing—all her friends were dancers. You forget how in the 80s that whole community was ravaged." After the show, she was dropped off at her house and she told Guy to keep the limo for the night. "I did that classic wanker thing, ringing up everyone I knew. 'I've got a limo.' I was going round every bar in L.A., but it was a Monday night and everyone was at home. The driver was probably thinking, Madonna's always home by ten thirty, but now I've got this asshole in the back." His experience seemed to mirror her emptiness. Going down an introspective road was hard for her, and, as if uncertain of the direction in which she was moving, Madonna turned back.

In February 1989, Madonna shot her next movie role as Breathless Mahoney in *Dick Tracy*. This was an important movie for her, the one that, after the failure of *Shanghai Surprise* and *Who's That Girl*, put her acting career on a more even keel. She took a little persuading though. When the director Warren Beatty approached her to discuss a part, Madonna put him off for a few weeks. Maybe she was unsure about taking on another film role, or maybe she just wanted to keep him guessing. Either way, the thought of working with Hollywood's leading man was too tempting, so she agreed to meet.

At fifty-two, Beatty had quite a track record as a womanizer. His name had been linked with every glamorous female star since the 1960s, from Catherine Deneuve to Faye Dunaway, Julie Christie, and Carly Simon. The latter purportedly wrote her hit song "You're So Vain" about him. But he was better known for groundbreaking cinematic work, particularly as producer and star of *Bonnie and Clyde* (1967).

By the time he met Madonna, Beatty had made numerous top-grossing films, including sharp 70s satire *Shampoo* and the 1981 Oscar-winning epic *Reds*. Aware of his celebrity status, and seeing his playboy notoriety as a challenge, Madonna immediately went into flirtation mode. Beatty offered her the part, but although he was entranced by the young star, he gave her only the Screen Actors' Guild scale wages. His preferred costar would have been Kathleen Turner or Kim Basinger, but both were unavailable. Madonna was to be a canny second choice, and perfect publicity for the movie. The two were intrigued by each other's reputations, and from that first meeting, there was a crackling attraction. Shortly after the film went into production, they started an affair.

With divorce papers served, Madonna was ready early on to "go legit" about her relationship with Beatty. The complete opposite of Sean Penn, Beatty was poised, subtle, and self-assured. He was an old-school movie actor, as smooth and perfumed as the air in Hollywood Hills. He persuaded her to give up the *Like a Prayer* angst and go back to the fizzy blonde that everyone knew and loved. "I had to dye my hair blond. I begged Warren Beatty, because it took me so long to grow my hair out and I really wanted to have dark hair," Madonna said. "Along with the album, which was much more personal . . . I felt great having my own hair color for the first time in years. . . . And then I had to change it, so I had a bit of an identity crisis. Women with blond hair are perceived as much more sexual and much more impulsive, not so serious."

Madonna's part was high glamour—an expensive gangster's-moll-turned-showgirl with bubbly blond hair and a silver dress. "Breathless Mahoney . . . falls in love with Dick Tracy in spite of herself. I don't think she's inherently evil, but she's quite accomplished in villainy," she remarked, with a degree of satisfaction. She knew that with *Dick Tracy* she was on a winning streak. Starring Beatty, Al Pacino, Dustin Hoffman, and Paul Sorvino, the film was set to be a blockbuster. It was shot in vivid comic-book colors; all the gangsters were stylized re-creations of the original strip cartoon, with their wide suits and bizarre prosthetic faces. Despite a weak plot, the effects were seductive, making it a diverting film to watch. And after her grueling stint on Broadway in *Speed-the-Plow*, Madonna knew how to project. Her screen performance was confident, and she seemed to enjoy playing the vamp. Although her lines were delivered in a slightly faltering, breathy tone, her wordless presence was luminous. In that respect, she exuded some of the appeal of 1930s and 1940s Hollywood. She would have been a dynamic silent-movie actress.

The renowned film archivist, John Kobal, predicted early in her career that "Madonna has the vibrancy required for stardom. . . . [She] has a curious kind of beauty, like Bette Davis, which she still has to establish." He compared her favorably with the movie icons she admired, women with classic cheekbones and sass, like Rita Hayworth, Ava Gardner, and Joan Crawford. For Kobal, what made an idol was personality rather than just the look. "All the great stars . . . could stand quite still and have a compelling quality which would make you ask, 'What is going on inside this person?' The talent of the great stars who endured was that they could keep regenerating themselves, keep us interested—that's why they're colossal."

Madonna lamented the end of the early twentieth-century studio system that cosseted its stars. "It would have been great in the old days [of Hollywood]. The studio system really nurtured and cared for you in a way it doesn't now," she said. "On the other hand, your life was not your own. Now you have more individual freedom, but you don't have anyone looking after your career in the way they did then." As previous filmmakers discovered, Madonna liked to have a lot of direction, and Beatty was sensitive to her needs. He took care of her:

he provided a masseuse on set, took her out for expensive meals, and flowers were sent to her trailer every day.

"I think by the time we met Warren, he had nothing to prove. He had made all these films. He was this lovely person who played great piano, he was always ready for people, smiling in his home," recalls Niki Haris. Beatty was delighted that Madonna was interested in him. Critics have suggested that their affair was a publicity stunt for the movie, but while it created a great deal of press interest, there was also genuine affection between them. When Madonna decided to record the *I'm Breathless* album separate from the soundtrack, Beatty was supportive. Bob Magnussun, bass player on the *I'm Breathless* sessions, recalls a very happy Madonna. "She was nice to everybody, she introduced herself to the musicians. One day Warren Beatty came in from the filming and he had that yellow Dick Tracy mac and suit on. Seemed like they were pretty contented with each other!" he laughs.

After the anguished split from Sean, Madonna had a few golden months. She was in a fairy tale. It seemed she had everything— Hollywood at her fingertips, a kind of sugar daddy, the respect of the community, a studio that was taking care of her in the old style. The *I'm Breathless* album reflects her lightness of mood, fleshing out the romantic fantasy. As the title suggests, she was in character, projecting the sense of a savvy Jazz-era nightclub singer. Featuring Beatty in his trilby and lemon-yellow coat, and Madonna all cleavage and corkscrew curls, the cover looked like a film poster. Described as "Music from and inspired by the film *Dick Tracy*," this record was essentially a promo for the movie, and seen as separate from her main mass-market albums. Produced by Pat Leonard and recorded with jazz musicians, it has the feel of 1930s Big Band swing. "It was a ten-piece big band, all really good, cream of the crop, players who captured that style of swing era music," recalls Magnussun, who has worked with everyone from Art Pepper to Buddy Rich and Sarah Vaughan. He admired Madonna's willingness to explore a different genre. "I'm pretty impressed when pop musicians move into another area. It takes a little courage to do that."

Most songs on the album reflect her showgirl persona, like "Hanky

Panky," a ballsy, cheeky paen to the art of spanking. Although the subject matter was a bit forced, the track had a rootsy, rocking jive. There was also "Something to Remember," a low-key, atmospheric ballad reminiscent of Dusty Springfield in its sense of regret. This song sounds more laid-back and soulful than the other tracks, most of which have a contrived air. That studied approach is most in evidence on the three Stephen Sondheim songs that Madonna tackles—"Sooner or Later," "More," and "What Can You Lose." She tries hard, pitching her voice deep and carefully holding and bending notes where required. She pulls it off—but like an actress, as if she's playing a part and performing a vocal exercise in technique. She had yet to do the vocal training that so transformed her voice after *Evita*. "She was in character. She started smoking. She actually bummed a cigarette off me," says Guy Pratt, who also played on the album. "Her character smoked, therefore she did."

This record was the flip side to Madonna's *Like a Prayer* persona—coquettish, pampered, and pandering. In places, it feels like over-annunciated musical theater. But her natural ebullience saves it from being a mere parody. On "Now I'm Following You (Part 1)," she duets with Beatty to a boogie-woogie rhythm. His soft, seductive voice echoes their easy rapport. For this track, they obviously didn't stretch themselves too much. "Warren came in and we did it in one take," recalls Bill Meyers, who played piano on the session. "Everyone's looking at each other. Pat said, 'Sure you don't want to do another one?' 'Nope', he said. 'That's it.' They'd paid for three hours, and the whole thing lasted fifteen minutes. I admire that. If you've captured the lightning in the bottle, why not?"

The final track is at odds with the rest of the album, yet it turned out to be one of her biggest hits. "Vogue" is a celebration of those 40s movie sirens, updated to the gay disco dance floor. It was the sound of summer 1990—catchy, defiant, with a delicious groove, and a classic video to match—one that crystallized her iconic status. As the decade turned, Madonna was at the peak of her game.

GIVING
GOOD FACE

In the summer of 1990, it looked like nothing could go wrong for Madonna. "Vogue," the video, is shot in luxurious black-and-white by David Fincher. Her hair is sleek, her makeup stark, she looks like a 1940s fashion plate. Her hands perform an expressive choreography, framing her face, reaching out to her dancers as they adopt the exaggerated runway-model poses of the gay underground. She inhabits this world, she controls it. She shows the beauty of style and surfaces, making this video a glorious celebration of image, an old Hollywood movie magazine brought to life. She is at her absolute apogee. Like the medieval Madonnas shining out from those wooden icons, she is the twentieth-century version, captured on celluloid.

She performs the song at the MTV Awards, and goes back to the etymology of the word 'vogue,' dressed up like Marie-Antoinette, her dancers moving around her in the powdered faces, wigs, and heaving bosoms of the eighteenth-century French court. It is a moment of inspired brilliance. "That level of production had never been done on MTV. The costumes, the fans, the drama," said Carlton Wilborn, one of her key dancers. "MTV had just no idea, we just came out and rocked."

"VOGUE" WAS THE BEGINNING OF A NEW PHASE FOR
Madonna. It was as if she got a sense of her immortality, and her
true power. Feeling secure in her status as a mainstream artist, she
began to play with that power and challenge her audience. ". . . In the
guise of a game you can find things out," she once said, explaining
the game Truth or Dare. "Sometimes it would turn into these really heavy sessions where it was all truths and no dares . . . the truth
brings people closer together. It's like being intimate with a lover.
The more intimate you are with somebody, the more an unspoken
closeness occurs."

In a key scene from her documentary *Truth or Dare*, the star responds to a dare by fellating a bottle of mineral water. In one fell
swoop, she solidifies her reputation as a sexual tease and agent provocateur, while exorcising the trauma of the sexual attack that happened
to her when she was a young girl alone in New York. She has often
referred to multifarious demons, and this was one of them. From
the early 1990s, Madonna began playing an elaborate game of truth
or dare with the world, and with herself. With each project—from
"Justify My Love," to Blond Ambition, to *Truth or Dare*, to *Sex*, she
began a journey of revelation, upping the ante in terms of nudity and
psychodrama. "She's always fishing for people to be real with her," a
friend once said wistfully, "but only a few people can." Layer after
layer comes off as Madonna chases the intimacy she craves. The *Sex*
era is a beautiful, bold, harrowing exercise in frustration and, despite
her attempts at invincibility, a curious act of self-destruction.

THE "VOGUE" video was assembled after a huge casting call in LA.
"There were about five hundred guys there. It was mayhem, with all
kinds of dancers," Wilborn told me. A performing arts graduate from
Chicago, he was the most experienced of the "Vogue" troupe. "At that
time, the dance environment was at a transitional point—L.A. was
show town and New York was all about technique. For this audition,
dancer dancers as well as commercial dancers turned out. It was red-

hot." Madonna quickly identified her main contenders. "That first day she saw, she cut, she saw, she cut, and ended up with thirty guys. When I got home, there was a message on my machine from her, saying would I meet her at a club that night." Wilborn turned up, along with two other men from the audition, and they duly partied the night away. To complete the test, Madonna invited them to a private dance class the next morning.

Within days, she had her "Vogue" troupe in place, which included Wilborn; the street-smart Oliver Crumes; Salim Gauwloos (aka Slam), a classically trained Belgian ballet dancer with smoldering Valentino looks; plus Jose Gutierez and Luis Camacho, original "voguers" from the gay scene. Directly inspired by Willi Ninja, the vogueing star of the 1990 documentary *Paris Is Burning*, Madonna wanted to incorporate his references to Fred Astaire, Olympic gymnastics, and Asian dance into her work.

When it came to shooting the video, Gutierez and Camacho set up most of the authentic "Vogue" steps, while choreographer Vincent Paterson embellished them. At first, not everyone was convinced. "I'd just finished ballet school, and this was my second video," recalls Salim. "I remember David [Fincher] said, 'Put him in this tuxedo jacket.' So I wore that, and they put me on some steps, and I was doing some poses, and it took like fifteen minutes, and I was like, 'OK, is that it?' I thought, This is not a good beginning. But then when the 'Vogue' video came out, I was like, 'Ah, OK! *Now* I get it!'"

"Vogue" became the number one hit of that summer, played in clubs across the globe, from London to New York to Bali. It rode the crest of the newly emerging dance craze, where club culture, house music, and techno met the mainstream. "Vogue" reflected the new hedonism: positive, upbeat, and totally inclusive. "Madonna was very much inspired by dance music. She liked our remixes for the *Immaculate Collection*, and she wanted to explore the club music from an original standpoint," recalls Tony Shimkin, who worked on the song with producer Shep Pettibone. Before it was recorded, they sent her a music track, "and on the flight to New York from her home in L.A., she composed the rap section. That song came about very quickly. I was impressed with the content of the lyrics. I'd heard rap over and over again, but it never told a story in that classy way, bringing you a visual picture of an era. And the video played a huge role in the song's success."

The seven male dancers in the video made such a dynamic team that Madonna later went on to use them for her Blond Ambition tour. Their ebullience leaped off the screen. Salim remembers that they all had a rapport from the start. "We used all the underground gay expressions, and Madonna learned them too. Like we'd say, 'Give face.' It's like giving good face, it means your skin is flawless and everything is on display. (This phrase was used in the 'Vogue' rap.) Another word we liked was 'ovah'—an expression for when something is so over the top but really good, it's like 'Ovah!'"

Emboldened by the success of "Vogue," Madonna chose to explore more "adult" territory for her next offering. The video for "Justify My Love" was filmed by Jean-Baptiste Mondino in an anonymous hotel in black-and-white, harking back to the breathy possibilities of European art cinema and the shimmering decadence of *La Dolce Vita*. Madonna is featured as a sex fantasist, exploring the erotic through leather, transvestism, and overtones of 1930s Berlin cabaret. Rapping with whispered intensity to a pared-down backbeat, she voiced the deep, private nature of female desire. Teetering between tension and sensuality, "Justify My Love" was dance ballad as art form. Recurring throughout the video were images of cross-dressing and camp, themes that reverberated in the work of her idols Marlene Dietrich and Mae West.

Many hailed Madonna for taking a bold new direction. Only she wasn't the sole author of this transformation. In the late 80s, a beautiful young Mexican-American woman named Ingrid Chavez was working on an album of spoken word tracks with her one-time boyfriend Prince. They were also shooting the film *Graffiti Bridge* in Minneapolis when Ingrid met funk rock hero Lenny Kravitz, and the two of them began an intense relationship. Kravitz invited Ingrid into the studio one day, when he was laying tracks with hip-hop auteur Andre Betts.

"They asked me if I wanted to lay something down, and the only thing I had on me was a letter to Lenny. I like letter-writing more than any other form. Beautiful books have been created from correspondence between two people. That's my way of expressing myself, in that intimate way," Ingrid said to me. "I did it in one take, and went back to Minneapolis."

The track they laid down that day was the original of "Justify My Love." Anxious to get a record company interested, Kravitz took a master copy of the song to Virgin. Meanwhile, the relationship between Ingrid and Kravitz petered out, and she changed her phone number. She heard nothing more from Kravitz until the day of the *Graffiti Bridge* premiere. "He came to my hotel room and said, 'Madonna's doing "Justify My Love." He asked me to sign a document saying that I'd get twelve and a half percent publishing, but no credit.'" Feeling strong-armed, Ingrid signed the paper.

She was then invited to the studio to meet Madonna while they did final mixes on the track. Ingrid was shocked by what she heard. "She did an amazing job of copying my vocals. I couldn't even tell the difference between my voice and hers. It was exactly like the demo. She got the honesty of the song, the intense emotion, and the real strong desire. Smart move on her part, she's always been smart. She's always just taken that thing that was unique, that would take her to another place musically."

Ingrid, however, felt uneasy in her "ghost writer" role, and sensed "weird vibes" from Madonna. "She said 'hi,' and then didn't speak to me. She watched me in a strange kind of way. Lenny told me that she had a thing for him, and that's why she was acting weird. That might have been his ego, I don't know. It was her birthday and there were about five of us hanging out in a room off the studio. She came in and said, 'Lenny,' and another person. She called out the two people who could have cake, and left the rest of us sitting there saying, 'OK! I guess we're not allowed to have a piece of that cake.' It's so odd to me. Maybe she just felt like she didn't want another woman to take credit for the creative style of the vocal . . . Madonna's voice when she speaks is not that voice on that song. She's copying the rhythm and the way I speak and the quality of my voice, which is probably my greatest gift."

Ingrid's speaking voice does have a captivating quality. Soft and quietly hypnotic, it was her signature tone on *19th May 1992*, the album she had recorded with Prince, which was yet to come out. And that posed another problem. "After 'Justify My Love' was on the radio, Prince called me up and said, 'Ingrid. What is up with Madonna's new song 'Justify My Love'? And I was like, 'Why?' He said, 'That's you, I know it's you, Ingrid. What is going on?' So I told him and he said, 'Are you a fool? You have a record coming out and everybody's going to think that you copied Madonna and nobody knows that you wrote that song?' I was like, 'Oh my gosh.'"

A local Minneapolis journalist then asked Ingrid point-blank if "Justify My Love" was her song. Feeling hurt and betrayed, Ingrid admitted she wrote it, and the story became widely reported. Although Madonna was criticized (*Chicago-Sun Times* rock writer Jim Derogatis later wrote that "'Justify My Love' represented a new low point in thievery"), she claimed that she was unaware of any deliberate copying. The "musical thief" accusation is one that has cropped up once or twice with Madonna. Eyebrows were raised when, a year after the Malcolm McLaren single "Elements of Vogue," Madonna's "Vogue" came out. And "Justify My Love" contained a beat sampled from the Public Enemy track "Security of the First World." In response, producer Hank Shocklee made the indignant answer record "To My Donna" with The Young Black Teenagers. In the same way that she once copied a girl's hairstyle at the Danceteria, Madonna absorbs her influences with an aplomb that some found worrying. With "Justify My Love," Ingrid ended up suing and reaching an out-of-court settlement, whereby she got twelve and a half percent of disc royalties and her name on the next pressing. Even now, though, her name doesn't always appear on compilations containing the song.

"Basically, I think Lenny wanted to say it was him who wrote the song and she interpreted it. I don't regret Madonna doing it," argues Ingrid. "I just felt betrayed, especially when it was a song so intimate. It wasn't *her* dreams, it wasn't *her* desire." Ingrid went on to release the album she'd recorded with Prince, and then retreated to New Hampshire. She married the musician David Sylvian, raised three children, and, more than ten years later, began to write and make music again. It took a long time for Ingrid to find her way back, on her own terms. "I consider myself a muse," she says—and a generous one at that.

"JUSTIFY MY LOVE" was the lead single from the *Immaculate Collection*, Madonna's first greatest hits package. An astutely assembled set of remixes, it was her second biggest album in the United States after *Like a Virgin*. A seamless marriage of high-octane pop and dance, it was the ultimate party record. It also established the tradition for dance remixes of all her future singles. The *Immaculate Collection* went on selling throughout the decade, and by the late 90s entered the Guinness Book of World Records as the highest-selling greatest hits album by a female artist.

"Justify My Love" also opened up a new creative avenue for Madonna, as she moved into more "adult" territory. She was photographed by Steven Meisel for *Rolling Stone* magazine, dressed in a suit, with her blond hair cropped short and slicked back 1920s-style, dancing and squeezing a flapper girl's behind. The pictures were directly inspired by the photographer Brassaï, who documented the gay clubs, brothels, and opium dens of Paris in the 20s and 30s. Then, because of its risqué nature, the "Justify My Love" video was banned by MTV. Outraged at American censoriousness, Madonna appeared on the ABC TV show *Nightline* and gave a defensive interview to the anchor Forrest Sawyer. But when the video became available in stores, it was a best-seller, and in Saudi Arabia, it was reputed to have been sold for large sums as black-market porn. At a time when female pop artists were expected to be sunny and straightforward, Madonna was pushing boundaries with her erotic cabaret style.

Both "Vogue" and "Justify My Love" were number one hits, while "Hanky Panky," her paen to spanking, did very well in uptight Britain. To her delight, Madonna was touching on taboo subjects and getting a positive response. Emboldened by this, she set about making her next tour the most memorable yet. With Who's That Girl, she began exploring conceptual musical theater, but it was on Blond Ambition that art, spectacle, and dance first really came together. According to tour choreographer Vincent Paterson (who'd previously worked with Michael Jackson), Madonna's intention was to "break every rule we can. She wanted to make statements about sexuality, cross-sexuality, the Church. But the biggest thing we tried to do was change the shape of concerts. Instead of just presenting songs, we wanted to combine fashion, Broadway, rock, and the performance arts."

The most iconic image from the show is Madonna's shiny, pink conical bra. This admirable piece of fashion engineering was the foundation on which the rest of the show was built. A comic masterpiece, it was designed by Jean-Paul Gaultier as both a parody and celebration of her voluptuous 34C bust. Once described by stylist Anna Piaggi as "a landscape gardener, an architect, and a technician all rolled into one," the French designer brought all his skills to play in making this garment. It was a labor of love; Gaultier remembers that period as one of intense stress, claiming to have gotten through 350 aspirins and 1,500 sketches before Madonna approved the costumes. "My clothes have always been in the same spirit as Madonna," he said, ". . . a tough outer shell protects hidden vulnerability." Or, as backup singer Niki Haris succinctly put it: "Cone bras, bustiers, platforms . . . anything she could do to make it bad, she went for it."

The bra was part of a corset that emphasized her newly sculpted, sinewy body. Although this physique had been on display on the Who's That Girl tour, here it was crafted anew, with strong muscle definition accentuated on the first leg of the tour by her hair in a scraped-back ponytail. The look was sensuous, severe, and immediately striking. The corset was invented in the late Renaissance to create a stiffened and upright carriage. As it prevented women from performing manual labor, it was meant to be a symbol of good breeding and wealth. By Victorian times, it had transmuted into the impossible hourglass shape that caused so many female fainting spells. The suffragettes of the early twentieth century rejected the corset in favor of freedom of movement, but it gradually crept back into fa-

vor as a way of flaunting female sexuality. Fashion historian Sarah
Cheang told me: "The modern fashion corset is a strategy that will
make women feel feminine, because it plays with the concept of a
submissive body and mind."

For Madonna, the association with sadomasochism and fetish
cultures was irresistible, and, in the same way she has always played
with double meanings, her Blond Ambition corset signaled both sub-
missiveness and strength. "When she pulled on that JPG corset and
showed the world her newly sculpted muscles, her combination of
body-toning and body-taming combined all senses of the notion of
discipline," says Cheang. "She was presenting a body that had been
subjected to a rigorous regime of self-discipline—an active body produced by exercise, but also a passive body that was contained, controlled, and disciplined by the pink corset." Hey presto, fifteen years
before the "new burlesque" of Dita von Teese, Madonna colonized
the concept of ultra-femininity and control. Ironically, von Teese
came from the same small town as Madonna (Rochester, Michigan),
and took her name from Dita Parlo, the same German silent-movie
star that Madonna later adopted as her alter ego.

The Blond Ambition look wasn't one of relaxation. According to
her U.K. trainer Jamie Addicoat, in order to achieve this improbable
body, her fitness routines had become almost manic. "Madonna was
in danger of burning out completely," he said. "She was doing five
hours physical workout every day (two hours running, one hour in the
gym, and two hours on stage)—more than most professional athletes.
It built up to the point where her percentage of body fat had dropped
way below what is healthy for a woman."

For Madonna, this was a small price to pay for a spectacle that
she controlled from start to finish. Blond Ambition was entirely her
concept. "Several months prior to the tour she showed me a legal pad
filled with notes and sketches of her own. She had conceptualized the
whole thing," recalls her lighting director Peter Morse. "The show
was a living representation of what was on that legal pad." He admitted it was a challenge, because "the scenes were incredibly removed
from each other. You'd go from an old city factory look to a beautiful

grand staircase to real pillars coming out of the ground looking like a cathedral. Nothing got used twice. It was a challenge getting a lighting system that would cover everything."

Such extravaganzas are now commonplace, but in 1990, nothing like this had ever been attempted before for a pop concert. "This was a big change for the general concertgoer. She created a direction and path for herself that hadn't been done before," says Morse. Madonna's journey from darkness to light opened at the Makuhari Stadium in Japan that April. From the outset, people were agog.

The show divided into four main segments, with Madonna moving through a series of characters—from sex siren to sinner to show-girl and dance diva. For the opening number, "Express Yourself," there was a *Metropolis*-style set that echoed the video with its industrial pumps, machine-like cogs, explosions, steam, and male dancers half-naked in chains. "'Express Yourself' was insane," recalls dancer Carlton Wilborn. "It was wild. I'd never had that experience before, the blast from the crowd. You couldn't hear the downbeats it was so loud, so you had to count inside your head and hope you'd got it right. You could feel the energy coming out from everyone around you." In this scene, Madonna is the androgynous dominatrix in satin corset and baggy trousers, doing an update of Liza Minelli's turn in *Cabaret* with the chair. She's also the leader of a girl gang, clowning around and sending up macho posturing with her homegirls Donna DeLory and Niki Haris.

The logical conclusion of this female bravado is a restyling of her song "Like a Virgin." Two male dancers in protruding conical bras dance a eunuch-like amalgam of classical Indian dance and vogueing while she rubs herself into a masturbatory frenzy on a crimson couch. It is beautifully bawdy. Gone is the white wedding dress and coy sexual references. Here is a woman in her early thirties celebrating the art of self-satisfaction and female desire. "I was very inspired by her," recalls Peter Morse. "For that number, it got frenetic near the end. She was simulating a climax, so I decided to help her along a bit (not that she needed any!). The scene could've been lit by one light, but I had fun with it and did strobe lighting. In rehearsals she gets a dancer to stand in for her while she looks and makes notes. You never get applauded by her. She'd say, 'OK, let's move on,' and that was her seal of approval. But when we rehearsed this song and I did the lights, she laughed and smiled at me. With her, you can try anything."

After her risqué version of "Like a Virgin," the lights dramatically go down, and we see Madonna in the spotlight as the penitent sinner, her head covered in a black veil, kneeling in a church nave while incense wafts around her. She sings for redemption and salvation, praying to a black-frocked priest (Carlton Wilborn) in a sober song cycle that moves from "Like a Prayer" through to "Live to Tell," "Oh Father," and "Papa Don't Preach." Wilborn recalls this section required "a lot of private rehearsal time." Its message was delicately balanced. "It's about her trying to find her way with religion. A side [of her] knew she needed it, another side was resistant, and our dance represented that battle inside," he says. "At the end, I push her head down and snatch it back up again—as the priest, I was trying to wake her up to the importance of it. I feel her open up to it and then decide to go her own way."

This dance is a battle of wills—he offers her strength, and she resists his dogma. He tries to enfold her, she walks away, looking back. From the black Puritan-style coats to the strongly grounded gestures, this section of the show has all the spareness and symbolism of her modern dance idol Martha Graham. The latter often explored mythical or religious themes, like *El Penitente* (1940), where she played a peasant madonna, a tempting Magdalene, and a saintly Veronica. With the same transformational energy as Graham, Madonna dances amid the dourly dressed men like a blond-haired sprite. She is the trickster figure, the sin-eater. In this confrontation with religious patriarchy, Madonna makes clear that there is a cost to her display of female sexuality.

The daring stage set heightened the drama in this scene. "For the church nave, Madonna insisted that the Greek pillars be real. There was a 3-D effect to it, not just flat sets," recalls Morse. "She had forty-foot aluminum castings rise up hydraulically from the floor. Nothing was phony or fake; it had real depth."

The sex and religion scenes were so powerful that on the North American leg, Toronto police threatened to arrest Madonna on the grounds of obscenity if she went ahead with the show. In response, she hammed up the masturbation sequence even more. After all the brouhaha, the Canadian Mounties maintained a polite distance and the show passed without a hitch. There was also opposition in Italy, when Catholic pressure groups urged a boycott of the concerts. They were very effective, as Italy was the only country where the Blond Ambition didn't sell out. According to musician Guy Pratt, she and Pat Leonard came up with the ruse to hold a press conference at the Leonardo da Vinci Airport in Rome in order to boost ticket sales.

With a sideswipe at the Vatican, she told the assembled press that she was proud of being an Italian-American and proud of having grown up in a country "that believes in freedom of speech and artistic expression." She said that her show was a piece of theater that takes the audience on "an emotional journey . . . I do not endorse a way of life but describe one, and the audience is left to make its own judgments." Despite the ensuing storm of publicity, the second date at the capital's Stadio Flaminio was canceled, the only tour fixture that didn't sell out.

Along with her yen for artistic expression, Madonna has always had an eye on the bottom line. The third segment of her show shamelessly promoted the film *Dick Tracy*, which opened as the tour progressed through Europe. Although the movie was a box office success, the *Dick Tracy* section is the least dynamic part of the show. Playing a nightclub singer in a striped vaudeville-style corset, Madonna lies across a grand piano, lip-synching the Warren Beatty duet with Salim dressed as Dick Tracy. For Slam, though, this was his most memorable experience of the tour: "I just left Belgium two years before, I went to a strict ballet school, and they all made fun of me going to America to pursue my dream, and now I'm here onstage, she's introduced me to twenty thousand people, and I'm lip-synching to Warren Beatty's voice. It was amazing."

Dick Tracy segues into a comedy sequence, where Madonna sings "Material Girl" as a suburban housewife wearing an embroidered dressing-gown and her hair in curlers, and performs "Cherish" to men in campy mermaid tails. Wilborn was less enamored with the kitsch element of the tour. "I've never been that drawn to that gay campness. Guys as mermaids, guys with cone tits," he says. "I am gay, but I'm not into camp. Madonna could sense that wasn't a comfortable place for me."

For the final segment, she was back on safer ground as party-girl Madonna, striking a pose for "Vogue," and ending "Holiday" in a Harlequin outfit. The final song, "Family Affair," has the cast in outfits reminiscent of *Clockwork Orange*. Resurrecting the *Cabaret*-style chair and bowler hat, Madonna intones the words "People together" with arms outstretched. This is the message that underlies the show; one that celebrates "love, life, and humanity."

THIS FOUR-month world tour broke records. Although Pepsi withdrew their $3 million sponsorship deal as a result of the "Like a Prayer" video, electronics company Pioneer were happy to take over as sponsors. Madonna was being paid $28 million for the Japanese shows alone. Eighteen trucks and a 747 plane transported the tour equipment, while the stage took a crew of a hundred to assemble before each show. It was a massive undertaking, and the tension of this became apparent in the documentary of the tour, *Truth or Dare*.

The backstage scenes are filmed by Alex Keshishian, then a twenty-six-year-old Harvard graduate who had made a few humble rock videos. He was brought to Madonna's attention by the Creative Artists Agency (CAA). She liked his graduate film, a popera based on *Wuthering Heights* with music from Kate Bush and Madonna. So, when her original director, David Fincher, pulled out shortly before the tour started, Madonna decided on Keshishian as a replacement.

His words—"I'll film you without makeup, I'll film you when you're being a complete bitch, I'll film you in the morning before your sleeping pill's worn off"—could have been a poster quote for the film. Part of *Truth or Dare*'s attraction is the implied struggle between star and director for authenticity. Although she was executive producer, she was canny enough to trust Keshishian's vision. "I would constantly disobey Madonna, to show her she wasn't directing me," Keshishian claimed. "I was completely prepared to be fired. That's when you do your best work—when you're not scared of being fired. I wasn't so blinded by the idea of working with Madonna that I'd do anything she asked." At first she resisted. "She was very demanding at the beginning. At one point my cameraman didn't know who to listen to. She'd shout, 'Cut.' I'd shout, 'Keep rolling.' Cut, roll. It would have been easier to recoil and give in. But I fought back and won. And when she gave me her trust, it was all-encompassing."

Keshishian shot backstage in black-and-white, cinema verité–style. It had a gritty, grainy feel reminiscent of D. A. Pennebaker's *Don't Look Back*, the documentary of Bob Dylan's 1965 tour of England. Keshishian's black-and-white scenes were at odds with the prevailing fashion for high-end-production concert films, and indeed, numbers from the show were shot in slick color by a different camera crew. The stark contrast between public and private was pivotal to the movie, and a source of critical debate. "I'm revealing what I wanna reveal," Madonna later declared. "While you *can* argue that I chose to show what I wanna show, I can also say that *what* I chose to show is very revealing."

What feels staged is Madonna's regal cartoon persona. The prayers before performance, the mawkish poetry delivered to her staff, and the way she casts herself as den mother constantly administering to the "emotional cripples" in her charge. Or the way she bawls out her hired hands. Tour production manager Chris Lamb said he practiced a disappearing act whenever the camera was around. "I always just kind of went the other way. I really didn't want to be onscreen being shouted at, so I made myself difficult to find. Y'know, when she has something to say, she doesn't mince words. Sometimes you get it between the eyes."

Actress and writer Carrie Fisher found this quality strangely appealing. "She often seems to behave like someone who has been under severe restraint and can now say and do whatever she likes without fear of reprisal." While Madonna revels in being a bitch, her ribald humor also comes across. "Why was I faced with three rows of assholes—all industry—up front?" she shouts to manager Freddy De-Mann after one of the U.S. shows. "Everyone looked like goddamn William Morris agents!" After Kevin Costner comes backstage to greet her and calls her show "neat," she pretends to vomit. "I've always thought it weird that celebrities assume a friendship with you because you're a celebrity too," she says. "It can get a little awkward."

Madonna's high-handed manner makes those more personal moments with her dancers feel like scripted intimacy. It draws attention to the central conundrum of the film: who is the real Madonna, and does it matter anyway? What is depicted on-screen is neither the two-dimensional tabloid picture of a female ball-breaker, nor an arch manipulator of Baudrillardian postmodern signs. Much cultural criticism focuses on Madonna as a symbol or a stereotype and misses the human being within.

The overriding sense in this film is of a woman under stress. The whole show rests on her shoulders. Madonna is the central, organizing point, the one keeping it rigorous, precise, and to the standard she desires. She conducts her business all day, in the rarefied air of those claustrophobic dressing rooms and hotel suites, never able to relax. "I'm so desperate for fun!" she exclaims to her friend Sandra Bernhard.

Madonna reveals moments of vulnerability almost despite herself. There is her deteriorating relationship with Warren Beatty. "Come here you pussy man!" she barks, but the insecurity shows on her face. Clearly disenchanted with the filming process, he berates her for living in an "insane atmosphere," and says the immortal phrase: "Madonna doesn't want to live off camera, let alone talk." At another point, she waits for him to call, but he doesn't, and she tries to mask her disappointment with a smile. "He wasn't around too much. He would just sit in the corner and say things with his dry wit," says Salim. By this time, Beatty was growing tired of his younger lover. He didn't appreciate her crude, roadie-like humor and the way she bossed him around. The constant, intrusive camera was, for him, a step too far.

Despite her bravado, it is evident that Madonna sometimes feels scared and exposed. When the Canadian Mounties in Toronto threaten to arrest her for obscenity, she brazens it out. But as she walks through the tunnel to the stadium, she needs the support of her girlfriends, clutching hold of Niki's hand as if unable to let go. And there's the phone conversation she has with her father, part exasperation, part little girl. "The show gets a bit racy sometimes," she says. "Can you tone it down a little bit?" he asks nervously. "No, that'd be compromising my artistic integrity," she trots out. After the show, however, she admits: "My father: I worship the ground he walks on. It was harder to do that [Detroit] show than the police in Toronto."

The darkest, most moving part of the film is when she comes to Detroit. It was "the hardest place we went to on tour," she says. "Going home is never easy for me." Here we see her relationship with her alcoholic older brother Martin. She eats a meal backstage, waiting for him. He is delayed, and she assumes he's not coming. When he finally arrives, all washed and brushed up, she's gone to bed. We see her awkwardness with an old friend, Moira McFarland. "She used to finger-fuck me," Madonna says inelegantly. And then: "Where's my idol?" as she comes out of the hotel room.

Her excitement turns to embarrassment when they meet and Moira, who has fallen on hard times, asks Madonna to be the godmother to her unborn child. "What was really weird was that here was this girl that I idolized from my childhood. I really thought she was the cat's pajamas, you know? Then it was like, Look what's happened to our lives," Madonna said later. ". . . I was touched she asked me to be the godmother but I don't have time to fly to North Carolina and participate in this whole ritual. Can you imagine me with all her family and neighbors? It would have been . . . like a creature landing from Mars." After the meeting, Moira calls Madonna a "little shit," but in the next moment forgives her when she remembers Madonna Sr. "I remember praying to her mother, Madonna, because it was the closest thing to God," she says, breaking down in tears. "When her mother died it was really sad."

Madonna's visit to her mother's gravesite has been criticized as overblown and staged. But, as she said later, she hadn't been there for years, and on that hot summer afternoon it took her and her brother Christopher nearly an hour to find it. No wonder she lies down with her head on the grave, searching for an emotional connection and sense of comfort. Christopher, though, felt uneasy. "[That] drove me crazy," he said later. "They filmed Madonna lying on our mother's grave, and then they were like, 'OK Chris, now it's your turn at the grave,' and I'm like, 'Fuck you, it's not for you.' That's why you don't see very much of me in that movie. I prefer the privacy that I have."

This part of the tour is not easy. As it rolls on to New York, tempers fray within the dance troupe, and Madonna has to reprimand her gay boys for picking on Oliver, the only straight dancer in their entourage. "You three together can be pretty ferocious," she says with unguarded directness. "He doesn't have the thick skin you have, the survival techniques you have." Salim recalls the teasing as a playful way of passing the time. "We made fun of Oliver because he wasn't ballet-trained, he was the only dancer who wasn't gay. You know how when you're a gay man and a straight man thinks you want him, and it's like, 'No!' He couldn't believe that Luis and Jose wore skirts, he was so amazed by it, so we had to make fun of him."

Salim admits that much of this was due to partying that got out of hand. "I was twenty years old, I was coming out, growing up, and dealing with all kinds of things. I wish I understood then what I understand now, because I would have enjoyed it so much more. We partied too much, in every city, it was just too much." Wilborn remembers "a lot of bitching among the dancers. Jose and Luis came in with the expectation that they had a certain position they wanted to hold on to. For me it was comical to watch. The other boys were a lot younger. I'd had success in my career already, and didn't get caught up in the whirl of it. Some of the boys had issues; they let the frenzy of it override their thinking."

For Madonna, after all "the tension and darkness" of the States, coming to Europe feels like "such a relief." Here we see Madonna joshing with her dancers, ordering one of them to "get your dick out" for fun, and looking on appreciatively while Salim and Gabriel kiss. That kiss was to become legendary. "We did the kiss, forgot about it, and then it ended up in the film. I was like, 'Oh my God!'" Salim said to me. "I was in a relationship; so was Gabriel. And his parents didn't know he was gay. This is where me and Madonna get a little weird, because he was really petrified. I remember him asking her not to put it in there. It was a little nerve-wracking. I didn't realize it would have such a big effect on people. What people are scared of is that guys might have had a little homo moment, you know, a little homo feeling, and that's the worst thing in America."

He also sympathized with Sharon, the makeup artist who was raped after her drink was spiked at a nightclub. What is astonishing is Madonna's knee-jerk laughter on hearing the news. When the reality of the story sinks in, Madonna stops cackling and looks concerned, but this cannot erase her moment of thoughtlessness. "They spiked her drink. To me that was really sad," says Salim. "I didn't get why everyone was laughing, maybe it's an American thing. But there's a lot of things I don't get about this country." Niki Haris, though, also was unsure about this scene. "Sometimes there was a mean-spirited energy, a nastiness. That's funny, Ha, ha, ha!" What the scene really showed was Madonna's discomfort with people who are victims. Maybe the incident brought up her own experience of rape in New York when she had been young, alone, and utterly helpless. Being in control was so important to her during this tour that she found it hard to deal with weakness and insecurity in others.

This is evident in the film's conclusion, as Madonna plays to the gallery, inviting each dancer into her bed for "intimate" chats in a way that feels like power play. The film is fascinating in how much it reveals about the stultified world of celebrity, how the pop business nurtures its own aristocracy, and has an almost feudal attitude to human relations. Although Madonna is looking for people to be "real" with her, most in her employ feel the pressure to indulge her or laugh too long at labored jokes (like the fellatio bottle). As even Jean-Paul Gaultier admitted: "I didn't stand up to her. She knows her own body so well, she knows what to wear to show it off best. The only person I know who wasn't scared of her was Sean; he wouldn't take any shit." Ironically, Madonna came closest here to a poignant picture of those haunted, self-obsessed Hollywood icons—Crawford, Monroe, Hayworth—that she had always so admired.

Black cultural critic bell hooks was unimpressed by the film, saying: "In *Truth or Dare* Madonna clearly revealed that she can only think of exerting power along very traditional, white supremacist, capitalistic, patriarchal lines." Critical of what she saw as a white woman star appropriating black radical chic, she quoted many grown black women grumbling about Madonna, "The bitch can't even sing."

According to hooks: "So why did so many people find it cute when Madonna asserted that she dominates the inter-racial casts . . . in her film because they are crippled and she 'likes to play mother.' No this was not a display of feminist power, this was the same old phallic nonsense with white pussy at the center."

hooks poses the question: "Plantation mistress or soul sister?" As a black female singer, Niki is aware of the argument, but says: "Not a plantation owner, not in my mind. More like an empress. Not a queen, more like a dictator."

WHEN THE film was edited and ready, Madonna knew she had a big hit on her hands. She exploited it by invading the 1991 Cannes Film Festival with all the efficiency of a German battleship. The night of its premiere, she sashayed up the red-carpeted stairs of the Festival Hall in a rose silk kimono. Turning around to the world's paparazzi, she dropped the kimono to show the silver Gaultier brassiere and matching pantie girdle she was wearing underneath. The crowd gasped. Mission accomplished.

From that moment, Madonna made her presence felt in Cannes. She stayed in a $2,500-a-night suite at the Hotel du Cap, and ordered her minders to throw everyone out of the pool when she went for a swim. She turned up at Spike Lee's *Jungle Fever* party, wearing big boots and a macho Gaultier Austrian Army–style jacket. She extended her stay so it would overlap with the appearance of Sean Penn, his girlfriend Robin Wright, and their new baby. Amid the melee, actors like Arnold Schwarzenegger, Mike Tyson's ex-wife Robin Givens, and Malcolm McDowell were ignored. "We wish she'd go home," said one of McDowell's friends. "She's a real pain. It's difficult to do business when they're being distracted by what's going on in her bathroom."

Madonna's concerted bid to make her movie the talk of the season had the desired effect. After its release that May, it quickly became a huge success. "A clever, brazen, spirited self-portrait," enthused the *New York Times*, while *Time* magazine praised it as "raw, raunchy and epically entertaining." The film went on to become the fifth highest-grossing documentary of all time.

But there was dissension in the ranks. The following January, three dancers on the tour—Gabriel Trupin, Kevin Stea, and Oliver Crumes—filed a lawsuit against Madonna, saying that their privacy had been invaded by the offstage footage, and that they weren't paid for their appearance in the film. According to dancer Salim: "They sued because the movie was shown all over the world and it made money and it was like, 'Why do we not get money?' It was like a slap in the face." Two years later, Madonna made a very modest out-of-court settlement. "I still feel a little resentment, because it's playing all the time and we needed it so much when the show was over," says Salim.

AFTER THE tour was finished, some of the dancers went through a dark time. Gabriel Trupin died of AIDS—"he had HIV, even on tour, but he just didn't know, you know?" says Salim. Most found it difficult to adjust once the artificial high of the tour was over and they had to go back to "normal" lives. "We used to make a good living as dancers doing videos, but then record companies didn't want to spend more money on dancers, so we would do the same for fifty dollars. We used to call them the fifty-dollar dances." After feeling lost for a few years, Salim found his way back via his roots in contemporary ballet. He now runs his own dance company in New York, and has made peace with the complexities of Blond Ambition. "It's OK," he smiles, "I forgive her, I don't hold grudges anymore."

MADONNA, TOO, crashed. "I thought I was gonna have a nervous breakdown. I couldn't take the crowds. I couldn't do the shows. It was too hot," she said. Comparing the end of the tour with somebody dying, she added: "I make my peace with it and when it happens I don't feel anything. . . . But I know I'm gonna feel something later. And it's really going to hurt."

She plowed on with her personal game of Truth or Dare. She had started it, so she may as well see it through. The next big venture, the next layer to come off, was with her book *Sex*.

FALLEN
ANGEL

IN 1991, MADONNA'S INFLUENCE REACHED A PEAK WITH a new music business venture. "It started as a desire to have more control, and became a kind of artistic think tank," she said of Maverick, the multimedia company she formed with TimeWarner, with a $60 million advance. "I want a real record label with real artists," she said. "I don't want to be Prince and have everybody be a clone of me. That's not having a label, that's having a harem." She then renegotiated her recording contract with a $5 million advance for each of her next seven albums, along with a 20 percent royalty rate. Rivaling Michael Jackson as the ultimate corporate artist, Madonna generated sales for Warner of over $1.2 billion in the first decade of her career, shifting 70 million albums. For some people, she had become too powerful, and they were just waiting to see her fall.

That winter, Madonna conceived the book that was to be her nemesis. Aiming for high-art erotica, she teamed up with longtime collaborator Steven Meisel and art director Fabien Baron. A graduate of the Parsons School of Design in New York, Meisel was a provocative photo-essayist who enjoyed lacing his fashion photography with a worrying undertow, from hyperreal high-society women to heroin chic. (His 1995 campaign for Calvin Klein jeans would be canceled amid accusations that it resembled child pornography.) In 1991, the combination of Madonna and a book of erotica gave Meisel an ideal opportunity to make mischief. He must have felt like a kid in a candy store.

The art director for the book was Fabien Baron, a French art student who moved to New York in 1982 and who, after a stint at Italian *Vogue*, guided the 1990 relaunch of Warhol's *Interview* magazine. He combined a taste for formal perfection with playful humor and anarchic typography. The *Sex* book had a range of influences—from punk to earlier fashion iconoclasts like Guy Bourdin (in its precise, choreographed surrealism) and Helmut Newton (in its stylized and sadomasochistic look). Along with writer Glenn O'Brien, a key observer of the New York pop scene and veteran of *Interview* magazine, this was the *Sex* dream team. It oozed style. According to London art critic Sarah Kent, the timing of *Sex* was impeccable. "'The Body' is in vogue: it's Today's Topic," she wrote, referring to artist Andres Serrano's "elegant come shots," and *The Jeff Koons Handbook*, which featured fairy-tale pictures of the artist having sex with his Italian porn queen wife, La Cicciolina.

Madonna presided over the production of her book, casting herself as dominatrix and sex evangelist Dita Parlo. "This is essentially something that comes from my mind. My mind is, you know, a catalyst for the whole thing," she said. "These are erotic short stories and erotic imaginings, visual and literary, and I've cast myself in the role in terms of pictorials." Her mission, she claimed, was to empower women and stimulate debate. "Sexual *repression* is responsible for a lot of bad behavior," she declared, taking the view that sex is a taboo subject because the Western world has a long tradition of silence on the matter. Social scientist Michel Foucault begs to differ, however. In his groundbreaking 1970s work *The History of Sexuality*, he argued that far from being ignored, sexual behavior in the West is constantly monitored and preached about. It's part of a society that "speaks verbosely of its own silence." Madonna is a case in point.

Her garrulous defense of taboo sex fits into a strong liberal tradition, one that particularly thrives in contrast to a coy mainstream

U.S. culture founded on Puritan fundamentalism. She is the equal and opposite of those religious forces—hence the note of missionary zeal in everything she does. "In all my work, my thing has always been not to be ashamed—of who you are, your body, your physicality, your desires, your sexual fantasies. The reason there is bigotry, and sexism and racism and homophobia . . . is fear. People are afraid of their own feelings, afraid of the unknown . . . and I am saying: don't be afraid," she argued.

Madonna also wanted to explore the notion of power in sex. "She was talking about gentle and hard, soft and violent. She was playing out all those elements in the book," says Charles Melcher, copublisher, with Nicholas Calloway, of the *Sex* book. "That was reflected in the materials: uncoated, soft paper on the inside and a hard metal binding on the outside." It was as if Madonna wanted to display her sexual knowledge as well as her body. As Foucault wrote: "Sexuality is tied to recent devices of power. . . . It has been linked from the outset with an intensification of the body—with its exploitation as an object of knowledge and an element in relations of power."

SOLD LIKE a piece of art in limited edition, with each copy numbered, the book was boldly presented, encased in a zipped Mylar bag and ring-bound with metal covers. The matte paper has the feel of newsprint or fanzine. As this was the first project for Madonna's new Maverick company, the packaging was crucial. The process hadn't been going too well at Warner Books, which was a mass-market publisher, and there was a "communication breakdown." At Fabien Baron's suggestion, the packaging job was transferred to Nicholas Calloway's bespoke Calloway Editions. "We did exquisite art books, $100 high-end, beautiful things. It was felt we might be a better creative fit," Melcher told me. "It was a challenge for us to figure out what the form would be. Madonna wanted the book to be sealed, something you had to violate in order to get into it and enjoy." They considered various kinds of clasps before hitting on the idea of the sealed bag "as a reference to a condom package."

The metal cover was Madonna's idea. "We were talking about materials for the cover, and we went into her kitchen. She pointed at the metal plate at the back of her stove and said, 'I want something like this.' I was very impressed with the way she interacted with her world to source things," says Melcher. Maybe she remembered that immortal postpunk band PIL and their 1979 album *Metal Box*, which was originally packaged in a metal canister. Making a metal book, though, was a nightmare. "We bought a million and a half pounds of aluminum, a pound for every book. We had to do front and back covers, and each one had to be rolled, stamped, and ionized. I don't recommend metal for books. It was a hugely difficult process," says Melcher.

Once the reader breaks their way into the book, Madonna appears in a variety of poses, exploring some charged sexual themes. First, we plunge directly into a dyke pantomime. Madonna sits bound in a chair flanked by two topless butch lesbians with tattoos and piercings. One holds a switchblade to her throat while the other sucks her nipple. In another picture, Madonna stands astride a bidet in a leather fetish bikini, PVC thigh-high boots, and a perfectly made-up face. Making a reference to cunnilingus, she clutches the head of a cropped-haired lesbian who's taking a drink from the water trickle beneath. What's notable about these pictures is that the butch lesbians are dressed in battered jeans and no makeup, while Madonna wears expensive designer clothes. Already there is an obvious power relation at work, with Madonna carefully controlling her image.

The lesbian theme reemerges later in the book, but it is more the "lipstick" variety—i.e., glamorous, celebrity-driven, beautiful. But within these pages, Madonna shows a vulnerable side of herself that's rarely seen in public. There she is, kissing her girlfriend Ingrid Casares, looking deeply into her eyes. It has the air of that old pioneer lesbian romance *Patience and Sarah*. Madonna has a softer look, as if she's saying: "This is really who I am." Ingrid is her haven, her caretaker. In another iconic shot, she is encased in the arms of Isabella Rossellini. With her mature, luminous beauty, Rossellini could easily be a replacement for the mother Madonna lost.

There has been much speculation about Madonna's sexual prefer-ences, but what emanates from her work is an uncomplicated, sensuous bisexuality. "She appreciates beautiful people, whatever their sex," says one friend. "She slept with girls and boys, and no one had a problem with that. Everyone was doing it," says another friend from her New York clubbing days. "All of my sexual experiences when I was young were with girls. . . . I think that's really normal: same-sex experimentation," Madonna declared in an interview with the *Advocate*. Then she went on to say: "I am aroused by the idea of a woman making love to me while either a man or another woman watches." All her strong female role models, from Marlene Dietrich and Mae West to Martha Graham and Frida Kahlo were actively bisexual. The written passages in *Sex* show an intimate, almost celebratory awareness of lesbian sex. "When she comes she cries out like the seagulls circling above us. Her body shudders again and again and I drink in every drop of her sweet nectar," writes Madonna/Dita in one sun-kissed scenario. After an interval of imaginative lovemaking, even the circling seagulls have become voyeurs. In another excerpt, Madonna refers to her female lover's ass as "pretty fucking righteous!" *The English Roses* this is not.

The lesbian character was one that had been a few years in the making. We first saw her unveiled in the video for "Justify My Love," kissing model Amanda Cazalet. "Because it was so unpremeditated, it was real. You can't act something like that," Cazalet said. "And yes, I'd say she's a good kisser." Then she was wearing a butch suit and grabbing a flapper girl's behind in Steven Meisel's mock Brassaï pictures. This was an adjunct to the very public parade of her friendship with comedienne Sandra Bernhard, going out on the town with her to New York lesbian clubs like the Cubby Hole, and appearing on the *Late Show with David Letterman* with her, both dressed in identical butch outfits. When quizzed about whether this affair was real, Madonna enjoyed keeping people guessing. "I'm not going to tell you yes or no. It's irrelevant . . ." she said at the time. "It doesn't make a goddamn bit of difference who I'm sleeping with—a man or a woman."

Many lesbians felt that it did matter. "Some said that she was ripping us off with her pseudo-lesbian antics," suggests Louise Carolin from *Diva*, the British lesbian lifestyle magazine. Writer/photographer Della Grace saw "interconnections" between *Sex* and her book *Love Bites*, a collection of documentary-style pictures of "lesbian camp and lesbian cock . . . an outlaw group of S&M exhibitionism" that was published the year that Madonna began work on *Sex*. Criticizing her for being a "sexual tourist," Grace claimed that Madonna was "the pure playing with the perverse . . . a voyeur . . . not dangerous, not real." Academic Jackie Goldsby called her a "cultural robber baron," while another writer, Russell Baker, said: "Madonna isn't the cultural elite . . . She's just Mae West for yuppies."

For Carolin, however, there were reasons to celebrate. "Madonna became meaningful in the early 90s with that lesbian chic thing," she says. "At that point lesbian culture was really changing. We were coming out of the 80s, which had been a vehemently political and anticommercial time. We looked at the fun gay boys were having and thought, We'd like some of that. Lesbians started to be seen as glamorous and playful. Madonna caught that wave very effectively. There was a hunger to see ourselves reflected in popular culture, and she made us visible."

Madonna did this in a way that chimed with the "coming out" of some high-profile women in entertainment, like alt-country star k. d. lang, rock singer Melissa Etheridge, and actress Ellen DeGeneres. When lang came out in an interview with the *Advocate*, Torie Osborne, executive director of the National Gay and Lesbian Task Force, said: "[She's] the first major woman pop star who's out and proud and fine about it. It signals a whole new era of possibility for celebrities." So-called lipstick lesbianism reached a peak when lang appeared on the cover of *Vanity Fair* "butched up," being shaved by supermodel Cindy Crawford. Before this point, to be an openly gay woman in pop was tantamount to commercial suicide. In the early 90s, a few women were testing the boundaries, including Madonna. "There she was, smooching girls in her 'Justify My Love' video. It was bold and transgressive," recalls Carolin. "Madonna did an *Advocate* interview where she talked a lot about her long love affair with gay male culture. It was inevitable that at some point she'd look across at the girls."

In that interview, Madonna upped the ante regarding the Sandra Bernhard question. Sick of preconceived notions about gay women being mannish and ugly, she said: "If I could be some sort of a detonator to that bomb, then I was willing to do that . . . If it makes people feel better to think that I slept with her, they can think it. I'd almost rather they thought that I did, just so they could know here was this girl that everyone was buying records of, and she was eating someone's pussy."

During this period, Madonna was linked with a number of women. It was rumored that she and Sandra Bernhard fell out because Madonna transferred her affections to Bernhard's girlfriend Ingrid Casares, the chic club owner from Miami. A furious Bernhard said: "I look at my friendship with her as like having a gallstone. You deal with it, there is pain, and then you pass it." Though she vowed never to speak again to "Schmadonna," some years later the two reconciled. They had too much in common, and the celebrity world is a small one. Ingrid, meanwhile, the self-confessed "spoiled rich kid" of Cuban exiles moaned that "I could discover the cure for cancer, and I'd still only be known as Madonna's best friend." Madonna also spent a while chasing the "Justify My Love" model Amanda Cazalet. "There was a lot of communication the following year (after the video) and I know if I'd been open to taking what was on offer, something would've happened," Cazalet said.

And one of Madonna's favorite lesbian friends was Japanese-American runway model Jenny Shimizu. "I believe she's a credit to gay culture," Shimizu told *Diva* magazine. "[Madonna] truly is what she represents: an open-minded individual who explores different lifestyles to educate herself about who she is. I can't imagine a better friend to our community than Madonna." Like Bernhard, Shimizu was a high-profile lesbian with an alternative glamour. She was first seen in her trademark tank top, jeans, and tattoos, modeling for Calvin Klein. Since then, her gamine, androgynous image has been muse to a succession of designers from Versace to Gaultier. "I think I'm attracted to powerful, aggressive, confident, sexual women. A lot of the women I've dated share those qualities," said the Harley-

driving model in 2006. One of her former lovers was movie star Angelina Jolie, and she has said that whenever Jolie called, she'd drop
everything and join her "wherever she was in the world." Madonna,
too, became an important friend.

"I met Madonna when I was in her 'Rain' video around 1994–95,
right about the time I started modeling for Calvin Klein, and we
ended up hanging out in L.A., Paris, and New York. I ended up feeling like I was this lesbian hustler getting on planes meeting women,"
said Shimizu. "One of my tattoos says HAULING ASS I; it's not
a reference to hauling my own ass around, but in reference to
my motorcycling—driving superfast. Madonna showed me a lot of
things—took me to the theater and museums, and it was nice to hang
out with her. She's a lovely lady; a totally smart, confident woman.".

In the early 90s, Madonna's woman-centered side was at its strongest. Many saw that as a positive rather than fake. "The lesbian subcultural references . . . borrowed by Her Madge to enhance her vision
of freewheeling female sexuality aren't our possessions," argues *Diva*'s
Louise Carolin, "they're our legacy, our contribution to the show."

Lesbianism wasn't the only taboo tackled by Madonna in her *Sex*
book. Another prominent theme was that of sadomasochism. As well
as being tied up by L.A. dykes, she plays with whips, ropes, and candles in a New York dungeon called The Vault. Dressed in a Nazi-
style black cap and boots, she whips a large lady in a PVC dress. In
other pictures, a menacing-looking biker nestles between her legs
and drinks a dubious liquid from her high-heeled shoe. Making the
connection between S&M and the self-punishment of religion, she
lies horizontal, with bound hands and feet, under a tall, bare cross.
This was echoed later, in a more modest form, on her 2006 Confessions tour, where she is tied to a giant mirrored disco cross. In *Sex*,
Madonna looks like a sacrificial victim, alongside a man lying prone
with candles on the back of each hand, placed like the nails of Christ
on the cross. Redolent of a theatrical self-abasement, this shows one
more aspect of Madonna's journey with the crucifix.

"There is something comforting about being tied up," she writes.
"Like when you were a baby and your mother strapped you in the

car seat. She wanted you to be safe. It was an act of love." In this
scenario, she shows how she has internalized her Catholic mother's
self-inflicted punishments. The crucifix wasn't just about pain and
martyrdom, however. It was Madonna's talisman, because it symbolized both spirituality and sex. According to the Spanish art historian
J. E. Cirlot: "Placed in the mystic Center of the cosmos, [the cross]
becomes the bridge or ladder by means of which the soul may reach
God . . . The cross, consequently, affirms the primary relationship
between the two worlds of the celestial and the earthly . . . it stands
for the conjunction of opposites . . . Hence its significance as a symbol
for agony, struggle and martyrdom."

Madonna's staged scenarios, however, are static and ritualistic.
"The definition of S&M is letting someone hurt you that you know
would never hurt you," she said at the time. This included the rape
scene in a high school gym, where she is pointedly laughing. When
asked by journalist Andrew Neil if her pictures might unleash "a kind
of evil, a dark side," she says: "I'm dealing with sexual liberation of
the mind. . . . This book is based on fantasies in an ideal world—a
world without abusive people, a world without AIDS. . . . It's a dream
world." Her viewpoint is at times vacuous and naive. "Generally I
don't think pornography degrades women. The women who are doing
it want to do it," she writes. And then later: "I think for the most part
if women are in an abusive relationship and they know it and stay in
it they must be digging it."

There is a dark side here, shot in basements and vaults, in the sub-
terranean gloom of an underground America. This contrasts with
the body-beautiful S&M—perfectly lit Helmut Newton–style shots
of Madonna biting the nipple ring of a statuesque black man, or a
shaven-headed man licking her foot encased in an impossible shoe,
like a deformed leather hoof.

Madonna moves through every taboo drama: young boys, old
men, gay men kissing at the Gaiety. There's a celebrity sex sandwich
with rapper Big Daddy Kane and supermodel Naomi Campbell, plus
shots with Madonna's then-boyfriend, the rapper Vanilla Ice. The
latter complained afterward that he had no idea the pictures taken

with her would end up in the *Sex* book. "I didn't want to be part of her slutty package. At all," he said later. The two began dating after she came to a concert of his in the early 90s. "It was fun. We were comfortable with each other . . . she was a sweetheart. Then the monkey wrench with the book came and flipped the whole deal." After the book came out, he refused to speak to Madonna. The more he slammed the phone down on her, the more she called. "That turned her on," he said in disbelief. "I'm not trying to turn you on, I'm just trying to turn you *off!*" Madonna didn't like to be refused, seeing rejection as a challenge.

Her extreme behavior, though, seemed to invite rejection. And with that in mind, she indulged in one of the most taboo—for women—subjects of all. Placed judiciously and gloriously throughout the book are images of masturbation. There's Madonna, astride a mirror on the floor, hand down her panties, gazing at her reflection; or lounging on a fleecy sofa in unzipped jeans, blowing smoke rings. And there she is, pulling down a pair of cutoff jeans and touching her bare backside. These pictures are taken in plain, dirty rooms that are empty apart from old carpet and a few props. They are the most erotic in the book, as Madonna captures the private, fevered world of female desire. It isn't stylized porn, manufactured for a male gaze with a come-hither expression. Instead, she has turned away from the camera, lost in her own pleasure.

Somewhere, though, something slips, and she is no longer a Brigitte Bardot goddess cavorting in the sand, displaying the joys of sexual freedom. By the end of the book, a tone of alienation creeps in. The photographs in Miami were done at the end of the shoot, in early 1992. By then she looks hardened, her blond hair brittle and her makeup smudged. There is that famous Technicolor shot of her walking naked down a highway hitching a lift, and her playing exhibitionist, eating naked in a pizza parlor while fully clothed customers look on. When this picture was taken, the owner was apparently so disgusted he threw Madonna and her entourage out of his restaurant. Among the final shots is Madonna playing a streetwalker, bare-breasted on neon-lit streets. There is an air of desperation, like the shots of rock star Courtney Love naked in a London taxi, taken years later for Q magazine. By the end of the book, Madonna had somehow crossed over from carefully managed erotica to bargain-basement soft porn.

Sex was problematic. A million copies were published in seven countries on the same day—October 22, 1992—and sold out. "There were lots of sleepless nights before the book was published," Charles Melcher recalls. "We had to sign our lives away before we saw any pictures upfront. It was all very top-secret and hush-hush. We had armed guards at the printing plant. What with the metal and the Mylar bag and the CD, it was like building a car. The assembly line was staggering, and all at super-speed, because Madonna had a lot of other commitments. Then the day it came out people went berserk. They lined up to get the book, and they bought stacks." At $49.95 a copy, the book was not cheap.

There was a storm of media debate. For some people, it went too far, for others, not far enough. "The desperate confection of an age-ing scandal-addict," wrote Martin Amis in the *Observer,* while the *New Yorker*'s Calvin Tomkins grumbled that the book was "more about lay-out than getting laid." For Melcher and others at Calloway Editions, the pictures were less steamy than they had imagined.

"One of the most amazing elements of that project was to show how fantasy is more powerful than reality. The build-up had us im-agining God knows what," he says. "We were excited about it be-ing a great erotic art book. I've been a student of this genre; it was unprecedented that a top celebrity pop star should do something so sexual. But I found the pictures to be a bit of a letdown. In the end the packaging helped to give them more of an edge, but they were not as forbidden as I thought they'd be."

Sex had a confusing philosophy. Most female critics pointed out the vacuousness of Madonna's remarks about porn and abuse. "She can dig her own abusive relationships, perhaps, and then swan out of them," wrote Marina Warner, "but a brief visit to the red light dis-tricts of most cities, to the prostitutes' haunts behind railway stations where women hitch rides to perform blow jobs for derisory sums . . . might give her pause."

In reality, it was not about the degree of nudity or the number, as Norman Mailer so elegantly put it, of "beaver shots." The book crossed over into pornography because, despite its ostensible call for human liberation and safe sex, it felt like an empty exercise in mass marketing. The premise was courageous, with genuine exploration of queer sex, but it drifted into the flippant and commercial. Madonna, finally, was overexposed. Pornography is cynicism about human feeling, with a dead-eyed aspect that is formulaic and antilife. It's no surprise that a few years after the book was published, one of the men featured in its pages, porn star Joey Stefano, was found dead of a drug overdose in a motel room.

Stefano had been thrilled to appear in the *Sex* book. "Here at last was a 'legitimate' gig of a sort, involving perhaps the biggest pop star in the field. But the pay was 'legitimate' too," wrote Stefano's biographer Charles Isherwood. Stefano complained that he was paid only $150 for the shoot. "When Madonna and Co. packed up and left the Gaiety, they took the tawdry chic that reeks from the pages of *Sex* with them. They left behind the mundane reality and the boys who had to live with it seven days a week . . . like Stefano's celebrity escort clients, Madonna had contracted with him for certain specific services. When those were duly rendered, he and the pop star parted ways." Despite her wish to appeal to the human spirit, Madonna was compromised by the cheap mundanity of the porn business that she passed through.

One young man I interviewed for this book was eleven years old when *Sex* came out. He was unaware of her previous Virgin incarnations; that was his first encounter with Madonna. "At school we all thought she was an old porn queen. We had no idea about the other stuff," he says. "There was the feeling that she was a bit *wrong*." One of Madonna's peers is singer/songwriter Tori Amos, who has always explored sexual issues in her work. She recognizes that many women artists feel the need to pillage "their own repressed self." For Madonna, this took the form of *Sex*. "Who am I to say?" Amos muses. "If you're not hurting anybody else, maybe on your path to self-discovery and the transmutation of a domineering ideology, you need to allow yourself to be defecated on. You can choose to explore that, it's part of your damage. Many women play it out behind closed doors. She chose to do it in public in front of voyeurs."

The general reaction to *Sex* was unease, the sense that underneath that nonchalant exterior was a troubled psyche. Madonna was upset when one of her favorite producers, Patrick Leonard, claimed: "If she doesn't marry soon she'll do herself lasting psychological harm." His tone was moralistic, but he anticipated her crisis. Shortly after the *Sex* book came out, her next studio album, *Erotica*, was released. The inset picture on the CD sleeve featured a blurred Madonna holding a black crop and wearing studded leather wristbands, her eyes closed and mouth open, with tongue hanging out in S&M porn pose. When set beside the cover of *True Blue*, the difference is striking.

The perfect iconic goddess of *True Blue* was all gone. In the same way that 60s beauties like Nico, Marianne Faithfull, and Brigitte Bardot, after they were famous, set about destroying their beauty, the very thing they felt limited them, Madonna annihilated hers. Within a few short years, she moved from teasing flirtation to a desperate sexual display. It is ironic that after the artistic triumph of *Like a Prayer*, she hits this bathos. But then she admitted unease when she had to dye her hair back to blond for the *Dick Tracy* movie. "I felt great having my own hair color for the first time in years . . . that was the avenue I was going down. But then all of a sudden I had to change it," she had said. Blond sent her off in the wrong direction. It was as if with the *Sex* book she showed the underside of the Hollywood dream. So many would-be actors come to L.A. dreaming of stardom and end up on the margins of adult movies. It can be argued that with its emphasis on the sexual attractiveness of its female stars, mainstream Hollywood is a glittery brothel. Many a disenchanted actor has lamented how Tinseltown can "turn your head."

In the *Erotica* pictures, Madonna is bound and gagged, sitting astride a table, the image cut with a scratched blue tint. She's worth millions, but here she portrays something worthless. Another picture has her Warholian image fuzzily superimposed on the trailer-trash B-movie porn look complete with slutty blond extensions and red nail polish. She looks like a woman on the verge of a nervous breakdown. Something, indeed, had gone wrong.

PART OF the package of the *Sex* book was a giveaway CD single of "Erotica," the opening track on her next studio album, *Erotica*. A marked departure from previous albums, it showed Madonna veering off in a darker, more experimental direction. Although *Like a Prayer* had been a thoughtful artistic statement, its thrust was still *Billboard*-friendly rock-pop. With *Erotica*, she was going deep down and dirty. When producer Shep Pettibone worked on the first batch of songs they recorded, he opted for a New York house sound and an "L.A. vibe." Madonna hated it, saying that if she'd wanted the album to sound like that, she would have worked with Patrick Leonard in L.A. She didn't need light and glossy. She wanted *Erotica* to have a raw edge, as if it were recorded in "an alley in Harlem."

Pettibone's first impulse was to top "Vogue," but Madonna told him sternly that she never repeated herself. They worked on the album in his New York City apartment from October 1991 to the following March, in between *Sex* book expeditions with Steven Meisel. The Dita Parlo character—dominant, playful, sadistic—influenced the album. Pettibone remarked that Dita seemed to bring out the "beast" in her, actually serving as a vehicle for the dangerous territory she was traveling.

There had been disappointment in her personal life. Her marriage broke up, and her affairs with high-profile men like Warren Beatty and Vanilla Ice had amounted to nothing. After Beatty she had a relationship with the model/dancer Tony Ward. This pretty boy had a predilection for submissive sex, and was one of the stars of her "Justify My Love" video. He moved into her Hollywood mansion, and they enjoyed playing sexual games together. But there were fundamental inequalities in their relationship: while he professed to be her biggest fan, she would always be the boss. Madonna grew tired of this dynamic and the affair petered out. She had a string of willing lovers, including her bodyguard Jim Allbright and nightclub owner John Enos, but that did little to dispel her loneliness and insecurity. "I have an iron will," she told writer Lynn Hirschberg, "and all of my will has always been to conquer some horrible feeling of inadequacy. I'm always struggling with that fear. I push past one spell of it and discover myself as a special human being and then I get to another stage and think I'm mediocre . . . And I find a way to get myself out of that. Again and again." She said her drive centered on that fear of being mediocre ". . . that's always pushing me, pushing me." Those closest to her worried about her inability to settle, not just with one person, but within herself. "Warren used to say I exercised to avoid depression. And he thought I should just go ahead and stop exercising and allow myself to be depressed," she said. "And I'd say, 'Warren, I'll just be depressed about not exercising!'" Her close friend and backup singer Niki Haris was aware of Madonna's denial. "I remember having a conversation with Warren. He said, 'She can't take that truth, it's too painful for her,'" she recalls.

Music was the one area where Madonna let her feelings out. The depression she had been avoiding seeped into the grooves of *Erotica*: all her anger, dismay, bewilderment, and passion ended up on this record. Apart from the power pop ballad "Rain," there were no sugarcoated top-ten hits. Madonna wanted to tell her stories. She was an experienced thirty-three-year-old woman with complex emotions, and she was determined to reflect that. From the opening track, "Erotica," the album is as confrontational as her book *Sex*. In her dominatrix persona, Madonna enters the velvet intimacy of her S&M world, coaxing a lover to submit to Dita's special mixture of pleasure and pain. The arrangement is sparse—snatches of Kool & the Gang's "Jungle Boogie," a grainy backbeat, sensuous Middle Eastern sounds, and Madonna's whispery, dry voice; half-spoken, half-sung. It has some of the trancelike intensity of "Justify My Love," but none of its vital force. Her voice is thin and surprisingly low on energy.

Her cover version of Peggy Lee's song "Fever" compounds the sense that Madonna has lost that sinewy feel so characteristic of her music.

Her sound usually reflects a dancer's agility and playfulness in its elasticity, but here it is brittle. More of a mental exercise, her version of "Fever" doesn't have the powerful sense of restraint and obsession that marks the 1956 original. With the next track, "Bye Bye Baby," Madonna is cool and minimal to the point of flatness. Her dance beat is usually like a strong heartbeat, but here it is barely discernible. She sends off an uncaring suitor with perfunctory lyrics, sounding like she is either not fully concentrating or doesn't have many inner resources to draw on—what alternative healers would call "scattered chi," a depleted life force.

But out of this flatness, this lack of feeling, something new emerges. "Deeper and Deeper" is more her trademark adventurous, ambitious pop. She creates her own female wall of sound with Donna and Niki's tense call-and-response back vocals. "For this track she needed a strong kind of sound," says Niki. "There was a good feeling in the studio. Madonna always had her note, right there. It had almost become telepathic between the three of us. I knew how to shape my voice more like hers, she knew how to shape hers like mine. By then we knew how to do that in the studio as well as live."

The song builds and builds to a compelling house beat and a gutsy flamenco guitar breakdown as she laments falling for the wrong love, again and again. "This was a disco dance number. I was able to have a little fun and came up with the middle bridge section with the Latin influence. Madonna went with it, and embraced it," recalls Tony Shimkin, programmer and cowriter of the song. With this track, she may have been thinking back to the simple advice her mother gave, that she should trust the healing power of love.

But maybe it all goes back to the lady garden, the source of life. "Where Life Begins" is her ode to cunnilingus, or, as it was dubbed in the studio, "Eating Out." Echoing vaudeville blues mamas like Bessie Smith, who sang about the "jelly" in her "jelly roll," Madonna rejoices in the power of metaphor and innuendo. Coproduced with Andre Betts, who also worked with her on "Justify My Love," this track is an intimate fantasy rendered even more sensual by its pulsating low-key jazz licks.

Madonna wearing that Jean Paul Gaultier corset, on the 1990 Blond Ambition tour.

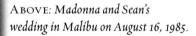

ABOVE: *Madonna and Sean's wedding in Malibu on August 16, 1985.*

LEFT: *Sean squaring up to the paparazzi in Tennessee, while an embarrassed Madonna hides her face.*

BELOW: *Sean and Madonna backstage before the Third Annual Commitment to Life Celebration at the Wiltern Theatre, Los Angeles, in 1987.*

Madonna and Sean on the set of Shanghai Surprise *in Hong Kong, 1986.*

Madonna's sister Paula Ciccone singing onstage in 1986.

RIGHT: *Performing the "Dress You Up" medley on her Who's That Girl? tour.*

BELOW: *Madonna and her comedienne friend Sandra Bernhard swap gossip backstage.*

Madonna as the streetwise Nikki Finn in the 1987 film Who's That Girl?

A scene from the 1988 Broadway production of David Mamet's Speed-the-Plow: *(LEFT TO RIGHT) Ron Silver, Madonna, and Joe Mantegna.*

RIGHT: *Dancing with thirteen-year-old Chris Finch at her British* Who's That Girl? *tour debut in Roundhay Park, Leeds.*

RIGHT: *A gun-toting Madonna in the* Who's That Girl? *film.*

LEFT: *Age thirty-one, with her more serious brunette* Like a Prayer *look.*

ABOVE: *The glorious triumvirate: Madonna and backing singers Niki Haris* (**LEFT**) *and Donna DeLory.*

BELOW: *Performing the masturbation scene on the Japanese leg of her Blond Ambition tour.*

ABOVE RIGHT: *Warren Beatty and Madonna on the set of* Dick Tracy *in 1990.*

RIGHT: *Al Pacino and Madonna in* Dick Tracy.

BELOW RIGHT: *Driving to dinner with Warren on her thirty-first birthday; and (*BELOW*) chatting to Warren at a New Year's Eve party in New York, 1989.*

A rapper/producer who grew up in the Bronx, Betts gave the album a lot of its "dirty" feel. Impressed with the work he had done on "Justify My Love," Madonna called him up saying she wanted to do some tracks in a studio where she wouldn't be recognized. He found her a small shabby jingles studio on West 21st Street in New York. "Madonna comes in with this big fur coat all the way down to her ankles," Betts told me. "She sits down and we start writing together. I'm on the piano and all of a sudden a rat runs across the room while she's writing lyrics. She looks at me and she says, 'Dre, did you see that?' I did, and I said, 'See what?' She goes, 'You didn't see that?' I was like, 'I didn't see nothing!' She goes, 'You're fucking lying, you saw it.' And I was like, 'Yeah I saw it, are you gonna leave?' She goes, 'Man, I'm not afraid of fucking rats!' And she just kept on writing. I was like, 'Wow', and she was just, 'Whatever!'"

So spoke the girl who had slept on studio floors and egg crates and eaten lunch out of garbage bins. Despite her superstar existence, there was part of Madonna that never lost touch with those early days scraping together a living in New York. And with this album, she was determined to evoke a sense of earthy reality. The day they saw the rat was the day she wrote "Where Life Begins." "I'm sitting there looking at her writing. She's blushing and she's got this smile on her and she goes, 'Gosh!' and I'm looking at her like, 'What the hell are you writing?'" laughs Betts. Though embarrassed to be writing about such an intimate subject in front of her new producer, Madonna clearly enjoyed the process.

Betts recorded several tracks with Madonna, including "Dear Father," which was chalked up to be "song four" on the record. "It was a song about her relationship with God. She was really loving it," says Betts. But when it came to organizing the publishing, Madonna was dismayed to learn that Mic Murphy from pop/dance act The System had played a bass line, and she nixed the song. Rumor has it that she and Murphy clashed a few times in the early 80s and Madonna never forgot it.

Despite the hiccup with "Dear Father," Betts took Madonna to more experimental places on *Erotica*, particularly with the crunchy hip-hop bass lines and low-slung groove of "Waiting." This bluesy, acid meditation on loving the wrong man is filled with resentment and brooding anger. What happened? She sounds a million years old. This is the sound of disillusion, as she almost spits the words out. There is a forceful addendum to this with "Did You Do It?"—a later track that has a reprise of the "Waiting" melody line, and some braggadocio boytalk. Madonna utters only one or two quiet words ("I'm waitin'"), but throughout the track there is the sense of her glowering presence. You can hear the power of her listening and her silence.

This track began as a joke. It reflects the rapport that Betts and Madonna had in the studio. "It was getting close to the end, and that day we were drinking gin and champagne and doing a little celebrating and she showed this mole that was on her hip. We had names for each other. She'd call me Pothead, and because her last name was Ciccone I'd call her my Chick Homie. And like everybody was calling her Mo, so I was calling her Mo Gizmo, all kinds of dumb stuff." Madonna had to go out for dinner, so she left Betts to finish work on some tracks. While she was out, he began to make up a rap. In a reprise of the provocative question that Madonna asked Camille Barbone all those years before, Betts recorded the guys in the studio saying "Did you do it?" while the music to her song "Waiting" was playing.

He improvised a rap over the top. "I'm talking about having sex with her. I'm doing this all over the 'Waiting' beat, the second verse I'm calling her a ho, all kinds of crazy stuff." Picking up on the events of the day, he invented a lurid scenario where they drank gin and had sex in her limo and he kissed the mole on her hip and quickly split. When Madonna returned from her dinner with Ingrid Casares and "some guys from the book," Betts couldn't resist making mischief. "I know she's Madonna but to me she's no different, I mess with my friends like this. I'm not going to disrespect her, but I'll be damned if I'm not going to have some fun."

Madonna asked him to play them the song "Waiting." "There's these guys in suits and everybody's all serious, so I cued up 'Did You Do It?' instead. I hit play, I'm facing the speakers, she's standing behind me and I can see her in the mirror. So I'm sitting there and all of a sudden I feel her lean on the back of my neck and I look up in the mirror and her eyes are just full of water and the song finishes and she goes, 'You're out of your fucking mind.' I go, 'I'm sorry!' She goes, 'You're crazy. Now can I hear my song?' And I look back and the guys are like, 'What the hell was that?'"

After the men in suits had disappeared, Madonna asked to hear "Did You Do It?" Nothing more was said until two weeks after recording was finished, when she called Betts saying she wanted the song on her album. "I said, 'Hell no! Are you crazy?'" he recalls. "Maybe," she said. "But I want to use the song on the album." Betts took some persuading, but she managed to convince him. "This goes to show how fair Madonna is. On every other song I got 50/50, but for 'Did You Do It?' I got 75/25. She gave me 75 percent of that song, so the convincing part was over. And because of my nasty foul mouth, she had to have an EXPLICIT sticker on her record." "Did You Do It?" fitted in with the gritty, urban sexual scenarios of early 90s rap. In calling his boss a ho, Betts was treading a fine line, but he did it with charm and an underlying admiration for her sense of daring. "The song was raw. It could've just been personal to her and she could've got a laugh out of it. But she put it out to the world."

In opting for a bare, minimal production, Madonna was able to express frustration and numbness as well as more easily orchestrated emotions like sadness and joy. She's left behind the dynamics of Pat Leonard's fulsome, string-laden pop to tell it like it is. The reality for her is "Bad Girl," a grungy tale of smoking too many cigarettes and seeking solace in lovers she doesn't care about. Or it's "Thief of Hearts," a scathing piece of disco house fired by a jealous mind. Or the verbose, complaining "Why It's So Hard." This was a difficult record for people to appreciate, and it wasn't until after the illumination of her later work that fans looked back to see how much this reflected her state of mind at the time. For her this was a concept album that explored the personal havoc of one's dark fears and desires.

With the song "In This Life," we get a sense of the other misery that propels her—the death of her friend Martin Burgoyne and the shadow that AIDS cast over her scene in New York.

"That was a touching song for her," remembers Shimkin. "She was very moved, you can hear that in the way she sang the lyrics. It was very personal to her, and you could see she was lost in the moment." But in uncovering that grief, she arrives at a new place, "The Secret Garden." Coproduced by Betts, this song has that early 90s Knitting Factory feel, with its downtown New York jazz riffs and drumming on the offbeat. Amid its warm, languid loops, this final track shows her moving toward transformation. She sings, with a kind of beat poetry and inner knowing, that despite the damage, despite a hardened heart, she can still find hope and beauty and a sense of self that soars free.

ALTHOUGH SHE could act the diva when she wanted to, in the studio Madonna was resolutely down-to-earth and realistic. Here the straightforward Detroit attitude came out. Tony Shimkin remembers composing with her and Pettibone in an apartment upstairs from the studio. "Shep was more about appeasing her and saying yes to what she wanted. I was younger and had more of a sense of humor. I was at the keyboard and she was sitting in the room saying, 'Are you done yet?' A few minutes went by. 'Are you done yet?' By the third or fourth time, I threw my pencil at her and said, 'No, I'm not fucking done yet. Go downstairs, get a bowl of popcorn, make some phone calls, and then come back to me. If I can't be myself, I can't enjoy what I'm doing.' She understood and respected that."

She was concerned about the tension between Pettibone and Shimkin. The young assistant felt he wasn't getting proper credit, and one day stormed past her out of the studio. He was in a local gym working out, when the pay phone rang. "They said, 'Tony, you have a call. It's Madonna,'" says Shimkin. "I was so surprised. She said, 'I feel bad for what's going on, I'd like you to talk to someone at my label.' It's easy for people to say she's a bitch, but she's not that type of person. She's very loyal."

Totally absorbed by the project, Madonna wanted to keep a calm equilibrium in the studio. She was also open to taking musical risks.

Keen to draw influences from unexpected places, she had Doug Wimbish play on several tracks. A pioneer hip-hop bass player, in the 1970s and early 1980s he was in the Sugarhill Records house band with Skip McDonald and Keith LeBlanc, playing on hip-hop classics like Grandmaster Flash's "The Message" and "White Lines." By 1984 he and his cohorts had moved to London and teamed up with dub producer Adrian Sherwood to create Tackhead—a funk-rock collision that stirred up the new "industrial" scene. Wimbish also did sessions with Mick Jagger and Living Colour, before his contribution to *Erotica* tracks "Where Life Begins" and "Secret Garden." Although he and Madonna seem unlikely musical bedfellows, he saw a connection right away.

"The thing about Mo is that she's always been linked to the underground," he says. "I remember seeing her at Danceteria wearing a big, huge multicolored jacket. You couldn't help but notice her. She was there with Bambatta, Grandmaster Flash. She was at the Roxy. She was really into the scene. She knew who I was and was curious enough to wanna have me on her record. If she's feelin' it, she's feelin' it. It was a very interesting community of cats that worked on this Madonna record."

Although the subject matter she was exploring was at times dark and difficult, Madonna still had fun. "She came into the studio with a box of old *Playboy* magazines, Hugh Hefner shit from the 70s," recalls Wimbish. "I guess she's researching the *Sex* book. I've met her before, I know her energy. I know how she is around men, how she can take control 'n' shit. She knows it—in a good way. You just can't be intimidated by it. Dre snatches one of the mags, looks at it, and goes, 'Damn! Oh shit, these bitches look like this back then?' I was like, 'Let me have a look.' Madonna says, 'Nah, nah, nah. You gotta do some playing.' 'I'm not gonna do no playing until I see some tits and some ass!' That's how we started our conversation. She started laughing. She was cool."

Madonna enjoyed the down-to-earth vibe that Betts fostered in the studio. "Dre's just straight ghetto at times, which is what I think she kinda likes," says Wimbish. "He's a straight up-and-down kinda

dude, he's not frontin'—not gotta get all dressed up and get engaged in some shallow conversation for a few years and that becomes
part of your character. No, he's really raw and honest but in a comfortable way."

Betts's easygoing nature allowed Madonna to be herself. Despite
her public image as a ball-breaker, she has a sweet side that comes
out when she feels relaxed and at home. Betts recalls how his friend,
aspiring designer Stephen Miller, used to come to see him in the studio. One day, Madonna asked Miller lightly: "What are you going to
design for me?" A few weeks later, he came back with a jacket for her
and a hat to match. "I've got something for you," he said. "Oh God,
thank you!" she answered. As Betts recalls, "She leaves, we didn't
know where she was going. She came back. She had taken her top off
and put the jacket and hat on. She came in and sat down with what
he'd just made for her, and that's what she wore for that day!"

There was also the time Madonna had a party at her house and
she was playing with a whip. Betts couldn't resist wrestling with it,
snatching the whip and using it to open her shirt. "She was wearing a
bra but the whole thing was cut out, so her nipples were out, it wasn't a
real bra. So she left her shirt off for a while and went around the party
like that," he recalls. It was a raucous party with people playing the
piano and singing, but Madonna didn't want to sing. "I said, 'What
the hell's wrong with you? Why don't you want to sing?' and she said,
'No, I would rather sing in front of thousands of people than sing in
front of a few.' Madonna might get mad at me for saying it, but she's
actually shy."

What Betts discovered is that once Madonna feels safe, her sweetness shines through. "I'd be honest with her and she'd open up and
tell me whatever, and I started realizing *Damn*, you're actually shy.
You put this whole big attitude on but underneath all that shit she's
a kitten, a little kitten."

ON SEPTEMBER 12, 1992, Shep Pettibone walked out of the studio
with a completed master copy of *Erotica* in his hands. A month later,

he saw Madonna at the launch party for her book *Sex*. While everyone around them got into Dionysian displays of simulated sex and live tattooing, he and she began talking about music. "After all, it was still the music that mattered, and it was the record we fawned over," he said. Betts has another view of the party. "There was a bathtub full of popcorn and a nude lady inside it. Then there was a lady walking around with sushi but with her bare breasts on the sushi tray. And there was a person hanging on a chain from the ceiling and all this leather and shit," he laughs. "But the crazy thing is, there are all these doors, and there were holes in the doors so you can look in and there's people having sex." What amused him the most, however, was when he saw a heavy macho guy he knew from the Bronx there on all fours with a dog collar around his neck. "I called his name and he looks back. He didn't know I was working on the record and goes, 'Oh my gosh!' I was the last person that he thought he'd see there. There were very few people from the hood and Bronx at this party. As a matter of fact, I think it might have been three! It was funny," says Betts. He also remembers Madonna wanting to go to her private chill-out room and asking Betts to hold hands and make a chain with him, her, and Stephen Miller to slide through the crowd. Even at her own party, she needed to feel protected and secure.

ALTHOUGH IT is one of Madonna's bravest and most personal records, *Erotica* is her least successful. It sold 5 million copies worldwide (compared to *True Blue*'s 21 million or *Like a Virgin*'s 19 million). Her sales dropped in the United States. In her home country, she had always sold upward of 4 million, but *Erotica* stalled at half that. Madonna realized that her *Sex* book had become a massive diversion. "What was problematic was putting my *Erotica* album out at the same time. I love that record and it was overlooked. Everything I did for the next few years was dwarfed by my book," she said. What the public wanted was the slick pop songs and the old cheeky, innocent Madonna they knew and loved. But she was never coming back; not in that guise, anyway.

Doug Wimbish feels that *Erotica* was a record ahead of its time. In the early 90s, Seattle grunge had kicked in, the bass-driven beats of jungle were emerging on the dance floor, and hip-hop hit a new level with the funky, conscious rap of acts like De La Soul. "Madonna's enough of an artist to take the hues and shades of what's happening and put a concept together. It's not just bash out a record," he says. "She had Maverick, she'd done the book, the film *Dick Tracy*, she dated a big-ass Hollywood actor. This was her first record with *her* concept. She just freaked everybody out. She turned the system upside down for a moment, and they had to deal with the shock and awe of it all."

He doesn't see *Erotica*'s 5 million sales as a failure. "In a sense, *Erotica* was the biggest one of her career. It was the one that molded her, that gave her the access code to what she's doin' now. *True Blue* and so on—it was good to get those numbers outta the way first. That's fantastic. She's much smarter now, when I look back on it. Absolute genius. Get those numbers outta the way when you're young. Set up the template for what you wanna do when you're older. Fifty million-plus records under your belt, you're good. If the label can't support what you're trying to do, fuck 'em. On one level, she's asking, how much do y'all really believe in me *now*?" Wimbish believes that Madonna forged a path for the next generation of female pop artists: "She was bringin' it from her point of view as a woman, bringing it to the forefront *for real*. That set the template now for your Christina Aguileras, Britneys, Beyoncés. She paved the road for a lot of that. You can be nice and clean and then a freak. And there'll be a lot of money for you in it at the end!"

M A D O N N A W A S experimenting with different guises, not just in her pop career, but in movie roles too. A pattern was beginning to emerge. With female directors she often expressed her strong, feisty side, notably as Susan in *Desperately Seeking Susan*. Then in *A League of Their Own*, Penny Marshall's 1992 film about a 1940s all-girl baseball team, Madonna summoned up the gutsy, gum-chewing spirit of her high school cheerleading days. Many male directors, however, couldn't resist a kind of assassination of her power, taking the strong female roles she chose and twisting them. In David Mamet's 1988 Broadway play *Speed-the-Plow*. Madonna understood her role as a kind of female avenger, a force for good, who persuades her cynical suitor to take up an inspirational story she has been reading instead of his usual commercial fare.

In the end, Mamet and director Gregory Mosher changed the emphasis of Karen's character, so that she came across as conniving and manipulative rather than innocent. "It was devastating to do that night after night," Madonna said. "I saw her as an angel, an innocent. They wanted her to be a cunt." She often took on the role of the fallen woman, an adversary between two men. In *Speed-the-Plow*, Karen was the toy of Bobby Gould (played by Joe Mantegna) and his gung ho producer Charlie Fox (Ron Silver). Two years earlier, in *Goose and Tomtom*, her first theatrical New York role, she played a brassy dame called Lorraine, who teased and tormented the two male protagonists. Conceived as a "Gnostic myth" by the playwright David Rabe, the play combined the supernatural with a criminal underworld. Art mirrored life, with Madonna's Lorraine stirring up the jealousy between these two deadbeat gangster hoodlums, one of whom (Tomtom) was played by Sean Penn. In real life, Madonna was to stir up Sean's jealous feelings in her friendship with Sandra Bernhard. A fan of David Rabe's writing, Sean had wanted Madonna to play the part of Lorraine. Their next joint foray into acting after the disastrous *Shanghai Surprise*, it ran for four days, before Madonna had to go off to shoot *Who's That Girl?* Although barely a thousand people saw it, this was one of her better performances.

"Madonna was the best Lorraine I ever saw. . . . There was certainly something in the part that seemed made-to-order for her persona—the Material Girl, which was all I knew before we started working together: sexy and materialistic, that sort of cynical, provocative thing she has," recalled Rabe. "She had lines like, 'I'm going to rule the world someday'; and she had probably been saying that all her life—as a child even."

In Woody Allen's 1992 film *Shadows and Fog*, Madonna plays the

girl on the flying trapeze, caught between her husband the strongman and the clown. "I have all my tricks for seducing," her character
says, almost guilelessly. Then, in the 1993 thriller *Body of Evidence*, she
plays Rebecca Carlson, a femme fatale who murders millionaire men
by having adventurous sex with them. "She's not only the defendant.
She's the murder weapon," the prosecutor declaims at her trial. "She
is a beautiful woman. But when this trial is over, you will see her as no
other than a gun, a knife, or any deadly weapon." For this film, shot
after her work on the *Sex* book, Madonna engages in full frontal nudity, taking costar Willem Dafoe on an erotic journey with candles,
nipple clamps, and cunnilingus in a parking lot.

The movie was directed by Uli Edel, who had made such provocative and atmospheric art-house films as *Christiane F*, a drama about a
Berlin heroin addict, and *Last Exit to Brooklyn*, adapted from Hubert
Selby Jr.'s novel about 1950s Brooklyn low-lifes. Conceived as a cross
between intelligent film noir and *Basic Instinct*, *Body of Evidence* was a
glossy, beautifully lit, but ultimately unconvincing film. Though Madonna's performance is accomplished, the movie was seen as part
of the *Sex* debacle, and when it was released, it was critically panned
(critic Leslie Halliwell denounced it as "too silly for words"). Audiences cheered when Rebecca was shot and fell back through French
windows to a spectacular death.

"We wanted to work together. We had been looking for a project
and when it came along we jumped on it," Edel told me. "But we did it
too quickly, and when it was finished it didn't succeed." He feels that
many critics overlooked Madonna's acting in their rush to condemn
the movie. "In the film, her acting was better than usual. People go
overboard in their criticism. She's a very brave woman, she takes a lot
of risks. Maybe over time people will look back and realize she was a
good actress."

By the time Madonna did *Body of Evidence*, she had become the
world's Sin Eater—depicted as using her sexuality in a destructive
way. The received story of early Madonna was that she was a glorious
groupie, sleeping her way to the top, and therefore that made her art
and her music suspect. As anthropologist Wendy Fonarow writes in

her book *Empire of Dirt*: "The female groupie is a disruptive figure. Basically, she is considered a specialized slut, not a slut who will sleep with anyone, but a slut who will sleep with anyone who has the right job." Early tabloid coverage of Madonna reeled off the litany of her useful DJ/producer boyfriends, implying that her creative output was not her own.

Madonna often found herself portraying in other people's plays and films a sexual woman who had to be punished. She was the trickster figure, a woman whose wayward power had to be diminished. The trickster is an archetypal character, usually male, who is both creative and destructive, who represents basic instincts and has an amoral, insatiable appetite. In ancient folklore, the trickster is a transient, running from one town to another, transgressing borders. He embodies the creative tensions in opposites: the sacred and profane. With his dedication to excess, the rock musician became the ultimate twentieth-century trickster. Madonna may not have trashed a hotel room or thrown a TV into the swimming pool, but she did her own version of that—belching loudly in public places, simulating masturbation, and exhibiting her private parts to the world. According to Fonarow: "Trickster needs to be punished for his violations." Madonna, too, found herself being punished and disapproved of both by right-wing Christian groups like the Moral Majority, and alternative-rock artists such as Courtney Love.

Love was a rock antiheroine, with split ends in her baby-doll blond hair and an asymmetrical grin. She had a caustic wit and wrote impassioned punk songs with her band Hole. "I'm not upper-middle class and I was never popular at high school. I have tattoos and I'm subculture, a teenage bag lady," she once said to me. Married to Nirvana singer Kurt Cobain, she had been dubbed the Queen of Grunge. Madonna immediately saw the commercial potential in Hole and offered to sign her to Maverick. Love declined, saying later: "Madonna's interest in me was kind of like Dracula's interest in his latest victim." Such were the misgivings that Love seemingly had about Madonna at this time, she convinced herself that a spurned Madonna had encouraged her friend Lynn Hirschberg to do a "hatchet job" on her. However, while a damming article about the Cobains written by Hirschberg did appear in *Vanity Fair,* there was no evidence whatsoever that Madonna had anything to do with it.

Three years later, Madonna and Love came face-to-face after the MTV Video Music Awards. Journalist Kurt Loder was interviewing Madonna for MTV when Love disrupted the proceedings by throwing her powder compact at the star and yelling "Madonna!" Sensing a scoop, Loder invited Love to join them. There followed an uneasy exchange, where Love did her utmost to annoy Madonna. The latter's response was to say "Who's got better shoes? Mine are Gucci," and walk off. "Was I bumming you guys out? Were you, like, talking astrophysics and stuff?" Love yelled. "Bye, Madonna. . . . Did I bum you out? Are you pissed at me?"

Madonna later described Love as "such a miserable person. She's incredibly competitive with people and anybody who's successful she's going to slag off." By the end of the decade, though, they reached a truce. Love even introduced her stylist, Arianne Phillips, to Madonna. When they both became Hollywood mothers, they found common ground, but back in 1992, Love symbolized the hardcore resistance to Madonna's charms. More and more female artists, from Love to Chicago songwriter Liz Phair, felt compelled to criticize her. "They slag me off any time anybody asks what they think of me or compare them to me. It's kind of like what a child does to their parent, they denounce you. They want to kill you off because they want their independence from you," Madonna complained. These competitive new rock heroines were anxious to establish themselves as the alternative to Madonna's grand pop spectacle. She was cast as manipulator and fake, a dark female force to be reckoned with.

But then, for vast swathes of her audience, she has the opposite effect, a kind of luminosity. John Izod identifies this as the female shaman. "This figure, an unconscious healer, also sometimes plays tricks on people, inflicting discomfort on them (which may well rebound upon him- or herself) in the process of breaking through to and healing the psyche," he said.

This effect was clearly seen in a little book that came out at the same time as *Sex*. Entitled *I Dream of Madonna*, it was a collection of women's dreams about Madonna, compiled by Texan folklorist Kay Turner. Madonna said she was flattered at the extent of theoretical writing about her: "I've so infiltrated their psyches that they have to intellectualize my very being. I'd rather be on their minds than off," she said. Here the dreams of women from a variety of ages and backgrounds show the pervasiveness of her influence, that she figures in women's lives as a healer, an enabler, a coconspirator, and a source of liberation. One woman, who had been the victim of sexual abuse, said that Madonna came to her in a dream, played with her children, and expressed concern about the problem of abuse. "She was interested in helping any way she could . . . She wanted to hear what it was like and how a message about this problem could penetrate society in a controversial way so people would pay attention."

There are other dreams where Madonna is leading the dance, where a hologram of Madonna lights up the night sky, where she's called Botswana—"because that means the Boss"—where she's a bitch, an erotic seductress, or a vulnerable child. She has an everywoman quality, and what was remarkable at this time was the pervasiveness of her influence. Despite the prevailing image of her as a conscious manipulator and conniving businesswoman, many women responded to her humanity. It was as if Madonna was taking on the role of the Virgin, granting prayers and intercessions. Turner described her book as "an unofficial response to *Sex*, in which Madonna used a new format to continue the dialogue she initiated early in her career about the importance of dreams and fantasies . . . this collection is a gift back to her: these dreams represent the other half of the dialogue."

Madonna was shown the book before publication and was moved by it. "It was a highly sexual little publication with a sense of what we called 'Vaginal Pride,'" says the book's British editor Peggy Vance. "Madonna liked the way it showed her human side as opposed to the posed, pornographic side. There was a gentler, homoerotic twist." With its quirky montage of images, *I Dream of Madonna* became a mass-market seller. "She's in the fabric of people's lives," says Vance. "She has a religious facet for people, a sense of charm and blessing. Not in the traditional way, but an empowering way. I saw people reading it on the tube, reading it everywhere."

But, to just as many people, Madonna was a nightmare of overexposure, with values that they didn't trust. With *Sex*, she had dared the world in an elaborate way, and some powerful men publicly picked up the gauntlet. In 1993, Madonna coproduced Abel Ferrara's film *Dangerous Game* with her production company, Maverick. In taking on the cult director of such darkly provocative movies as *Driller Killer* and *Bad Lieutenant*, she was asking for trouble. It became an intriguing game for Ferrara, who's been described by some as a mischievous misogynist, to see if he could break her spirit. In a reprise of previous movie themes, Madonna played yet another woman caught between two aggressive men. In this film within a film, she plays a Hollywood actress called Sarah Jennings, who plays an abused wife, Claire. Having undergone a religious conversion, Claire no longer wants to partake in the drugs and sex games she once played with her suburban husband (James Russo, a close friend of Sean Penn). Dismayed, her husband tries to humiliate her in ever-escalating ways, and eventually shoots her to death. Russo's actor character has trouble separating art and life, and his on-screen violence becomes a little too real. The film's director (Harvey Keitel), too, finds his marriage falling apart as the film progresses.

Madonna initially thought she was playing the role of a catalyst, an agent of transformation. But, like her experience with *Speed-the-Plow*, the director had other ideas. Ferrara elicited strong performances by throwing away the script and encouraging his cast to improvise. To an ordered and organized Madonna, this was unthinkable. However, over the three-month filming period, he gradually broke down her resistance until her unscripted self began to emerge. "Look in the mirror. What do you see? I see a two-bit cunt having a nervous breakdown," Russo sneers, while a bruised Madonna looks tearfully at her reflection. As he smashes the mirror, it's as if she's acquiescing in her own destruction. It is clear that at one level the film is about Madonna, or the public perception of her. "We both know she's a fucking whore and she can't act," Russo shouts at one point, as his character hacks off her hair the way Sean Penn once threatened to do.

In another scene, Keitel's director character provokes Sarah by saying: "Who the fuck are you, you commercial piece of shit?" But perhaps most telling of all is a small scene where Sarah confesses to the director her experience of rape some years before. True to the spirit of improvisation, Madonna digs deep into the memory of the sexual assault that happened to her as a young woman in New York. This is what film auteur David Lynch would describe as "the eye of the duck," a pivotal scene that lies at the heart of the movie.

Quietly, nervously licking her lips, Madonna's character recalls how her attacker made her strip naked and lie down. He tries to rape her, but her body is so rigid, he has to resort to fellatio. "I remember this horrible choking feeling," she says, recounting how the man then dragged her to the side of the roof by her hair and held a knife against her throat. "He said, 'I dunno if I should slit your throat or push you off the building.'" She looks up at Keitel. "And I would've done anything, *anything* for him."

There in that scene is the reason why Madonna did *Sex*. Why she stripped her body bare as a mode of confrontation as much as eroticism. Why she feigned masturbation onstage and constantly upped the ante in terms of shock and control. Underlying her seamless pop tunes, driving her music and her declarative images is a sense of white-hot anger. Writer John Izod was onto something when he described her as not "celebrating love and sexuality in their own right so much as playing with the idea of them."

It's not so much grief at her mother's death that drives her as the sense of abandonment that left her unprotected. She encountered her own worst possible scenario, becoming a victim of male violence, and thereafter turned that full-tilt into her work, reversing the equation at every opportunity. This is why women respond to her on such a gut level, why so many heterosexual men feel ambivalent. The story she is presenting is not just one of charm and seduction, but anger and revenge. It's the dark undertow, the id, the sense of righteous indignation that made much of her mainstream audience feel uncomfortable and turn away. The aptly titled *Dangerous Game* was a critical and commercial failure, and many found it too bleak to watch. They didn't want to see Madonna in this light. In the same way that people saw Oscar Wilde as a wit and a raconteur and missed the poignancy, or read Noël Coward as lighthearted comedy of manners, without seeing his savage sense of social injustice, so many critics did not go beyond the shimmering surface of Madonna's pop persona to understand the troubled rage within.

It was at this time that songwriter Tori Amos released "Me and a Gun," a devastating song about her experience of rape that led to her founding RAINN, a national U.S. support service for victims of sexual abuse. There are parallels with Madonna in the way Amos turned the tables on violence and used it to fuel her art. "It's about accepting the violence that had occurred, that had seeped in through every part of my being. Rape can crawl inside and live with you as another voice," she says. "You can't deploy a SWAT team to get this shaming voice out of you. The only way to deal with destruction is creation. That's the key to a victim consciousness—to change that pattern so you don't become a tragedy. You go after the rapist that has set up a stall inside your mind."

Madonna expressed the turmoil within, and then, frightened by the result, tucked it back inside. It took five long years before she had the courage to return to it again.

I Only Shoot
What I Need

"I DIVIDE MY CAREER INTO BEFORE AND AFTER THE *Sex* book," said Madonna. "Up until then I was just being a creative person working and doing things that inspired me and I thought would inspire other people. After that I suddenly had a different point of view about life in general. *Sex* was my fantasy and I made money off of it. That is a no-no . . . It's all part of a strong woman in control terrifying people." *Sex* gave Madonna sleepless nights. Unnerved by her confusing and confrontational stance, the public stayed away in droves, and her popularity dipped to an all-time low. Compelled to find a way back into people's hearts, she chose a medium that for her had always been successful—the live show. Running from September to December 1993, The Girlie Show wasn't as audacious as Blond Ambition, but it showcased Madonna as a comedienne, an arch proponent of modern vaudeville and burlesque.

The choreographer Alex Magno was impressed with her ideas. "It was a very organic show, based on pure performance. It didn't rely on special effects and gimmicks," he told me. Many of the moves were choreographed by Magno, a Brazilian street dancer who came from a poor background in Rio de Janeiro. After making his way to the United States, he formed L.A.-based dance company Personna Dance

Theater and, combining ballet with jazz, built up a considerable reputation within the dance community. It was shrewd of Madonna to
call him for her Girlie Show. "She picked me out of fifty different
choreographers. And she tends not to go for the most famous in their
field, she wants something different. She wanted to personally meet
me first—she might like your work but if you don't connect with her
on an energy-vibe level, you don't work with her."

Among the dancers, Carlton Wilborn was the only one from Blond
Ambition to join her for the new tour. "The Girlie Show was my favorite, it was much more elegant, with a more sophisticated visual
effect," he says. There was a stringent rehearsal process beforehand.
For "La Isla Bonita," for instance, where the entire cast were dressed
as sailors, there was some complicated choreography. "We knew Madonna had been rehearsing on her own. Alex then brought her in to
do her spots. We didn't realize that she'd be moving as much as we
were. There was a lot of motion upstage and downstage, and she knew
every single thing. She was *unbelievable*. I went, Oh shit, that's why the
woman is *who* she *is*. She's got her shit down. Real organic emotion
came through that number, with a Latin flair. Madonna doesn't have
to put herself through that, but the side of her that's pure artist needs
to stretch herself physically." As with Blond Ambition, Carlton took
on some leading roles, particularly for the dramatic segment "The
Beast Within," a theme that would reappear in Madonna's later work.
"That was about the ways we hold things within us that can kill us. If
we don't come face-to-face with it, it'll destroy us," he says.

For the opening number, though, Madonna concentrated on the
circus theme, with barrel-organ music, a big top, and a girl (Carrie
Ann Inaba) descending from the ceiling on a rope. Inaba had taken
lessons from a professional circus acrobat to get the right effect—only
there was one difference from the normal family spectacle: she was
wearing nothing but a G-string. This was a dynamic introduction to
the first song, "Erotica," where Madonna posed in the full Dita Parlo
regalia of short hair, tall boots, and a riding crop. It was a gamey
image, performed with slow, controlled movements that set the tone
for the whole show. A sophisticated production, it reflected Madon-

na's state of mind at the time, with moments of sheer brilliance and other points that were less focused, where it seemed she was treading water.

The Pantomime Dame routine, for instance, was one she had performed several times before, and a rehash of old comic ideas. Here it was done in Bette Midler's style, with flouncy blouse, blond Afro wig, and 70s hot pants. "Express Yourself" and "Deeper and Deeper" were turned into discopops, complete with mirror ball and dancers shimmying from one side of the stage to the other. After her upset with the *Sex* book, Madonna was going firmly for the gay vote, appealing to her most loyal audience. "She isn't really a fag hag, she's got a gay sensibility herself—not as a gay woman, but a gay man. That's what comes across," cultural commentator Peter York told me. "She *knows* what the gay boys are thinking, and she's exploited them *mercilessly*."

There were moments of high camp: the "La Isla Bonita" sailors, for example, or her delighted dance between two men baring six-pack muscles on "Fever," or her donning military garb and shouting orders for "Holiday." All this was diverting, but it didn't match the power of her Dita Parlo character. The high points of the show were when Madonna gave full rein to her sense of theater. As she told Alex Magno: "This is the way I work: everything I do has to have a motivation, every step has to have a reason. I work like an actor."

What resonated most was Madonna as an early 1900s showgirl, holding herself taut in an Indian-style headdress for the intricate movements of "Vogue." Or Madonna in top hat and tails aping Marlene Dietrich in the film *Morocco*. In an image as classic as the conical breasts, she became the female ringmaster, singing "Like a Virgin" with a heavy German accent and a knowing wink. "In rehearsals we asked ourselves, What is she doing? We all thought that was gonna die, it was so clichéd," recalls her lighting director Peter Morse. "But when it came to it, the crowd loved it. Madonna knew what response she'd get."

There was also the sequence for "Bye Bye Baby" where, reminiscent of the Japanese cross-dressing all-female dance company Takarazuka, Madonna and backup singers Donna and Niki dressed as bawdy Vic-

torian gentlemen and grabbed the lady dancers. It was during this
tour that she, Donna, and Niki really came into their own. For the
song "Rain" they sat together dressed in black like three wise crones,
with the focus purely on their voices.

"That was the first time we sat down together and felt our harmonies," recalls Niki. "Madonna's voice was starting to get strong. I
could see a difference. She was into trying new things and trusting
herself. It was great to sing with her. The three of us had a good balance—Donna was a good cover when Madonna was dancing, and I
would do the gospelly, big-voiced stuff that complemented her and
said something about being strong. We tried our best to emphasize
what she did, rather than embellish it." By now, the fans were seeing
Madonna, Niki, and Donna as a powerful team. They also looked
striking together. "We emphasized the different ways women looked.
People embraced the fact that we weren't just skinny dancers sitting
next to her. We were inviting and inclusive."

The most compelling scene in the show was for the finale, "Justify
My Love," where Madonna and her cast strode gracefully onto the
stage, wearing Dolce & Gabbana period costumes. With top hats,
crinolines, and jackets of dove gray, white, and black, they looked like
a majestic Edwardian mural. As the track, with its pared-down, atmospheric beats, drew to a close, the dancers exited the stage one by
one, until Madonna was left alone. She turned her back to the audience, her bustle behind her, and silently drifted off, like a ghostly
woman in black.

As in her performance of "Vogue" in eighteenth-century garb at
the MTV Awards, Madonna's talent for visual theater came into focus with this tableau. "There's something about the way she stages
things," says Peter Morse. "This scene was on the edge of reality, very
surreal. It painted a vivid picture." For Carlton, too, this was a key
moment. "Energetically, it was still, but it has *so* much power to it. We
wore original vintage costumes from old movies, rented for the tour.
There was something about the way she and her brother Christopher
were raised that has a natural class to it, and it came out there."

It was scenes like this that made art director Christopher Ciccone proud of the tour. An artist, interior designer, and businessman, Christopher has collaborated with his sister at various points in her career. He danced with her when she first started out in New York, and he helped to conceptualize the dramatic sets of Blond Ambition. Madonna liked working with him and trusted his vision, so his promotion to artistic director of The Girlie Show tour was a logical next step. "I think that was a high point in both our careers. Both of us at our peak, creatively and vocally and performance-wise, it all came together perfectly, in my opinion," he said. Morse, however, had his reservations. "Christopher had some good ideas, but they were creative, not realistic. They were difficult to manage from a technical, theatrical point of view. For instance, he wanted the whole stage to be surrounded by red drapes—but you can't put lights on that, it just goes black, green, or brown. He is an artist in his own right, but ideas on paper didn't always look good on stage. We worked it out, though!"

This concert also showed how far Madonna had developed her choreography. The Girlie Show's forceful movements echoed those of her modern-dance heroine Martha Graham. "The Graham technique is very hard physically, with very strong movements. It's not good if you're tall, but it helps if you're short, like Madonna," says British choreographer Jane Turner. "Madonna's got great control. She's completely at ease in her body, and has immense technique. She has the ability to sustain movement, and dancing that slowly is very hard. Every muscle is being worked. It denotes power and strength. She's a bit like Tina Turner in that she often poses with slightly splayed legs, in a way that's quite macho. She's unashamed of her muscularity."

The Girlie Show ended on a high note with her revisiting the song "Everybody" dressed in shorts and a T-shirt. And as the lights went down for the final time, she emerged from behind the mask of a Pierrot, affectionately singing "Everybody Is a Star." When there is nowhere else to go, it's good to go back to where you started. The Girlie Show was Madonna's homage to gay culture, a tribute to those suffering from AIDS, and a celebration of life. It was well received,

but although she won back a large section of her audience, the fallout
from the *Sex* book continued into 1994, resulting in one of Madonna's
most notorious TV appearances.

On March 31, 1994, she was interviewed on the *Late Show with David
Letterman*. The biting, bantering host introduced his guest as having
"slept with some of the biggest names in the entertainment business."
At that, Madonna strode on wearing a long, black velvet dress and
Doc Marten boots, her black hair cropped short and slicked back. She
seemed brittle and nervous, her body language defensive. Within seconds, Letterman began provoking her with sexual innuendo, and she
soon rose to the challenge, calling him a "sick fuck." When he looked
shocked, she continued using the word "fuck" throughout their conversation. "This is American television," he said. "You can't be talking
like this." She smoked a cigar as they traded awkward insults. Although she tried to make jokes and laugh, her hostility came through.
"You used to be cool. Money's made you soft," Madonna accused Letterman. "You just kiss up to everybody on the show." As Letterman
tried to coax her into playing the talk-show game, she became more
militant, saying, "Can't we just break the rules? Fuck the tape, fuck
the list. This is contrived." By then the crowd was heckling. Letterman continued to goad Madonna, asking if she had a boyfriend. "Why
don't you ask if I have a girlfriend?" she retorted.

Letterman finally tried to wind the interview up, but Madonna
sat resolutely in her chair. "Don't fuck with me, David. Don't make
me act the fool," she snapped. By then, though, the damage was done.
The star had uttered the word "fuck" thirteen times, given Letterman
a pair of her underwear, and talked about peeing in the shower. The
next day Madonna was lambasted in the press as having run out of
ideas and "built a career on smut." Her popularity was once again at
an all-time low. Since then many people have criticized the "thirteen
fucks" interview, but Madonna was reacting to Letterman's intrusive
questions about her sex life. Sensing the hostility of the crowd, she
went into overdrive. That night she truly became the nation's Sin
Eater, the trickster. Her words had the same vitriolic charge as Steve
Jones of the Sex Pistols saying, "You dirty fucker" on prime-time

British TV at the height of 70s punk. "I'm happy you could come by now and gross us all out," Letterman said to Madonna. She knew she wasn't showing herself in the best light, but she was feeling victimized and lashed out. "That was a time in my life when I was extremely angry," she said years later. "Angry with the way I was brought up. Angry about how sexist this society that we live in is. Angry with people who assumed that because I had a sexuality that I couldn't also be talented. Just everything."

When the furor died down, Madonna realized that it was time for damage control. She put in a more toned-down appearance on *The Tonight Show*, with Jay Leno, and then publicly made up with Letterman at an MTV Awards ceremony. But she knew the only sure way back into people's hearts was through her music.

IN 1994, Madonna went back into the studio, building on what she had started with *Erotica*. When she began work on the new album, *Bedtime Stories*, R&B and soul were in the ascendant. Janet Jackson was outselling her brother, Toni Braxton had gone global with her self-titled debut, and Salt-N-Pepa and En Vogue joined forces for "Whatta Man," one of the biggest hits of the year. There was also Mary J. Blige—the sound of Southern Pentecostal meets street soul—and the mischievous, hip-hop-inspired TLC. Madonna took cues from this for her new record. Shep Pettibone's house rhythms were gone, to make way for more fashionable beats. "I wanted a lot more of an R&B feel . . . The idea going in was to juxtapose my singing style with a hardcore hip-hop sensibility and have the finished product still sound like a 'Madonna record,'" she said.

She began the process by meeting with hip-hop producers she admired, opting first for Babyface (aka Kenneth Edmonds), who had produced songs for an array of artists from Whitney Houston to Toni Braxton and TLC. Concerned that *Erotica* had been too dark and "ahead of its time," she decided to write songs in a lighter, more romantic vein. With Babyface, she came up with the straightforward love ballad "Take a Bow," which became a massive U.S. number one hit. Vintage romantic Madonna, it was slightly saccharine, compared to the rest of the tracks that ended up on the album, but it sold throughout the world. Babyface's manager Ramon Hertz remembers when Madonna performed it live at the San Marino Music Festival in Monaco. "As big as I knew Madonna was, it didn't hit me till we went there. We were driving down the street in convoy, with me, Madonna, and Kenny (Babyface) in a Mercedes-Benz up front. We turned a corner into a small village. It was crazy, bedlam. The streets were jam-packed on both sides with people shouting 'Madonna! Madonna!' It was like the pope. We could barely get the cars through. We laughed when Kenny said, 'They don't have a clue who *I* am.'"

Madonna, though, was sensitive to artistic protocol. When it came to the live performance of the song, she made sure that Babyface (who was singing backup) was near to her. "In rehearsals he was on a platform behind her, but she brought him closer and made him a featured part of the song. That was sensitivity from one artist to another. You don't often get that," recalls Hertz.

After their collaboration, Babyface introduced her to Dallas Austin, a young hotshot producer in Atlanta. He had already made a name for himself doing edgy, socially aware numbers for TLC, and his collaboration with Madonna resulted in two of the best songs on the album: "Secret" and "Sanctuary." With its chunky backbeat, gentle strings, and funky guitar motif, "Secret" is both languid and tense at the same time. The song has the air of quiet revelation and a relaxation of spirit. Madonna insisted later that the song wasn't just about love but also about spiritual self-empowerment. "It's about God being in us all and not on a pedestal," Madonna said. It was originally produced by Shep Pettibone under the title "Something's Coming Over Me," and Austin reworked the demo, bringing out a new warm, soulful tone in her voice, and making her swoony, humming sound a central feature of the track. "Sanctuary," meanwhile, went further into mystic territory as a reflection on sex and fertility. But unlike the declarative stance of former albums, this was about Madonna seeking refuge, burying herself in a hidden love. For this, apocalyptic imagery is fused with fluid pictures of unconscious desire.

Madonna then teamed up with Mariah Carey's esteemed producer Dave "Jam" Hall for one of the quirkiest tracks on the album, "Human Nature." A fierce riposte to all the critics of her *Sex* book, it combined a loping En Vogue–style rhythm with a hip-hop backbeat. Complete with the sound of doors slamming and a startling sample from "What You Need" by hip-hop band Main Source, it throbbed with a tightly restrained but devastating anger. The accompanying video, shot in black-and-white, with Madonna being shut in boxes, padded cells, and narrow rooms, shows how trapped and claustrophobic she had been feeling. Now an acclaimed video director, Dustin Robertson remembers working as assistant to Jean-Baptiste Mondino on the shoot. "That was when I first met Madonna. She stepped out of her trailer wearing the patent-leather outfit and stiletto-heeled boots. She stepped carefully yet confidently across a stage floor covered in electrical wires and boxes, and *silence* hushed over the entire set. She was *stunning.*"

As with "Open Your Heart" and "Justify My Love," Mondino knew how to capture Madonna's essence. "Their energy is *nothing* alike, which is why the combo works so well," Robertson told me. "He is cool and laid-back—she's a stickler for details. He is an energy wrangler and has a wonderful way of handling M. She demands and prefers a strong handler to pull out the best she's got to give." Though it was a striking video and a masterful song, it was one that her American heartland wasn't yet ready to embrace. When it was released as a single, "Human Nature" stalled at number forty-six in the *Billboard* charts.

Madonna took some adventurous musical steps with Dave Hall, creating the grainy neo-soul of "I'd Rather Be Your Lover." The song was augmented with a bluesy rap by the neo-soul artist Me'shell Ndegeocello. A lesbian bass player and songwriter with cropped hair and cool tones, Ndegeocello was one of the first signings to the Maverick label. Andre Betts introduced her to Madonna after the *Erotica* album came out, and the latter didn't waste any time signing her up. Ndegeocello's 1993 debut album *Plantation Lullabies* helped to pave the way for a new organic soul movement of such 90s artists as India.Arie and Erykah Badu. Using the image of the plantation as a metaphor for modern-day ghetto life, Ndegeocello said, somewhat earnestly, "My lullabies are the calm before the revolution of the people of color." She wasn't as successful as Maverick's later signing, Alanis Morissette, but Ndegeocello gave the label some cool credibility.

Though Madonna was anxious to make an impact in this burgeoning soul market, her work with top R&B producers underscored her vocal limitations. At this stage, her voice just wasn't powerful enough to hold and bend those deep, soulful notes. There are moments on *Bedtime Stories* where she sounds unsure and tentative, as if she is trying to get acquainted with the new self that's emerging. Needing another flavor to expand the album, she looked to the United Kingdom, where club and dub sounds were being fused by acts like Björk, Massive Attack, and Soul II Soul. Brilliant studio remixer Nellee Hooper had written and produced for all three. "He has a very European sensibility, which I appreciate," Madonna noted, and brought him to L.A. for her album.

So began her journey with English studio wizards: via their electronic textures, she found the perfect setting for her voice. Along with Nellee Hooper, Madonna hired his right-hand man, the programmer/producer Marius De Vries. "I'd always been interested in sound design and poking around with old machinery and plugging in patch chords," says De Vries, an ex–Saint Paul's choirboy who ran a reggae sound system before hooking up with Hooper and becoming part of Björk's team in the early 90s. When he and Hooper came to work on tracks for *Bedtime Stories*, there was slight trepidation at the number of producers already on board.

"It was very much a multiproducer record. Nellee and myself had to stay conscious of who else was working on it, and be speaking the same language," De Vries told me. Opposed to the "variety pack" approach, Madonna was determined to make her album as seamless as possible. Some suggested that already there were too many cooks. "No, because the cooks weren't all in the room at the same time," De Vries demurs. "But one had to be careful the thing didn't end up sounding too unfocused. I don't think there was a lot of communication between the various producers at the time of making it. It was to Madonna's credit that she kept an overview, and the album ended up sounding relatively coherent."

The sessions with Hooper and De Vries took place that summer at Chappell Studios in Encino, California. On the first day of the session, De Vries mistook Madonna for the cleaning lady. "I was at the studio early to set up my stuff. I hadn't put my contact lenses in so I was a little bit blurry-eyed. I stumbled into the place, started plugging things in, and there was this girl sitting in the corner of the room. I went, 'Oh, hi' (very noncommittal), and carried on setting up. I didn't realize Madonna liked to get there quite so early. It took us about half an hour to disentangle that first misunderstanding!" laughs De Vries. "She was very charming and forgiving and actually quite enjoyed it. She has a sense of humor."

Hooper produced three tracks on the album. First was "Survival," a lush, summery song that captured her state of mind—she was burned by the *Sex* backlash, but she had still kept her self-belief intact. This was followed by "Inside of Me," a "missing you" love song, by turns arrogant and vulnerable, about keeping face and saving face. And "Bedtime Story," a minimal trance track with deep, bubbling beats and lyrics about a journey into the subconscious. It was written for her by Björk. Madonna had been eager to meet and work with the alternative Icelandic star, but Björk preferred to keep her distance. "I had written the song specially for her, but my intuition told me that it would be wrong for me to sing on the song," Björk said. "I also refused to meet her officially when she asked. When I meet her, I want it to be by coincidence, when we're both drunk in a bar or something." Friends close to Björk say that she was perturbed when Madonna began working with members of her own production team—Hooper, De Vries, and, later, Guy Sigsworth. The truth is, Björk is unique; there was no danger of Madonna sounding like her.

Still, "Bedtime Story" was a vivid track that foreshadowed Madonna's move toward electronica. "That was a very brave choice," says De Vries. "Although it wasn't a Björk cover version, Björk has such a particular and idiosyncratic approach to the construction of lyrics and phrasing. Every aspect of the architecture of her writing is distinctly Björkian. To try to perform one of those songs is a brave undertaking. It's difficult for the singer to be infected by the way the lyric is so stamped with Björk's approach to language. Having said that, Madonna captured the atmosphere of it beautifully." Tackling that song seemed to set something free in Madonna. "She was straining at the leash a little bit, to find some other languages to speak," suggests De Vries. "'Bedtime Story' was an embryonic moment that went a lot further on the next few albums."

It also caused a swing in her popularity in Europe. Released as a single, the track didn't dent the U.S. top forty, but it went top five in the United Kingdom and became a huge dance-club hit, with remixes by Orbital and Junior Vasquez. It also inspired one of her most experimental and expensive videos. Shot by Mark Romanek for a reputed $5 million, it was a Daliesque epic in which Madonna floats through the air, gives birth to doves, lies on a surreal operating table, and has her eyes and mouth switched, Frida Kahlo–style. Strongly influenced by Remedios Varo's painting *The Lovers*, the video entered the portals of high art, screened in art galleries and kept in the permanent collection at London's Museum of the Moving Image.

The collaboration with Nellee Hooper seemed to add something to Madonna's aesthetic. She was so pleased with their tracks that she had him remix ones laid down by other producers—such as "Forbidden Love" and "Sanctuary." "She appreciated Nellee's sure-footed approach to building rhythms, and his sense of space and spaciousness," explains De Vries. "She likes attention to detail and good craftsmanship, and demands that. If you can prove yourself to her in that respect, she'll respond well."

De Vries was also struck by the fact that it took them just two and a half weeks to construct, record, and mix five tracks. "That's remarkable for a major artist. I was amazed at how quick the process could be, and how decisive one had to be under those circumstances. You had to make strong decisions and not second-guess yourself too much. It was a very focused process. 'Forbidden Love,' for instance, was done and dusted in two days. You have to have a special mind-set when you're working that fast. I'd construct something that was fairly close to how it would sound and then she'd sing it in a few takes. Madonna's rarely unsure about the sounds she wants." By contrast, a U2 record could take two years, "and then no decisions will have been made until the last minute. That's a different way of approaching it—drafting and redrafting. Madonna is much more Hitchcockian—I'll only shoot what I need."

When it was released in October 1994, *Bedtime Stories* received mixed reviews. *Rolling Stone's* Barbara O'Dair praised its "lush soul and creamy balladry," yet she added that the "Express Yourself" message "comes not with a bang but a whimper." And Mat Snow at Q magazine condemned the album as "tepid," saying that despite the input of top producers, "the girl remains obstinately and perversely recessed. It's as if the whole body of her voice has been electronically filtered out to leave only its outline. For all the inventiveness of production . . . the star of the show seems to have faded to processed featheriness."

What reviewers picked up on was Madonna in retreat. Still smarting from criticism over the *Sex* book, she was evolving a softer, gentler image. Yet despite the pastel tones of her new look, there was also a sense of grit. She combined this, strikingly, with the video for "Secret," the first single from her new album. Shot in black-and-white in Harlem, the video portrays Madonna as a 1950s-style nightclub jazz singer in a mixed-race relationship. Intercut with scenes of "street" people, misfits, and freaks, it is one of her most distinctive videos. Madonna knew that a lot was riding on her first release after *Erotica*, and she wanted to create a startling effect.

"She was ready to go there. At the time she wanted to bring it down a little, instead of the glamour glamour," the video's director, Melodie McDaniel, told me. "Madonna had a blond Jean Harlow look at the time. I wanted to combine that old classic Hollywood mix with the edginess of modern contemporary, but make it feel timeless. I was trying to think of something different, something real."

Madonna's choice of director was astute. A young Jewish and African-American graduate from the prestigious Art Center College of Design in Pasadena, McDaniel was an aspiring photojournalist,

who liked to work with a "Cassavetes approach," bringing people together and documenting the results. Her compelling images led to her
being signed to Propaganda, a production company with a Bauhaus
mixture of art and commercial work, which launched careers of such
directors as its cofounder David Fincher. McDaniel had done only
two videos—for bands Porno for Pyros and the Cranberries—when
Madonna approached her. But what Madonna was most interested
in was one of McDaniel's early short films, where she staged a scenario of a baptism combined with voodoo, in the style of 1940s avant-
garde filmmaker Maya Deren. This film later was projected on giant
screens on Madonna's 2001 Drowned World tour. "She was drawn to
the rawness of my work," recalls McDaniel.

Though flattered by Madonna's attention, she was also terrified.
"It was awesome I got this break. I went to meet her and she said,
'Give me your references, I wanna see what you want to do.' I was
blown away by the song 'Secret,' and found it inspiring, but I was
freaked out. I was jumping from young artists to working with an icon."
McDaniel presented Madonna with pictures by some of her favorite
1970s photographers, like Bill Burke, "who took pictures of people
from the South, most people might think of as freaks or inbred. I was
drawn to these images, a certain feel." She also showed Madonna *East
100 Street*, a book of photos shot in Spanish Harlem by controversial
70s photographer Bruce Davidson.

"She likes you to bring her stuff for inspiration. She was drawn to
those books. That was enough for her," says McDaniel. Madonna let
the director stay at her New York apartment on Central Park West
for a week, to do research. "She bought a couple of my photographs
before I did the video, and when I went to her beautiful apartment,
they were hanging on her wall next to some pictures of Muhammad
Ali and a few Frida Kahlos. She wasn't in town; she said, 'Look at my
reference books, use what you want.' She had lots of books on paint-
ers, books by Helmut Newton and Richard Avedon. I didn't realize
what a voracious reader she was. She was incredibly bright. I had this
idea that pop stars were, not exactly lazy, but they'd sit around being

the artist and let everyone do everything for them. Madonna runs the show. She does her research well."

Madonna was happy to work with a few people from McDaniel's team, including a young stylist called Brigitte Echols. "I was never into doing celebrity things. At that time, there was a Herb Ritts kind of thing in videos—not a lot of emotion and depth. I came from a punk background, not a pop background 'at all. I didn't want to do Madonna, but I'd go to the ends of the earth for Melanie," remembers Echols. "Next thing, I'm driving up to Madonna's gorgeous house in Hollywood. It's early 1900s Spanish style. I enter the house through an underground tunnel and go up in an elevator. The first thing I see is a Frida Kahlo's painting. I can see she appreciates art, it's not just a rich person's trashy home."

The next scene is etched on Echols's memory. "It was eleven in the morning and the house was full of light. Her assistant says, 'Madonna will be down in a minute.' Then Madonna appears at the top of the stairs, freshly showered, in a white sheer dress. You could just see her rose-pink nipples and panties through it, and she looked absolutely gorgeous. She was so sweet and nice. Her first words were: 'What were you thinking of putting me in?'"

In preparation, Echols had gone to a low-rent mall called Crenshaw Swap Meet and had a gold necklace made with the name MADONNA on it. "It cost $180, with a teeny diamond chip, and it came in a cheap jewelry box. Her eyes lit up when she saw the jewelry box. She opened it up—she was like a child who'd got the best present— and she said, 'It's lovely. Could I have it a little bigger?' It was so nice to find her something that she didn't already have."

They sat on her living-room floor and Madonna chose swatches of material she liked. Echols then had an $80 skirt and $50 top made up at her local dry cleaners, plus vintage clothes she had picked up from costume houses, a La Perla bra, and one or two pieces by budding designer Marc Jacobs. "She didn't know who Marc Jacobs was, but she could see the *value* of what it was," recalls Echols. "She knows clothes. That woman knows clothes."

McDaniel and her team scouted out suitably scuzzy locations for the video, doing street-casting—a naturalistic approach that was later copied by countless directors and designers, including Calvin Klein. Wanting to capture a low-rent, speakeasy feel, they assembled a striking cast of offbeat "nonmodel" characters, from transvestites to card tricksters and edgy Harlem teenagers. So far so good, but when it came to the actual shoot, McDaniel had a baptism by fire. "I like the voyeuristic thing—just let the cameras roll and improvise. No, Madonna wanted direction, direction, direction," recalls McDaniel. "She was sitting there; I was waiting for her to be natural. I'd call, 'Action,' and she'd sit there saying, slightly impatiently, 'What am I doing? What am I *doing*? Hello?' I felt a bit frazzled." Madonna had sailed into Harlem with a fabulous, decadent entourage of Hollywood trucks, trailers, and security. Even Donatella Versace stopped by for a visit. "When it all rolled up, I remember thinking, Oh my God. I tried to give direction to some of her creative team, and they just kind of looked at me like, Yeah," McDaniel says.

Overawed by the entourage, she was too shy to tell Madonna that she wanted her raw around the edges, like Jennifer Jason Leigh's prostitute character in *Last Exit to Brooklyn*. "When she came out of the trailer, her team had made her look very mild and glamorous, with no edge. All clean and neat and safe. I didn't communicate clearly enough what I wanted. We did a take. Then I remember pulling Madonna to the side and explaining. She was really annoyed. 'Why the fuck didn't you tell me?' she said, 'Wasting all this time!' They went back into the trailer, her team rolling their eyes. It was so painful. I felt humiliated, but it was my fault, I should've spoken up."

Madonna had her hair and makeup redone, and the result is the famously sleazy, romantic image that appears in the video. Her creative team loved it, and so did she. "I realized that she's game for anything, and I should have really pushed it, really driven it home," says McDaniel. "I've seen her be hard on people, but it wasn't being mean. There's no room for dilly-dallying around. She gave me a wake-up call."

Echols has a more prosaic memory of the shoot. "The first scene has

Madonna walking down the street in Harlem. Fatima, the assistant director, had a great black leather coat on, with a fur trim, She said, 'Wow, that's a great coat!' and ended up wearing it. Then she comes out of her trailer. The guy's done her hair. I don't know where that hair fucking dude came from. It was all tight pin curls, such a *hairdo*. Not Mel's deal, it's gotta look natural. We felt intimidated by these fancy makeup people. Celebs have their people become a wall around them. That's the only time we felt separation. We weren't sure how to express ourselves in this situation." When the misunderstanding was straightened out, though, each side appreciated the other.

Echols noted the close relationship Madonna had with her director of photography. "All famous beautiful film women know their DP. They have to trust them entirely. Madonna knew how to make everything work right—the lighting, the angles, how to play with the camera. She knows what looks good on her. She has a beautiful body, she can do different kinds of looks, she has that composure. She's fascinated by all the different things she can be, she can see herself in many ways." Echols sees Madonna's approach to style as collaborative. "We had ideas about the outfit. She agreed to it and made it work. She wore the necklace for a year after that. And we saw photos of her in the outfit we'd made at Crown Cleaners."

Echols gets irritated when people claim Madonna is not so beautiful in person. "That's bullshit. She's luminous. Marilyn Monroe had it. It's a quality that reacts with film and takes on its own life." She recalls seeing her at the Propaganda offices one day, dressed like Jean Harlow. "I didn't know her then, and I said, 'Who is that woman?' She had on a big coat, heels, sunglasses, and platinum-blond hair. She looked like a movie star from the 30s. Amazing." Six months after Echols worked with Madonna, the star was on the cover of the U.K. *Sunday Times* magazine, looking the epitome of high glamour in a shimmering Versace gown, with platinum hair and eyebrows dyed blond. Madonna was fond of Gianni Versace. The charismatic Italian saw himself as a tailor rather than a designer; he was inspired by Andy Warhol and abstract art, and used Madonna as a muse for his creations. But there was something eerily prescient about the *Sunday*

Times cover. Under the headline MADONNA FALLS FOR VERSACE, she lies spread-eagled on a flight of steps, as if she is dead. Two years later, Versace was gunned down on the steps of his Miami beachfront mansion. Madonna mourned his death, and it is notable that she never really went back to that high-octane Monroe-style glamour again.

THE "SECRET" video was a huge hit, replayed endlessly on MTV, while the single went top five worldwide. McDaniel and Madonna stayed friends, working on a few more ideas together. "She has an entourage of people, but she brings you in," says McDaniel. "You go to great places, not just fabulous places—she'd take us to some unknown underground club and just go for it. She loves new discoveries. She knows how to live in both places. It was genuine." McDaniel doesn't view Madonna's impulse as vampiric. "I didn't feel that at all. Everyone is influenced by everyone. You can take something and make it your own."

Madonna gave McDaniel a copy of *Push*, a hard-hitting novel about childhood abuse, by New York writer Sapphire. The two of them wanted to develop it as a feature-film idea, but Sapphire wasn't interested. Madonna presented a large package with McDaniel's show reel, and got Russell Simmons involved. Sapphire's response was: "Absolutely not, I don't want to have anything to do with Hollywood." McDaniel collaborated again on a fateful photo shoot for *Vibe* magazine, with star basketball player Dennis Rodman. "They were flirting and they wanted to meet. He came to her house in Miami. It was challenging to me to figure out how to make them look real and natural and different. I scouted a neighborhood in Little Havana. It was very raw: the people from the neighborhood didn't even recognize her. It was a little run-down. I snapped them being playful and cuddling, but it later all went sour."

The photo story never ended up in *Vibe* magazine, and Madonna's affair with Rodman became one of her biggest regrets. But when they first got together, there was an intense physical attraction. Rodman shared her flair for getting attention. The six-foot-six-inch player had a penchant for flamboyant cross-dressing, and once he appeared at a function in a coffin, like the 50s rock 'n' roller Screamin' Jay Hawkins. At first, Madonna appreciated Rodman's style.

"Basketball players to Madonna are like ballet dancers or any kind of dancer . . . graceful and elegant. Very sleek," he claimed in his autobiography *Bad as I Wanna Be*. "Athletes are a real turn-on for her because she appreciates anybody who can move with such fluid motions. Madonna's a connoisseur of bodies. She studies them and watches them closely." According to the indiscreet Rodman, Madonna hounded him for several months, viewing him as a perfect physical specimen, and a potential husband and father. "I think Madonna was getting some good lovin'," said her friend Niki Haris. "I think Madonna might've got turned on by the brother!" But the relationship soon fizzled out. Hurt by the fact that Rodman gossiped about her in his book, Madonna was judiciously brief in public—the chapter about her, she claimed, had "made-up dialogue that even a bad porno writer would not take credit for"—while remarking in private that he wasn't that great in bed, and the affair was short-lived anyway. "I feel exploited once again by someone I trusted and let into my life," she said.

What their affair highlighted was her vulnerability. Now in her mid-30s, Madonna was anxious to have children. In an elusive search for Mr. Right, she had brief relationships with various unlikely men. She even had a dalliance with rapper Tupac Shakur, the year before he was killed in a drive-by shooting in Las Vegas. "I went to a restaurant with her that was full of black rappers," says Alison Clarkson, formerly U.K. singer Betty Boo. "Tupac Shakur sat with us for a bit. She was going out with him, but then it came to an end, because homegirls were saying to him, 'I can't believe you're going out with a white girl.' She was open about the fact she'd been dumped."

It was in the summer of 1994 that Madonna met a more promising partner, Cuban-American fitness trainer Carlos Leon. She'd noticed him jogging in Central Park and arranged an introduction via her assistant. The affair grew slowly, away from the limelight. Though an aspiring actor, Leon was a proud, private man, wary of Madonna's superstar friends. She enjoyed meeting his parents, a hardworking couple living in a modest East 91st Street apartment, and going on anonymous dates with him to Lincoln Center and Central Park. For a while, she could make believe this was just a normal relationship. Here was someone she could have been at school with. Many people called him "sweet," while Tobias Nunez, a friend from high school, remembered Leon as "a nerdy guy; he was very straitlaced . . . shy and innocent." Despite this, Leon had a hint of Latin machismo in his temperament, and didn't relish playing second fiddle to Madonna the star. "Carlos was lovely, but unfortunately met her when she was in the realm of 'I want to be a superstar, but you gotta treat me as any other girl you'd date.' It was confusing. She'd want him to be 'normal,' then say, 'I'm flying to London tonight and you should come too,'" recalls Niki Haris.

LEON'S DEDICATION was severely tested when Madonna took on one of the most high-profile film roles of the 90s, that of Eva Peron in the movie *Evita*. It had taken over fifteen years for Tim Rice and Andrew Lloyd Webber's hit 1978 musical to be turned into a Hollywood film. Plans had passed through the hands of a number of directors, including Oliver Stone and Ken Russell, along with a host of possible leading ladies, from Meryl Streep to Michelle Pfeiffer. "For years we never got the right team together," recalls lyricist and coproducer Tim Rice. "Studios were suspicious about musicals on film—they felt they were more successful on stage. By the mid-80s things went cold, but it perked up in the early 90s, and that was largely because Madonna showed an interest."

When the project finally got underway with British director Alan Parker at the helm, Pfeiffer was a firm favorite for the lead part. An avid fan of musicals, Madonna had been obsessed with the role for years, and didn't want this one to slip through her fingers. She felt that this could rehabilitate her battered movie reputation. She managed to convince Tim Rice that she was born to do the part. "I was always pro the idea of Madonna," he told me. "I didn't want a conventional film actress. I wanted someone accustomed to putting over a story and emotion in song. Madonna acts so beautifully through music. Better actresses, like Meryl Streep, weren't right because they're not singers. They can hold a tune, but they're not brilliant *interpreters* of songs. I wanted Elaine Page at first, but she was too old by the time we got the film together."

With Rice on board, Madonna just had to convince a wary Alan Parker—so she sat down over Christmas 1994 and wrote him a four-page letter, explaining why she was passionate about the part. She claimed that as she wrote the letter, "it was as if some other force drove my hand across the page." Thanks to Rice's petitioning, and the fact that Pfeiffer had just had a baby and was therefore unavailable for the grueling film schedule, Madonna landed the role. Andrew Lloyd Webber was still unconvinced about her ability to sing the part, so she enlisted the help of esteemed voice coach Joan Lader to develop her vocal technique.

Those sessions in Lader's Manhattan apartment paid off. Lader taught Madonna how to sing from her diaphragm rather than her throat (strange that it took the star so long to grasp that, even though she had been touring for years). She learned how to project in a much more structured way. Every night Madonna would go home, thrilled at the sounds she could create. She would call friends and sing to them over the phone at full volume. By the time she arrived for soundtrack rehearsals at CTS Studios in London that September, she felt confident that her performance would be up to snuff. The first day of recording, however, was a bewildering experience. She was used to singing in the intimate surroundings of a studio, with one producer and maybe a couple of musicians. On what Alan Parker later dubbed "Black Monday," Madonna had to sing "Don't Cry for Me, Argentina," the most difficult song in the musical, in front of Andrew Lloyd Webber and an eighty-four-piece orchestra. Not surprisingly, she felt unprepared. This was an environment that she couldn't control, that had a completely different protocol and set of expectations. The sheer scale of the operation was so intimidating that she found it difficult to perform.

By the end of the day, Madonna was distressed and tearful. "I was so nervous," she said later. An emergency meeting with Lloyd Webber and Parker was called, at which it was agreed that she'd record her vocals in a smaller studio, and the orchestrations would be done elsewhere. Recording was a painstaking process, with the cast working for four months before the soundtrack was complete. But the result, a seamless combination of gung ho musical theater, pop, and proficient musicianship, was worth the effort.

On this record, the sweetness and power of Madonna's voice comes out as never before. It is displayed to best effect on tracks of the young Evita, like "Oh What a Circus" and "Buenos Aires," where she could inject some of her pop funkiness. Where she comes slightly unstuck is the later songs—on "I'd Be Surprisingly Good for You," for instance, her duet with Jonathan Pryce, she gives a pulpy, romantic reading, ignoring the scheming, manipulative side of Evita's character. Then on "A New Argentina," the track where Evita is proselytizing in front of the workers, Madonna's limitations are exposed. What's needed here is a rich, operatic voice, but in contrast to the mass choir, hers comes across as bare and one-dimensional. And there is the party piece itself, "Don't Cry for Me, Argentina," delivered with a sense of vulnerability rather than strength. But despite the lack of emotional complexity in her voice, Madonna still makes it a compelling show tune. Right up to its grand orchestral finale, she gives it her all. This is her perfect moment, the one that she has been understudying for her whole life. For Madonna, this was a point where everything came together—song, film, and a major starring role.

There is also pathos in the way she sings "You Must Love Me," a completely new addition to the musical. It was Rice's stab at an Oscar, because one can only win an Academy Award for a new song. Madonna's reaction to the song was typical of the way she lobbied throughout to have a more sympathetic portrayal of Eva Peron. Alan Parker intended to emphasize in the film the shrewd manipulator, who connived her way to success, whereas Madonna, overidentifying with the part and concerned about her own image, wanted to project a softer, quieter strength. In many scenes, she got her way, but with this song, she lost out. "'You Must Love Me' was written and rewritten five or six times," recalls Rice. "I remember taking lyrics to Madonna and she was trying to change them. Her view was that Peron loved Eva, but my view was more cynical. The scene can be interpreted in different ways, but my lyrics were kept, thank God!"

THOUGH SHE performed well for the soundtrack recording, Madonna still had to fight feelings of inadequacy. In an attempt to prove herself, she launched into a month of assiduous research, becoming a virtual ambassador for *Evita*. She delved deep into the story of Eva Peron. Born Eva Maria Duarte, in 1922, the first lady of Argentina was an illegitimate child from a poverty-stricken background. In her teens, she left her rural town and went to Buenos Aires to "make it," scratching a living as a prostitute before becoming an actress. By her twenties, she was well known for her portrayal of self-sacrificing, patriotic heroines. She met and soon married Colonel Juan Peron, then minister of labor for the military regime. When he was ousted from that post and arrested in 1945, Evita encouraged the unions to strike for his release, and to back his presidential bid the following year.

A valuable aid in his campaign for popular support, Evita was a national inspirational figure. A highly glamorous woman, she mixed Dior with politics, and campaigned for women's suffrage. She initiated welfare reforms and was the frontwoman for the Social Aid Fund, a massive program of public spending. Although Evita was elevated to near-sainthood after her death from cancer in 1952, there was ambivalence about the way she exploited her fame and wealth and her working-class origins. She was despised by the ruling class, who considered her an upstart, and violently opposed by the army, who were suspicious of a woman in politics. Undoubtedly, Madonna saw parallels with her own experience, her picture of Evita fitting some of the more grandiose notions she had about herself.

Because of this, *Evita* is one of Madonna's better roles. Filming began in February 1996, with a $55 million budget and a cast that included Antonio Banderas as revolutionary leader Che Guevara and Jonathan Pryce as Juan Peron. In the first half of the movie, Madonna makes an effortless good-time girl; she is less convincing as a political leader, rousing the workers with bouts of self-conscious brow-furrowing. Toward the end, though, she comes into her own, portraying Evita's deteriorating health with a real sense of sadness. It's here that her research paid off.

In a journal she kept for *Vanity Fair* magazine, she details how Peron was so revolted by the smell of his wife's cancer that he would wave to her from the bedroom door but refuse to come in. Aware of how important she was to his popularity, Peron decided that he would put her body on display after her death. Before she died, Evita was injected with chemicals to preserve her organs and flesh, and not allowed painkillers that interfered with the process. "I can only imagine how she must have suffered," wrote Madonna. She dreamed of Evita. "I was not outside watching her, I was her. I felt her sadness and her restlessness. I felt hungry and unsatisfied and in a hurry." Throughout the strenuous filming schedule in Argentina, Budapest, and London, Madonna came to realize why Evita lived at such a feverish pace. "She wanted her life to matter."

What also gave depth to Madonna's portrayal was the experience of her mother's death. When acting the hospital-bed scenes, she imagined how her mother must have felt when her father told her she was dying, and this brought on floods of tears. Madonna painfully missed her real mother on Mother's Day, and bonded closely with her screen mother. "Her English is as good as my Spanish, but we speak the language of hurt people, so all is understood." The actress, Victoria Sus, told her about a dream she'd had, where Madonna was a child pressing her head against her belly and saying she wanted to go back inside her womb. "If only she knew how close to the truth this is," wrote Madonna.

While filming *Evita*, she discovered she was pregnant with Carlos Leon's baby. This gave an added charge to her performance. There was a potent irony in the scene where she dances as Evita in an empty ballroom with Banderas's character, and falls to the ground, clutching her cancer-ridden womb. At the time she was over three months pregnant, trying desperately to disguise her shape. By contrast with the character she was playing, snuggled within Madonna was a new life, her baby daughter. She writes of an afternoon off, when she had gone riding for the first time at a very slow trot. With remarkable prescience, she says: "I imagined myself galloping through the countryside at full speed without a care in the world, the wind in my hair. I thought to myself, I could have this life if I wanted it. Children and a husband waiting to have lunch with me."

Madonna said after the filming: "My life will never be the same." *Evita* marked a transitional point. When it was released in December 1996, the film was a box-office success. It was also critically acclaimed, earning Rice and Lloyd Webber that coveted Oscar for "You Must Love Me," and a Golden Globe Award for Madonna. For some of her fans, though, *Evita* was a perplexing move—a straight, decorative role in a mainstream musical, miles away from the subversive undertow of *Erotica* and *Bedtime Stories*. But the role reflected a side of Madonna that needed to be fulfilled and understood. Finally, she felt she had proved herself as an actress. And finally, too, she would become a mother.

Book Three
ABSOLUTION

BITS AND ZEROES
AND ONES

ON OCTOBER 14, 1996, MADONNA'S DAUGHTER, LOURDES (Lola), was born at the Good Samaritan Hospital in Los Angeles. Soon after the birth, her relationship with Carlos Leon foundered, fueling rumors that he had been a mere sperm donor. Madonna was indignant. "There is speculation that I used the father as a stud service, implying that I am not capable of having a real relationship," she said. "It's just all part of the view the media likes to have of me. . . . That I don't have any feelings and I don't really care for people. That I'm just ambitious, cold, and calculating."

The truth was that, although Madonna was fond of Leon, she felt he wasn't the life partner she desired. She found him jealous and possessive, particularly of her friendship with Ingrid Casares. He, meanwhile, chafed at her fame and her career, which would always relegate him to second place. When Lola was seven months old, they parted ways, and Leon granted Madonna sole custody of the baby. Leon went on to pursue an acting career but has maintained strong ties with his daughter. Feeling that the father had an important nurturing role to play, Madonna allowed him to see Lola from the start, and has encouraged them to develop a close relationship.

Having a child transformed her life, bringing out a gentler, more compassionate side to her personality. It also gave her work a new kind of emotional depth. Madonna christened the baby Lourdes, because she felt her daughter would be a healing influence on her life. "Lourdes was a place that my mother had a connection to. People were always sending her holy water from there. She wanted to go there but never did." With the birth of her daughter, Madonna continued her own Marian cult tradition in naming her Lourdes.

At the time of Madonna's birth in the late 50s, U.S. Catholicism was undergoing a growth spurt with a huge expansion of churches and convents. It was also at the height of a booming Marian cult in America. Each May, millions of Catholic schoolchildren, college students, and parishioners marched in processions to honor the Virgin during her sacred month. They decorated maypoles, crowned statues with flowers, sang hymns, and recited prayers together. A form of popular Catholicism, Marian devotion was a "lived religion" that came from village-centered European immigrants, such as Madonna's Italian grandparents.

As theologian Paula M. Kane writes, "Catholics believed that Mary would intercede with Jesus to answer their wishes, cure their diseases, secure employment, find them spouses, and protect their children." By the 1950s, Mary had come to represent conservative ideals of womanhood. In the Cold War era, she also stood for nationhood and the papacy, with Catholic women encouraged to be models of virtue, to counter the godless influence of the "Red Dragon of Russia."

Mary symbolized spiritual purity and self-sacrifice. Periodicals such as *Immaculate Heart Crusades* and *Our Lady's Digest* focused on Marian crafts and etiquette, with features like "Do-It-Yourself Madonna" and "Here's How to Make a Simple Marian Shrine." Part of Madonna Sr.'s schoolgirl reading would also have been Saint Francis de Sales's *Introduction to the Devout Life*, a seventeenth-century Catholic text that contained instructions on how to preserve one's chastity and purify the soul. Under such strict moral codes, Madonna Sr. would have found her daughter's pursuit of sexual expression deeply shocking. She would feel she had failed in some way. Maybe the explicit nature of Madonna's work was a rejection of all her mother stood for. Maybe in her eyes, all that daily devotion and modesty didn't do any good, because it hadn't kept her mother alive. Madonna's reaction to her mother's piety was radical, choosing to cut off identification with her from the start. "If she were alive, I would be someone else, I would be a completely different person," she once said.

But having a daughter made Madonna see her mother in a new way, and it also reestablished a connection with religion. She experienced a kind of resurrection, and part of this was her interest in Kabbalah. Madonna has said that while she was pregnant with Lola, she felt she should have something to teach her daughter. In the same way that Madonna Sr. handed down the Catholic faith to her daughter, Madonna felt she needed a faith to pass on to Lola. "What should I tell her about life?" She had been practicing yoga, reading the *Bhagavad Gita*, and taking an interest in Hinduism. This was enhanced by the latest man in her life, the young aspiring screenwriter Andy Bird. A tall, thin Englishman with pre-Raphaelite hair, Bird introduced her to yoga and Eastern mysticism. She met him through director Alex Keshishian, and the two had a passionate relationship that led to her spending some time in London, living with Bird in a rented house in Chelsea. Madonna began to dress like Bird, in a looser, more free-flowing style. She went with him to hip but casual places like the Metropolitan Bar and Nobu, and took yoga classes at the Innergy Center in northwest London. Although eager to downsize her life at this point, she was still superstar enough to cause a distraction. A leading instructor at the yoga center was apparently so disenchanted with the kerfuffle that surrounded Madonna every time she came, he asked her to go elsewhere.

Andy Bird helped to initiate her search for the divine, but it wasn't until one evening in 1996 when she went with Sandra Bernhard to the Kabbalah Center in Beverly Hills that her world lit up. Here she found a system of belief that not only fitted her life but transformed it.

Kabbalah was to inspire the album *Ray of Light*, and frame every-thing Madonna did from then on. Derived from an ancient Judaic philosophy, Kabbalah is about reaching higher states of consciousness through reflection and meditation. It is about rigorously setting aside the ego to effect change in oneself and the world. Having spent several decades immersed in the material world, Madonna was ready to undertake a kind of spiritual rebirth.

WITH HER next album, she tore up the rule book, and, in the same way she could move dramatically from one persona to the next, she essentially tore up the old life. *Ray of Light* had quiet beginnings. Early in 1997, when Lola was just a few months old, Madonna began casting about for collaborators. She began writing with Pat Leonard again, and also approached songwriter Rick Nowells. A musician with early 80s New Wave bands in San Francisco, Nowells cut his songwriting teeth with Stevie Nicks, and made a name for himself writing huge hits for Belinda Carlisle, as well as Celine Dion's best song, "Falling into You." Initially, it seemed, Madonna wanted to go for a big pop sound. "She invited me over to her house to check me out," recalls Nowells. "She let me hold Lola. I had a three-year-old boy at the time, so I was in that space." Their shared experiences as new parents, as well as his songwriting skills, helped Nowells to get the job.

They met again in late April for a two-week songwriting session at his modest studio in the Hollywood Hills. "Madonna would drive up by herself every day at three p.m., walk in the door, chat for a few minutes, and then get to work. I played keyboards and she sat on the couch with a mike and her lyric book. She'd be improvising melodies, I'd be writing chords. She'd jot down lyrical ideas, or have some ready. Before I worked with Madonna, I never believed you could get a song together in an hour, but she would channel it. We'd have a melody within half an hour. She would always leave bang-on seven p.m. to go to see Lola, but we'd always have a song written and demoed. We wrote nine songs in ten days."

Nowells is adamant that though they worked at such a pace, Madonna didn't stint on quality. "She's a real artist. She understands how to channel and compose a song. It's not just jamming melodies.

She understands what a chorus and verse should do, where to put a bridge, how to work her melodies." When they wrote the song "The Power of Goodbye," for instance, he was struck by her lyric-writing. "It was deep, poetic, and intelligent. When she's on and at her best, she's on a par with Joni Mitchell or Paul Simon," he enthuses. The economy and elegance of her writing, especially on this album, was a reflection of her voracious reading. She took particular inspiration from Shakespeare's sonnets and spare, provocative 60s female poets like Sylvia Plath and Anne Sexton.

Nowells describes "The Power of Goodbye," a meditation on ending, as "a beautiful poem. I was knocked out. Touched. I had a jungle drum beat, a soft pad sound and some minor chords that she jammed to. Later in the studio William Orbit cut the jungle beat in half and morphed it into a reggae beat, so it ended up with a different feel." As each day passed, they explored new genres, trying out varied textures. It wasn't always straightforward. One day they spent hours struggling with one idea—Nowells had a soundtrack sample from the cult German 70s film *Vampyros Lesbos*. "Madonna liked it, thought it was a cool title, and good to create something around the sample from this weird, freako film." By six o'clock, however, they had to admit it wasn't working. "I was panicking a bit, I wanted to have a good day," recalls Nowells. "Then I just started playing three chords, and Madonna started singing. I followed her, and the rest was stream of consciousness."

The result was "Little Star," a warm, loving lullaby to her daughter. Probably because it was approaching the witching hour of seven p.m., Lola was on her mind. Madonna had spent all afternoon away from the baby and missed her. Within the hour, she and Nowells had a complete demo, a song that expressed some of the awe and overwhelming love that a new mother feels for her baby. Inspired by the moment, Madonna sang of how much hope and healing this new bond held out for her. The tenderness of the song also made a deep impression on Nowells.

"The next day I was driving to the studio and played back the demo in my car. I started crying because it was so beautiful. It affected me—to be able to create a song about a child that was so moving and carefully expressed."

The other song they cowrote for the album was "To Have and Not to Hold." Nowells wanted to create a beat around a Latin samba feel. "The verse came quickly—Madonna had it prepared—but I was struggling with the chorus. I got lost in the key relationships, and was having difficulty with the B-flat minor." For inspiration, they listened to the music of Brazilian artist Astrud Gilberto. There was something in her technique, the subtly shifting modulations and re-mote harmonic leaps, that unlocked the puzzle for them. "Then I got the right chords, and we went on to finish the song. That was on our first day. You never know when you jump in with somebody. Early on you have to make things happen—a lot was tied to how successful we were that day. I was so pleased we ended up with this track that sounded smart, elegant, and European."

Madonna also cowrote some songs with Kenneth "Babyface" Ed-monds, but they were abandoned because, according to him, they had a "'Take a Bow'–ish kind of vibe and Madonna didn't want, or need, to repeat herself." The favorite to oversee the album was William Wainwright (aka William Orbit), then a relative unknown who had emerged from the underground U.K. rave scene. Seven years earlier, he had done a memorably atmospheric remix of "Justify My Love," and Madonna felt that Orbit could take her music into a totally new direction, giving the album a coherence that *Bedtime Stories* had lacked.

Orbit came out of a scene that had changed the face of dance cul-ture. Acid house was described in Bill Brewster and Frank Broughton's groundbreaking book *Last Night a DJ Saved My Life* as: "weirdly, disrup-tively, creatively universal. In the sixties you could tune in, turn on and drop out, but only if you were a hip photographer or if daddy kept up the rent on the Kings Road flat. This time, a voyage of discovery was opened up to nearly everyone." Brewster and Broughton assert that it was a cultural revolution.

"You couldn't fully understand today's Britain without knowing the changes it brought. As [then–Prime Minister] Margaret Thatcher swept away the post-war community ideal and replaced it with the free market and its cult of selfish individualism, here was a youth movement that proposed the opposite. Here was music that meant little unless you shared it, and a drug that reminded its users that humanity's greatest achievements are social."

A key figure on the scene, Orbit had made a number of lush house tunes as Bassomatic and Torch Song, and, under the name Strange Cargo, released some ambient, instrumental albums. Although she always allied herself with clubland, the Ecstasy-fueled soundscape was one that Madonna had yet to incorporate into her music. She decided that Orbit's abstract beats and classical sweep would be the perfect setting for her new songs. "I love the haunting, trancelike quality of William's records," she said. "I've always found something melancholy about his music. Since I'm attracted to that sound, and since I tend to write a lot of sad songs, we seemed like a good match." She also later described her new album as one that would "sound great on drugs. It'll make you feel like you're in the K-hole. It whips you into a frenzy . . . You can imagine what it would be like to be high and listening to it."

The tall, gangly Orbit was an unlikely collaborator. A self-effacing English gent, he found musical inspiration in the psychedelic trance-like states of club culture. He took a lateral approach to music-making, more organic and less governed by the clock than Madonna was used to. "*Ray of Light* was exceptional because it did take a long time," says Marius De Vries, who was brought in to coproduce a number of tracks after his work on *Bedtime Stories*. "The gestation, which is very much Will's thing, was a long process."

The working relationship between Madonna and Orbit took a while to develop. Used to creating at his own pace, he was thrown by her need for control, while she bridled at what she saw as a lack of professionalism. When she first started working with him, she was shocked that he didn't have a flashy studio, just a small setup with an Akai sampler and a few keyboards. And when Orbit turned up at her house one day with the wrong DAT, he had to beg for a week in which to get properly organized. Feeling that she needed a safety net, a worried Madonna called up her old friend Pat Leonard, asking him to help out. Before long, though, she became more comfortable with Orbit's working process and changed her mind, acknowledging his "mad musical genius." Orbit insists that he didn't reinvent Madonna. "She's much more of a self-directed person than that," he said. "It was more that she produced me producing her. She turns me on to far more stuff than I do her." When they went to gay London nightclub Heaven to see techno mischief-maker Aphex Twin, that was her idea, not his.

Madonna wrote an apologetic letter to Leonard, saying that it was going to be all right and she wouldn't need him, because she and Orbit could do it alone. She had to follow her instinct, she said. She didn't know why, but she felt that this English eccentric was going to be very important for her career. Although four songs they had worked on would appear on the album, Leonard was to take a back seat as a producer. Leonard was purportedly very upset, especially when Madonna said afterward, somewhat dismissively, that he would've lent the songs "more of a Peter Gabriel vibe."

Sensitive to Leonard's awkward "demotion" on the record, Orbit said: "It was hard for Pat. He did a great job of being manful about it, but Madonna was deconstructing his songs and tearing layers away from them. I'd try to help him by putting things back in, but she wouldn't have it. Pat writes beautiful melodies, though. We were never going to destroy them completely." With this record, Madonna was deconstructing her past, and Leonard was a living embodiment of that.

Sessions began in the summer of 1997, in a studio near the Universal Theme Park in L.A.'s Studio City. From the outset, she had greater depth of expression in her voice. "I noticed how much her voice had developed and improved, and how much her confidence had come along," observes De Vries. Rick Nowells agrees, saying that her experience with *Evita* had given her the ability to project. "In doing *Evita*, she had six months of singing those proper theater songs. She had to do a lot of training and building her voice."

On the opening track, "Drowned World/Substitute for Love," Madonna reflects on her compulsive desire for fame, how that burned through relationships and made them shallow and fleeting. Over Orbit's backward tape-loop effects and bleeps, she sings with bell-like clarity. This song sets the tone for the whole album: as if the ghost of her former self is supplanted by the spirit of what she's to become. At the time, she described her fame as "a cross to bear, the real thorn in my side. I wouldn't trade my life for anything—I've been blessed with so much, I've had so many privileges—but, being famous, it's like the agony and the ecstasy."

WITH *Erotica* and *Bedtime Stories*, Madonna had made some tentative trips into her subconscious, but here she does so with greater focus and intent. On "Swim," for instance, she evokes the sacrament of baptism as she dips into metaphorical waters, washing her sins away. "Water is a very healing element," she said. "There's water in birth and . . . in baptism, and when you go into the bath or the ocean there's a feeling of closing, a feeling of starting all over again. That's what's going on in my life and I'm exploring that element in my songwriting."

Filled with apocalyptic Old Testament images, the song has the sense of her sloughing off not just her own misdemeanors but those heaped on her by the world. As Catholic theologian Richard McBrien says: "The Church has always taught that Baptism is necessary for salvation. . . . Ideally the rite of Baptism is celebrated during the Easter Vigil. When not, the celebration should be filled with the Easter spirit." It's an interesting coincidence that her album was released at Easter time. Starting with a simple guitar riff, the track is filled out with a bubbling psychedelic undertow. The song is an adaptation of the 70s song "Sepheryn" by hippie musicians Clive Muldoon and Dave Curtis. Muldoon died from a drug overdose at the age of twenty-eight, but his niece, Christine Leach, happened to sing the lyrics while in the studio with Orbit, and that inspired Madonna.

By the title track, she is ready to be reborn. With its speedy acid electronica, "Ray of Light" is an ecstatic hymn to the skies. Marrying her melodic pop with bleep-driven techno, Orbit creates a sensur-round for her voice. It is as if she's being carried effortlessly by the sound. Orbit said later that he was lucky to be able to work with her post-*Evita* voice. "'Ray of Light' is just a semitone higher than she's comfortable with, but we thought the strain really helped. She got frustrated when we were recording, but you want that bit of edge with singers, that thing of reaching. You can't fake it, and you can hear it when she cracks it on the record."

From here she plunges back into the ghosts of desire, with the dark Garbage-style distortion of "Candy Perfume Girl." She's all tingled nerve endings, ultra-awake and aware. She moves into "Skin," bass-driven, abstract, with a submerged sense of yearning. "I really like that one," says Marius De Vries, who coproduced the track with Orbit. "We were working in parallel studios, running back and forth between them. Inevitably it was competitive and edgy. We hadn't met before and our work covered the same sort of territory, so we circled each other warily at first. 'Skin' was an icebreaker. The track started as a couple of simple beats and a lyrical idea. We constructed that in a very collaborative way, from the ground up—which is why it was so packed with detail. We were trying to fill out each corner of it with our own favorite sounds!"

From here Madonna lunges into the vigorous "mea culpa" song "Nothing Really Matters," where she condemns herself for living self-ishly and celebrates the fact of having a child. "[Lola] doesn't know about me being famous, and it's completely unconditional love, which I've never known because I grew up without a mother," said Madonna. "When you have children you have to step outside of yourself.... You look at it from a different perspective." The ferocious party girl was a memory. Madonna described her mood for *Ray of Light* as "complete wonderment of life ... I was incredibly thoughtful and retrospective [sic] and intrigued by the mystical aspects of life." Motherhood had transformed her in a positive way. De Vries notes: "She was more set-tled. Calmer. Lola was around all the time. One of the leisure rooms in the studio was converted into a kind of crèche. She was very cute. She was just beginning to make a nuisance of herself and walk."

For this song, Madonna employed her psychological strategy of pitting two producers against each other, so that each would raise their game. According to De Vries, "Nothing Really Matters" was the song that he had most prepared beforehand. "I had my vision of how the song should be finished, and Will found that off-putting. On all the collaborations I'd left a lot of space for him, but for this I wanted to put something on the table and say, 'This is what I think,'" he says.

The track begins with a strange, electronic, slightly broken noise. "Will said, 'I hate that noise. It sounds like the DAT's broken.' I was like, 'Yeah, that's the point.' It's quite slow for a dance tune of that nature, not a pacey tune." Despite Orbit's protest, the breaking DAT sound stayed in, because Madonna had the casting vote.

Then, with the song "Frozen," Madonna changed the mood and slipped into a Pat Leonard chorus as easily as if she were coming home. This is one of her finest moments—taut and theatrical, with delicately shifting tones. She moves from liquid sweetness to icy drama, shape-shifting much like the video, which was shot after dark by director Chris Cunningham in freezing temperatures in the Mojave Desert. In the video, she flies through the sky like a witch with her familiars, dressed in flowing black, with her long dark hair streaming behind her. The gothic goddess is one of her most powerful images, echoing the ghostly themes of the record.

The first single from the album, "Frozen" was a suitable epic. But it took a while to get right. De Vries was brought in at the end to add his distinctive programming to the track. "Madonna felt the song hadn't quite achieved its potential. So I had the song for a day and a half and I messed around with it," he says. "I programmed up some beats and effects, and gave it the right amount of detail without cluttering it too much. I'm quite theatrical in my production. Camp, some would say. I try and consciously make every sound *do* something. I want the effect of every sound to be maximized. At the risk of overcrowding a record, there need to be sonic hooks that are less to do with melody than sound and dynamic."

Toward the end of the album, Madonna moves into her Rick Nowells trilogy—"The Power of Goodbye," which has the devotional charge of a church hymn; "To Have and Not to Hold," a brooding mood piece; and "Little Star," her dedication to Lola. "The subject matter in itself is quite dangerous. It's easy to get sentimental," says De Vries, who produced the latter track. "It's a delicate tune. I knew it had to be handled with butterfly-like delicacy, but also knew it needed an engine room to it, an energy, so it didn't become mawkish. That's why I did something with this skittery, unsettled, never quite resolving beat—to counteract the warmth and coziness of the central idea."

After the tenderness of "Little Star," the final track is shocking. "Mer Girl" is another key point in Madonna's life, her second Lynchian "eye of the duck" moment. With Orbit, she went on a psychic journey, as he encouraged her to look deep inside herself. Becoming a mother seemed to spark off a revelation about her own mother and the effect of her death. We move through a threatening dreamscape, as Madonna, her voice half-spoken, half-sung, describes running from her house, from a restless baby who won't sleep and a mother who haunts her. She runs through a childhood landscape—a lake, a hill, some trees, the cemetery—as the rain beats down. The ground opens up and in spare, sparse words she conveys a sense of being buried alive with her dead mother, smelling her rotting flesh and her decay. She runs away in fear. She realizes that she has been running all her life.

When she recorded this vocal in the studio, the effect was immediate. "She stepped out of the vocal booth, and everybody was rooted to the spot," says Orbit. "It was just one of those moments. Really spooky."

When the album was finished, everyone knew they had made something resonant and groundbreaking. "It's a very fine, courageous record," says De Vries. "Madonna really explored the edges of production and sound design, and crafted something that wasn't just about being radio-friendly. It was populist, with an artistic dimension, and that does take time. She started with more unfinished songs than usual. A lot of the writing was in the process of construction. And she had to allow Will to take his time. He doesn't always immediately arrive at where he wants to get. He has to make a journey of it."

As Orbit said later, "I walked into Madonna World and emerged, blinking, five months later." He learned from Madonna's ability to make quick, focused decisions. "She kept telling me, 'Don't gild the lily,'" he recalled. "And the other thing she'd say, as I was ready to crawl home exhausted, was, 'You can sleep when you're dead.' In the studio she's completely sleeves-rolled-up. You think of her as a . . . pop icon. . . . You don't perceive Madonna as a great producer, but that's exactly what she is."

There were a few snags to be sorted out before the album was ready for release. Orbit's liberal use of sampling led him into tricky territory, particularly on the track "Swim." The song featured a flute sample by musician/producer Pablo Cook, a fellow member of Orbit's band Strange Cargo. "He sampled that particular melody from my first solo album *Geronimo*, which I released under the name Exact Life. We recycled things a lot in those days," says Cook. He enjoyed being on Madonna's album, but felt that "technically, if a melody goes on a record, you should take a percentage of the publishing. Madonna is very strong and hard and down to the wire. I admire that in a woman, but when it enters your own backyard, it's a different thing. I remember William calling me, trying to get me to give the sample up and accept a buyout. I could hear Madonna in the background, going, 'Who is this guy? Who *is* this guy?' I had Italian solicitors trying to buy me out. I took it to the wire until I could see my relationship with William falling away. I had people calling me up who'd worked on the album, saying, 'Do you want to go to court?'" Cook ended up capitulating for the sake of his friendship with Orbit. "It was not an easy ride, but we're good buddies now," he says. Motherhood may have ushered in a kinder, gentler Madonna, but in business, she still favored the hard-headed approach.

RAY OF LIGHT was released in March 1998 to widespread critical acclaim. *Rolling Stone* called it "brilliant," while *Slant* magazine in the United States dubbed it "one of the great pop masterpieces of the 90s. Madonna hasn't been this emotionally candid since *Like a Prayer*," and

U.S. entertainment channel E! bestowed an impressive accolade with its mark of A-. The only note of caution also came from *Rolling Stone*, with Rob Sheffield's comment that William Orbit "doesn't know enough tricks to fill a whole CD, so he repeats himself something fierce." This didn't deter people from buying the album. Since its release, it has sold an estimated 17 million copies. It won four Grammy Awards, including Best Pop Album and Best Dance Recording. Finally, it won over the undecided. This was the record that brought on board "serious" music buyers, the music press demographic of twenty- to thirty-five-year-old male readers. With *Ray of Light*, Madonna achieved the thing that had eluded her since *Like a Prayer*—full artistic credibility. "I've been in the music business sixteen years and this is my first Grammy (well, actually I've won four tonight)," Madonna said, blinking furiously, in her acceptance speech at the 1998 awards show. "It was worth the wait."

The record also signaled greater success for her in Europe. In the United Kingdom, for instance, the album went to number one and was registered six times platinum, while in the United States it peaked at number two and sold four times platinum. Maybe this gave weight to Madonna's decision to relocate to London. For her, *Ray of Light* was more than a comeback; it was a resurrection. Approaching forty, she had finally, it seemed, grown up. Gone was the arch, glittering blonde of *Erotica*; now she reemerged with burnished golden ringlets, subtle makeup, and a flowing, Eastern-tinged look. Mario Testino's album cover artwork was shot through with radiant blue, from her shiny satin shirt to the aquamarine background. The emphasis was on Madonna as natural and unaffected, her head thrown back in laughter, her wild hair streaming behind her. This record encapsulated her growing maturity. She was doing well in her career, and she had a beautiful baby daughter. The only thing missing was a lover to share her life with.

BY THE summer of 1998 she and Andy Bird were drifting apart. Although the Warwickshire-born man was ambitious, it seemed he could never quite follow through with his plans. Madonna often paid his way and rented an apartment for him when he came to Los Angeles. Although she enjoyed mothering him for a while, she had her reservations about him. With his black clothes and motorcycle boots held together by tape, he never really fitted into her London smart set. As they were breaking up, Madonna went through an emotional crisis when she found out she was pregnant. She desperately wanted another baby, but only in a secure relationship. While she agonized about whether to keep the child, the decision was apparently made for her when she suffered a miscarriage.

This experience threw Madonna's personal life into sharp relief. Her priority now was to find a suitable husband, someone who was equal to her, who had his own career, but who also wanted to have a family. For years, this had proved elusive—partly because Madonna was too focused on her work to give serious attention to a man, but also she hadn't been emotionally ready. Unresolved pain from her childhood had left her reluctant to commit, and it seemed to friends that she was adept at sabotaging relationships that mattered. "There were whole chunks of my life where I was so lonely . . . and wondered if it was ever going to be possible for me to have a relationship that was going to last. I did wonder if it was possible to find a man who could handle me, as well as a man I could handle," Madonna said. "But then, just when I wasn't looking, I found one."

Just a few months after the release of *Ray of Light*, Madonna met her match. "You know when people say 'he turned my head'? My head didn't just turn—my head spun around on my body!" she exclaimed. When she met Guy Ritchie at that summer lunch party at Sting's Lake House in Wiltshire, she met someone very like herself: driven, determined, and adept at reinvention. The son of an advertising man and a model, Guy was a bright but restless child. His parents divorced when he was five, and his mother married Sir Michael Leighton, the holder of a three-hundred-year-old baronetcy. Although Guy spent holidays in Loton Park, the Leighton family estate near Shrewsbury, most of his growing up was in a series of boarding schools. A severe dyslexic, he ended up at Stanbridge Earls, a school for children with special needs in Romsey, Hampshire. It is a pleasant, enlightened school set in acres of countryside, but Stanbridge Earls couldn't contain him. Expelled at the age of fifteen for playing truant and bringing girls into his room, Guy left his expensive education with just one qualification in film studies. Years later, he claimed that he was expelled for taking drugs, but his father countered, "Guy says those things on occasion. I think it's rather modern to say it. He likes to pretend he's been a bit of a scallywag, but I don't actually think he was."

Guy's initial ambition as a teenager was to be a gamekeeper, or, like his grandfather and great-grandfather before him, to go into the army. His grandfather Stewart was a family hero, a major in the Seaforth Highlanders, decorated in World War I and killed at Dunkirk. Although Guy abandoned such ideas when he moved to London and got a job in a Soho film company making promos, he brought that taste for military strategy into his filmmaking. He worked hard, wrote well, and took risks. He hung out with his private-school cronies on a stretch of road in Fulham called "The Beach," mixed with savvy working-class guys from the East End, and tried hard to get funding for his film scripts. Full of bravado as a young man, he used to drive his Triumph sports car "like a lunatic," and once got his face cut for getting on the wrong side of some unsavory people. Struck by stories of London gangland, he affected a Cockney accent, and imagined himself living a life more dangerous than the one he had been used to at Loton Park. For someone who was distantly related to the late princess of Wales, the chirpy Cockney was quite a reinvention.

After making a short film called *Hard Case*, in 1995, Guy managed to get money from a variety of backers, including Sting's wife, Trudie Styler, to make his first full-length feature film, *Lock, Stock and Two Smoking Barrels*. Set amid rival gangs in London's criminal underworld, the film is shot with fast edits, musical flourish, and an array of directorial tricks. It incorporates themes that would crop up time and again in later work—guns, games, and homophobic gags. Though ruthlessly violent, *Lock, Stock* was essentially lighthearted, and it became a commercial success. "For the first time since I left school I know what I'm doing," he said. With its references to *Performance* and *The Italian Job*,

Lock, Stock earned Guy a reputation as the English Quentin Tarantino. His characters were more stylized, however, and he didn't have the latter's cinematic range. Guy had yet to really develop his oeuvre; this would come later, with his film *Revolver*.

Shortly after *Lock, Stock* was in the can, he went down to Sting's house in the country. "I was very pally with Trudie at this point, because we'd just made the film," he told *Interview* magazine. "On my way to the train station, I called and said, 'So who else is coming for lunch?' She said, 'Just a couple of people.' And I said, 'Well, who?' And she said, 'Madonna.' I've gotta tell you, it did knock my socks off a bit." The pair of them hit it off immediately. Both appreciated words and wit, and both loved film. "She's very dry. Very funny," he said.

At the time, he was planning work on *Snatch*, a crime caper about illegal betting and bare-knuckle boxing that was to star Brad Pitt. Ten years younger than Madonna, with a charming smile and a hint of aggression, Guy was his own man, with his own career. He seemed like the perfect partner. In the same way that Madonna's world is hyper-female, with her Hollywood glamour and addiction to high fashion, so Guy's style is hyper-male. His version of masculinity is all about strategizing and game-playing. His films are full of riddles and word tricks, and the women are as diamond-hard as the dudes. At the epicenter of each movie is the gun, whether it's a revolver, rifle, or a huge Kalashnikov. A gun gives the illusion of control over one's environment. To a small boy packed off to boarding school after his parents' breakup, this was irresistible. As a teenager, he was a good clay-pigeon shot, and later on, he cultivated an interest in shooting real birds. Like Madonna's first husband, Sean Penn, Guy took from guns a sense of power in a world that was beyond his control. Madonna has called Guy her "soul mate." Maybe they both recognized a childhood pain and the need to cover it up to survive.

Despite this, the romance took a while to get off the ground. Guy was still seeing the model Tania Strecker, so when Madonna came to London, she had to meet him in secret. This was infuriating for Strecker. Madonna and Guy had passionate trysts in a tiny but well-appointed film-production apartment in Wardour Street. While he filmed *Snatch* on location in the United Kingdom, she shot the whimsical, half-baked comedy *The Next Best Thing* with Rupert Everett in Los Angeles. In the film, she plays a yoga teacher, desperate to find a man and have a baby. In real life, Madonna had the man within her sights, and she pursued him with admirable determination, but as long as she lived in Los Angeles, he was reluctant to commit. As far as Guy was concerned, his films were about London characters and subcultures, and although he had some tempting offers for big features, he didn't want to be "emasculated" by the Hollywood studio system. "It's about finding that edge and staying on it," he declared. Guy was also a little intimidated by Madonna's success, obliquely referring to her in an interview as having "a work ethic that crashes mine. It makes me feel like I'm not doing enough . . . that I've got so much to learn." As obstinate as Madonna, he refused to compromise. Eventually, she was the one to back down and relocate to England. That, she claimed, is when their relationship took off.

BY THE beginning of 2000, she found herself pregnant. There was no question in her mind about whether to keep the baby, but the timing was difficult. At that point, she and Guy were still having an on-again, off-again affair, and although he was excited at the prospect of fatherhood, at first he was ambivalent about settling down. Plus Madonna had just started work on her next album. Buoyed up by the success of *Ray of Light*, she was eager to get back into the studio. She was well-disposed toward Orbit, but by the year 2000, his sound was pretty ubiquitous. It even underlay pop-lite songs, like "Pure Shores," the number one hit for U.K. girl group All Saints. Although she was happy to keep him on board for a few tracks, Madonna knew she needed a distinctive sound to stand out in a market now dominated by young, fresh fillies like Christina Aguilera and Britney Spears. She was introduced to the Paris-based electronic artist Mirwais Ahmadzaï by the photographer (and Kylie Minogue's ex-boyfriend) Stephane Sednaoui. The latter had made an erotic video for Mirwais's single

"Disco Science," a crunchy house track built around a sample from the opening to the classic Breeders' song "Cannonball."

Madonna liked Mirwais's pitch-shifting, his pulverizing rhythms, and his way with acid bass. "I truly believe this man is a genius," she told *Billboard* magazine's Larry Flick. "I listen to his stuff and think, This is the future of sound." The Swiss-born, half-Afghani Mirwais shared her delight in genre-hopping. "Each new scene is a system," he said. "And I don't want to be part of just one scene. I want to do something different." Like Madonna's, his background was rooted in 70s disco and New Wave. He was lead guitarist for one of France's key alternative 80s bands, Taxi Girl. Sounding like a cross between The Stooges, Kraftwerk, and Giorgio Moroder, they were a major influence on latter-day mischief-makers like Daft Punk and Air. "With Taxi Girl we were involved in drugs; we were so desperate and we were twenty years old," he said. Seeing music as political, he didn't want to just sell records, he wanted to "change the culture." Mirwais would have agreed with French theorist Jacques Attali that "music is prophecy. . . . It makes audible the new world that will gradually become visible." Mirwais's worldview was melancholic, politicized, and intellectual, and it was almost a point of principle for him to take musical risks. That is what made his collaboration with the commercially aware Madonna so edgy and futuristic.

Mirwais maintains that working with her was an "accident" rather than the dream of a lifetime. That is why he was able to keep a level head and concentrate on getting out of her the best music he could. "The challenge was to make something current appear," he said, "something hidden in her personality. Everybody knows her as a chameleon, or a businesswoman. I wanted to show her potential as a musician." Mirwais had already recorded his debut album when he met Madonna. Its bold title—*Production*—was a deconstruction in itself. While Orbit fashioned ambient soundscapes for Madonna's voice, Mirwais cut them up, filled them with glitches, and sent the beats spinning. Her *Music* album was the inevitable meeting of two arch postmodern minds. Recording sessions began at SARM studios in West London in September 1999. By then, Madonna had been having a relationship with Guy for over a year, and her mind was jittery. She had led a very domestic life while Lola was a baby, but now that her daughter was in preschool, the world was opening up again. "I feel like . . . an animal that's ready to be sprung out of a cage. . . . I miss performing, and dancing, and being on the road, that kind of energy," Madonna told *The Face*. She wanted to make a party record, and, overwhelmed by her feelings for Guy, she also wanted to make a statement about love.

The opening title track is a resurrection of the disco girl. Like Prince in his prime, Madonna can sometimes pull out a single that stops you in your tracks. "Vogue" was one; "Justify My Love" another. And "Music" has that same genre-defining quality: robotic, tinny, trashy, and audacious. The beats are fractured, minimal, and loud, the lyrics deliciously tongue-in-cheek. She resurrects the Madonna imperative: Dance. Party. Surrender. You are slaves to the music. In a way, she had come full circle to the Danceteria, an element in the video, where she appears as a ghetto-fabulous female in a feather boa and Stetson, all diamonds and bling, going to lap-dancing bars and traveling in the back of a luxury limousine driven by comedian Ali G.

A series of young nubile girls had been auditioned for the roles of her girlfriends, but they were too stiff and posed. In the end, Madonna called up old clubbing pals Debbie Mazar and Niki Haris, and they sat carousing in the back with her, giving the video its sassy, flowing energy. "I was at home when Madonna called me. She said, 'I need my girlfriend, not these fake girlfriends trying to be my girlfriends. Throw on some clothes and come down,'" recalls Niki. "We laughed all day."

The video was made by Jonas Akerlund, a Swedish director who once played in an early-80s death-metal band called Bathory, and who had a vivid, anarchic style. He came to Madonna's attention in 1996, when he did the "Smack My Bitch Up" video for Maverick hardcore techno-band the Prodigy. The song had already been slammed by the National Organization for Women (NOW) as hav-

Madonna performing the song "Fever" on the Girlie Show tour in 1993.

IN BED WITH
MADONNA.

Madonna.
Like you've never seen her before.

DINO DE LAURENTIIS COMMUNICATIONS PRESENT PROPAGANDA FIL
IN BED WITH MADONNA DIRECTED BY ROBERT LEACOCK EDITED BY BARRY ALEXAND
STEVE GOLIN AND SIGURJON SIGHVATSSON PRODUCED BY TIM CLAWSON AND JAY ROB

LEFT: *A poster for Madonna's 1991 tour documentary* In Bed with Madonna, *a.k.a.* Truth or Dare.

BELOW: *On set with director Alan Parker for the 1996 film* Evita.

The launch of Madonna's book Sex at a Virgin Records store in New York on October 22, 1992.

ABOVE: *A candid moment in* Truth or Dare.

BELOW: *Madonna on set with Woody Allen, John Malkovich and Mia Farrow for the 1992 film* Shadows and Fog.

ABOVE: *Simulating an orgy with female dancers in the Girlie Show.*

LEFT: *Madonna in her Dita Parlo dominatrix character, singing "Erotic."*

ABOVE: *In Jean Harlow mode at the launch of her 1995 album* Bedtime Stories.

BELOW: *At nearly forty years old, Madonna's "new age" look for the album* Ray of Light.

LEFT: *Madonna jogging in Central Park with her former lover John F. Kennedy Jr.*

BELOW LEFT: *Appearing on the* Arsenio Hall Show *with her father, Tony, in 1992. This was a surprise reunion for Madonna—Hall arranged the meeting without her knowledge.*

BELOW: *Madonna with her daughter, Lola, and friend Ingrid Casares in New York, 1998.*

LEFT: *With Ingrid Casares and Guy Oseary at a party for* Vibe *magazine in 1994.*

ABOVE: *Madonna listens to President Bill Clinton during a 1994 political rally.*

ABOVE RIGHT: *Modeling her best assets at the 1992 John Paul Gaultier show in Los Angeles.*

RIGHT: *Two-year-old Lourdes Maria (Lola).*

BELOW: *With Carlos Leon, her boyfriend and the future father of Lola, at the 1995 Versace Fashion Show in Paris.*

*Madonna performs on her
Drowned World tour at Earls
Court, London, in 2001.*

Madonna and Guy Ritchie on the steps of Dornoch Cathedral, Scotland, carrying their baby, Rocco, after his baptism in December 2000.

BELOW: Madonna and Guy's wedding banns at Dornoch Registry Office.

LIST OF INTENDED MARRIAGES

MARRIAGE (SCOTLAND) ACT 1977

M11(R)
581

Section 4(2) of the Marriage (Scotland) Act 1977 requires the district registrar to display a list of marriages for which he has received statutory notice. This list shows the names of the parties to intended marriages and the proposed date of the marriages.

Any person who claims that he may have reason to submit an objection to an intended marriage may inspect the entry relating to that marriage in the Marriage Notice Book which is held by the registrar.

Entry number in marriage notice book	Bridegroom's name	Bride's name	Proposed date of marriage
2000/30	Jamie Robert Neal	Tessa Morrison	20/12/2000
2000/32	Andrew Davies	Jane Elizabeth Tooze	24/12/2000
2000/33	Roy Alexander McGlynn	Catherine McGarry	14/02/2001
2000/34	Guy Stuart Ritchie	Madonna Louise Ciccone	22/12/2000

ing "dangerous and offensive" lyrics, and the video was just as provocative. Filmed from the point of view of someone going clubbing,
ingesting large amounts of drugs and alcohol, getting into fistfights,
and picking up a prostitute, the trick ending reveals that the subject is
a woman. (So that's all right then.) Because of this video, Wal-Mart
and Kmart pulled The Prodigy's album *The Fat of the Land* off their
shelves. Appreciating Akerlund's graphic imagery, and the stir it created, Madonna made him director of her "Ray of Light" video. Shot
with lasers and lurid colors, the groundbreaking video was crucial to
her late 90s "comeback." Then his glittering promo for "Music" restored Madonna to her throne as reigning queen of dance culture.

The song works because it is the real thing; it is sung by someone with a history. When Madonna urges the groovers to dance, and
chants "Yeah," they follow. "It's not experimental, but it's not completely easy," Mirwais said about the song. "It's a small victory for
underground music."

With the next track, "Impressive Instant," she leads them into a
heady mix of acid techno and pop trance. Hers is an abstract world
of nonsense lyrics, disco balls, and glitz. The mood is still up-tempo
for the William Orbit–produced "Runaway Lover," a vigorous parry
to Guy, the man who's turning her world upside down. He's taking the wind out of her sails, confounding her with his maddening
mix of coolness and devotion. This is a theme she develops with the
other Orbit-produced track, the spine-tingling "Amazing." "They're
all I-love-you-but-fuck-you songs," Madonna explained. The latter
is about "loving someone that you wished you didn't love. Because
you know that you're doomed, but you can't stop yourself, because it's
amazing."

With "I Deserve It," the key love song on the album, we are introduced to an extraordinary new texture. If *Music* had all been electronic
funk, it would have dated. But what lifts it into the first division is the
unexpected moments of acoustic folk rock, where everything drops
out and all we hear is warm, Neil Young–style guitar, and Madonna's
melodic voice. "It's a love song, but there's something lonely about it,"
she said, ". . . the juxtaposition of the acoustic guitar and then that

synth siren sound—to me that strange combination makes it a little bit uncomfortable." Here Mirwais shows the other side of his musical persona, the man who played for ten years in melancholy acoustic band Juliette et Les Independents.

With these intimate guitar riffs, Mirwais and Madonna created the soft inner heart of the album. That romantic sentiment is best expressed on "Don't Tell Me" (another fan favorite), where Madonna seems to forget herself. Her voice has a sinuous quality, and she sings like a dancer, easy on the beat, with just the right amount of tension and release. It's a declarative song that conjures up the Midwest of her childhood and teenage years, where the fluid rock of Carole King and Lynyrd Skynyrd would have been the soundtrack of her high school peers. What's startling about this record is Mirwais's mix of the organic and analogue with space-age effects. The two work in tandem, but only because they are an expression of Madonna's own musical history. She is the force that pulls it all together. Just as when she sings with that dragging, electronic vocodervoice on "Nobody's Perfect," or projects vulnerability and uncertainty on the Japanese haiku–like track "Paradise," she is translating her experience into music.

"The main thing that struck me was her presence in these songs," says Guy Sigsworth, who produced one of the standout tracks on the album, "What It Feels Like for a Girl." "She said to me, 'Guy, I'm really good at simple. I do simple really well.' She was playing me roughs of other tracks on the record, Mirwais and William's songs. I'm a great admirer of their work and the way they play with technology, but as soon as she entered, it was like she took a big flag and stuck it in the middle of the territory. It made the album cohere really well. I can see how she was producing them as much as they were producing her. She was giving a directness of purpose to what they were doing. That's quite a challenge."

Sigsworth was another member of the Björk team that Madonna admired. A Cambridge music graduate with a love of Stockhausen and Kate Bush, Sigsworth had worked on several of Björk's albums, including *Post* (1995) and *Homogenic* (1998). A producer who's worked with everyone from Seal to Britney Spears to more alternative artists like Gem and Kate Havnevik, he has a particular way with the female voice. "I've always felt that ladies in music are more vocally adventurous. A lot of male singers are from the Liam Gallagher school, more limited in their range because they've got guitars behind them. Women often experiment with the melody and take it to different places," he maintains.

Sigsworth also has a love of technology, but unlike Mirwais, he revels in understatement. "People talk about music on computers and say, what's the mystery in the bits and zeroes and ones? I say there is mystery there—what I like doing with computers is finding the mystery in the digital glitches of modern sound." Madonna had been keeping an eye on Sigsworth—she was one of the few thousand people who bought a record he produced, by U.K. trip-hop act Mandalay—and when she wanted to add a more ambient electronic feel to the *Music* album, she got in touch with him.

He sent her a CD with a backup track and a sample of Charlotte Gainsbourg in *The Cement Garden*, a cult 90s film about teenage brother and sister who have an incestuous affair. The daughter of French musician Serge Gainsbourg (who, with his wife, Jane Birkin, created "Je T'aime," the most notorious love song of the 70s), Charlotte had a deadpan but sensitive delivery. "It's OK to be a boy, but not OK for a boy to look like a girl, because being a girl is degrading," she says in the film. Madonna took this idea and ran with it.

"She wrote this lyric, taking a phrase from what Gainsbourg said, and made a beautiful melody out of it," recalls Sigsworth. Feeling unsettled and hormonal, because she had just found out she was pregnant with Guy's child, Madonna expressed her exasperation with a world that compels women to be less of who they are. "Men are quite intimidated by women who accomplish a lot," she said. "There have been so many instances where I've said to myself, 'Oh I wish somebody would have said to me, Be great, but don't be too great because you're going to limit your options. It is a game that all strong women have to play . . . the song is . . . a realization about the politics of the sexes. It's a complaint."

Sigsworth recorded the track with Madonna at SARM studios

rather than his own place, "because I was terrified of fucking up, basically. I knew she'd worked in that bed-sit environment with William,
but I wanted to make sure I had backup. I remember the first day in
the studio, pretending to be cool, but inwardly punching the air and
yelling, 'I'm working with Madonna!'"

Soon after they started, though, Sigsworth realized they had a
problem. "The way she'd written her verses, they were out of sync
with my music. I said, 'That's OK, we'll stick an extra bar in here
and your melody and my music will catch up.' She said, 'No.' The
genius of what happened was finding interesting ways to cut up what
I'd already written, put it in the computer, and reposition it around
her voice in more unusual ways," he recalls. "The end result made the
song more fluid and magical. That was her challenge: not to take the
cop-out solution. It made me raise my game. I'm very proud of what
we came up with."

He also found Madonna's impatience with knob-twiddling a challenge. "She understood the studio process. Rather than let me work
on something for two hours, she'd say, 'Just give me a rough idea, an
approximation of the sound. Then, if I don't like it, we don't waste
time.' I'd protest, wanting it to be perfect, but she'd say, 'No, that's
OK.' She's worked with so many people before, she just wants to get
it done."

With its restrained production, "What It Feels Like for a Girl" has
a barbed and beautifully executed sense of anger. Along with "Express
Yourself," it has become one of her best-known "femme-pop" songs.
It's not exactly a call to arms, but it develops the idea she expressed in
her *Vanity Fair* "*Evita* diary" several years earlier: "If I had known that
I would be so universally misunderstood, maybe I couldn't have been
so rebellious and outspoken. . . . Could an idiot have come this far in
life? I wonder if I could ever have been the kind of sweet, submissive,
feminine girl that the entire world idealizes."

Guy Ritchie directed the video for the song. With his background
in pop promos, he was eager to make a video for Madonna, and went
about it with his customary "guerrilla filmmaking" attitude. She rises
to the occasion, playing a trigger-happy revenge queen, merrily crash-

ing cars and eradicating any men who get in her way. Condemned for its violent imagery, the video was banned by VH1 and MTV, which squashed its chances of being a big hit. Although tongue-in-cheek, the video was also fueled by a barely disguised anger. One of the issues that irks Madonna the most is not being taken seriously as an artist.

Like many producers who've worked with her, Sigsworth feels that Madonna has been underestimated as a musician. "She had an omnivorous appetite for music. She would bring a box of CDs into the studio for me to check out. She's fascinated and truly in love with music." To him, she was a remarkably resourceful singer. "She knows her limits and what she can do vocally, but within that she's very creative. I like the fact that she's not showy with her singing. It's about the song. She'd be the last one to try and out-roulade Mariah Carey. She has a very direct way of telling the tale." He noticed that she didn't need to grandstand in the studio. "Most singers want themselves as loud as possible till it's almost painful in the mix. Madonna's not like that. She likes to hear herself *in* the music, not on top of it. That shows a kind of self-knowledge. She's very aware of the musical context. I love flamboyant singers, but I get tired of that American school of the Olympic five-thousand-yards vocal. It's the vocal version of guitar solos."

To Madonna, the most important thing is communication. "She goes direct to the listener's ear," says Sigsworth. "She tests out her music by going out on the town with her nanny, her personal assistant, and girlfriends—what she calls the Pussy Posse—and playing it to them on her car stereo. She trusts their reaction much more than the record company." Madonna's female audience is uppermost in her mind; she knows the importance of good melody lines, because that will make a hit song. DJ/producer Norman Cook once told Sigsworth: "When I play a record in a club, I know it's going to work if the girls go for it. I know the guys will go for it if it's got the right rhythm, groove, and attitude. But if the girls go for the melody lines, then I know it'll be a big hit."

The album was completed by the spring of 2000. The only goof track on it was her version of the Don McLean classic "American Pie." It was an odd choice for her, a folk-based protest song that was far out of her disco background, but it was featured on the soundtrack of her critically panned movie *The Next Best Thing*. She regretted its inclusion on the album, claiming she was "talked into it by some record company executive." Apart from the "American Pie" track, though, Madonna could barely contain her excitement about *Music*. She primed her fans by telling the official fan club that "the single is going to drop very soon. I worked on it with a French guy named Mirwais, and he is the shit."

Life was going smoothly. Guy had long finished his relationship with Tania Strecker, and he and Madonna were now "legit." As the expectant father, he even gave up alcohol while Madonna was pregnant, so she wouldn't be tempted. The only bum note was hit when Madonna told an L.A. radio interviewer that she wouldn't have her baby in a British hospital because they were too "old and Victorian." This didn't endear her to the British public, so she had to do some damage control, saying how much she loved London and Europe's creative attitude toward the arts. In reality, she was nervous about her pregnancy. She had been diagnosed with placenta previa, a condition that can cause the mother to hemorrhage and cut off the baby's blood supply, and had to take extra care. On August 10, 2000, a month before her due date, Madonna began bleeding and was rushed to the L.A. Cedars-Sinai Hospital. Guy had been at a private screening of his film *Snatch*, and when he arrived at the hospital, she was hemorrhaging badly and going into shock. Although she had a Cesarean scheduled closer to the due date, Madonna had to have an emergency procedure. Her son, Rocco (named after one of her uncles), was born on August 11. Jaundiced and premature, he was kept in intensive care for five days before Madonna and Guy were allowed to take him home.

It was her forty-second birthday, and she was ecstatic. Little Rocco had made a good recovery, and was a calm baby. "I feel complete," she said. Guy, meanwhile, was bursting with pride. "He was small and came out early, but not alarmingly small. He was sweet small," he said. When he was talking about his son, Guy's defensive bravado melted away. "Fatherhood does change you . . . It's like a huge wave of love, but much stronger." There was something that softened in Madonna, too. In early pictures, she looks at Rocco with an amused devotion that only a mother can give her son. Having a daughter makes a woman think about the female in herself, and be fiercely protective of her. Having a son ignites a different kind of love. It is no less intense, but the bond is almost romantic. Madonna's joy at having a family of her own was compounded when the day after Rocco got home, Guy gave her a diamond ring. "I never liked big rocks on my finger—well, I do now," Madonna gushed. To her friend Rosie O'Donnell, the truth was simple. "Madonna first fell in love with her daughter, and that taught her how to fall in love for real," she said.

A MONTH after Rocco's birth, the album *Music* was released. There was an authority about this record. It stood out at a time when pop (particularly in the United Kingdom) was dominated by the karaoke of young stage-school-trained acts like Steps and S Club 7 massacring 70s disco hits. There was also the legacy of The Spice Girls, where girl groups were manufactured with alarming speed, all formulaic hooks and moves, and scant attention paid to the music. Madonna criticized people for panning The Spice Girls, saying, "I was a Spice Girl once," but she was putting herself down. Madonna had a vision and musicianship that was beyond most of her young female imitators.

To her annoyance, some tracks had already leaked onto the Internet. She sued the music-download site Napster, but that didn't hurt the impact of the record once it was released. The "Music" single went to number one in numerous countries, including the United States, and was her biggest hit since "Take a Bow" (1994). The album won a Grammy, and in 2003 reached the dizzying heights of number 452 on *Rolling Stone*'s list of greatest albums of all time. For *Music*, Madonna created her cartoon cowgirl persona, relishing Americana while at the same time sending it up. The CD artwork was pure camp, with pink and blue Stetsons, bales of hay, 1950s cars, guitars, and embroidered jeans. Gone was the gothic goddess of *Ray of Light*; now her hair was back to sun-kissed blond. After moving to London, Madonna found herself looking at America with new eyes, with a sense of fond irony. Although now a mother of two, she had no plans to stay quietly at home. *Music* signaled her willingness to get out into the world again and engage directly with her audience. It was during the launch party for the album (a high-bling affair in L.A., with pole dancers and champagne) that she hatched plans for a tour. For the first time in eight years, she would be back on the road.

Hard-working and Hard-laughing

"I HAVE TO STAY CURRENT. GOD HELP ME, BUT I GUESS I have to share radio air time with Britney Spears and Christina Aguilera," Madonna told friends early in 2000. She was privately fretting about being overtaken by the younger competition. She knew that she could reassert her position as queen of pop with a world tour, but with two small children, it would take some planning. She dipped her toe in the water with a low-key set at Manhattan's Roseland Ballroom, showcasing tracks from *Music*. "This is a chance to get my feet wet again," she said. "It's been a while." Wearing a black rhinestone cowgirl outfit and a Britney Spears T-shirt, she performed for a select audience that included celebrity friends Gwyneth Paltrow, Donatella Versace, and Rosie O'Donnell.

After the show, she sat in a downtown bar talking to the *Rolling Stone* writer Kurt Loder. With some expansion, couldn't the Roseland gig become a full-scale roadshow, he asked. "I'm thinking about it," was Madonna's reply. On November 29, soon after she had won Best Dance Record and Best Female Artist for *Music* at the MTV Europe Awards, Madonna did a short set at London's Brixton Academy. What had been billed as a party for an invited audience of 3,500 became a media feeding frenzy. With a Microsoft deal to broadcast her first live online event, the buzz reached fever pitch, and tickets were going for a reputed $3,500. The police presence outside the venue was considerable, while inside, the auditorium had been transformed into a giant TV-studio-cum-hayloft. Wedged at the front were a gaggle of fans in cowboy hats, while upstairs was crammed with assorted industry people, including Kylie Minogue.

At ten p.m. sharp, Madonna bounded onstage wearing black jeans and a T-shirt with her son's name emblazoned on it in glittering letters. She opened with the song "Impressive Instant," backed by a band led by Mirwais on guitar. Her voice was strong, if a little breathless. Being at home with baby Rocco and not having toured for several years had obviously taken its toll. By contrast, she was more comfortable with the mid-tempo "Don't Tell Me." She then shouted gleefully: "I'd like to dedicate the next song to all those pop bitches out there!" before launching into "What It Feels Like for a Girl." The old Madonna was back—girlish, teasing, and appealing directly to her female fans. She segued into "Holiday," with dancing girls in Union Jack T-shirts, slightly awkwardly strutting her stuff atop a pickup truck. The mood was celebratory and camp, with a video montage of Madonna's stylistic history flickering behind her, from "Material Girl" to "Vogue" and beyond. It was as if she was throwing down the gauntlet to the new generation of young Britneys and saying: "Top this!" Nine million fans logged on to her live Webcast, shattering Paul McCartney's world record for the three million who tuned in to his performance at Liverpool's Cavern Club the previous year. Her publicist Liz Rosenberg said: "Madonna is thrilled to pieces." Plans for a tour were now a "distinct possibility."

By the end of the year, the publicity circus surrounding her became surreal, with Madonna and Guy supplanting David and Victoria Beckham at the lead of the media aristocracy. Despite the absence of official photographs, their wedding on December 22, 2000, at Skibo Castle in Scotland became a world event. Mindful of the Malibu helicopters that had turned her wedding to Sean Penn into such a farce, Madonna wanted to keep the ceremony secret, and she and Guy went to great lengths to keep the paparazzi out. "Fuck 'em all," she said, "I've given enough." It was rumored that there had been negotiations with celebrity magazines *Hello!* and *OK*, but the £2 million Madonna asked for was too much, even for them. She had probably priced herself out of the market to get a little peace.

For this event, Madonna was to star in her own fairy tale. She originally wanted to get married at Althorp House, the place where Princess Diana is buried, but Earl Spencer was worried about security and turned her down. Guy then persuaded her to go to Skibo Castle in the Scottish Highlands, a place that appealed to him because of his Highland family roots.

And—just as important—the 7,500 acre estate was near a prime partridge shooting area. Dubbed "heaven on earth" by Andrew Carnegie, the Scots-born steel tycoon who restored the castle in 1898, the Edwardian pink-turreted building is set in breathtaking countryside. The word "Skibo" is derived from the Celtic for "fairyland," and Madonna has said since that she felt the place was enchanted and magical.

This oak-paneled, mock-baronial folly was once a retreat for esteemed guests like Edward Elgar and Rudyard Kipling. It was then used as a summerhouse for the Carnegie family, until financier Peter De Savary bought the place in 1990 and turned it into an exclusive country club, wooing Hollywood players like Sean Connery, Michael Douglas, and Jack Nicholson. For the last week of December, Madonna and Guy turned Skibo into a luxury fortress, hiring a crack security team and getting hotel staff to sign four-page confidentiality agreements. All guests had to turn off mobile phones, and there was virtually no contact with the outside world. Except that the world was busy looking in. Paparazzi were chased from the bushes and TV crews were stationed in the local town, desperately trying to sniff out information for their news bulletins.

They were granted one brief photo opportunity on December 21, the day of baby Rocco's christening at Dornoch Cathedral. Dressed in a three-quarter-length cream coat, her hair in a chignon, Madonna gave a regal wave on the steps before disappearing into a waiting car. She and Guy weren't seen again until after Christmas, but news of the wedding filtered out regardless. That she wore a strapless £30,000 ivory silk dress designed by her maid of honor, Stella McCartney. That he was kitted out in a kilt of the finest Macintosh plaid. That she had around her neck a thirty-seven-carat diamond cross, and a quarter-million-dollar 1910 diamond tiara on loan from Asprey & Garrard. That four-year-old Lola walked down the grand Skibo staircase, as a flower girl, tossing rose petals in her mother's path. That Rocco was dressed in a miniature kilt cut from the same cloth as Daddy's. That the bride wore Gaultier at dinner, and Versace at dancing. That guests, including Gwyneth Paltrow, Sting, Trudie Styler, Rupert Everett, Matthew Vaughn, and Ingrid Casares, were to dance the night away to jigs, reels, and—oh, joy!—Madonna songs. That the wedding cake was three feet high and stuffed full of profiteroles.

The grand affair struck the public imagination, probably because the media blackout gave it a mysterious, deeply romantic air. Her emotional father gave Madonna away. "My God, just look at you," Tony said before the event, his voice trembling. Finally, it seemed, they were reconciled, and any awkwardness between them had disappeared. The prodigal daughter had returned. Reverend Susan Green, the only female rector of a Scottish cathedral, presided over the ceremony, while Madonna, keeping her feminist credentials to the last, promised to "cherish, honor, and delight in family" rather than "obey." The only warning note was her row with Guy before the wedding, when he went shooting with his mates rather than help her with the arrangements, and she admonished him for "murdering small birds." This was a prelude to a much deeper conflict that would develop later, but for now, the couple were harmonious and happy.

AFTER THE New Year, the honeymoon (at Sting's Wiltshire estate) was over, and Madonna was back in work mode. Plans for her world tour were getting serious. "I'm finally going to fucking drag my ass into a rehearsal studio," she said. "I don't see the point of doing a show unless you offer something that is going to mind-boggle the senses. It's not enough to get on the stage and sing a song. It's all about theater and drama and suspense. . . . I'm looking forward to it, but I'm also nervous." In March 2001, anticipation of the tour was stoked with a very public open call for auditions for her elite dance troupe. Hundreds of hopefuls queued for hours in the biting cold along Manhattan's Lafayette Street. Twenty-one-year-old dance student Janelle Gilchrist had spotted an ad in the New York magazine *Back Stage*. "I was like, Ohmigod, I gotta go," she gushed to MTV reporter Rob Kemp. Another applicant was less relaxed. "This is as bad as it gets," said twenty-one-year-old Mollie Black. "Usually it's fifty or eighty people. Obviously every dancer wants to dance for Madonna." Her friend Cherilyn Caulfield agreed: "It's more of a media event than anything else."

In the end, of Madonna's ten-strong Drowned World troupe, only Ruthy Inchaustegui from The Girlie Show had danced with her before. The musicians were new recruits as well, with her musical director a hip twenty-two-year-old DJ/composer Stuart Price. Otherwise known as Jacques Lu Cont, the London-based artist had his own cult electronic act, Les Rhythmes Digitales, and later became part of dance/rock band Zoot Woman. Before he took the call from Madonna's management, Price was used to making records that sold maybe five hundred copies. He described his 1996 album *Darkdancer* as "club house music with 80s production values bleeding through." This obviously appealed to Madonna, but Price was shocked when he received the summons early in 2001.

"I wasn't expecting it," he told me in 2003. "I was doing promo in Cologne, staying in a hotel room so small that the door opened out into the corridor. I was hired first just to play keyboards, but there was a certain direction she was looking for, and she put me in control of making music the right side of cool. For me it was an opportunity—there's no other major artist on that level who'd take the risk of having someone like me, not well-known, control the music. I didn't have a burning desire to be a musical director, but with her it was different. Her style of working was different." On the song "Holiday," Price suggested that she drop part of an obscure Ibiza bootleg of Stardust's "Music Sounds Better with You" into the middle section. "Madonna said, 'Yeah, fuck it, let's do it.' You don't see Whitney or Tina Turner doing that."

Band rehearsals began in Los Angeles that spring at Culver City Sound studios. For the first month, Price, guitarist Monte Pittman (who was also Madonna's guitar teacher), percussionist Ron Powell, and drummer Steve Sidelnyk concentrated solely on the music, putting in thirteen-hour days, five days a week. "After finishing a rehearsal at ten p.m., I'd go to the production studio and get ready for the next morning. I'd get a few hours sleep, then get up to go to rehearsal again," says Price, who claims not to have minded the rigorous schedule. "Madonna's a notorious hard worker, but she's also good fun. She's hard-working and hard-laughing! I felt relaxed, which made me feel useful."

Once the first stage of rehearsals was done, Warner Records announced dates that were due to start in Cologne that June, claiming that her tour would be "the most extravagant stage spectacle of her illustrious career." The global box-office frenzy was unprecedented, with tickets selling out within hours. Meanwhile, the second month of rehearsals took place at the L.A. Lakers' Stadium, where Madonna worked out the nuts and bolts of the stage show in an arena context. "With the massiveness of it all, there were so many things we had to achieve, and things just ran over," Price recalls. With a show that was using over a hundred tons of equipment, including giant TV screens and a mechanical bull, there were bound to be teething problems. Madonna's traveling entourage came close to two hundred people, and eight juggernauts had to transport equipment from venue to venue, including a stage that covered 4,900 square feet. Inevitably, the first German dates were canceled due to "technical problems." The queen of pop did not seem overly apologetic, so some German fans threw away their Madonna CDs in protest.

The delay was soon forgotten, after the grand opening night at the Palau Sant Jordi arena in Barcelona on June 9. Here she unveiled a set that was more performance art than greatest hits, sending Warner executives into a spin. Madonna was adamant, however, that this was to be a personal statement, focusing on the new musical direction she'd taken with *Ray of Light* and *Music*. "Her music for that moment was really kind of introspective and dark, so the tour had to reflect that phase," said the tour director Jamie King. "I thought it was really important that Madonna didn't sell out and that she didn't just do the hits, but she did really cover her new material because that was who she had evolved into and . . . who she was." A former dancer with Michael Jackson, King was also a protégé of Prince. His anarchic, energetic style was suited to Madonna's new direction. "Madonna for so many years has been . . . about beauty, great light, powerful, positive images. So it was interesting to see her transformed into this sort of darker character. It was really intriguing," he said.

The set designer Bruce Rogers created a vivid, apocalyptic backdrop for the show. He claimed his inspiration lay in his West Texan childhood. "I grew up in an area known as the 'oil patch.' The weather there was as much a part of life as anything. We had thundering rainstorms with lightning and tornadoes, windstorms, mud storms, flash floods, hailstorms," he said. "We had such large skies I sometimes felt that I was in the midst of God's theater."

Lighting director Peter Morse was a little skeptical at first. "She took on Jamie King as a new director. He has very bizarre ideas—'this is a dark show with a dark feel.'" But then Morse understood that what was important was the unseen, what symbolized the unconscious. "It's not so much about the notes that make the music, but the space between them. I kept in a lot of shadow and not much direct light, to keep it mysterious."

Like a cross between commedia dell'arte and high-end Las Vegas spectacle, Drowned World was a deliberate challenge to concertgoers. The first section featured a rather clichéd reference to punk nihilism, with Gaultier-designed bondage gear, cyberpunk gas masks, and

Madonna dressed in a 1977 punk-style kilt. She cursed at the audience and played guitar Stooges-style, funneling her rebellion into the "anti-fame" tracks like "Substitute for Love" and the grungy "Candy Perfume Girl." According to Oasis guitarist Gem Archer, who saw the show at London Earl's Court, she was a passable guitar-player. "I thought, Yeah, get on there, you've learned a few chords. But it looked like the barre chord still hurts."

It was a quirky opening, but the show really got into gear with the Geisha section, where for the song "Frozen," Madonna appeared onstage in black wig, kimono, and forty-foot sleeves. For "Nobody's Perfect," she turned into a hobbling geisha girl, suppliant and submissive before her male oppressor. In an echo of the long-ago fight with Sean Penn, when he had threatened to cut off her hair, the samurai swordsman hacked off her ponytail and held it aloft like a trophy, while Madonna fell to the ground. She moved into "Mer Girl Part 1," an atmospheric piece about the death of her mother, which was interrupted by the spectacular sequence of "Sky Fits Heaven," where dancers flew *Crouching Tiger, Hidden Dragon*–style from one end of the stage to the other. Turning into the vengeful female warrior, she slit the samurai's throat with ostensible satisfaction. Then, with "Mer Girl Part 2," she pulled off her wig and shot him dead. Projected behind her was a ghostly Madonna, chalk-white, with blue bruises and blood seeping out of her nose. She has the avenging air of Goddess Kali, and the terrifying intensity of Japanese horror films like *Ringu*. Against a Moroder-style backbeat, this section of the show concluded with violent manga-like cartoons and dark, pornographic imagery.

It wasn't an easy ride. It looked beautiful, and it had elegance and fragility as well as lurid color. At her London show, while many people in the audience were spellbound, just as many chatted in the aisles, waiting for her to sing the hits. For those involved, it was an artistic and technical challenge. "It was extremely hard to choreograph, because of the different martial arts," recalls choreographer Alex Magno. "Madonna and the dancers had to be trained. All the flying was very dangerous. 'Frozen' took us two days to work out, but 'Sky Fits Heaven' took two weeks."

Morse found this section a tricky one to light. "I didn't want to follow people as they flew, I just wanted to accent their flight. They had to get their timing right. And Madonna wanted to highlight these kanji characters from the ancient Japanese alphabet. I managed to make the symbols appear on those forty-foot-long sleeves. It was so perfect I couldn't believe it. That was one of those magic moments."

And Magno had to be inventive with the choreography, because Madonna wanted to sing with a mike. "She had Rocco, he was very young. She hadn't performed for eight years and she needed to get back into shape. She didn't want to dance so much, she wanted to sing live and sound good. She didn't want to wear a headset—she wanted to hold a wireless mike and sing everything live. I found that very limiting. She's always asking, 'What're the *words*?' She's very picky about that. It's not just the music, she's like an actor saying, 'What's the word here?' She remembers all those songs with the steps."

The song "Frozen" is a personal favorite of Magno's, so he was delighted to be asked to choreograph it. He loved the video—"where she's in black with henna tattoos and birds flying. Brilliant, the strings and the lyrics. It was, OK, here's a goddess. That music makes her a myth." But faced with the forty-foot arm-span, Magno was stumped. "In the video her hands move so beautifully, like a ballet," he says. "But with those huge long sleeves she wasn't able to use her hands. You want to move the hands. So I had to make it with the movement of the slaves and the dancers."

What he also found testing at times was getting his instructions from Jamie King. "Madonna would communicate with Jamie and then he'd communicate with me. Sometimes there were misunderstandings. It was hard, but we survived!" King was a hard taskmaster. Dancer Jull Weber said, "He is very demanding. He likes everything to be done quick and precise. He also has an amazing eye for error, so he can detect anything that goes wrong. He deserves all the success he's had." King was the perfect foil for Madonna, creating a show that was like "a well-oiled machine." This time around, she needed to delegate; she was in a different place from when she had done The Girlie Show eight years earlier. "Madonna had changed a lot as a person," recalls Magno. "For The Girlie Show tour she was much more involved. She knew every detail, even the guy that was cleaning the floor. Then I had a direct connection with her. She was consumed by her work."

By the time of Drowned World, she had shifted focus. "Her work was her husband; he was her lover, her everything. She was much calmer as a person, more sensitive. She was still a perfectionist, but more forgiving. The mother side came out." Although forcing her to divide her time between work and family, becoming a mother had given new emotional depth to Madonna's live show. "I feel between The Girlie Show tour and Drowned World she evolved immensely as an artist," says Magno.

This calmness was apparent in the third segment of the show, where Madonna transmuted into the cowgirl. Sitting comfortably on a couple of haystacks, in a Stetson and diamante, playing guitar and singing "I Deserve It," she smiled widely at her screaming fans as if to say, "Look, I can sing and play guitar at the same time!" It was an engaging moment. With the Americana section, Madonna was fully at home. She did a line-dancing hoe-down for "Don't Tell Me" and sat astride a bucking mechanical bull for the defiant "Human Nature." Quite what country-and-western fans would have made of her stereotypical renditions is anybody's guess. But Madonna was determined to have her fun. By the time she sang the song "Secret," the psychodrama was complete. Behind her were projected images of spiritual awakening—from Melodie McDaniel's baptism film to shots of Jews praying at the Western Wall. Here, for a moment, was a reference to her own religious conversion.

Then Madonna shifted gear once more to early 80s New York Danceteria, with a triumphant version of "Holiday." The neo-disco of "Music" provided a celebratory finale, as she spun on a giant revolving seven-inch single, while a huge screen behind her projected image after image, from Material to Geisha Girl. For Stuart Price, this was a personal high point. "A big part of the rhythmical structure of 'Music' is taken from Kraftwerk's 'Trans-Europe Express,' so we decided to

re-create it wholesale and make it the intro to the live song. It's basically one note played a million times—it can sound minimal on your
kitchen stereo, and it can be massive in a stadium. I found it really
exciting as the climax of the show."

Right to the end of the show, she was a stickler for detail. Peter
Morse remembers the opening night of the U.S. leg of the tour,
in Philadelphia. By then he had an assistant who took care of the
lighting, but Morse decided to visit the venue that night. "There's a
point during 'Holiday' when she and the girls go down in an elevator,
and the spotlight shines on her face. The guy was an instant too late,
just half a second. 'That's nothing!' he said. 'It'll be big tomorrow,'
I told him. And it *was*. 'Peter Morse, you fucked that up.' 'I was just
visiting . . . !' We were always on the edge of our seats with her. We
didn't dare disappoint her, or she'd kick your butt."

ALTHOUGH MANY people talked about a kinder, gentler Madonna
since her interest in Kabbalah, some close to her felt she had changed,
and not necessarily for the best. That, ironically, the more compassionate her outward persona became, the more businesslike she was
with some of her oldest friends. During this tour, Niki Haris, in particular, noticed a rift developing. "There's what you'll do at twenty-
two, and what you won't put up with at forty. Madonna was my friend,
this amazing girl from Michigan, someone I was doing a gig with,"
Niki told me.

Problems arose when Niki expressed disapproval of the costumes
and creative direction of the songs. "I remember it was hard for me
to tell her after the 'Like a Prayer' video, 'It's tough for me to see you
dancing in front of burning crosses.' Then she was so understanding, but for Drowned World she didn't seem to like me voicing my
opinion.

Over her years with Madonna, Niki had shared a lot as a friend.
She had also been given more responsibility on the live tours. "By
The Girlie Show, she was letting me help with choreography. And

on Drowned World, I was doing the girls' numbers with Jamie and singing her parts during sound-check to save her voice. She relied on us for a lot of things." But Niki saw her status subtly change.

"There's a time in an artist's life when they just want to be around their fans. I kept it real with her. I'm not going to sugarcoat it 'cause you're Madonna. But there comes a time when if all the people are saying 'yes' and there's this one voice saying 'no,' well, you're no longer a friend. All I do is frustrate her." Although Niki felt uneasy about the atmosphere surrounding Madonna, she bit the bullet and continued with the tour. And the show was shaping up to be a hit.

Drowned World was Madonna's most complex piece of musical theater yet. It elicited a passionate, if mixed response. In the United Kingdom, the *Mirror's* Kevin O'Sullivan dubbed the show "An immaculate misconception . . . tedious nonsense." The *Daily Mail* hyperventilated over how much money she was earning from the London shows (£27,000 a minute), but said: "There's plenty of material in the old Material Girl yet." In the United States, she did a grand slam of thirty dates, determined to beat the younger competition. *USA Today* praised her for still being "the canniest provocateur in pop," while the *New York Daily News* raised the old chestnut "42-year-old mother-of-two," yet celebrated a show that "doesn't stoop to the corn and contrivance of Vegas." Although she was focused on the show, Madonna made sure that her family traveled with her on as many dates as possible. That is why she always tours in the summer, so her children can come too. At this point, she and Guy were in post-wedded bliss, and the latter didn't mind too much that he was playing the supporting role to her career. It wasn't until her Re-Invention tour three years later that his resentment began to emerge.

After two nights in Philadelphia, Madonna performed five hysteria-surrounded dates at Madison Square Garden. By early August, the strain was beginning to show, as one of her New Jersey nights was canceled due to laryngitis. She took a few precious days off before returning to the fray. As the tour snaked across the United States, the Madonna publicity machine was in full swing, whether to announce her plans to do a remake of Lina Wertmüller's 1974 film *Swept Away* with Guy, or the Sotheby's online auction of her memorabilia, with the beaded Dolce & Gabbana bra from The Girlie Show fetching a record $23,850. Then the festivities came to a complete stop. "The end of the tour usually builds up to a big party," remembers Price. "But this ended on a very somber note."

On September 11, terrorists hijacked two passenger jet airliners and crashed them into the World Trade Center towers in New York. A third plane smashed into the Pentagon, and another, retaken by the passengers, went down in Pennsylvania. Nearly three thousand people died in these attacks. Madonna postponed her concert that night at Los Angeles's Staples Center, and pledged all proceeds from her final three dates to the victims and their families. "There was a moment's silence every night," recalls Price. "It was a poignant end to the tour." Dancer Jull Weber said that Madonna turned the final shows into a "commemorative event. She talked in all the concerts about the tragedy that happened. We weren't just continuing our tour, we were performing to celebrate joy and happiness, especially in that time of difficulty."

On the closing night of September 15, Madonna wore an American flag for a skirt, instead of a kilt, and led the crowd in prayer, encouraging President Bush to practice restraint. "Violence begets violence," she told the twenty-thousand-strong audience. "What happened was horrible, but I'd like to think of it as a wake-up call. There's terrorism every day all over the world . . ." The crowd obliged her request for a moment of silence, but then some fans began frantically chanting, "U-S-A!"

"OK, USA—but start looking at the whole world. If you want to change the world, change yourself," she countered, the heat of the moment making her unusually candid. "We're not doing this show because we want to forget, but because we want people to remember how precious life is." With that, "Holiday," extraordinarily, became a call for world peace.

AFTER THE Drowned World tour had ended, the receipts were counted. According to the Amusement Business database, Madonna's

Drowned World was the number-three grossing concert tour in the United States in 2001. Her stint at Madison Square Garden alone, for instance, earned her over $9 million. But, claims Stuart Price, it's not just about business. "When someone goes through that financial barrier, they don't do it to be rich, they have a desire to be exceptional. The lady isn't just a businesswoman, she has a deep ingrained musical sense."

In February of the following year, at America's prestigious Orville H. Gibson Guitar Awards, Madonna was nominated for Most Promising Up-and-Coming Guitarist. There were a few raised eyebrows, but for the ever-ambitious Madonna, this must have been the best payback of all.

THE WORLD Trade Center attack threw a pall over the next few years. The cultural mood was one of bleak soul-searching and paranoia. After the high hopes and global parties of the beginning of the millennium, a raw truth seared through Europe and America that there was a price to be paid for free-market domination, that Western beliefs were not unassailable, nor were they perfect. Terrorism had been a blight on the political landscape in Europe for several decades, but in the United States, that expression of hatred took many citizens by surprise. "But what's not to love?" many asked about their culture and the American Dream, which for so many had been a long-lasting ideal.

In her next album, *American Life*, Madonna questioned those values, and questioned herself. Hers was an appropriate response to the 9/11 disaster and the ensuing Iraq War. Although she didn't address those issues directly, the confusion, disorientation, and anger they created seeped into the grooves of each song. Recording started late in 2001, then was put on hold while she filmed *Swept Away* in Malta and starred in the West End play *Up for Grabs*. Then Madonna returned to the studio in the summer of 2002, just as the debate about America's planned invasion of Iraq was heating up. At one level, there is no separation between political and personal life, and her record expressed that. She would later mutter about Mirwais's downbeat existentialism and the long discussions they had into the night, but the French producer only brought out a sense of anxiety that existed deep within her. At first, the proposed album title was *Ein Sof*, a Hebrew word meaning "endlessness." It was rumored to be Madonna's religious record, but as the months went on, it became more a meditation on the difficulty of leading a spiritual life in the A-list bubble, and the album title was changed to *American Life*. "It's a reflection of my state of mind and a view of the world right now," she said.

She was forty-four years old and experiencing what amounted to a midlife crisis. If *Like a Prayer* was her "divorce" album, *American Life* is her psychoanalysis. She even references Sigmund Freud, and throws out countless questions: Who am I? Where am I going? What does it all mean? Much of the album is suffused with sarcasm: right from the disaffected ennui of the title track to the belligerence of "Nobody Knows Me," Madonna is kicking against the claustrophobic effect of celebrity worship. As movie star Brad Pitt once said: "Celebrity is bestial. It is the worst type of karma, because of the huge solitude it brings. You are like a gazelle that finds itself straying from the flock. And soon your path is cut off by lions." His statement is a little self-pitying—most people would give their eyeteeth to have his money and power—but there's truth in the weirdly antisocial nature of fame and materialism.

The cult of celebrity fosters social division, the sense of separation into "us and them." According to cultural theorist Terry Eagleton: "There is an erotic enticement in the idea of being able to do anything you like, just as there is phantasmal fulfillment in the idea of resources that can never be spent. Celebrities are the postmodern version of the horn of plenty, the Land of Cockayne, the fairy-tale purse that can never be empty. In a world running out of both oil and elbow room, this vision has its allure." He adds that in a "drably unheroic" world, the "magic has to be artificially manufactured." Madonna called this "the allure of the beautiful life. Look like this, you're gonna be happy. Drive this car, you're gonna be popular. Wear these clothes, and people are gonna want to fuck you. It's a very powerful illusion, and people are caught up in it, including myself. Or I was."

Her friend, the director James Foley, saw the impact that fame had on Madonna. As quoted earlier: "She gets home, takes off her coat, and takes off her personality. Her accent even changes from fake Brit to native Detroit. I'm fascinated by fame—what a radical experience it must be for someone like her. We all have a perception of the world outside of us, but to have that world looking back at you—it's bizarre. You can't turn it off. It's amusing for a while, then it becomes claustrophobic, a horrible trap."

Madonna has had her celebrity moments. There was the time in the late 80s when she was introduced to Billy Steinberg, writer of her "Like a Virgin" hit, at a party. "It was a bit comical really," Steinberg recalls. "I was sitting on the terrace with Steve Bray when she walked toward us with Warren Beatty. Steve said, 'Madonna, this is Billy Steinberg who wrote 'Like a Virgin.' Warren starts to laugh. I say, 'Gee, I've wanted to meet you for so long.' She snapped, 'Well, now you did,' and walked away. I was crestfallen. She must be slightly resentful she didn't write her signature song."

Her Hollywood actor friend Rupert Everett recalled a night during the *Truth or Dare* years, when he invited Madonna to dinner and she ignored his guests. "Madonna was approaching the dizzy pinnacle of fame, and at those heights you don't bother to disguise your feelings. If she was bored, she let you know. Manners were something she had discarded at base camp," Everett said. There was also the New Year's Eve when Madonna went with Sean Penn to Helena's, an exclusive club in Los Angeles. Sean didn't dance, so she brought her choreographer along just in case she wanted to hit the floor. The only snag was, he had to leave his gay lover outside. Witness to this event was Dennis Fanning, a no-nonsense policeman who was helping Sean with research for his role as a cop in *Colors*. Fanning went to the door and pulled the man in, telling security he was with Madonna's party. "I sit his ass down next to his boyfriend, turn to [Madonna], and go, 'C'mon, you want to dance with him? Dance. But why should his boyfriend be outside on New Year's Eve? The fuck is that all about?' She's looking at me like she hasn't been talked to like that in years."

Manners were in short supply in later years too, when Kabbalah was meant to have tempered Madonna's ego. One evening in L.A., her former makeup artist Sharon Gault saw Madonna at a Kabbalah meeting. She said hello, and the star apparently looked straight through her. "As if she doesn't know her, as if she'd never seen her in her life," recalls Niki Haris (whom Gault related the story to). "Yet Sharon did her makeup for years." The "beautiful life" was still very alluring to Madonna. "The line between the haves and have-nots was wider. The superstardom became out of hand. She was so inaccessible," says Niki. "After the Kabbalah thing, I'd go to her house and there'd be Jewish men sitting by her pool, and answering her phone. It was off-putting. It went from her being a super-close friend to me having no access to my friend."

Though Madonna was politicized and penitent in public, Niki had yet to see her newly compassionate side. "In 2003, just before I gave birth to my daughter Jordan, Madonna threw a baby shower for me. I was touched, because things had been strained between us since the Drowned World tour," she says. "But after that she never contacted me again. Phone calls weren't returned, she changed her e-mail address. I had witnessed this with Madonna for years. In a way, we were all employees, pure cattle. A friend said, 'You're not that important to her.' I realized then it was all over."

Other friends of Madonna, though, attest that her pattern of severing ties is justifiable. "I don't think she enjoys or intends to hurt anybody," maintains Tony Shimkin, her friend and cowriter from *Erotica* days. "So many people who work with her want to keep in contact and get more and more out of her. She lets people get close, but not for too long. When I sensed it might be an issue, I ceased to call. She has to protect herself."

And many see her as nothing but loyal. Her former dancer Carlton Wilborn, for instance, recalls her lending him her Hollywood chateau for a few months when he was "between work and having a hard time. She was out of town a lot. She brought me in, taught me the security system, and let me have the run of it. I will always be indebted to her.

She could've dropped me $10,000, but she did this for how I needed to feel. There was me and the security guard and that was it. She trusted me and that was fantastic."

Niki Haris went on to have a successful solo career, making seven jazz records, supporting Gay Pride events worldwide, and singing for the Dalai Lama in Tibet. She is happy with her lot, and asserts that she is grateful for the time she had with Madonna. "When she's being the best she can be, she's amazing—loving, giving, and charitable," she says. "But due to her inaccessibility to me now, I have a stinging feeling in my heart and questions that were never answered."

At one level, Madonna was well aware of the corrosive effects of stardom. Celebrity has an ugly side, and she wasn't afraid to ridicule that. On the song "American Life," she sends herself up, rapping (rather badly) about having a jet pilot, a private Pilates teacher, and three nannies, yet still feeling unsatisfied. It is a frank, contradictory critique of the culture that spawned her. Although Madonna has benefited immeasurably from the American Dream, she knows its pitfalls and feels qualified to draw attention to them. "I'm saying celebrity is bullshit. And who knows better than me?" she declared. Disruption is a feature of this record. On her previous album, *Music*, Mirwais's stops, starts, and electronic glitches symbolized the force and fun of hedonism, whereas here, they just signal discomfort. His twitchiness perfectly suited her mood. "The music has to jar my brains in terms of lyrics," she said. "Different things inspire me to write. I could be having a guitar lesson and something will just come to me. Or Mirwais will send me over music—rough stuff that doesn't have an arrangement, basic chord progressions. *American Life* itself came about like that."

The next track, "Hollywood" is old-school Madonna in the way her voice glides over sumptuous pop beats. You could almost be in the car with the top down, cruising Sunset Boulevard, smelling the magnolias, sensing promise, looking to be noticed, looking for that lucky break. But the song's breezy momentum is rudely interrupted at the end by Madonna chanting in a distorted, robotic voice. She sings with wry sensuality, capturing that illusive sense of sunshine, freedom, and desperation that so characterizes Los Angeles.

Then, on the track "I'm So Stupid," Madonna reclaims the geek inside. Though she writes with pithy dexterity, sometimes her lyrics seem to be aimed squarely at the audience for whom English is a second language. This song is a case in point—a confession almost idiotic in its simplicity. But then maybe it's the voice of the teen-age Midwestern girl hell-bent on making it. The dazed-sounding track "Nobody Knows Me" also has a sense of childlike defiance, dismissing critics who have no knowledge of her jealously guarded inner self.

The concept at the knotty heart of this album is "nothing." It is there in the titles—"Nobody Knows Me," "Nothing Fails"—it's there in the repetition of "no" in the song "Love Profusion." With her strong use of the words "no" and "nothing," Madonna is sarcastic about people's assumptions about her and emphatic about what she knows. That romantic love is her lodestone, her source of power. As a hymn of devotion, "Nothing Fails" is the most majestic song on the album.

It began as a humble track that musician/producer Guy Sigsworth wrote for his wife. "I never write love songs, but I was moved to write one for her," he says. "I've never had a problematic relationship with her, there's not been a lot of drama. But I wanted to write some-thing naive and honest." Sigsworth developed it with female artist Gem Archer to come up with something understated yet moving in its simplicity. In demo form, it sounds like an offbeat folk song. They decided to send it to Madonna. She loved it, and asked if she could rewrite it a little. What is interesting is how she changed the melody line on the chorus to make it more instantly pop. Her version adds to the original, giving it a melodic lift. This, coupled with Mirwais's generous production, lends it a dramatic, theatrical air. "It was very different sonically from our demo, but I was happy with what they did," says Sigsworth.

Complete with London Community Gospel choir and strings, the song becomes revelatory and ecstatic, honoring the transforming power of love. "They were a bunch of great singers giving it loudly," recalls the strings engineer Geoff Foster. Madonna's mysticism seeps through, with her references to the Kabbalistic "tree of life." Orthodox rabbis were infuriated with the way she played fast and loose with the name Yahweh, but, misguided or not, her thirst for spiritual sustenance led to the creation of a ballad, awe-inspiring in its beauty.

In its wake come the acoustic guitars and quiet reflection of "Intervention" and "X-Static Process," tracks with the bell-like clarity of a 1960s Joan Baez folk song. The warm, rudimentary guitar sounds symbolize a private sanctuary that's distinct from the techno clutter of other tracks. These "songs for Guy" then lead into her equivalent of *Ray of Light*'s "Mer Girl," the song on the album most striking for its autobiographical intimacy. Propelled by pneumatic disco pop, "Mother and Father" is another paean to the mother she lost. Detailing the hurt and neglect in her family, Madonna moves from nursery-rhyme singsong to frantic rap to sounding like a demented twelve-year-old Bessie Smith. It's a triumph, both as pop psychoanalysis and as a piece of mangled, innovative dance music.

"That song is a way of letting go of the sadness and moving on," she said later. Much of her life she has felt surrounded by death, with the death of her mother, close relatives, and her beloved friends in New York. "I've always been aware of my own mortality. I've always had that feeling of, What is the point of living and life?" That altered when she had children and realized that "we're here to share, to give, to love," and death wasn't necessarily an end in itself.

Disrupting this reverie is "Die Another Day," which Elton John later lambasted as "the worst Bond tune of all time." With its stabbing techno strings and disembodied voice, it was almost an anti-Bond theme. The fact that she won a Golden Raspberry Award for Worst Supporting Actress in the Bond movie didn't help. "They wanted something big and brash and in yer face," recalls Geoff Foster. "Mirwais didn't want strings in the traditional sense, with that big bed of lushness. She'd done that with 'Frozen' and moved on. There's something sacrosanct about having an orchestra, so it's vaguely blasphemous to take it and cut it up and mess with it. The original arrangement was more complete and flowing, and Mirwais totally cut it up. Which is fine—that's part of the process!"

Much easier on the ear is the final song, "Easy Ride." Cowritten with Monte Pittman, this track is about the wayward Midwestern girl returning home, working for the good life with blood, sweat, and a few tears. Her priorities are warmth, security, earth, life, and family. Post-9/11, this seems fair enough. But over and above that soars the longing to live forever, to remain transcendent. Its filmic strings give the close of this album a sense of open space and cautious hope. We feel that Madonna's spiritual journey is complete—for now.

IN LAUNCHING the album, Madonna opted for a radical image. As in 1989, with *Like a Prayer*, she dyed her hair dark brown to signify "serious." On the album cover she resurrects the classic 1960s image of Che Guevara. Wearing a black beret and anarchist colors, she is Madonna the revolutionary. Some also saw a parallel between the album cover and an infamous 70s photo of kidnapped newspaper heiress Patty Hearst. There are torn fragments of the U.S. Stars and Stripes, and two red stripes daubed like warrior paint on her face. The letters AMERICAN LIFE bleed blood-red, punk-rock style, and the parental-advisory sticker signals a very "adult" record. In the CD booklet, she totes an Uzi submachine gun, her body in various martial-arts poses spelling out the letters of her name. The photo shoot, photographed by Craig McDean and packaged by the French design team M/M Paris, cost a rumored $415,000.

Despite the introspective nature of the songs, Madonna still wanted *American Life* to be a hit album. "If she doesn't shift units, she's disappointed. Maverick is a multimillion dollar machine that has to be kept going," says Foster. "During recording she was really focused, with a machine-like stamina. There was a sense of camaraderie, but you've got to make sure you're on top of your game."

MADONNA MADE sure she was up to the minute with the "American Life" video, an extension of the provocative artwork for the CD booklet. Here she plays a gun-toting resistance fighter, with her crack team shooting from the runway into the crowd at a fictional fashion show. She ends up throwing a grenade at a President Bush look-alike. It would have been more powerful had the target been more political than vacuous fashionistas, but it still caused a stir. "It is an antiwar statement," she said. "But it's not necessarily against [the Iraq] war. At any given moment, there's at least thirty wars going on in this world and I'm against all of them." The main problem with the video was the timing of its release.

Part of the fallout from the 9/11 disaster was the U.S. administration's determination to invade Iraq. U.S. Congress gave President Bush authority to attack Iraq if Saddam Hussein didn't give up weapons of mass destruction (WMD) he supposedly had. On February 15, 2003, 10 million people in over sixty countries in the world (including a million in the United Kingdom) demonstrated against the war. But the U.S.-led Operation Iraqi Freedom began on March 20, in defiance of the United Nations Security Council's resolution. Although coalition troops included soldiers from the United Kingdom, many claimed that this was a violation of international law, breaking the UN Charter.

It was a sensitive time, as countries including France, Russia, and China signaled their opposition, and America and the United Kingdom were increasingly isolated. There was a McCarthy-like atmosphere of paranoia in the United States—only this time, the "reds under the bed" were Muslim terrorists or non-patriots. In this highly charged climate, many musicians and actors felt pressured to support the war or remain silent. All-female country band the Dixie Chicks became the focus of a hate campaign when their lead singer, Natalie Maines, spoke out against Bush, saying, "I feel the president is ignoring the opinions of many in the U.S. and alienating the rest of the world."

As a result, the band received death threats, had their music banned by many radio stations, and lost a large section of their country audience. Branded "Dixie Sluts," "Traitors," and "Saddam's Angels," they were told to "shut up and sing." Bruce Springsteen and Madonna came out in support of the right of the band to express their opinions—though, faced with the prospect of low sales and public condemnation, Madonna toned down her own political rhetoric. On April 1, she postponed the release of the "American Life" video, and then withdrew it, saying: "I have decided not to release my new video. It was filmed before the war started and I do not believe it is appropriate to air it at this time. Due to the volatile state of the world and out of sensitivity and respect for the armed forces, who I support and pray for, I do not want to risk offending anyone who might misinterpret the meaning of this video."

Many fans saw this as Madonna copping out, fudging what could have been a radical artistic statement. Some even suggested it was just another carefully orchestrated publicity stunt. It would have been courageous of Madonna not to dilute her message, but, ever aware of her megastar status and the bottom dollar, she was nervous about a backlash.

As the months wore on, the campaign against the Dixie Chicks showed no signs of abating.

In May, a Colorado radio station suspended two DJs for playing the Dixie Chicks in violation of a ban on their music. There were boos at the Academy of Country Music (ACM) Awards in Las Vegas when the group's nomination for Entertainer of the Year was announced. The academy gave the award to Toby Keith, an outspoken critic of the group. Then the U.S. Red Cross refused a $1 million donation from the band. Maines said at the time: "The entire country may disagree with me, but I don't understand the necessity for patriotism. Why d'you have to be a patriot? About what? This land is our land? Why?"

Though the Dixie Chicks lost many fans, they gained a new audience. "I'd rather have a smaller following of really cool people who get it," band member Martie Maguire said, "than people that have us in their five-disc changer with Reba McEntire and Toby Keith."

272 M A D O N N A : L I K E A N I C O N

As it was, Madonna lost out with both her mainstream and her hip audience. Withdrawing the video annoyed those against the war, while for others, she hadn't gone far enough in support of Bush. Even though the album was more about fame versus love than an explicit antiwar statement, it was deemed unpatriotic. Reviews were mixed— "Madonna has absolutely nothing to say to us," yawned the U.K. *Sunday Times*, while the *Independent* claimed she sounded like "some lady of the manor swanking it over the plebs." In contrast, BBC Radio 1 praised the record as "brave and strong," with "attitude and balls." Many reviewers were perplexed by the contradictory nature of the title track—you detest the trap of fame and money, but love the American Dream? You hate the celebrity pecking order, but have to be top dog? What gives?

In the end, the beauty of her love songs got overlooked, and the acoustic rock tone didn't appeal. Sales suffered. *American Life* has posted the lowest sales of any Madonna album to date, both in the United States and worldwide. It went to number one the first week of release, but then quickly fell down the charts. By mid-2006, it had reached 666,000 copies sold, compared to the 3 million of its predecessor, *Music*. But it has grown as a cult favorite among fans, and became a huge remix success on the club scene. It was the only album in history to have seven top-ten hits on the U.S. Hot Dance Music/Club Play chart. Later, Madonna compared Mirwais to Jean-Paul Sartre, describing him as "very intellectual, very analytical, very cerebral, very existential, very philosophical." On a slightly disparaging note, she added: "We both got sucked into the French existentialist vortex. We both decided we were against the war, and we both smoked Gauloises and wore berets, and we were against everything. . . . I was in a very angry mood, a mood to be political, very upset with George Bush."

Although Madonna's hardcore audience never abandoned her, *American Life* marked a significant dip. Like a lot of her peers, she had been compromised as an artist. "There is an atmosphere of fear in America right now that is deadly," said Sir Elton John. "Everyone is too career-conscious. They're all too scared. In the 1960s, people like Bob Dylan, the Beatles, and Pete Seeger were constantly writing and talking about what was going on. Now hardly any are doing it." But by mid-2004, it was apparent that Iraq's WMDs were nonexistent, and the U.S. administration came under scrutiny. This, combined with the box-office-breaking success of Michael Moore's antiwar film *Fahrenheit 9/11*, meant that artists felt able to nail their colors to the mast. The Dixie Chicks were joined by artists including Jon Bon Jovi, Dave Matthews, James Taylor, Wyclef Jean, Ozzy Osbourne, Mary J. Blige, and Pink in their condemnation of the war. And though Madonna was to steer well away from the subject for her next album, the controversy surfaced in her live tours instead.

By the beginning of 2004, she was eager to go out on the road again, if only to promote the hell out of *American Life*. Once again, she had to take on the younger stars snapping at her heels, and prove she was the best.

MOMMY
POP STAR

IN AUGUST 2003 AT THE MTV VIDEO AWARDS, TWO young pop "virgins," Britney Spears and Christina Aguilera, appeared onstage dressed in wedding white, singing "Like a Virgin." They were joined by Madonna, the bridegroom, dressed in vampiric black. The latter swooped in on Britney and gave her an emphatic French kiss, before launching into "Hollywood," her caustic tale of Tinseltown. The crowd was ecstatic. "I kissed Britney Spears. I am the mommy pop star and she is the baby pop star," Madonna said later. "And I am kissing her to pass my energy to her."

At that point, Britney was her biggest rival. Her 1999 debut album *Baby One More Time* had sold over 27 million copies worldwide. With her pneumatic grace and Barbie-doll looks, Britney was the quintessential teen diva. There was something compulsive about her performance, about the way she attacked dance routines with vim, vigor, and a strange kind of pent-up anger. "I practiced so hard I was delirious," she once said of a night rehearsing a video routine. Like Madonna in her early days, Spears was no skinny supermodel, but had a robust quality that appealed directly to her teenage girl audience. She combined sex and spirituality with the raunchy schoolgirl look. Coming from a devout Baptist background, she said that she intended to remain a virgin till marriage (hence the "Like a Virgin" joke). No wonder that "Britney naked" became the most popular request typed into Internet search engines.

Later that year, Madonna dueted with Britney on the latter's single "Me Against the Music," and the suggestive video had them dry-humping each other with a wall between them. The general verdict was that this was a rather desperate attempt at titillation. "It's just the stupidest video either of them has ever made and they both know it," says Dustin Robertson, editor of the promo. "Madonna almost took herself out of the edit, until I saved the performance with shots she signed off on. Didn't love, but signed off on." The two stars didn't collaborate on anything else. Britney had a lot of Madonna's moves (and even her interest in Kabbalah), but that is where the similarity ended. Coming from a poor background in Louisiana, Britney worked as an off-Broadway child actor and was a veteran of the Mickey Mouse Club at eleven. Groomed by producer Eric Foster and Swedish songwriting maestro Max Martin, she launched a pop career and was world-famous by her teens. Her success ushered in a new era of manufactured pop.

In the face of this, Madonna felt compelled to assert her position. "I arrived at a different time," she said. "Before the time of Svengalis holding talent searches; finding a girl that looks right and can carry a tune, and then figuring a way to market her. I'm not saying those girls can't grow into something, but . . . everything is so homogenized."

But all was not as perfectly stage-managed as it seemed. It was inevitable that having been groomed so rigorously for stardom, Britney chose to rebel. And she differed from Madonna in the way she so publicly fell apart. By early 2007, after a failed marriage to dancer and aspiring rapper Kevin Federline, and a custody battle over their two baby boys, a troubled Britney got tattoos and went off on an alcohol-fueled bender. In a moment of disintegration, she roughly shaved her head in front of the paparazzi and ended up in rehab for alcohol and drug abuse. Unsurprisingly, Madonna distanced herself from the rather tarnished pop princess.

By 2004, Madonna was confronting her aging self. It was rumored that she told the producer of her Drowned World tour video to airbrush out any lines or wrinkles. By her own admission, it was taking longer and longer to get her image together. But at the age of forty-five, there was no question of growing old gracefully. Determined to seize time and trends and mold them to her wishes, Madonna simply devoured her prey. The Britney kiss brings to mind Roger Corman's 1959 horror flick *Wasp Woman*, in which cosmetics magnate Susan Cabot develops a rejuvenating beauty cream derived from an enzyme secreted by wasps. It's intended to make women look forever youthful. Obsessed with restoring her fading charms, Cabot insists on being the first test subject. The solution is at first remarkably effective, transforming her into a sultry, dark-haired vixen . . . until she begins to take on the predatory traits of a giant female wasp, setting out on a nocturnal killing spree. After she devours her victims, nothing—not even shoes, belts, or cardigans—is left.

By virtue of its sheer size and scale, and its dedication to her greatest hits, the Re-Invention tour that summer was one way of gobbling up the competition. From the moment she started auditions, Madonna began filming the process with Jonas Akerlund, director of her "Ray of Light" and "Music" videos. By enlisting Akerlund for her tour film, she hoped to create a fiercely edited and fast-paced documentary that had some of the spirit of *Truth or Dare*, twelve years later. It was as if Madonna had one eye on posterity. At the same time, all her albums were reissued and remastered in acknowledgment of her considerable legacy. Once again, Jamie King was employed as artistic director of the tour. "Madonna came up with that name (Re-Invention) because for years everyone has been always saying she re-invented herself," he said. "And in typical Madonna fashion, she played on that and used it against . . . the users."

As ever, Madonna had a clear idea of what she wanted from her new cast of dancers. "She's really attracted to *characters*, people who can take on roles," says Raistalla, a striking black female dancer who assumed many of Re-Invention's androgynous parts. "Her ideas for shows are so lavish and theatrical, as a dancer you have to know how to project yourself and portray something within that." Born in Miami, Raistalla comes from a musical family, and started dancing at a young age. She wasn't a personal fan of Madonna's, but "my mom was a *big* fan. She had *all* her albums!" When it came to the audition, Raistalla thought that she didn't have a chance. "Madonna's dancing usually fits a certain criteria, with a lot of acrobatic and physical stuff. But once I got toward the end of the audition, I realized I *did* have a chance. I knew her energy, that it was competitive, so at the end, when I had to do ten one-handed push-ups, I was staring her dead in the eye, thinking, I'm this person you want me to be. I was giving it to the character, I pulled in everything I knew. What sold it to her was the way I did the tango, with lots of passion and emotion."

From the opening scenes, Re-Invention was a very passionate, sensual show. Filmmaker Chris Cunningham (who has made disturbing avant-garde videos for artists like the Prodigy and Aphex Twin) shot the introductory film *The Beast Within,* where Madonna writhes on a dirty old bed like a deranged demigoddess, being barked at by wolves and reciting from the *Book of Revelations.* The film was projected onto enormous screens, the biggest size available at the time. "We had them custom-made. It was outrageous," said Jamie King. The effect was one of overwhelming the senses. "We were gobsmacked," recalls Dan Holden, a fan who saw her London Wembley Arena show. "I was so floored that when Madonna first appeared doing her yoga moves, I couldn't quite take it in."

After the upside-down glory of "The Beast Within," the show slipped into the song "Vogue," which was set in a 3D-style Regency interior, with the dancers wearing minimalist Renaissance costumes. With its strong visual flair, Madonna likened the show to an art installation that slightly changed every night. She sang "Nobody Knows Me" as laser light words zipped around her. She dressed up in military garb and danced to simulated explosions for "American Life." Violent images of war and suffering were projected behind her as the dancers paraded in religious costumes: an Orthodox priest, a rabbi, a nun. "Religion breeds fragmentation. We're taking off the things that separate people, so they can all be one," Madonna said later, conveniently ignoring the fact that Kabbalah is a religious belief system. Raistalla remembers that song as a high point of the show. "I loved performing that one. I'm a militant person, I like projecting a strong, commanding presence. We were soldiers and we had to manifest issues of life in America. I had similar feelings to Madonna, and was able to express what I felt about the situation with Iraq—I was displaying that in my body."

On the back-screen projection, a President Bush look-alike cozied up to a Saddam Hussein double. Madonna's anger at the Iraq War was still raw and on display. The connection between religion and fashion was accentuated by a V-shaped catwalk that rose above the crowd.

It was an emotive spectacle, one that didn't let up, as Madonna moved into a jazz/circus section. Cloud, one of her most gifted dancers, entered stage left as an acrobatic huckster in a top hat, dancing to a remixed version of "Hollywood." Here we had icons of multiethnic U.S. culture—the tap dancer, the skateboarder, the fire-eater, the Hindu dancer. Madonna then turns this contemporary vaudeville into gothic horror as she sits and sings in an electric chair, wearing a Wild West costume made out of the stars and stripes. Every possible button is pushed.

Having dispatched with a tango version of "Die Another Day," Madonna reappeared in bohemian black with a hippie bandana, looking like her Maverick protégée Alanis Morissette. Complete with acoustic guitar, she performed moving versions of "Nothing Fails," "Like a Prayer,"and "Mother and Father." The only mawkish note was her rendition of John Lennon's "Imagine," on a par with "American Pie" for underscoring pointedly what Madonna is not. Her renditions of other people's protest songs sound like karaoke, whereas her uplifting dance anthems are inimitable. For the final section, she brought in Lorne Cousin, a bagpipe player from the Scottish Highlands. "It was Madonna's idea. It was the link between 'Imagine' and 'Into the Groove.' The idea was that it would start off slowly, like a lament, to follow the mood of that song and then build up in tempo so that it led to 'Into the Groove.' I think it worked really well," recalled Cousin.

To suit the mood, all the male dancers were kitted out in long tartan kilts. This audacious look became one of the most enduring images of the show. "That was the other high point for me," recalls Raistalla. "Performing 'Music' in Celtic skirts. It was supposed to be all boys. I could pull off the boy roles really well, so Madonna threw me in too. I felt we exchanged well when we were dancing together. My energy bounces back and forth and in and out, like hers. The times we shared onstage, we were connected."

At the end of the show, while performing "Papa Don't Preach," Madonna wore black T-shirts with various "Do It Better" lines, referencing the famous ITALIANS DO IT BETTER T-shirt from the 1987 "Papa Don't Preach" video. One night, it was KABBALISTS DO IT BETTER, while on other nights it was BRITS or IRISH. Her message was all-inclusive and declarative. As the final notes of "Holiday" rang out, projected behind her on the giant screens were the words REINVENT YOURSELF.

The tour was a major undertaking, with fifty-six shows in twenty cities. It became the highest-grossing concert tour of the year, with estimated takings of $124.5 million. Reviews were favorable: USA Today, for instance, praised it as "splashy and stylish" with (thank God) "sexy but age-appropriate costumes," while Washington Post writer David Segal confessed to being "entertained into submission." Although Madonna's showbiz hybrid of Broadway, Cirque du Soleil, military drills, and rock concert left him reeling, he couldn't help admiring it: "Here's the weird part: It's not a mess," he wrote. "It's actually kind of amazing. Pretentious and annoyingly preachy at moments, yes. Strangely devoid of titillation and almost tame by the standards of her naughty-naughty phase, sure. But measured in verve, nerve and technical wizardry, it's hard to leave this epic extravaganza feeling anything less than awe." For fans, too, the show was a favorite. "Because it was a greatest hits, everyone knew the songs and everyone in the auditorium was singing along. With Drowned World, you sometimes felt detached, but with this, everyone felt part of it," recalls fan Dan Holden. "It was very uplifting."

Despite the plaudits, however, Re-Invention somehow slipped beneath the mass-media radar. Although it eventually became the year's best-selling tour, Madonna had to promote hard, particularly in the United States, to sell out the shows. Part of the problem was the vastly inflated ticket price—in the United States, for instance, she was charging up to $300 a seat. Also, many people underwhelmed by *American Life* saw it as a bid to shore up sagging album sales with "a quick-buck oldies tour." Although musically it had a retro feel, Re-Invention showed how Madonna had entered a new phase with her utilization of visual art. In plundering her back catalogue, she began to do the one thing she professes never to do: reflect. The seeds of this had already been sown in a little-known fine-art installation that had a brief run in New York in 2003.

X-STaTIC PRO=CeSS is one of Madonna's most fascinating projects. In a series of photographs, shot in 2002 with Stephen Klein, Madonna deconstructed her own myth to devastating effect. She was a mature woman growing tired of posing for glorified fashion shoots, and she had a critical distance from all those pristine pop-culture images she had created. "I'm not interested in going to a fashion shoot and just trying on a bunch of clothes," she told W magazine. "I can't tell you how boring it is posing for pictures. It's so boring. If I don't feel like I'm creating something that means something, I don't want to do it."

Madonna had always admired avant-garde fashion photographer Stephen Klein, a graduate of the Rhode Island School of Design. Klein's approach combined a sense of surrealism with the erotic. He and Madonna had worked together on various shoots and formed a rapport. After lengthy e-mail exchanges, they came up with the idea of "the process," because Madonna sometimes felt that her most interesting thoughts occurred during rehearsal rather than in the final piece. Their proposal for the *X-STaTIC PRO=CeSS* exhibit was "a performer in her rehearsal space where she creates and brings her ideas to life or death." Like many photographers before him, Klein used Madonna as his muse.

"Madonna's always been more of a performance artist to me," he said. "So I created a landscape for her to respond to, using things she's explored in the past, like the wedding dress, the pole, fire, death, the bed, religion." During a break in her recording of the *American Life* album, they had a marathon ten-hour photo and filming session. In the bare surroundings of an anonymous studio, some key themes emerged: first, there was the coyote, a feral, prairie wolf with wild eyes. In ancient mythology, the wolf is a symbol of evil, the chaotic and destructive potential of the Universe. This theme was developed in the accompanying "Beast Within" video piece, where Madonna recites apocalyptic words inspired by the *Book of Revelations*: ". . . As for the murderers, fornicators, sorcerers, idolators, and all liars/Their lot shall be in the lake that burns with fire," she intones.

Madonna uses the elemental force of fire in vivid piece of deconstruction. A pristine white wedding dress, like the one in the "Like a Virgin" video, sits on a tailor's dummy. In a series of images, we see the dress devoured by flames until there is nothing left but charred, blackened pieces of lace. Over forty pages in this five-hundred-page work are devoted to the dress on fire. Copyright on the entire exhibit is credited to Boy Toy Inc., a tongue-in-cheek reference to the 80s persona that she cheerfully destroyed. In fact, the triptych of albums, *Ray of Light, Music*, and *American Life*, are all about her systematically dismantling images that no longer served her—the virgin/whore tease, the fame-hungry star, the blond ambition virago. "I'm not a pop star, I'm a performance artist," she once said haughtily to a TV interviewer. With this exhibit, she stripped away the pop glitz to reveal the real performer underneath.

We see Madonna wearing an off-white leotard and fishnet tights, holding ballet and yoga poses. There is something Puritan yet faintly erotic about her outfit. She poses with her head down on a bare bed, her hair riven with plain brown hair grips. There is a sense of austerity, of solitary confinement and anguish. In other shots, her knees are bandaged, her tights laddered, and her leotard torn, showing the exhaustion of constant rehearsal. And there's the vaudeville: Madonna as a circus contortionist, legs behind her head and blue high heels on her feet.

In these pictures, the emphasis is on her body, not her face. Klein has created a painterly impression, like a mangled Degas. Most striking of all are her "queen" images. Here she is wearing a jeweled mask, a dark red damask crinoline, and an ornate headdress. Her face implacable behind an animal-like mask, she looks part Elizabethan, part magical high priestess. Like the ladies of the Renaissance court, with rotting faces beneath their white lead powder, this image is magnificently decrepit. I can show you what lies beneath this glittering showbiz exterior, she seems to say, I can show you what is corrupted.

Madonna's session with Klein ended up as a short exhibition at the Deitch Projects in SoHo, in the spring of 2003. The gallery was transformed into a dark, blue-lit postindustrial theater by Klein and designers from the architecture firm LOT/EK. Images of the bed, the queen, and the coyote became photographic animations valued at up to $65,000 a piece. And many of the pictures ended up in a $350 limited-edition art book made up of delicate tissue-like pages in a slip case.

Originally a one-off, X-STaTIC PRO=CeSS provided inspiration for the Re-Invention show, and as the tour progressed throughout 2004, Madonna and Klein added to the exhibition. It was shown in London and Berlin after the tour ended, and then again two years later, in augmented form, in Japan. It is an installation that keeps on mutating. It's Madonna's pure artistic license, and an indication of where her creative heart lies. For her, this started off as an anti-fashion shoot.

"I can enjoy fashion—sometimes," she said. "Some of my very good friends are designers. Jean-Paul Gaultier is a real artist. And I can see the beauty and the art that is involved with couture and design. . . . But with everything going on in the world right now, I just feel we are too preoccupied with the wrong things. I'm just not that interested anymore in fashion per se. . . . Now, actresses look like models and models become actresses. Yuck. Who has any individuality?" Away from the commercial bottom line, this was her opportunity to explore the avant-garde within herself. "This is the inner landscape of a performance artist. And I think, if you look at the pictures, they're not even in the most flattering positions, you know? It's not about that."

With her work, Madonna registered a deep change in herself, one prompted by having a family. This was apparent to all those who came in contact with her. "She was much calmer as a person on the Drowned World tour, but before the Re-Invention tour, she was a *completely* different person again," says choreographer Alex Magno. "She was very calm and peaceful, just not the same. She was *tamed*, not a wild beast anymore."

Whether this was due to Guy Ritchie is a moot point. "Guy's a very manly man. Whenever he comes around she completely crumbles, she loves him so much," her dancer Raistalla told me. "She's such a boss, but when he's there she turns into a little kitten. It's funny to see." Keeping her family together is a key priority for Madonna. "Rocco and Lola were around a lot of the time. She let us hang out with them in rehearsals and play with them at her house." In turn, Madonna kept an eye on her dancers. "She's very motherly; I thought she took good care of us," recalls Raistalla. "I got injured a couple of times—she was on top of it, making sure we were healthy, that we saw doctors. She took us to see other artists who might inspire us, like the French pianist Katia Labèque." Madonna also wasn't averse to teaching them a little Kabbalah. "She was like a mother in that she was into our self-improvement. She introduced us to Kabbalah. I absorbed it, I liked the sessions, and I wanted to explore it. But in the end I didn't continue with it, because Kabbalah can be very confusing and mind-wrecking if you take it too far."

By then, Madonna had been studying Kabbalah for eight years. What began as tentative quest prior to the *Ray of Light* album developed into a full commitment to the Kabbalah Center and its teachings. As she pursued her spiritual interests, more and more fans began to follow suit, becoming part of a popularization of this ancient philosophy. Dating back to first century A.D. in Palestine, it essentially transcribes the way the Universe works. It is encapsulated in the *Zohar*, the primary text of Kabbalah, which was said to be "written in black fire on white fire" and revealed to Moses at Mount Sinai. Within the text are the seventy-two Hebrew names of God, an arrangement and rearrangement of twenty-two letters coded within the first books of the Bible. There is the surface meaning of the words and stories, but concealed within are hidden messages of divinity that keen students can understand only through dedicated prayer and meditation. Scholars and rabbis have been cracking the code for centuries. Modern Kabbalists refer to this code as a kind of DNA for the Universe. For Madonna, who loves the power of words, and who used layered meanings of the Catholic liturgy on her *Like a Prayer* album, this was irresistible.

Kabbalah has a rich history, one that emerged in its modern form in twelfth-century Provence, with the doctrine of the sephiroth, the ten emanations of God. They are represented as branches on a tree, parts of the body, or steps from earthly chaos to the spiritual world. One of the major Kabbalists from this period was Abraham Abulafia (1240–95), among the first to create the written letter combinations of the Kabbalah, as keys to altered states of consciousness. Later, in the thirteenth century, a Spanish Jew called Moses de Leon published the *Sepher ha Zohar*, or *Book of Splendor*, which became the key text of Judaic Kabbalah. By the eighteenth century, though, Kabbalah went into decline, with many Jews dismissing it as mere superstition.

CONCURRENT WITH the development of Jewish Kabbalah was a liberal, humanist interpretation that flowered during the Renaissance, becoming a major influence on European occult philosophers and magicians. The Kabbalah that Madonna adheres to is firmly rooted in the Judaic Old Testament. Although it went into decline for a while, there was a revival in the late 1960s, along with the wider trend for spiritual exploration. Kabbalah received a commercial boost when New Yorker Karen Berg and an orthodox Hasidic Jew called Shraga Feivel Gruberger came up with a new, modern interpretation of the ancient system. When they met, she was a secretary in his insurance firm and both were married to other people. She didn't see him again until eight years later when, as a young divorcée, she found herself "strangely flustered" when asking him about his Kabbalah studies.

By 1971, Gruberger had left his wife and children, reinvented himself as Dr. Philip Berg, and married Karen. She referred to their affair as the working of a higher power. It was revealed to her in a dream that her job was to wrest this centuries-old tradition from the mantle of Jewish men over forty and make it accessible to all. "I insisted that this wisdom be made available to the peoples: to everyone, of any age, gender or religious belief. . . . I said, 'If I can understand it, then anyone can,'" Karen declared.

Soon after their marriage, they set up a learning center in Tel Aviv, followed by one in New York. Karen trademarked the name "Kabbalah Center," and it grew rapidly, so that by 2006 there were fifty-one centers worldwide and 3.5 million converts. It now boasts a range of celebrity A-listers from Lindsay Lohan and Demi Moore to Michael Jackson, the Beckhams, and Britney Spears. Like Hinduism in the 1970s and Nichiren Shoshu Buddhism in the 1980s, Kabbalah was the new system of belief for spiritually hungry stars. It has been given a twenty-first century spin, with scientific-sounding buzz-phrases like "spiritual DNA" and "technology for the soul," designed to reassure young skeptics. This is what drew Guy Ritchie, a committed Darwinist, to Kabbalah. "It's challenging. It's like a physics lesson, the bridge between science and spirituality," said Madonna. Though he was cynical at first, she persuaded Guy to come to a class, and he began to study it further. "I think he was kind of embarrassed, [as] he doesn't want to subscribe to anything that's perceived as being religious. . . . But the bottom line is that it's very scientific, and that's what appeals to Guy."

The Kabbalah headquarters in London reflects its elevated status. Based in Stratford Place in the West End, it is a large building with deep pile carpets, shining pastel-pink chandeliers, and luscious flowers in strategically placed vases. This contrasts with the more basic, homey surroundings of the Beverly Hills HQ, one of the oldest centers. Though the decor is different, the philosophy is the same worldwide. I went to an open-day early in 2006, and browsed at the bookstore. With such a rich, varied tradition of writing on Kabbalah, I expected to find an array of different texts. Instead, there were about fifteen titles, all beautifully produced and all written by either Rav, Michael, Yehuda, or Karen Berg. Hmm. Judging by their bookstore, it would be hard to counter the suggestion that Kabbalah Center is a family cult and "Kabbalah Lite." While Madonna prides herself on her intellectual rigor, it's strange that the version she opted for ignores all other scholarly writing on the subject.

Still, there were some engaging talks at the London center. I found out about Kabbalistic astrology ("tuning into the energy of the cosmos"), Kabbalah and health ("cancer is a confusion of the body"), and its perspective on women. While much of the center's transformative theology is persuasive and positive (Yehuda Berg's *The 72 Names of God* being a key text), its attitude toward women is less enlightened. Nestling amid the feminist sound bites of Karen Berg's *God Wears Lipstick* are some reactionary ideas. "Men and women are two entities," said speaker Ruth Nahmias. "A man is the channel of energy, the woman is the vessel . . . like an electric lightbulb, he is the plus, she is the minus. It's like pouring water into a cup, she reveals the light." In this determinist universe, men are the active force, women the passive.

Some women in the workshop began to demur: What about lesbians? What about single career-women? Then, when Ms. Nahmias declared, "I don't want you to be feminist," several openly walked out. This perhaps wasn't the smartest way to attract independent twenty-first-century women. On one level, Karen Berg's assertion that she wrested a four-thousand-year-old philosophy from the hands of a male elite and made it accessible to women contradicts her deeply traditional view of women's "special spiritual role."

It is ironic that Madonna, seen as one of the strongest women of modern times, gravitates toward Kabbalah. She rejected Catholicism for its patriarchal rigidity, only to adopt a system that echoes the fundaments of Old Testament Christianity in its polarizing of men and women. In the Bible, conception is an act of magic—the Son of God is born without sex taking place, therefore the ideal woman is one who doesn't have sex. Women were seen as earthly creatures with base instincts, while only men had the potential to perceive the higher planes. In Kabbalah, the emphasis is on transcending the "garbage," the earthiness of life. "Intent on journeying from a lower to a higher level of being," the Kabbalist needs to reach a state of "purification." The notion of clean clothes without matching a pure soul within echoes the very Jansenist Catholicism that inspired Madonna's mother. Maybe that is what was behind Madonna's spiritual search—and, on a more base level, her demand for a new toilet seat to be installed at each venue she visited on her 2006 Confessions tour.

More progressive is the Kabbalah Center's Spirituality for Kids foundation, which works in schools and youth and community centers to help children develop into "strong, clear, happy human beings." This is the area of the Kabbalah Center where Madonna has most focused her energies. It's not surprising that she has donated all her profits from her children's books to the foundation. The idea for the books first emerged in the early 90s, when her American publisher Nicholas Callaway watched Madonna read one of his books, *Miss Spider's Tea Party*, for MTV, to promote her album *Bedtime Stories*. The audience of feisty teenagers were spellbound. "I thought then that she had an uncanny ability to tell a story," said Callaway, "and that's when I first suggested to her that she might make a terrific children's book author."

After becoming a mother, Madonna decided to take him up on his offer. Impatient with traditional "princess" stories, she decided to write one of her own. "The women in *Cinderella* or *Sleeping Beauty* or *Snow White* are really passive. They don't move the plot along at all. They just show up, they're beautiful . . . the princes tell them they want to marry them, and then they go off and live happily ever after," Madonna remarked. "I thought, 'Well, what's a girl supposed to get out of this? That's such a load of crap.'"

Her first book, *The English Roses*, was inspired by her daughter's schoolfriends, whose names were (as in the book) Nicole, Amy, Charlotte, and Grace. It's a gentle lesson in dealing with jealousy, as the girls are nudged by a fairy godmother to be kind to another girl, Binah, whom they have ostracized. Binah is beautiful and good, but leads a sad existence and she is seen by the other children as an outsider. In a story that echoes Madonna's childhood, the heroine's mother is dead and she has to do household chores all day for her father. Her life is transformed when the girls bring her in to their elite circle. "First they invited Binah to a tea party, and then they started walking to school with her, and not long after that, they were doing homework together," writes Madonna. "Binah even taught them how to bake an apple pie. They soon found out that she was very likeable indeed."

This was the first of five stories that she presented to Callaway in 2002. Wanting to make books that had a classic feel, she and her publisher searched long and hard for suitable illustrators. Warhol protégé Jeffrey Fulvimari was their first choice, and he illustrated *The English Roses* with a sophisticated, whimsical style that echoed 1930s French classics like *Babar* and *Madeleine*. The book became an event, published simultaneously the following year in thirty languages and more than a hundred countries. On the day of publication, Madonna hosted a children's tea party in London. Dressed in a flowery dress and glasses, looking every inch the demure housewife, she read from her book. One of the onlookers noted with bemusement the bizarre crowd, saying: "It was a mixture of fidgety children, gay men weeping, and skeptical journalists."

For children's literature expert Wendy Cooling, the party was memorable. "It was a beautiful day on a roof terrace in Kensington, a posh champagne launch party where we all had a bit of fun," she recalls. "Madonna read to the children, but they found it difficult to listen—they were all a bit young. Madonna was very charming. She was delightful to her children, she obviously has a good relationship with them. Afterward, she was sweet to me, giving me roses from the display, saying, 'Take something home, take a rose, take a butterfly.' I warmed to her, but, sadly, didn't warm to the books."

The English Roses was soon followed by *Mr. Peabody's Apples*, a three-hundred-year-old Ukrainian Kabbalah tale updated to 50s America and lusciously illustrated, with a nostalgic "innocent art" feel, by Loren Long. In 2004 came *Yakov and the Seven Thieves*, adapted from another story by the same Ukrainian rabbi, Baal Shem Tov. This one preached that "all of us have the ability to unlock the gates of Heaven—no matter how unworthy we think we are." There was also *Arabian Nights*–inspired *The Adventures of Abdi*, and, in 2005, *Lotsa de Casha*, a story reflecting on the age-old adage that money doesn't buy happiness.

Though eyebrows were raised at the thought of the *Sex* book heroine writing for children, in some ways Madonna wasn't taking a huge leap. Some of her songwriting is in a nursery-rhyme style, and woven through her music is a sense of childlike innocence—whether it's "Dear Jessie" on *Like a Prayer*, or "Mother and Father" on *American Life*. Sometimes her lyrics are clumsy, as if English is her second language, as though she's keeping it simple for the mass demographic—"Impressive Instant" from the *Music* album being a case in point.

As theorist Roland Barthes once wrote about pop music in "On Popular Music," "The music, as well as the lyrics, tends to affect such a children's language . . . [like] repetition . . . the limitation of many melodies to very few tones, comparable to the way in which a small child speaks before he has the full alphabet at his disposal . . . also certain over-sweet sound colors, functioning like musical cookies and candies."

Madonna is great at "simple." As she told producer Guy Sigsworth, "I do simple really well." But while this works in her songwriting, her artless approach to children's books isn't quite so effective. She tells the tales in a straightforward, rather dry way, interrupting the flow at points with self-conscious humorous asides. Although they have sold moderately well, the critical reception has been muted. "I found them too moralistic, too obvious," says Wendy Cooling. "I suspect if they'd been [written] by anyone else, other than Madonna, they wouldn't have seen the light of day. They don't read aloud terribly well. A book for young children has to have a kind of rhythm and an element of surprise."

Children's expert Julia Eccleshare agrees: "Her books are very message-ridden. These celebrities think that writing a children's book should be easy. It isn't that simple. It's like trying to hit a moving target. *Charlotte's Web*, for instance, [is] a story about a pig and a spider. Who'd have thought that would become a classic? But it has a lot of humanity and warmth, and the story drives along in an exciting way." By the time *Too Good to Be True*, Madonna's 2006 sequel to *The English Roses*, appeared, various celebrities, from Fergie, Duchess of York, to Julie Andrews and Kylie Minogue, had tried their hand at children's literature. "Childhood is the new nirvana. Being a good parent is part of celebrity status," remarks Eccleshare. "Also with Madonna we get the sense of strong messages she wants to convey."

As well as the Kabbalah themes and the promotion of Spirituality for Kids, the underlying message in Madonna's children's stories was one of retreat, a nostalgia for stability, tradition, and family values. This was strikingly expressed in her next persona, the Lady of the Manor.

AMERICAN WIFE

UP AN ANCIENT ROMAN ROAD ALONG THE ROUTE TO Salisbury from Winchester, on top of a hill near Cranborne Chase, the valleys and rolling hills of a Wiltshire countryside are in full, decadent bloom. Down a steep path, past bald signs that say KEEP DOGS ON LEASH, a tree-lined path opens, giving way to rearing pens for pheasants and partridges. Game is everywhere, primed for shooting. The turrets of a house are nestled behind a screen of trees. A black ornamental gate and fence protect a sloping garden filled with more rearing pens.

Ashcombe House is a modest red-brick country manor with a brown roof and bedrooms tucked in the eaves. It exudes a reassuring, cozy, storybook air—seeming completely private, but then not. Madonna's back garden skirts a public right of way.

A path from the house leads down to the village of Tollard Royal, comprised of a few cottages and a pub called the King John Inn, run with flair by an attractive brunette, Michelle Birks. "Madonna used to come in here for a pint. Not so much now," she says tersely. The pub interior is dark wood and crushed velvet, with a photo montage on the walls of themed Rocky Horror party nights. It has the same

1970s bikers' feel as pubs on the Isle of Man. In the country, nothing changes.

In August 2005, Madonna was featured in U.S. *Vogue* sitting astride a horse, wearing tweed and jodhpurs, leaning down to put one arm around Guy, who stood in front of her in his flat cap and country woolens. She also appeared in twinset and pearls, feeding the hens, blond hair coiffed like a 1930s American heiress. "Speaking in carefully modulated tones . . . making polite but distracted small talk, she has the air of an Edwardian dollar princess—the moneyed American belles who were married off to impecunious British nobles in the golden age," wrote *Vogue*'s Hamish Bowles.

The magazine displayed photographs of the interior of her £9 million country home, Ashcombe House, former residence of 1930s society photographer and diarist Cecil Beaton. Madonna and Guy bought the house when it came on the market a few years before. Initially, Guy was the one eager to buy a rural retreat. "Guy has always wanted to live in the countryside," said Madonna. "He's the country person, not me. He loves nature and animals." Loves animals so much, in fact, that he wants to shoot them. Propelled by boyhood memories of Loton Park, his stepfather Sir Michael Leighton's estate on the Welsh borders, Guy has always been passionate about hunting and fishing. "We did a couple of days in West Yorkshire. Fantastic birds—150 feet high, at least. We were stood in this deep valley. These birds were seriously high—fucking fantastic shooting," he once said. "But I'm out for the *craic* as much as anything. All I want is seven mates to go and have a scream with." He realizes that not everybody approves. "If I was an outsider looking in, I would not approve. . . . I would think everything about it was Machiavellian and slightly macabre," he admitted.

For Madonna, country life offered a fantasy escape. In the *Vogue* article, she waxed lyrical about the romance of Ashcombe; how it "has something very mystical about it . . . in the summertime it's the most beautiful place in the world." She talked with glee about the Cecil Beaton–style parties she hosted, weekends of folly where she created a makeshift stage and invited all her friends to stay. "We put red velvet curtains up. Gwyneth and Stella and Chris composed a song together, which was brilliant—a spoof on 'American Life,' only they called it 'American Wife,'" laughed Madonna. Tracey Emin and well-groomed art consultant Zoe Manzi wrote a poem and recited it, while Sting played the lute and Trudie read a Shakespearean sonnet. Madonna herself performed a bawdy scene from a 1930s mock-Restoration play *The Town Wench or Chastity Rewarded*. There was something slightly cloying about this charade, as if Madonna was playing dress-up with her self-congratulatory friends.

But deep within there was also a wish for artistic tranquility. "You can choose to go there to work in a very undistracted way . . . or you can go there and get lost in the environment," she said of Ashcombe. "You feel protected because you're sunk into that valley, and as far as the eye can see you can't see another house. It's a kind of buffer against the world." The snag was, her private world abutted a very public right of way. There was consternation among local people when shortly after the couple moved in, they tried to restrict the use of the public footpath. In 2004, she partly won her attempt to prevent ramblers from walking across the estate. A planning inspector ruled that the public should not be granted access to much of the land under "right to roam" legislation.

"It was a source of some interest to us in the profession as to why the path hadn't been identified during the legal process," says Adrian Neale, an estates manager based nearby in Winchester. "Diverting a public right of way has to be done through the county council, and it's difficult, time-consuming, and costly." Outweighing the problem of the public footpath, though, was the quality of the 1,200 acres of land attached to the house. It is an optimum site for game shooting. "It's a trophy estate. The topography is perfect, with low valleys and high ridges," says an insider. "Guy Ritchie takes his shooting seriously. He buys a day at a premier shooting venue and travels around the country. He and his party are very demanding, apparently."

Madonna embraced her husband's hobbies. "I see England as my

home. I now know how to ride. I know how to shoot. I know how to
fish," she said proudly. She hosted shooting parties, with guests including Vinne Jones, Marco Pierre White, and notorious pro-hunter
A. A. Gill, who once wrote in GQ magazine of deer-stalking and "that
heavy, delicious, repellent scent of cud and blood." He posed with a
gutted stag strewn over his Land Rover like a fashion accessory, his
hunting partner proudly wearing blood from the deer entrails like
a bizarre face pack. It reminded me of having tea in the home of a
wealthy woman who frequently went hunting with her husband. Her
drawing room was impeccable, with expensive drapes, antique furniture, and silver cutlery. Which made it all the more strange to see the
arrangement of splattered and dismembered fox carefully attached
to her beautiful wallpaper. This was the mind-set that Madonna was
welcoming into her life.

In October 2005, she was listed tenth in *Country Life* magazine's
"Power 100 of the Countryside." At a time when the Countryside
Alliance was fighting the Anti-Hunting Bill that was passed through
Parliament, Madonna was being feted as one of the most powerful
figures in rural Britain. "She successfully fought access legislation that
affected her privacy, her participation in shooting helped boost the
rural economy, and her foray into the world of riding . . . will surely
provide a welcome fillip to an equine industry increasingly beset by
health and safety . . . legislation," declared the magazine.

This was a perplexing incarnation for Madonna fans, particularly
British ones. The United Kingdom is still a class-based society with
a wealthy monarchy and landowning aristocracy. Unlike most other
European countries, Britain is not a republic. Despite decades of re-
branding, marketing, and selling off country estates piecemeal to the
"nouveau riche," there is a lingering feudal mentality, a sense of "us
and them." In becoming the rarefied Lady of the Manor, Madonna
transmuted from "us" into "them," she was the "toff" swanking it over
the "plebs." To those who loved her meritocratic rise from New York
City streets through club culture and cutting-edge pop, this adoption
of such a conservative persona seemed like betrayal.

"Madonna has little to add and nowhere to go as a cultural radical. She could genuinely embrace oppositional politics to mark herself as definitively radical in the early twenty-first century, but has instead embraced the trappings of an English aristocratic lifestyle," wrote cultural theorist Sean Albiez. "She thinks she the Queen of England," remarked her former backup singer Niki Haris. "The difference in her voice from, say, the Blond Ambition era and now is marked," agrees UK voice expert and acting coach Louise Kerr. "Her voice now is fuller, less nasal, more 'trained.' She has gone from being American (which is a classless society) to identifying with a class that doesn't resonate with the fan base. People don't aim to be part of the aristocracy."

An American fan expressed to me dismay at her "elitism," at the way she appeared to turn her back on the United States. The unease at Madonna's Lady of the Manor persona has historical foundation. Many of those aristocratic country estates were the result of ill-gotten gains from the eighteenth-century slave trade in the Caribbean. This aspect of history has been obscured, now that the days of the big houses like Blenheim, Chatsworth, and Longleat are over. The countryside is no longer dominated by the rigid hierarchy that Robert Altman so precisely pictured in his 2001 film *Gosford Park*. The old landowners are gradually being replaced by a new breed of city businessmen and "high net-worth individuals," but this breed is just as interested in protecting its financial assets. Madonna is not the only one buying up land—she is in the company of bands and musicians like Genesis, Sting, and former Pink Floyd guitarist Dave Gilmour. "Those rock stars who've made it earn a lot of money. It's not just the purchase price of a country estate, they need to be pretty wealthy to run it thereafter," says Neale. "You have to afford the staff to upkeep these listed properties. There's also the farming, which is not particularly profitable, and capital-intensive, plus game-keeping, etc. Still, it's regarded as a bit of a trophy."

It is also a serious piece of investment. Madonna's move to the United Kingdom takes on a new light when one considers that "for overseas buyers, the United Kingdom is regarded as a very secure place to live. They can freely move their money in and out of the

United Kingdom without fear of government interference through taxes." This has provoked a reaction with some of the old guard. "There's great sadness from long-standing country folk at seeing the great estates being broken up," says Neale. "There's a feeling that the asset breakup has tipped over into new money, into countryside, with these 'outsiders' coming in. But you can't pickle a rural property in aspic and expect it not to change."

Madonna has talked about meeting Prince Charles. She was very amused at the way he flung his lettuce around at dinner. Maybe eating with royalty was proof that she had made it. The question is, can a wild-card pop star really buy her way into the British upper class? "It's entirely possible. It takes about two minutes. The British upper class is very keen on money," asserts cultural commentator Peter York. "All you need is a flattering tongue, some money, a house, and someone to organize parties for you. Any sensible duke will come and drink your good wine."

There has long been a history of rock 'n' rollers, from Mick Jagger to Bryan Ferry, hobnobbing with the gentry. For York, the issue is why "any intelligent, self-starting human being would want to do that. But it is a fact that quite confident, achieved, and modern people do find certain aspects of the British upper class rather attractive. We're not talking about the stuffy older end. They like the idea of louche, rather beautiful people who can do what they want. It's like being a pop star without groveling on the dole at the beginning. What the upper class have is a way of life legitimized and proven by *centuries*, therefore it can't go wrong. A lot of these stars are aspirational, they know what the good stuff is, and go for it with a sort of homing instinct." Marrying ex-prep-school Guy Ritchie was a wise move. "With him she didn't just have an entree, she had a permanent conduit."

The other location for Madonna's bespoke British lifestyle is her town house in London's Marble Arch. "London is now the biggest metropolitan area for the international rich, more so than New York," says York, sitting in his well-appointed abode a few streets away from Madonna's. He points out of the window. "If you were to throw a brick out of here, you think you'd hit a nice, sensible British person behind these Regency facades. Well, you wouldn't. There's a sweet French investment banker there. Two gentlemen sharing there, one Swiss, one German. An Italian restaurateur. A French hedge-fund dealer. In South Kensington, it's all French Eurotrash. And here there are so many Americans because it's near the American embassy. This city is very receptive to everybody, and it's now at the pinnacle of its decadent multiculturalism. Madonna chose to be here. It's actually very clever of her." York saw her one evening at the nearby members-only club Home House. "She was small and not very noticeable—like a tiny little Victorian wax doll stuck up on cushions."

For Madonna, London was a place she had to learn to love. "I never thought in a million years I'd live in London. In fact, I quite disliked the place for a while," she said. "When I started out as a singer, the press was so terrible to me. . . . So this was always a city I'd get in and out of as quickly as possible. Then I met my husband. . . . He was a filmmaker, working mostly in London. It just seemed like it was my move to make, which I did. Then I just fell in love with London. If I was in America for a while, I'd begin to really miss [it]. . . . It's funny the way things turned out." U.K. tax laws, which favor the super-rich, also probably helped to ease the way. Since the late 90s, London in particular has become "the world's conduit of choice for private wealth." As *Guardian* writer James Meek says, "Its generous treatment of the mega-rich, particularly those born abroad, makes it in some ways a virtual tax haven."

By 2004, Madonna was overhauling her business empire. Six years earlier, she had "let go" of her manager Freddy DeMann with a reputed $25 million payoff. Complaining that he worked her too hard and made her tour too often, she hired female managers (first her former secretary Caresse Henry, and then for her "Semtex Girl" management team, "Semtex Girl" Angela Becker), who, she felt, were more sympathetic to her needs. "I consider my manager to be one of my best friends," she said of Becker. "I like to keep people around me that I've known a long time. I have lots of surrogate mothers!"

Once DeMann was out of the picture, she encountered problems with Maverick, the label that she had set up with such high expectations in 1991. A former partner in the company, DeMann had been a steady influence, and his exit coincided with a downturn in the label's fortunes.

From its inception, Madonna regarded Maverick as more than a vanity label. Taking her CEO role seriously, she and partner Guy Oseary worked hard on the A&R front, spending a lot of time wooing and recruiting acts. Her most successful signing was Alanis Morissette, the Canadian singer/songwriter, whose 1995 debut *Jagged Little Pill* went on to sell 30 million worldwide. Although Morissette told me that the album was "written from a desperate, dark, almost pathetically sad place within my subconscious," her anthem-like tales of survival and revenge struck a chord. Like Carole King's *Tapestry* in the 1970s, *Jagged Little Pill* captured the feelings of a female generation. "She reminds me of myself when I was young," Madonna had said indulgently. And Morissette's manager Scott Welch picked up on this during her first world tour, saying, "I saw the same thing with Madonna. The girls caught on first, and it was mainly women at her gigs. Then they brought their boyfriends along, and the thing went mainstream."

Although Madonna did well with other Maverick acts, such as the Prodigy, Seattle grunge band Candlebox, and singer/songwriter Michelle Branch, her label never repeated the spectacular success of that Morissette debut. The latter's follow-up albums—*Confessions of a Former Infatuation Junkie* (1998) and *So-called Chaos* (2004)—were well received but not nearly as popular, with steadily declining sales. Communications between Maverick and its parent company, Warner Bros., grew tense, until in March 2004 Maverick sued the latter for $200 million, claiming breach of contract and fraud. The following month, Warner countersued, saying that since 1999, Maverick had lost $66 million, and as far as they were concerned, the parent company had fulfilled its commitments. That June, the two parties reached a settlement, whereby Warner agreed to buy Madonna out of Maverick, and Guy Oseary took over as the sole CEO. By 2006, Maverick had a considerably lower profile than in the heady days of the early 90s.

Madonna's exile from Maverick symbolized her move away from the United States (where the label had its L.A. headquarters), to focus more on family life in Britain. So assimilated was she into the culture that she was often seen drinking a pint with Guy, not just in their London local but on the Isle of Wight, near Southampton, where his father, John, had a holiday home. Like Princess Margaret drinking with the "great unwashed," Madonna has been spotted in some rather unprepossessing venues in Nettleston, a small place on the northeast coast of the island. "She's often been in this pub where the lunch ladies from the local school hang out. It's all sticky Axminster carpets, nasty beer, and Simply Red on the jukebox," says musician Jake Rodrigues, whose parents live nearby. The pub was a far cry from the Ivy or other exclusive eateries of the stars, but there is a side to Madonna that almost relishes the frugal.

It has been noted that both she and Guy like a bargain. Careful about cash, Madonna was reluctant to pay the going rate for a large house in London, declaring that people want to exploit her celebrity status. "I cannot believe how expensive real estate is here," she said. "I'm just too middle-class to throw my hard-earned money away like that." She once had a meeting with an interior designer who gave what she considered to be a reasonable estimate for custom work on her study. "Madonna said no, it was too expensive. But what she wanted was very expensive!" says the designer. "I found her to be a bit of a spoiled brat, actually." Inside Madonna still beats the heart of a thrifty girl from hard-working Michigan. She is said to sign every single check herself, which, considering all her various projects and households, is quite a feat. She has an eye for detail: one musician who had been well paid for a session was amused to later receive a bill for the fruit he'd eaten in the studio. Once she was asked to model a designer's clothes from the Paris collection for a magazine. She said yes, on the condition that she gets to keep the clothes. The designer's staff demurred, saying, ahem, the models will later need them to wear on the runway. "In that case I won't do it," she declared. Madonna always keeps her eye on the bottom line. In her early days struggling in New York, she would let other people pay out first, and that became a survival tactic that stuck. Like many wealthy businesspeople who've worked their way up, she still feels the urge to scrimp and save.

Madonna is often kind, generous, and gracious (she has donated large sums of money to AIDS charities, for instance), but when it comes to business or dealing with hired hands, she is more hard-line. *Times* journalist Ginny Dougary was dismayed when Madonna imperiously told off an assistant before even acknowledging Ms. Dougary's presence. "It's one thing to be *epater le bourgeois* when you're twenty-something, but it is neither cool nor classy—both of which Madonna aspires to be—for a grown-up woman in her forties to humiliate a member of her staff in front of a stranger. And, for that matter, it's a pretty poor display of manners to the stranger, too."

This graceless, materialistic side seems at odds with the Kabbalah teachings of compassion and spiritual development. But, in the same way that people joked about 80s Nichiren Shoshu Buddhism as "chanting for a Porsche," there is a strain of the Kabbalah Center philosophy that celebrates material gain. By 2003, the center was a vast nonprofit, tax-exempt charity with assets of approximately $60 million. In 2005, its L.A. center alone grossed $27 million. The head of the charity, Karen Berg, is a woman with a taste for real estate, designer clothes, and a domestic staff of forty full-time volunteers— or *chevra*. "They look after my lifestyle, which is great for me!" she enthused.

Regular Friday-night shindigs at the center in Beverly Hills are also networking opportunities for the well-connected. Madonna's friend, the songwriter Gardner Cole, noted with bemusement how he was courted by Kabbalists after he was seen talking to her at the center. "I'm highly recruitable," he says. "They recognize the power of celebrity. I got a lot of phone calls after that—How're you doing? How are your studies going?" Niki Haris saw a shift in her boss after the latter developed an interest in Kabbalah, saying, "Madonna used to laugh at the absurdity of celebrity-ism. But then she only wanted to hang around celebrities and people with money." A close friend from New York remarks that "I don't see her so much now. Her friends are mainly those also into Kabbalah."

With her life revolving around Kabbalah, Guy, and the children, Madonna was less in touch with the rest of the Ciccone family. Relations with her siblings haven't always been easy—Madonna has said that their mother's death left them all "emotional cripples"—and they are ambivalent about their sister's fame. Madonna's sister Paula, for instance, was incensed when video editor Dustin Robertson came to work in her film production office wearing a Madonna T-shirt. "She *refused* to work with me until I took it off," he recalls. The loss of their mother so early has affected them in different ways. Some dealt with it by channeling their feelings into work—Melanie is a music business manager, while Christopher has a multifarious career as an artist, interior designer, and restaurateur. But other siblings have had difficulties. Madonna's older brother Martin has struggled with alcoholism, and his relationship with her is fraught. Her half-brother Mario, once described by a family friend as "a lovely little guy who was great with video equipment," is a former cocaine addict with a police record. Although she had bailed them out on a number of occasions, Madonna felt exasperated with her brothers, particularly Martin. She once said that she wanted to feel that the latter loved her and not just her money.

MAYBE KABBALAH was just one aspect of a significant change in Madonna's life—that marriage and motherhood were bringing out a conservative side.

Madonna has homes in Los Angeles and New York, but when she settled in London with her family, there was a sense of hunkering down. Apart from anything, it made financial sense. According to James Meek, "The fact that many of the wealthiest 'British' residents actually reside everywhere and nowhere, between London and Moscow or Monaco . . . deflects attention from a deeper truth—that often the thing which most concerns the very rich is time, rather than geography. Their only true domicile is their own family." To Madonna, her family is a top priority. Determined that her offspring should stay in one place and socialize with other children in a normal way, she has sent both Lola and Rocco to the Lycée, a prestigious French school in South Kensington. Nancy Andersen, who was at school with Lola, remembers her as "very nice and quite quiet. There was no favoritism. If she was talking in class she would get told off. Teachers would tell us to leave her alone and not bother her because she had a famous mother. They said, 'She's normal, like you.'"

Nancy has a strong memory of Lola getting a lead part in a school circus production. "It was when she was about five. She was playing a cactus on stilts. She wore a green outfit with straw sticking out like spikes, and at one point all the straw came out." Discipline at the Lycée is strict, and the workload intensive. "All the lessons were in French. If you don't understand, the teachers don't help you, they expect you to know it," remembers Nancy. The school is popular, with impressive results and a certain cosmopolitan flair. One parent recalls that "The headmistress of the upper school was a creation in Dior. She had platinum blond hair, like Eva Peron, and a ferocious reputation. The school had a swap-meet every year, but instead of old rubbish they'd be selling off £80 plates."

The school's combination of rigorous work and Continental style appealed to Madonna; "after all, I'm half-French," she once said. As far as her children's education was concerned, she was leaving nothing to chance. Even as a preschooler, Lola was being whisked by her nanny around London art galleries and museums, and she has always been precociously bright. After her stint at the Lycée, she was sent to Cheltenham Ladies College, the most academic and prestigious private school for girls in the United Kingdom. Her brother Rocco, too, has flourished at the Lycée, being moved up a school year when he was six.

An attentive mother, Madonna has always tried to be home in time to give supper to the children and put them to bed. Following in her disciplinarian father's footsteps, she believes in rituals and routines, and providing a strong, nurturing family environment. She has come a long way from those days in New York when ex-boyfriend Mark Kamins noted that "she wasn't a homemaker."

In the summer of 2005, Madonna showed this new domestic side when she was featured on the cover of the woman's bible of Middle America, *Ladies' Home Journal*, wearing a dove-gray top hat, Marlene Dietrich–style, and reading a book. The photo shoot within, taken by U.K. photographer Lorenzo Agius, was inspired. Here was "Mrs. Ritchie," got up like a starched Edwardian lady, reading antiquarian books in a dark library. Here was "Mrs. Ritchie," in black chiffon and leather lace-up boots, wearing a small black confection of a hat and a monocle. And here was "Mrs. Ritchie," in velvet and tweed, lounging in a crusty brown armchair. She inhabited a bookish world of magic realism, miles away from the usual glitzy studio shoots.

"When we were planning the shoot, she was exhausted with the kids, she'd been recording, and she just came across as a very ordinary person going about her day as a mother. It's nice to see that side to someone; I warmed to that," recalls Agius. Madonna said she didn't want to do a fashion shoot—"she doesn't really like fashion, but she obviously loves clothes"—so Agius decided to have her dress up period-style and pose in a "fairy-tale kind of children's book setting." After weeks hunting for the perfect Harry Potter library location, they ended up at a prop house in the London suburbs, which had an eighteenth-century Spanish library installed in it.

"She loved it," recalls Agius. "But it was interesting, because when we started shooting, she said, 'What are we going to do?' It was a bit of a surprise that she needed direction and guidance. I mistakenly assumed that someone that experienced, doing it for twenty-odd years, working with the best photographers in the world, would instinctively know, but that was my mistake. We were trying to get something different, not for her to be Vogue-ing or hamming it up in front of the camera."

Agius said to her, "Just kind of pose, just act . . ." to which Madonna replied, as quick as a flash, "Strike a pose, there's nothing to it." They had fun with the shoot, but the most abiding memory Agius has of the day is that Madonna is not just street-smart, but intelligent. "I laid this massive book out for her, a religious book in Hebrew, and she was reading it. She's pretty impressive, very well-read." This twilight world of antique books and mahogany tables seemed to chime with her psyche. The pictures symbolized how far removed she felt at that point from the shiny world of current pop.

BUT MADONNA'S pattern has never been straightforward. Once the children's books, the house in the country, the cozy marriage were all in place, something happened to disrupt it. On August 16, 2005, her forty-seventh birthday, she was riding a new polo horse on her Wiltshire estate when the animal stumbled and hurled her to the ground. She suffered three cracked ribs, a broken collarbone, and a broken hand. She was rushed to the casualty department at nearby Salisbury District Hospital. According to a source, "Madonna's voice was shaking when she gave her name and date of birth. She was wearing her riding gear and was trembling. And she was obviously in a lot of pain, but she was lucid." Guy wasn't there when she had her accident, but drove to the hospital as soon as he heard, arriving about ten minutes later, "looking very worried."

Madonna was given a private room and discharged that night with an armory of painkillers. She was told to rest up, and that she couldn't dance or do yoga for three months, until her injuries had healed. The accident literally stopped Madonna in her tracks. "It was the most painful thing that ever happened to me in my life, but it was a great learning experience," she said later. Over the next few months, that brush with mortality seemed to subtly change her. In the *Ladies' Home Journal*, she talked about her life, saying, "Marriage is hard. [It's] a tool for each and every one of us to ultimately make the world a better place." She described in detail the discipline regimen she followed with her kids—how if Lola was messy with her clothes, she got them taken away until she learned to tidy up. "I'm the disciplinarian. Guy's the spoiler . . . I'm doctor's appointments, lessons, homework. I'm the boring one." She talked quietly, relentlessly, about the minutiae of her life. "We eat dinner at nine or nine thirty; my husband [it's always "my husband," never "Guy"—L. O.] does ju-jitsu and doesn't finish until then, which is irritating. We eat dinner late, we go to bed late, I get up early—not a lot of sleep goes on here. I don't see a lot of my girlfriends." She said that she just stayed at home and worked. "I hardly ever go out to parties, or even to restaurants." This, it seemed, was a Madonna in retreat. And some wondered if that was the end of her story as queen of pop.

ABBA ON
DRUGS

A MONTH AFTER THE ACCIDENT HAPPENED, MADONNA
began to reemerge. As the bones healed, she felt the urge to get out
in public again. And with an extraordinary volte-face, she pulled the
show girl out once more. The Lady of the Manor period and her riding
accident had left her emotionally cautious and artistically becalmed.
She was about to return, and, as it always had been, she found her way
back through music . . .

"After the accident she was forced to lie low for several months.
Then, when she came out, it was like a bullet from a gun," says a close
friend of Madonna's. All that pent-up energy was expressed on her
new album, *Confessions on a Dance Floor*, a seamless mix of club tracks recorded with her DJ/producer Stuart Price. The album was conceived
after the Re-Invention tour, when Madonna had scrapped plans for
a musical she had been working on with film director Luc Besson.
One element survived, however: a disco section where Madonna told
Price to do something that "sounded like ABBA on drugs." That was
"Hung Up," the opening track and first single from the album, which
liberally sampled from ABBA's 1970s disco hit "Gimme Gimme
Gimme (a Man After Midnight)."

One of Madonna's most spectacularly successful songs, it grew out of a brainstorming session in Price's tiny apartment in Maida Vale, west London. When it was finished, she realized they had something explosive on their hands. In much the same way she demoted Pat Leonard on the *Ray of Light* album after she met Orbit, Madonna bumped Mirwais (originally scheduled to produce the record) to the sidelines to work with Price. She would come to the latter's apartment every day at three p.m., climb the stepladder to his loft, and make music, almost as an escape. They worked under impossibly cramped conditions—"My apartment consists of a couch, a mixing desk, an Apple computer, as many vintage keyboards as I could fit into one room, and a kettle," said Price—but that was reassuring to Madonna, reminding her of early creative days in New York. And having worked on initial demos in this way with Orbit for *Ray of Light*, she wasn't fazed by the primitive surroundings.

"I couldn't have made this record anywhere else. . . . Where you record is very important," she told the *Observer*'s Simon Garfield. "It can't be too nice, it can't be too expensive, it can't have a view to an ocean or a field. I'd rather be in a prison cell with Pro Tools. . . . I want it to be exactly as it was when I wrote my first song. In a small space with hardly any frills." Ever one to watch the pennies, she didn't relish recording in a large, swanky studio, feeling she had to create twelve number-one hits to justify the money.

To Price, it was simple: "What we're doing now is what she was doing at the start of her career. She said, 'I used to hang around the DJs long enough to force them to make records for me,' so nothing's changed there. . . . On 'Into the Groove,' if you solo the vocals, you can hear the cars going by outside in Manhattan. These records weren't manufactured pop records. She was literally going around a DJ's house and saying, 'What's the best music you've got?' and singing over it."

The album was an homage to records they had both grown up with—ABBA and Giorgio Moroder being the obvious influences. "If there are references to earlier records it's probably done unknowingly, part of our molecular structure," Madonna said cheerfully. It is ironic that a guitar riff from one of her earliest demos, "High Society" on the Gotham tapes, ended up on the album track "I Love New York," while a keyboard sample from Price's favorite the Pet Shop Boys graced the song "Jump."

From the opening bars, it is clear that this bold, ambitious, noisy record was a reaction to all those nights she spent twiddling her thumbs in Wiltshire. From the first screaming ABBA sample above the grinding disco rhythm, to the section where everything drops out and all we can hear is a muffled backbeat, the song "Hung Up" is a triumph. In Madonna's voice—vulnerable, tentative, yet deadpan—we hear her history. In a sense, this album has thirty-year-old influences, but with new technology. "'Hung Up' is about grabbing a chance when you can or 'You'll wake up one day and it'll be too late,'" she later explained. The song echoes Robert Browning's poem "Two in the Campagna," which is about the need to seize "the good minute." If you don't take an opportunity in love, the minute is gone. "I believe in the good minute," she once declared.

A compelling slice of euphoria, it was the perfect antidote to the more downbeat *American Life*, and therefore crucial to Madonna that she could release the track as her first single. There was just the tricky question of copyright. She had to approach the notoriously difficult Björn Ulvaeus and Benny Andersson in order to get permission. "I had to send my emissary to Stockholm with a letter . . . begging them and imploring them and telling them how much I worship their music, telling them it was an homage to them, which is all true," she said. "And they had to think about it. They never let anyone sample their music. They could have said no. Thank God they didn't."

Another key sample is the dramatic synth sound of the Jacksons' 1981 hit "Can You Feel It." The Jacksons' rhythm builds with an unrelenting pace, like a monstrous undertow on the track "Sorry," her multilingual rant that was written, one presumes, after a row with Guy. Later released as the second single from the album, it went top ten throughout Europe and reached number one in the *Billboard* dance charts. The video, the first made by her tour director Jamie King, continued where "Hung Up" left off, with Madonna and her crew leaving a club and picking up men to dance in their disco-style van. There was a roller-rink sequence for which all the dancers, including Madonna, had to learn how to roller-skate from scratch.

The homage to 70s disco continues with a sample of Donna Summer's "I Feel Love." That song's unmistakable rush laces the sound of "Future Lovers," the sole track produced by Mirwais. Like the others, the rhythm pounds like a runaway train, its generous bass lines punctuated by ebullient synth loops. When she was writing this track, Madonna was mindful of Gloria Gaynor's "I Will Survive," the song that she danced to all those years ago at Menjo's club in Detroit, and considered "Sorry" a kind of follow-up. In fact, the whole album is Madonna's tribute to all those soulful disco divas who inspired her.

There's also the ghost of Iggy Pop (and the ghost of her Gotham past) on the irreverent "I Love New York." Many took offense at the way this song mocked cities like Paris and London. "I *love* London and Paris [but] . . . I have a history with New York that I don't have anywhere else in the world," she told *Attitude* magazine. "Even though I grew up in Michigan, I really grew up in New York. Aside from when my mother died, the toughest time in my life was living in New York; being broke, having no friends, and struggling, trying to find my place in the world. . . . New Yorkers have this thing with people, that they know you have survived New York too." She admitted that the city was "kind of brutal," but she loved its "insanity and noise . . . it's like putting your finger in a socket."

In all these tracks, Madonna's voice is just another texture. She had come far enough in her career to let her voice just signal a mood. This album was less about foregrounding her as the "star," more about surrendering her to the dance floor. In songs like "Get Together" (which recalls the freestyle beat of her Danceteria days), the spacey, futuristic seduction of "Forbidden Love," and "Like It or Not," produced by Bloodshy and Avant, there is a sense of psychological intimacy. Lyrics rise up through the mix like private thoughts, capturing the meditative aspect of standing on a dance floor lost in your own world. And Madonna has plenty to think about. Her fame, once again deconstructed and set aside; and her spiritual passion, which soars through the astonishingly lush track "Isaac." But over and above it is the gravitational pull of her driving energy, pulsating through the standout track "Jump," an inspirational song reiterating one of her earliest messages: face the fear and don't look back. Charging through life like a bullet train, taking all her influences with her, Madonna ended up full circle, returning to her dance roots with *Confessions on a Dance Floor.*

No wonder people responded so favorably to the album. When it was released in November 2005, it was a best-seller from the start, and has since become one of her most successful albums, holding the record for topping the most charts in the world. The lead single, "Hung Up" was number one in forty-one countries. To many, it felt like the old Madonna: upbeat and reassuring. Buyers also responded to a very powerful marketing campaign. Disappointed by the sales of *American Life*, Madonna decided to do a little market research for her new album. Before the record was finished, she had Price slip a few mixes (with her vocals turned down) into his live DJ sets. He filmed the crowd reaction with his mobile phone, to give her an indication of which tracks went down best on the dance floor. In this way Madonna used club audiences as a focus group.

"It suggests she feels a need for endorsement," commented Claire Beale, the editor of U.K. advertiser's bible, *Campaign* magazine. "Like a lot of people who work in advertising, she is far older than her target audience. She may feel this is a useful way of reconnecting with a younger generation." Determined to reach every age group in a quest for sales, Madonna did indeed appeal to teenagers as well as the over-forties. Even my four-year-old son began chanting the opening lines of "Hung Up."

She matched this marketing drive with a brand-new image: long, strawberry-blond hair curled back Farrah Fawcett–style, and a shiny purple 70s disco leotard. All complete with a mirror ball. And she made sure she wore this outfit everywhere, even to her belated birthday party hosted by interior designer David Collins a month after the album's release. "When I came to the door, I couldn't believe it," said one guest. "Madonna looked like she'd just stepped out of her latest video." The message was loud and clear. "I want to dance," she declared to the world. "I wanted to lift myself and others up with this record." Madonna made strategic appearances at various clubs, taking the Semtex girls from her "Semtex" management team to the Roxy in New York and G.A.Y. and the Koko Club in London. The latter was originally the Camden Palace, one of the first London venues she played back in the early 80s. She engaged in the ultimate publicity stunt—riding down the center of Manhattan on a horse for the *Late Show with David Letterman* (and she chose the biggest horse). Part of "Hung Up" was featured on a global ad for Motorola's new mobile phone, and became a master ringtone. Filtered through every possible medium, *Confessions* was touted as Madonna's big "comeback" record.

"With her last album, many naysayers were questioning her relevancy. This new album puts all that to rest," said Warner Bros. CEO Tom Whalley, with an almost audible sign of relief. Virgin Megastore merchandise manager Jerry Suarez summed up the prevailing mood by saying: "It's all about Madonna right now . . . The last record suffered because she got so political. Less guns. Less tanks. More disco balls. More ABBA. We're good."

This was a woman fiercely engaging with her public, making the most of branding opportunities with MTV as well as Motorola and iTunes. "I'm a businesswoman," she said. "The music industry has changed. There's a lot of competition and the market is glutted with new releases—and new 'thises and thats.' You must join forces with other brands and corporations. You're an idiot if you don't." She reassured the "naysayers" by announcing: "I don't need to be going on about the war in Iraq. I made a lot of political statements. . . . I don't want to repeat myself, so I moved to another area and that's 'God, I really feel like dancing right now.'"

THE DANCE-FOCUSED "Hung Up" video was shot by Swedish director Johan Renck, who had fashioned the Japanese kabuki theater style of Madonna's 1999 video "Nothing Really Matters." This time Renck kept the concept simple, but still with his snappy images and elegant lighting style. An homage to John Travolta and *Saturday Night Fever*, the video was filmed in catacombs, on the London Underground, and in a Tokyo slot-machine arcade. "Madonna wanted to do a video where her music confronts all types of subcultures in the world of dance," said Renck. One of the most arresting moments is where the music drops down to sub-bass, and the camera travels from a giant boom box to Madonna writhing in the disco lights. It is as if she is inside the music. "It's a surreal, dreamlike piece of music, with Madonna looking like she's within a disco ball," Renck enthused. This image, with the purple leotard and the revolving, spacey lights, became her iconic Confessions look. She then set it off with the shot of her Travolta-style strut down the street in an original 70s hooded leather bomber jacket. Bought for a few dollars by a stylist in a church thrift store in Utah, the jacket echoed the tone of the video—sweaty, subcultural, and real. As ever, Madonna's dancers were street rather than stagey, their lithe, inspired movements spurring her on, bringing out the dance diva that lay dormant inside. In the video, she has a muscular, sexy beauty, strolling along, looking taller, more substantial somehow, than her actual five feet four inches.

Although the video was one of the first things she did after her riding accident, Madonna's fiery energy is palpable. "When I shot the video, none of the bones had gone together," she said. "Pharmaceuticals and my will got me through the shoot. So, to come out of that, I felt so much inspiration and so much joy to have my body back and to feel strong again."

Madonna's body was her temple, and a much-discussed one at that. In the weeks after her album release, much was made of how young this "forty-seven-year-old mother of two" looked. In maintaining that perfect body, though, Madonna was leaving nothing to chance. Every day she did an hour of Olympic-level ashtanga yoga, an hour of Pilates, and an hour of aerobic exercise. She took business calls on her Stairmaster, and ate a finely tuned macrobiotic diet, allowing herself one glass of wine with Sunday lunch. A large proportion of her working day was spent, effectively, working out. According to fashion historian Sarah Cheang, there was rigorous method to this madness.

"The 1980s aerobics, 1990s workout, and twenty-first-century yoga trends have all encouraged women to create an internal corset of muscles that flatten the stomach through hard work and self-discipline," she says. "These are active bodies that subscribe to norms of beauty and must be continuously on show to the approving gaze of others." Back in the 1980s, the late Dusty Springfield complained to me that being a female pop star required "a lot of upkeep. All those hair extensions and the exercise. It's too much for me." Within fifteen years, that upkeep would be de rigueur for any girl conforming to twenty-first-century standards of beauty.

"In the simpler world of the 80s and 90s, girls needed the right dress, hair, and flowers for the prom," says psychologist Margo Maine. "These days, preparation for a special event takes weeks, starting with tanning; waxing their eyebrows, bikini line, and legs; manicure and pedicure; coloring their hair; having their makeup done by an expert; maybe even having a cosmetic plastic surgery procedure. The dress and the date have become almost incidental. The body is the project, and the process is endless."

In the global Barbie culture, more and more young women have fallen prey to disordered eating and excessive exercise to achieve the skinny look of runway models and celebrities. And an estimated 8 percent of young American women have serious eating disorders, such as anorexia or bulimia. This, despite the fact that posed celebrity photos are regularly retouched, so that what we see is a distortion of their body appearance—in other words, what "ordinary" women aspire to isn't real anyway. There was also the problem of the "lollipop ladies"—celebrities like Nicole Ritchie, Brittany Murphy, and Victoria Beckham, who were so thin that their heads appeared too large for their bodies. Although she seemed pleasingly fleshy in her "Hung Up" video, Madonna has often come perilously close to the "lollipop" look. One TV makeup artist at this time said that she looked "a bit gaunt." Although some delicate cosmetic surgery might be tempting, the improbable bodies of older stars like Cher and Joan Collins would not be something that Madonna aspires to.

"A body sculpted by the knife of the surgeon would not signal Madonna's power and discipline in the same way as a body sculpted by hard work and strength," comments Sarah Cheang. "To support the Madonna myth, her body must display the signs of strength above the signs of beauty." This was a goal that would present more and more of a challenge for Madonna. She felt the pressure to look young and vital in a market where her competitors were twenty years younger, but at the same time she wanted to stay cool, not seem aging and desperate. Already the critics were closing in: "Even with Muscles Like These, Madonna Can't Beat the Hands of Time" screamed a *Daily Mail* headline. The article gleefully pointed out the "virtual roadmap of veins" in Madonna's hands, "something the toughest exercise regime just can't solve."

Madonna continued her battle with time, regardless. There was an underlying tension to her strenuous efforts to stay young and beautiful. Rumors were beginning to surface about problems in her marriage. She has made no secret of the fact that it has been a struggle. "When I first met Guy, I couldn't believe I had met someone as strong-willed as I was," she said. "Guy has a very forceful personality with very specific likes and dislikes. He doesn't back down one iota if it's something we disagree on, but I respect that." Although Madonna appreciated a man with mettle, she didn't feel totally secure with him. "She complains that he never compliments her on the way she looks and that makes her paranoid about the ten-year age gap between them and him not finding her attractive anymore. That is so hard for a woman like her," said a friend. Madonna's response was to accentuate her beauty in every manner available to her, and stick religiously to her exercise regime.

As long as she could get away with it, she would—and for the promotion around her *Confessions* album, she flaunted her toned body in a way she hadn't done for years, as if she was having one last final fling.

AT THE other end of the spectrum, another forty-seven-year-old female star released a high-profile album. British artist Kate Bush couldn't be more different from Madonna in terms of personality and approach. *Aerial*, her eighth album, was released on the same day as *Confessions on the Dance Floor*, but she gave only a handful of interviews and eschewed the limelight, preferring the music to speak for itself. Blending folk, reggae, classical, and Renaissance styles, *Aerial* was a graceful, surreal record, including a song about a washing machine and "King of the Mountain," a comment on Elvis Presley and the excesses of fame. Portrayed as an eccentric recluse by the U.K. press, Bush retired from the spotlight for twelve years to give her son, Bertie, a normal childhood. In contrast to the worldwide headlines about Madonna's babies, Bush didn't release news of her son's birth in 1998, and it wasn't until two years later that the story broke. But though they were at opposite ends of the pop spectrum, both Bush and Madonna related to music in a way that was intensely personal. While Bush depicted in painstaking detail on *Aerial* the imaginative power of a woman's domestic world, Madonna recorded on *Confessions* the private meditation of someone joyfully lost in the hedonistic, external world of club culture.

But Bush would never choose to make a film about herself or her artistic process. Madonna exposed that side of herself again, with *I'm Going to Tell You a Secret*, the backstage documentary of her Re-Invention tour, with a large section on Kabbalah thrown in. Premiered in November 2005, just after the release of her album, *I'm Going to Tell You a Secret* was directed by Jonas Akerlund with his customary verve. Unlike *Truth or Dare*, which has an air of spoiled Hollywood about it, *I'm Going to Tell You a Secret* signals early on that its goal is spirituality and maturity. It opens with Chris Cunningham's slightly disturbing film of Madonna and coyote in *X-STaTIC PRO=Cess*. Powerful and dark, this snippet suggests right away that Madonna wants to experiment with her own myth. "I refer to an entity I call the beast . . . the material world we live in right now . . . the world of illusion," she intones in a voiceover narrative. "We're enslaved by it." This from the woman who wanted a Paris collection for free. She was obviously still fighting her demons.

The film then focuses on her dance auditions, as dozens of young hopefuls queue up to make an impression. They're a brave bunch. "I'm glad I'm not a dancer anymore," says Madonna. "It's a dog's life." Then, with her chosen few, she goes into battle, saying: "The stage becomes a beast that we have to tame." As in *Truth or Dare*, the performance scenes are in vivid, high color, while the backstage interaction is shot in black-and-white. Here we have revealing moments with her husband, Guy. Clearly embarrassed and awkward to be on film, he, by turns, mocks her and ignores her. At their local pub in London's Mayfair, he sings after-hours folk songs, while she lies asleep on a bench. After one performance, she sits mad, defensive, and sweaty in her limo, disappointed that he went to the pub instead of coming to the show. Like Warren Beatty in *Truth or Dare*, he is an elusive presence, uneasy with the camera, not fond of being seen as playing second fiddle to his wife.

Observer critic Kathryn Flett asked, quite understandably, why in the edit Madonna "picked so much footage of her 'old man' looking like an utter jerk? But perhaps all that real ale-drinking and maudlin Irish balladeering dahn Mr. and Mrs. Ritchie's local . . . is what passes for cute if you're born in Bay City, Michigan." Maybe this was Madonna's attempt to show the reality of marriage. "I got married for all the wrong reasons," she says wistfully. "There's no such thing as the perfect soul mate. The perfect soul mate is the person who pushes all your buttons and pisses you off. It's not easy having a good marriage . . . [but] easy doesn't make you grow."

What's more touching is her interaction with the children, as a four-year-old Rocco and seven-year-old Lola wander in and out of the frame—sparky, tenacious, and engaging. "I'd like to see her more. I'll be happy when the tour is ended," says a solemn and impossibly pretty Lola. Madonna sums up her dilemma as a mother when she tells her dancers: "Sorry I didn't get to hang out with you guys more. I have another family. And one day you'll know the pull of work and family and the struggle to keep it all balanced."

As in *Truth or Dare*, the film is fascinating for what it inadvertently reveals, that strange isolation at the heart of stardom. After a show, with the crowd still roaring in the background, Madonna goes backstage to an empty dressing room. "Where is everybody?" she asks uncertainly. "As you can see, I've got no friends!" In that odd celebrity world, there is a pecking order, one that iconoclastic rocker Iggy Pop was forced to acknowledge when he played the support slot at her Dublin gig. "I hope he doesn't take a shit on my stage," she remarked, before going to his dressing room to say hello. The two native Detroiters air-kiss warily. Afterward, he mimics the bland way she says: "Have a great show!" It is a telling moment of punk rock meets mainstream pop.

Madonna shows her friendship with the high-profile filmmaker Michael Moore, whom she salutes from the stage one night on tour. "Jesus, she stuck her neck out there for me tonight, which is a crazy thing to do," said the seasoned activist. On the one hand, Madonna shares time with radical left-wing campaigner Moore, and on the other, her Republican dad. The shots of Tony Ciccone in his north Michigan vineyard are as homey as apple pie. He gives a bland assessment of her live show: "Very good," he says, while his wife, Joan, echoes, "Very nice." God only knows what frustration seethes at this under Madonna's cool exterior. But Tony makes some astute comments about his daughter's character: "The entertainment business was the avenue she needed to express her needs. . . . To me it was a growing process. She's growing up. And instead of growing up with us, she grew up with the world."

There are parts of the film that seem affected. The backstage party, where everyone strenuously has "a good time," for instance. Or Madonna being told by her manager that they have to reschedule a flight because the queen of England will be in the air. "Her Madgesty" quips: "There's not room for two queens in that country." The high-handed manner with the dancers, when she introduces them to classical pianist Katia Labèque, saying off-camera that this will be good for them "because they might not even know what classical music is." And that odd sixth-grade poetry that Madonna and crew keep delivering to each other. There are not many people who could get excited about a poem eulogizing their ability to pick up someone else's sweaty underpants.

Madonna is better when she's unself-conscious. "This is stinky," she exclaims, sniffing the corset she's worn for dozens of shows. "These big fat Italian thighs . . . I stink." And there is that compelling sequence, arguably the most important one in the film, where Madonna describes what it feels like doing a show. She's onstage at Slane Castle, Dublin, in front of eighty thousand people. Just as she starts her show, a full moon sails over the stage and the rain pours down. She and her dancers are in constant danger of being electrocuted. "I felt such love. People stood there for six hours in the rain and didn't move . . . the rain was pelting me," she says, "I felt I was in a war zone, constantly worried for the dancers . . . traumatized . . . and when the show ended, I can't remember what happened."

Here Madonna describes with forceful simplicity the suspended, out-of-body nature of performance. There is no spin, no irony, just pure emotion and experience. Key parts of the film are those capturing the trancelike pull of being on stage: "BAM, right back to the crowd," announces her skateboarder, who in the "Hollywood" medley shoots from one side of the stage to the other. "This light we're supposed to shine back . . . the more we're fed by the crowd the more we give back," he riffs, like the surfer looking for the perfect wave, the perfect high. No wonder the dancers find it difficult making their way after the tour has ended. "They need to remember it's about the experience. You live it and you move on," the show's director Jamie King says coolly.

"Dancing is best in the moment," says Re-Invention dancer Raist-alla. "I don't remember what happens. Things go by really fast. Everything is really light and bright. It's a complete rush." At the back of her mind, though, she always knew that it was going to come to an end, and that she needed to establish herself in her own right. "It gets lonely being on tour. No matter how much you connect with your coworkers, there's no place like home," she recalls. "I was in a different mind-frame from them. I was waiting to transition to being an artist." Since the Re-Invention tour, she has been working on her own music, cowriting some snaky electro-funk with Miami producers Kas Gamble and Jack Oates. While working on her self-titled debut album in 2005, Raistalla sent a few tracks to Madonna for feedback. "She loved the originals, and told me to make sure I know what I'm getting into, 'cause it can be a hard business. She was being very motherly again." And circumspect. Raistalla's album has been drawing people in from unexpected places—"not just those into electronica, but a lot of rock and hip-hop fans. If it grabs all types of people, that's my goal." Raistalla found her way quite quickly after the tour. Many dancers, though, still hit that proverbial dip. The light from the Madonna show is so bright it overwhelms anything beside it.

The only element in this film larger than her is Kabbalah and its almost evangelical undertow. In the final scenes, Madonna goes to Israel to address the Spirituality for Kids foundation, wearing a demure dress and acting like a global ambassador. "I'm here not to represent a religion but as a student of Kabbalah," she announces, before imparting a message of unity. *I'm Going to Tell You a Secret* was an important film for her. She spent several months in the cutting room with Jonas Akerlund, keeping him a virtual prisoner in her home while they pored over shots. Before Madonna released the film, she invited a select audience of friends and coworkers to see a three-hour rough cut in a Notting Hill cinema, and write their comments afterward on a questionnaire. The remark that came up time and again was "too much Kabbalah," resulting in substantial pruning before the final edit. The DVD released the following year was a longer "director's cut," complete with Madonna's trip to Rachel's tomb outside Jerusalem, where she was hounded by paparazzi. Even though she had been advised by Israeli security not to make the trip, she insisted on going. She becomes irate with the attention, but needs it at the same time. This paradox of scorning the press yet living her life in public is one that would reappear later to dramatic effect with her bid to adopt a Malawian boy, David.

"She has a messianic attitude, she wants to break rules," said her producer Mirwais. With *I'm Going to Tell You a Secret*, the final fusing of Madonna the Icon with Madonna the Saint began.

EARLY IN 2006, Madonna did a photo shoot for W magazine with Steven Klein that, like *X-STaTIC PRO=Cess*, was packed with psychodrama. Shot in a gigantic Hollywood soundstage with six black and white stallions, these pictures featured her as a heroic horsewoman. As well as exploring the trauma of falling off her horse and surviving, with these pictures Madonna was stirring up the age-old fantasy of pubescent girls, horses, and early sexual experience. Only here she turns it on its head as a middle-aged mother. These pictures emanate all the eroticism that her *Sex* book lacked. There's Madonna standing with her bare back to the camera, wearing nothing but black rubber panties, fishnet tights, and long PVC gloves. She holds a riding crop à la her Dita Parlo character from *Erotica*, but, nearly fifteen years later, she exudes more natural authority. There is strong muscle definition on her bare back. The skin isn't smooth, and it isn't a young body, but there is more sexual suggestiveness in this one cool pose than an entire collection of *Sex* photos.

Madonna lies face up on a supine black stallion, smoking a postcoital cigarette; she wears a hat with a horse's tail, and there's a saddle, so she's half-woman, half-horse. With obvious tones of S&M, she is decked out in a jeweled bridle and black gloves. In the most surreal, dreamlike pictures, she confronts a white stallion, raising her arm as if to tame him. With the Equestrian, Madonna invented a new character—a kind of haughty, erotic, Edwardian horsewoman.

She developed the equestrian idea for her next tour, testing it out well before it hit the stage. One day during rehearsals in L.A., she marched into the sound studio next door, where the photographer Steven Meisel was on a fashion shoot. She and Meisel hadn't been getting on for a while, but Madonna was anxious to get an audience reaction. She strode in with a riding crop and high boots, saying, "My dancers are trying out some new steps, tell me what you think." The assembled fashionistas were then subject to an impromptu five-song set. Feedback was positive, so Madonna continued with the provocative theme, making it the opening section of her new Confessions tour.

From the day it opened on May 21, 2006, Madonna was determined to make this her biggest spectacle yet. With musical director Stuart Price, she turned it into a two-hour disco extravaganza. On the night I went to the show in early August in Wembley Arena, she had the air-conditioning turned off in a deliberate attempt to create a sweaty nightclub atmosphere. A huge Swarowski- and diamond-encrusted mirror ball descended from the ceiling and, like a beautiful alien exiting her space pod, out stepped Madonna, wearing Gaultier jodhpurs, cravat, and horse-tail hat. She and her dancers pawed the stage, combining equestrian moves with pole-dancing and 3-D gymnastics. At times, there was almost a Monty Python—esque effect to their cantering.

This show was all about visuals, about emotions and feelings writ large, and inclusive, powerful statements. As ever, she wove her life into her art, displaying X-rays and MRIs of her eight broken bones on massive video screens while she sang "Like a Virgin." Another witty reinterpretation of her best-known song, it incorporated footage of violent riding accidents and jockeys being flung perilously from horses. As Madonna rode a merry-go-round pole dance on a diamond-encrusted saddle, you could sense the trauma, and see the breaks.

Like the London artists Gilbert & George, who turned their daily life into an art installation, Madonna sees herself as a living sculpture, feeding her own experience into her work. *"Je suis l'arte,"* she said to Sebastien Foucan, a *parkour* hero and the main advisor behind the next number, "Jump." It is an homage to *parkour* (PK), a physical discipline that combines extreme sports and martial arts. Adapted from French military obstacle-course training, it is a dynamic form of movement that revolves around the notions of "escape" and "reach," where the *traceur,* or participant, uses physical agility and quick thinking to overcome obstacles. The *traceur* moves around his or her surroundings—from walls to buildings, bridges, and railings—with complete mental dedication. Like for champion surfers or skateboarders, *parkour* for them is a philosophy and a way of life.

In the same way that Madonna recruited Vogue dancers from the New York underground for her Blond Ambition tour, for Confessions she used original *traceurs* from the Parisian suburbs. She was inspired to do this after seeing her friend Luc Besson's *parkour* movies, *Yamakasi—the Modern-day Samurai* (2001), and *Banlieue 13*, which came out at the same time as the Confessions tour. The "Jump" sequence was a thrilling moment in the show, with the dancers performing acrobatic stunts against a backdrop of 3-D buildings.

This was their most physically difficult number. "It took quite a bit of work getting used to, I'm not going to lie," one of her star dancers, Mihran Kirakosyan, told me. Despite coming from an athletic family—his father was a choreographer, his mother an athlete—and being a dancer all his life, Kirakosyan found this song a challenge. "We had many injuries during the rehearsals and practice. That is what I love about dancing for Madonna. She's not afraid of pushing us or trying new and creative ideas." It seemed that after having been laid low and severely restricted after a riding accident, Madonna was fully exploring the notion of physical freedom. With the riding, roller-skating, and *parkour* sequences, she was forging a link with sport, movement, and dance.

After the intense activity of "Jump," the first act concluded with a quiet, darkened stage, and voiceover confessions from her dancers. "I live with my past tucked away deep inside of me," said one. "I cut my arms," said another. Their words hung in the air as Madonna rose up with one of her most provocative images—standing in a Christlike pose on a gigantic mirrored disco cross. Many felt it to be in poor taste, including some Jews, Christians, and Muslims, who all complained about the way she played fast and loose with the image of Jesus. "Jesus would have loved it," she declared in an open statement to the press, and she invited Pope Benedict XVI to one of her shows in Rome. In her eyes, it was a remarkable piece of Catholic kitsch, as vivid as the brightly colored Sacred Heart statues in her mother's living room. Members of the city's Orthodox Standard Bearers Union in Moscow failed to see the humor, and burned a huge poster of the star outside her concert. For some, the cross was proof that Madonna finally believed her own hype, that she truly saw herself as a Messianic figure sent to save the world, a kind of a self-appointed twenty-first-century Christ. "We thought it was a bit flashy, a bit L.A.," says her former dancer Salim Gauwloos.

But there were also some in the Catholic Church who saw her show as an endorsement of the faith. Jesuit priest Father Carlos Novoa, for instance, wrote in the Colombian daily *El Tiempo*, that Madonna's parody of the crucifixion "is not a mockery of the cross, but rather the complete opposite: an exhaltation of the mystery of the death and resurrection of Jesus." He went on to say that the song "Live to Tell," in which Madonna is crucified, "is one of the best sermons I have witnessed in my life."

Whatever the shock value, it was an arresting visual image. As she sang "Live to Tell," above her cross was a screen with figures that started at zero and ticked up to 12 million, signifying the number of children who had been orphaned by the AIDS epidemic in Africa alone. This disturbing statistic led into the second, "Bedouin" section, where Israeli singer Yitzhak Sinwani sang his glorious vocal on "Isaac." Here Madonna interspersed footage of the Iraq War with famine in Africa, making the link with global suffering. A woman danced, wearing a hijab, the Muslim veil, and when the dance finished, Madonna "liberated" her by taking off the garment. "She's a caged bird and she eventually takes her veil off and emerges from the cage," Madonna later explained. Although the hijab is a garment designed to keep women submissive and hidden from the male gaze, it was rather arrogant of Madonna to imply that she was this woman's liberator. Many Muslim women use the hijab in more complex ways, both as a source of protection against unwanted male attention and as a defiant sign of cultural difference.

The "Bedouin" section was followed by an abrupt change of mood, with a New York skyline on the backdrop and Madonna in black swan feathers and bomber jacket strumming a guitar, Courtney Love–style, to "I Love New York" and an ecstatic "Ray of Light." The energy in the room at this point was palpable, the audience's reaction rapturous. It was like the moment in a nightclub, when everyone on drugs "comes up" at once. When the song subsided, Madonna finally sat down on the stage and addressed the crowd, as if talking to a few people in her living room. "Aah," she sighed. "It's good to be home."

The London crowd cheered, as she went into an acoustic version of "Drowned World." One of the edgiest moments of the show followed "Let It Be," when she staggered around the stage, as if punch-drunk from fame. Throwing her body into disturbing shapes, she gave an artful evocation of how fame can corrupt and eventually disintegrate a character.

But as soon as she had touched on those themes, she dived into the hedonistic rush of the "Disco" section, with an Electribe 101–ish version of "Erotica" and the techno charge of "La Isla Bonita," complete with *Hawaii Five-O*–style Technicolor backdrop. At one point during this song, she skipped up the catwalk with her dancers, grinning from ear to ear, looking like a teenage girl just having fun. For those few seconds, you got a glimpse of why she does this, how that uncomplicated girlish *love* of what she's doing is at the root of her appeal. She then set "Hung Up" loose on the crowd, like a giant tidal wave, strutting along the catwalk with her surprisingly fleshy yet taut body encased in that shiny purple leotard. Then it was over, and the biggest disco in town picked up its baubles and trundled on through Europe, playing Russia and the Czech Republic (both firsts for Madonna), before finishing in Japan on September 21.

It had been an epic summer for her—one that started with a low-key set in a tent at the U.S. rock festival Coachella, to a full-blown world tour. Making nearly $200 million, it was the top-grossing tour ever by a female artist. Madonna had played sixty shows to 1.2 million people. She proved she was once again the reigning queen. Maybe it was time to hang up her baubles and rest. But she couldn't resist the lure of the limelight—within a month, she was back in the news, but this time for an issue that was to nearly tear her apart.

COMING
FROM GOD

"I WAS SO HYPED UP WITH ADRENALINE THAT I DON'T recall it actually happening. That was the biggest crowd I've ever played to and the closest to home I've ever played. I think my kids could hear me singing," Madonna said after her appearance at Live 8. Family was Madonna's priority in the summer of 2005, when anti–Third World poverty campaigner Bob Geldof wrote to her, asking if she could take part in a second Live Aid he was planning. At first, she said no. "I was going on holiday with my children and wanted to spend time with them. Then I thought again." Using his considerable powers of persuasion, Geldof managed to get her to sign up for Live 8, a massive concert in London's Hyde Park that was to raise awareness about famine and debt relief in Africa. Timed to coincide with the G8 superpower conference in Edinburgh, the event took place on July 2. There was an audience of 200,000 in Hyde Park, and millions more at a network of simultaneous rock concerts across the globe. In London, performers included Annie Lennox, The Who, and Pink Floyd, who got back together specially for the occasion.

Madonna's set was a high point. Dressed in a sharp white tuxedo, she performed "Like a Prayer" with the London Community Gospel choir. Just before she started the song, Geldof showed the crowd a picture of Birhan Weldu, a starving girl at the time of the first Live Aid event in 1985. Twenty years later, there she was, in the audience, a beaming, beautiful, healthy young woman. Grabbing the moment, Madonna took Birhan by the hand and led her onstage while she sang the intro to "Like a Prayer." Some criticized Madonna's emotional gesture as opportunist, noting the rapidity with which Birhan was dispensed with once the song got underway. Even so, Madonna's set was entirely appropriate: succinct, dignified, and vibrant. She obviously enjoyed the day. There was a point during the set when she rested onstage by the drum kit, watching her dancers body-popping, with the slightly proprietary, relaxed air of someone used to being in control. She knew that her trio of songs—"Like a Prayer," "Ray of Light," and "Music"—were going to metaphorically raise the roof.

Her performance was a key point in a concert that stimulated awareness to such an extent that the G8 leaders later pledged a doubling of aid to Africa by $25 billion a year. Although the World Bank was to water down the debt relief, imposing conditions on recipient nations, Live 8 brought the thorny issue of Third World poverty to the attention of a younger generation.

It also politicized Madonna in a new way. In 2003, she gave an interview to the *Sunday Times*, in which she admitted to being ignorant of Fair Trade coffee—"one has to be educated about these things and I didn't know." At that point, the politics of developing nations clearly wasn't high on her agenda. But the Live 8 concert marked the beginning of a love affair with Africa, leading to her Kabbalah-inspired Raising Malawi campaign, and, in 2006, the adoption of a young African boy.

THREE YEARS earlier, Madonna was desperate to have another baby. She was having fertility problems. "Because of my exercising and this, that, and the other, I've kind of screwed up my cycle a bit and I'm going to the doctors to make sure I'm OK to have a baby," she said at the time. In order to mask the disappointment at not conceiving, Madonna did what she has always done, and focused on her work. As time went on, there were reports of Madonna and Guy drifting apart and seeking solace with other people. Some sources singled out Stuart Price as having a "special relationship" with Madonna, though that was probably more to do with their shared enthusiasm for the work than anything else. Much of the strain came from Guy's reluctance to play second fiddle. "He feels totally hemmed in by her career," said a friend. "It's as if work is the only thing that interests her."

IT COULD not have helped matters when, in September 2005, Madonna was the one in the limelight at the premiere of his new film, *Revolver*, a Kabbalah-influenced gangster flick that had already been panned by the critics. Before the film, her publicist had apparently told the throng of paparazzi that Madonna would "only answer to the name of Mrs. Ritchie." Of course, when the star and her husband arrived, the "paps" took great delight in yelling: "MADONNA! MADONNA!" She snubbed the photographers, and the story was all over the papers the next day. On what was meant to be Guy's night, Madonna still managed to steal the show.

It was unfortunate that Guy's film, *Revolver*, didn't get the attention it deserved. Starring Ray Liotta, Jason Statham, and Vincent Pastore, it was a conceptual movie involving chess, gambling, and toe-curling violence that operated on a number of levels. "[It's] based on the formula of a game: where does the game start, where does it stop, and who's conning who," said Guy. Compared to his other films, this was his best-developed. "It took three years to write this film, whereas *Snatch* took me three months," Guy admitted. His previous offering, *Swept Away* (2002), had been such a disaster, that with *Revolver*, he stayed firmly within his area of expertise.

Swept Away had been a sobering experience for him. A remake of Lina Wertmüller's 1974 social satire about a spoiled socialite on a yachting cruise, who is tamed by a wild deckhand, it was Guy's first attempt at making a feature starring his wife. A longtime fan of Wertmüller's dynamic, socially aware filmmaking, Madonna in particular was attracted to the idea. Shot in Malta in the summer heat, the film was a glorified holiday for the cast and crew. Their enthusiasm for the production, however, didn't translate to the film. "I had no idea [it] would be such a disaster . . . we had so much fun making it," said Madonna's stylist Arianne Phillips. The dialogue was unconvincing, though, and the acting strained. And Madonna's character was rather unpleasant. Because the heroine was named after Guy's mother, Amber Leighton, one wonders if this was Guy's way of getting back at all the controlling women he perceived in his life.

Once Amber (portrayed as a Fascist) is shipwrecked on a desert island, she is forced to submit to the Communist deckhand (Adrianno Giannini), and when she is broken down, they fall in love. Once again, Madonna found herself in a role where her character is degraded and dominated. Maybe her power and wealth makes the idea of submission strangely attractive. Either way, it didn't appeal to reviewers, and the film went straight to video in the United States and the United Kingdom. Swept Away was lambasted by the critics and won five Golden Raspberry Awards. Incensed by the reaction, Madonna vowed never to act again. She felt that people were unjustly harsh, and she was probably right. In places, the film is like an extended music video, but it has its moments. Madonna's performance is slightly wooden, but then many leading Hollywood actresses, such as Nicole Kidman and Demi Moore, have a brittle air about them, because they are so stylized. We have seen a lot worse: G.I. Jane, for instance.

After Swept Away, Guy knew that he had to contend with the fact that many people saw him as Madonna's man. The very thing that made him hot property—his independence as a filmmaker—was being compromised. His way of dealing with that was to affect a tough exterior in public, calling Madonna "the missus," and rarely openly showing affection. "Deep down he blames her for his career nosedive," said a friend. By the end of 2005, their marriage was in trouble. Some close to the couple said that Guy could be a little macho (Gwyneth apparently found this so irritating she was seeing less and less of her old friend), while Madonna found it hard to shift the focus away from her own concerns. In an effort to shore up their marriage, they worked on a series of pledges, which included spending more time together, and Guy's idea for an hour a day of "Madonna time"—her designated hour for talking about work. They even sought marriage guidance from a counselor in Harley Street.

It seemed to be working. When the marriage was in a more settled phase, they put on hold their efforts to conceive and considered plans for adoption, turning to friend Brad Pitt for advice. In 2005, his partner, Angelina Jolie, had adopted a daughter, Zahara, from Ethiopia. They represented a growing trend for intercountry adoption, with prospective parents looking for children as far afield as China, Eastern Europe, and Africa. *Sunday Times* writer Steven Swinford said: "In Africa, babies have become a rapidly growing export. The number of Ethiopian children adopted between 2001 and 2004 more than doubled, to 1,535. Madagascar, Mali, and Burkina Faso are also proving popular."

With Africa in mind, Madonna and Guy began the eighteen-month-long vetting process required by the British authorities. Because of her work with Raising Malawi, a charitable organization focused on helping orphans in one of the world's poorest nations, Malawi was an obvious choice. Hard-hit by drought, this landlocked country in southeastern Africa has a spiraling AIDS crisis and an average life expectancy of forty. More than half the population lives below the poverty line.

Before she first flew out there, Madonna requested a list of twelve children for possible adoption, and the one that caught her heart was David, a thirteen-month-old boy at the Home for Hope orphanage. In October 2006, she and her entourage (which included security guards, publicists, and a camera crew) drove in a convoy of three Nissan 4×4s down a dirt track thirty miles outside of the capital, Lilongwe. Though Madonna was filming this as part of her own campaigning documentary about Malawi, the visit had all the pomp and circumstance of a royal delegation. When she and Guy arrived at the orphanage, one of the village elders said it was as if she "was coming from God."

Many of the orphans were in a desperate state. More than 250 children slept in the five dormitories, and despite the dedication of the small staff who ran it, many of the children were malnourished and vulnerable to killer diseases, like malaria. According to one of the teachers, Madonna was carrying David, "smiling and saying, 'Ah, beautiful.'" David's mother, Marita, had died after giving birth to him, so his father, Yohame Banda, who could not afford to feed his son, took his son to the orphanage. He eventually gave him up for adoption. "They told me a *mzungu* (white foreigner) had seen a picture of David and liked him very much," said thirty-two-year-old Banda. "My family and I agreed this was a very good opportunity for David to get an education and grow up healthy."

Madonna spoke with Banda, promising to take good care of his son. Malawi has strict laws regulating foreign adoptions of children, which normally mean that would-be parents must foster the child in the country for eighteen months before moving abroad. But because of the "special circumstances" of the case, the high court in Lilongwe granted Madonna an interim adoption, with the eighteen-month trial period to be completed in Britain. She and Guy flew home, to be joined by baby David just over a week later. Adopting her new "Ray of Light," however, was not going to be that simple.

After her visit to Malawi, a media storm broke out. A coalition of more than sixty aid agencies and children's charities mounted a legal challenge to get the adoption blocked. Under the umbrella organization the Human Rights Consultative Committee, they claimed the adoption was unlawful, because Madonna hadn't lived in the country for eighteen months. "The rich shouldn't get preferential treatment," said Emmie Chanika, director of the Civil Liberties Committee in Malawi. "Do we have checks so people cannot grab our children? I am fine with the idea of adoption but I want people to go through the system." However, a Malawian government official insisted that Madonna had been "pushing papers for some time" before David was taken out of the country.

The case was adjourned once the interim order went through, but the debate grew more heated, as other organizations weighed in with their opinions. "Where possible, we work with our partners overseas to keep children within their families," said Alison Sanderson from the International Children's Trust. "Psychologically and emotionally . . . the [local] family is the best place to bring up the child." David's extended family in Malawi, including uncles and a grandmother, were worried about the situation. "People have taken advantage of my brother because he has little education," said the boy's uncle Profera. There was concern that Yohame didn't fully understand what adoption means. "He doesn't know the boy is completely and forever going to be out of his custody. The issue is about awareness and ignorance of the whole process," added Undule Mwakasungule, director of the Center for Human Rights and Rehabilitation in Malawi. Yohame Banda confused matters by sending out mixed messages. He said that he had never agreed Madonna could take his son on a permanent basis, but then later said he would not contend the adoption.

Opinion was polarized. Some saw Madonna's £1.6 million pledge to help 900,000 orphans as a bid to fast-track the adoption process, while others saw it as a valuable gift to the country. "We must be frank. We can't afford to look after the thousands of babies that are being orphaned every day," said Mirriam Nyirongo, a retired nurse working in an orphanage in northern Malawi. "If rich people like Madonna take just one child, it will be a major boost for [the country]."

The contrast between David's life in Africa and his prospective one in England was huge. In the Lipunga village he left behind, the primary school has 892 children and six teachers. Four of the eight classrooms do not have desks. The village is fourteen miles from the nearest clinic and forty miles from a hospital. With his new family, David would shuttle by private jet between mansions in Mayfair, Wiltshire, New York, and Beverly Hills. He would be educated at top private schools and have access to the best health care. One of the first presents Madonna bought for him was a £5,000 rocking horse from Harrods. Although Madonna enjoys a privileged life, she and Guy still had an unnerving wait from when they met baby David to when the interim adoption order came through. "Madonna was so happy when this worked out," said an associate of the Raising Malawi project, "she has such a strong image, you never think of her as crying, do you? However, I saw tears when she got the news that the adoption was going through. She was very emotional about it." Madonna said simply: "It's so worth it. He's just the best little baby ever. Guy and I have never been happier."

Throughout October and November, the story refused to die down, with online polls and letters passionately voting "for" and "against." Madonna went shopping for a baby like he was a fashion accessory. She did this as her latest PR stunt. She should adopt from her own country before swanning off to Africa. If Madonna wants to help Malawi, she should pay off its national debt—she'd still have some to spare. But there were other voices: that the star should be saluted for her courage, that she should be allowed to bond with her new baby in peace. That "angel Madonna" has highlighted the problem of all children suffering in Africa. "How dare anyone question her motives?" railed Guy. "It's so preposterous that anyone would be critical of Madonna for wanting to share her love and wealth."

Once again, Madonna had become a lightning rod for criticism. Feeling victimized, she issued a defensive statement: "After learning that there were over one million orphans in Malawi, it was my wish to open up our home and help one child escape an extreme life of hardship, poverty, and, in many cases, death, as well as expand our family.

"Nevertheless, we have gone about the adoption procedure according to the law, like anyone else who adopts a child. Reports to the contrary are totally inaccurate."

Rather than lie low and wait for the furor to die down, she launched her own media onslaught, giving a tearful interview on the *Oprah Winfrey Show*. She said that David was severely ill with pneumonia the day she and Guy drove up in their 4×4. "I was in a panic," she said. "I didn't want to leave him in the orphanage, because I knew they didn't have medication to take care of him." They managed to get him to a clinic to give him a bronchial dilator and antibiotics, so he began to recover. "I was transfixed by him. I was just drawn to him," she declared.

There was speculation about the fact that, despite being "transfixed" by little David, Madonna found time to go to the gym and conduct a global publicity tour for her new children's book, *The English Roses: Too Good to Be True*. She spoke to the BBC *Newsnight* anchor Kirsty Wark in a room dressed with drapes and candles; she appeared again on national TV in the United States, inviting talk-show host Regis Philbin to be the godfather of her new son. In an interview with NBC's *Today* show, she said: "I didn't expect to be demonized. . . . I didn't expect to be accused of kidnapping or doing something illegal." She speculated that much of the criticism was motivated by racism, the fact of a rich white woman adopting a black baby. "That's underneath a lot of people's prejudice about me adopting David," she claimed.

Unrepentant and angry, Madonna seemed unable to retreat from the limelight, thus laying herself open to more condemnation. Fellow celebrity Angelina Jolie felt compelled to comment, saying she was "horrified" by the attacks on Madonna, but then said she would choose children only from countries where adoption rules are clearly defined.

Madonna didn't help her case by going on a shopping channel to promote her book. And there was the bizarre paparazzi shot of Madonna jogging in Central Park followed close behind by her nanny running along with David in a pushchair. Guy lambasted Madonna for getting involved with the publicity circus, saying it made it look like the adoption was just about her, rather than their joint decision. Critics said that if Madonna had really wanted privacy, she should have gone to Malawi without the cameras. After all, other stars, like Ewan McGregor and Meg Ryan, had adopted children from overseas and managed to keep it low-profile in the media. This was ignoring the fact that Madonna has always resolved her issues in public. Compelled to seek mass love and attention, yet overly sensitive to criticism, she creates her own vicious cycle. When the BBC's Kirsty Wark dared to suggest to Madonna that she must find the situation bewildering because she was used to being in control, the star retorted: "I'm a detail-oriented person, [but] I often don't have things my way. The world's reaction was quite shocking. There's no way I could have prepared myself for that."

Within weeks, fuel was added to the media fire with rumors that Madonna wanted to adopt another African child, this time a girl. Guy wasn't thrilled, because he wanted to assimilate David into the family first—but Madonna was on a crusade. "I saw this child in the village, with questioning dark eyes and the saddest smile," she said. "I thought, 'She looks just like me.' I told Guy, 'We must give this child a home too.' We may still. The conditions here devastate me." The adoption was bringing up old traumas from the past, and memories of how she felt abandoned as a child. There seems to be a pattern in the way wealthy menopausal stars like to create their own rainbow tribe—with women like Josephine Baker, Audrey Hepburn, and Mia Farrow embarking on a personal odyssey to save the world's children. Approaching the end of their "natural" childbearing years, it is as if a menopausal crisis is triggered and projected out into the world. Their urge to create another, bigger family is a way of healing old, long-buried hurts. In solidarity with Madonna, Mia Farrow felt moved to comment: "She's a wonderful woman and I think that child at least will have every opportunity and I'm happy for the child and for the family."

Underlying this issue is the world's continuous unease with a powerful woman, particularly one who provokes Western anxiety and guilt over global poverty. There is envy of Madonna's millions, a need to curtail her influence, to cut her down to size. But there is also admiration at the way she pursues her goals and tells the world in the process, dragging the issues that concern her into the open. With the adoption of baby David and her pledge to Malawian orphans, she did more than most pop stars in highlighting the desperate poverty in Africa.

The twenty-first-century star resurrected that ancient image of Madonna and child, only this time it was in modern form, with modern issues. She had launched a crusade that in time will either backfire on her or lead to her universal respect as a humanitarian. By Christmas 2006, though, she was exhausted and unhappy. There was a Friday-night ceremony at the Kabbalah Center in London to bless David and welcome him into the fold. "Guy was there, looking jowly and comfortable, with Rocco on his shoulders. Lola was talking loudly and running around, like the precocious free spirit she is," remarked a friend. "But Madonna sat on her own, with David. She was gracious, but she did not look happy. She seemed kind of isolated." The media frenzy had taken its toll.

At this point, a defensive Madonna felt that even her closest friends had let her down. She had clashed with Stella McCartney, in particular, over the animal rights issue. A fan of fur, Madonna upset Stella when in 2001 she wore a £1,000 Philip Treacy fox fur hat. Then, in the December after her adoption of David, she was pictured coming out of Cecconi's restaurant in London's Mayfair wearing a £35,000 coat made out of forty chinchillas. This, plus the fact that Madonna and Guy regularly rented out their Wiltshire estate to shooting parties, was too much for Stella. They exchanged some frank words, with the result that from the New Year 2007, Madonna agreed not to have shooting parties at their country house. This decision was also affected by complaints from local residents saying that birds from the shoot were flying into high-voltage power lines and causing power outages in the area. She must have been aware that the image of a caring, spiritual Madonna didn't quite fit with wearing real fur and killing birds. "Someone in Madonna's position should act more responsibly," said Mary Brady, of the Animal Rights Coalition. Once more, Madonna felt the heat of public disapproval.

It had been a year of career highs and emotional turmoil. She had a bestselling album and tour, but also personal struggle in her marriage and an ongoing battle over the adoption of David. By the New Year, she had called it quits. For the moment. Guy and Madonna renewed their wedding vows in a low-key ceremony at their home in Wiltshire and then went to an island in the Indian Ocean over Christmas. "I don't usually go on vacation but it was great," said Madonna. "But with three kids, you need a vacation to get over the vacation!" She sounded settled and renewed, but already an edginess was creeping

*Madonna kisses Britney
Spears at the 2003 MTV
Video Music Awards.
"I am the mommy pop
star and she is the baby
pop star," Madonna said.*

LEFT: *One queen meets another at the premiere of the 2002 James Bond film* Die Another Day.

BELOW: *Madonna at the London launch of her first children's book,* The English Roses.

BACKGROUND: *A poster for Guy Ritchie's 2002 film* Swept Away.

RIGHT: *Madonna and Guy at the world premiere in Toronto of his film* Revolver, *2005. Her arm is in a sling after her riding accident a month earlier.*

RIGHT: *Guy (seated) and Madonna (with bag) on location in Malta for* Swept Away.

RIGHT: *Madonna performs a military-style "Express Yourself" on her Re-Invention tour in 2004.*

Madonna strikes an impressive ashtanga yoga pose during the Re-Invention tour.

LEFT AND RIGHT: *Performing the "equestrian" section of her Confessions tour in 2006.*

RIGHT: *Madonna sings at the Live 8 concert in London's Hyde Park in 2005.*

BELOW: *Creating an iconic image on the giant mirrored cross of her Confessions tour.*

With Bob Geldof onstage at the 2005 MTV Europe Awards in Lisbon.

ABOVE: *Madonna and Guy with their bodyguards, visiting the tomb of Rabbi Ashlag in Jerusalem during a Kabbalah conference in 2004.*

RIGHT: *Madonna with Rocco and Lola, leaving a Kabbalah service in New York.*

Guy and a glamorous but tense Madonna at the Vanity Fair Oscar party in West Hollywood, 2007.

ABOVE: *Madonna and family relaxing in Hyde Park.*

BELOW: *Walking with a crowd in Malawi, during the October 2006 visit when she first met baby David Banda.*

Madonna with
adopted son David
and daughter Lola,
returning to the
Home of Hope
orphanage in Malawi
in 2007. Locals
called Madonna a
"heroine."

in. It turned out that for much of the holiday Madonna had worked out furiously in the gym, while Guy took the children to the beach. Not a fan of the sun, because she didn't want to risk the wrinkles, Madonna often stayed indoors. On a deeper level, she and Guy were drifting back to more separate lives. After the brief patch of harmony during the adoption crisis, former difficulties resurfaced, and they began having verbal battles in public.

Rebelling against Madonna's controlling behavior, Guy went out drinking, shooting, and fishing with his friends. She would call his drinking haunts, looking for him, wanting to know when he was coming home. Often he would turn off his mobile phone. In trying to prove that he was his own man, Guy was going overboard. "Guy is really tough on her. He won't let her get away with anything," said a friend. "It's not good news. It's as if he thinks it's his duty to put her in her place every now and again. She just gets tired of it sometimes. She wishes he was nicer to her." Both desperately wanted to make the marriage work, because of the children, but it was under strain. She was homesick and wanted to move back to New York, whereas he wanted to stay in London and not disrupt the children's schooling. They put on a brave face in January, when they went as a family to the opening of *Arthur and the Invisibles*, a Luc Besson animation, in which Madonna was the voice of Princess Selenia. Although she clung on to Guy as if for dear life, it was rumored that she was privately considering plans to move back to New York, with or without him. And she was plowing on with her career: designing a collection for Swedish fashion giant H&M, producing a documentary about Malawi, starting work on her next record. In April 2007, she went into the studio with the two hottest names in the business—Justin Timberlake and Timbaland—to create a " hip-hop inspired" album. She also directed her first short movie, a low-budget comedy called *Filth and Wisdom*. And she found time to go back to Malawi with David, so the little boy could see his father again. Despite previous criticism from aid agencies there, many Malawians welcomed Madonna back as their heroine.

As Madonna sings in her song "Jump," there was too much to do, too much life to live, and never, ever, did she intend to stay in one place when she had learned from it all she could.

WHAT NOW for the icon, as she approaches fifty? "Madonna's over it now. She'd say she isn't, because she has to, but she is," says her video editor Dustin Robertson. "How can she say good-bye? How can she let go of all this? It's an epic process to go through for the woman, the artist, the icon. Let alone to watch from the sidelines, as we all surely will." Maybe Madonna will move further into the political arena, using the power that she has with her mass audience. Presidential candidate Hillary Clinton is one of the few women alive that she looks up to, and Madonna makes no secret of her friendship with Hillary's husband, Bill, and other prominent Democratic activists, like Michael Moore. Madonna's Raising Malawi campaign has raised her consciousness to such an extent that we could expect her, Bono-style, to become more involved in the global campaign against poverty. In July 2007 she appeared at the global Live Earth event, and released the charity record *Hey You* for the campaign. In the 80s and 90s, her goal was to liberate women. Now, it seems, she wants to be part of liberating the world.

"People underestimated me, didn't they?" she said in 2006. "They thought that what I was doing in the 1990s was all that I was as a woman. . . . I'm not ashamed of anything I did. But so much of it was coming from a place of anger and defiance, of trying to be in-your-face about feminism. It took Kabbalah for me to see that all of that controversy wasn't necessary, that women can better send a message of empowerment by the example of living their lives in a good way . . . what they do with their time on this planet." Traditionally, a woman in her fifties was seen as "past it," no longer useful to society. The best she could do was wind up her work and retire gracefully to look after the extended family. Now more and more women are reaching key career positions at fifty, and making a major cultural impact in the world. Female heads of state today include German chancellor Angela

Merkel; Finnish president Tarja K. Halonen; Luisa Diogo, the prime minister of Mozambique; and Helen Clark, prime minister of New Zealand. Back in the early 1980s, a slogan we liked was "The Future Is Female," if only because that seemed a distant dream. Maybe Madonna sees that in the political world, that is where the real power lies. Maybe, like her old flame Warren Beatty, she will even seek the presidential nomination from the Democratic Party.

Even if it isn't overtly political, Madonna will always have a public role. A huge collector of visual art, she once said that when she was "very, very old," she would like to be like Peggy Guggenheim, a patron of artists. Madonna has always had the ability to draw a wide range of people under her wing. According to cultural theorist Andrew Ross, she functions "like what environmentalists call a charismatic mega-fauna: a highly visible, and lovable, species, like the whale or the spotted owl, in whose sympathetic name entire ecosystems can be protected and safeguarded through public patronage."

The world Madonna lives and breathes is her art. There is no doubt she will continue to make music—but where will she go as an artist? She would hate to become a parody of her former self, like her heroines Mae West and Marlene Dietrich, wobbling onto the stage at eighty in a wig and heavy makeup, singing "Like a Virgin." In her fifties, will she still be trying to defeat the aging process? Or will she go within and explore something more artistically radical, as did her dance icon Martha Graham, who, at the age of fifty, choreographed *Herodiad*, one of her most powerful pieces?

THERE ARE many parallels between Madonna and her idol. A former Graham dancer, Jane Dudley, has a vivid memory of Graham's *Herodiad* performance: "When she performed it, it was unreal. . . . She would take you into herself in a way that was almost hypnotic." Madonna has done the equivalent with "Like a Prayer," with "Justify My Love," with "Mer Girl," and "Mother and Father." And it's not just those moments of psychodrama that have a transformative power: Madonna still understands the inclusive, celebratory dynamism of dance—from "Into the Groove" to "Vogue" to "Music" and "Hung Up." She has given her fans a glorious array of images and years of enticing live shows. She will continue to express in her body and her sound what she sees as the zeitgeist. Whatever the outcome, Madonna's story is long, her influence far-reaching. She was born at a boom time for the Virgin Mary in U.S. Catholicism. She rose to fame in the 80s, when the Virgin was worshipped at shrines throughout the world. And there has been a resurgence of Madonna's fame during a period of global uncertainty and conflict. In her desire to save Malawi, she is moving beyond the pop world to take on a role of spiritual mother. As fellow pop iconoclast Tori Amos says: "She introduced the new paradigm that the Virgin Mary may have been spiritual *and* sexual. Whether or not the Madonna of modern times fully understood the implications does not matter; she was christened Madonna and she saw the gift in a song called 'Like a Virgin.' It represented the resurrection of the Virgin Mary as a woman. We have long equated spirituality with a denial of the sexual being, but Madonna challenged this."

Though flawed and all-too-human, it's her fearlessness that inspires. Like the icon who originally bore her name, this Madonna is here in perpetuity.

ACKNOWLEDGMENTS

Thanks first and foremost to Malcolm Boyle, for his love, humor, and inspiration. Huge thanks to my researcher Rob Diament (lead singer/ songwriter of the band Temposhark and an impressive Madonna archivist). His intelligence and enthusiasm inspired me whenever the going got tough. Thanks, too, to my agent, Jane Turnbull, and my editors: Doug Young and Sarah Emsley at Bantam Press, and Mauro DiPreta at HarperCollins U.S. for their belief in the book. Also Robert Sabella, for his support and insight.

Thanks to the interviewees, all of whom were so generous with their time and their recollections. I was struck by the sheer force of creativity and dynamism of so many who have known and worked with Madonna. There was such a wealth of material that it couldn't all be included in the book. Thanks, then, to the interviewees, including Edward Acker, Lorenzo Agius, Tori Amos, Nancy Andersen, Camille Barbone, Jimmy Bralower, Gardner Cole, Ginger Canzoneri, Louise Carolin, Wendy Cooling, Andrae Crouch, Andre Betts, Jimmy Bralower, Ingrid Chavez, Pablo Cook, Marie Cooper, Wyn Cooper, Kevin Cummins, Marius De Vries, Kim Drayton, Bill De-Young, Johnny Dynell, Andy Earle, Julia Eccleshare, Brigitte Echols, Ulrich Edel, Maripol Fauque, Deborah Feingold, James Foley, Geoff

Foster, Randy Frank, Bruce Gaitsch, Salim Gauwloos, Jon Gordon, Niki Haris, Ramon Hertz, Richard Hojna, Barney Hoskyns, Antony Jackson, Mark Kamins, Mihran Kirakosyan, Danny Kleinman, Pearl Lang, Alex Magno, Bob Magnussun, Brian McCollum, Melodie McDaniel, Charles Melcher, Bill Meyers, Peter Morse, Rick Nowells, Melinda Patton, Guy Pratt, Princess Julia, Raistalla, Tim Rice, Dustin Robertson, Sandy Robertson, Earle Sebastian, Susan Seidelman, Tony Shimkin, Guy Sigsworth, Peter Sparling, Billy Steinberg, Peggy Vance, Carlton Wilborn, Doug Wimbish, Dick Witts, and Peter York.

And many thanks to Heather Bradford, Sarah Cheang, Wendy Fonarow, Louise Kerr, Adrian Neale, Susan O'Brien, Daniel Theo, and Jane Turner for their wonderful help with research. Last, but not least, thank you to my family for everything.

NOTES

*Unless otherwise indicated, all interviews for this book were conducted by the author in the United Kingdom and United States between 2004 and 2007.

INTRODUCTION

xi *"I am . . . l'art,"* The Confessions Tour—Live From London DVD, 2007.

xi *"Her [eyes] . . . the room."* Everett, Rupert, *Red Carpets and Other Banana Skins* (Little, Brown, London, 2006), p. 181.

xii *"has rejoined . . . the harlot."* Paglia, Camille, *Sex, Art, and American Culture* (Viking, London & New York, 1992), p. 11.

xiv *"she . . . secretary to herself."* Mailer, Norman, "Norman Mailer on Madonna: Like a Lady," *Esquire*, August 1994.

xv *"I haven't . . . deserve this?"* Price, Richard, "War Over Baby David," *Daily Mail*, January 25, 2007.

xv *"Her most . . . experience."* From *Naked Ambition*, UK Channel 4, December 2000.

1. THE DEATH OF MADONNA

3 *"My grandparents . . . with."* Worrell, Denise, "Madonna: Why She's Hot," *Time*, May 27, 1985.

5 *"She was . . . facial structure."* Ibid.

6 *"I was considered . . . my father."* Ibid.

7 *"She was . . . my mother."* Ibid.

7 *"I remember . . . better."* Ibid.

9 *"Sometimes . . . dark beyond."* Zehme, Bill, "Madonna: The Rolling Stone Interview," *Rolling Stone,* March 23, 1989.

10 *"the most frightening . . . moving."* Bowlby, John, *Attachment and Loss, Volume 3, Loss* (Pimlico, London, 1998), p. 371.

10 *"For five years . . . strangle me."* From *Truth or Dare* documentary, 1991.

10 *"compulsive caregiver."* Bowlby, op cit, p. 368.

11 *"I think . . . regulations."* Thompson, Douglas, *Madonna: Queen of the World* (John Blake, London, 2001), pp. 16–17.

11 *"Mother stands . . . martyr."* Eichenbaum, Luise, and Orbach, Susie, *Understanding Women* (Pelican Books, London, 1985) p. 60.

11 *"It promoted . . . Jansenist influence."* McBrien, Richard P., *Catholicism,* 3rd ed. (Geoffrey Chapman, London, 1994) p. 639–40.

12 *"My mother . . . in common."* Laskas, Jeanne Marie, "Immaterial girl," *Harpers & Queen,* November 2005.

12 *"Until Christ . . . beautiful."* Madonna, "Madonna's Private Diaries," *Vanity Fair,* November 1996.

12 *"It's a central act . . . the movies."* Chinnici, Joseph O.F.M., "The Catholic Community at Prayer, 1926–1976," from O'Toole, James, ed., *Habits of Devotion: Catholic Religious Practice in Twentieth-century America* (Cornell University Press, Ithaca & London, 2004), pp. 9–87.

13 *"When a woman . . . second-class citizen."* Eichenbaum and Orbach, op cit, p. 40.

13 *"the link . . . to do."* Ibid, p. 62.

2. A MAGICAL PLACE

16 *"I'm a . . . star."* Ciccone, Christopher, "Oh Brother!" *Attitude,* July 2006.

17 *"I resented . . . Cinderella."* Worrell, Denise, "Madonna: Why She's Hot," *Time,* May 27, 1985.

17 *"I wouldn't . . . investment."* From *Madonna: The Unauthorized Biography,* M.I.A. Video, 1993.

17 *"Bitch . . . next phase."* Ibid.

22 *"Madonna . . . not be denied."* Taraborrelli, J. Randy, *Madonna: An Intimate Biography* (Sidgwick & Jackson, London, 2001), p. 28.

23 *"None of . . . their group."* Interviewer not named, "Madonna: Virgin Pop," *Island* magazine, September 1983.

24 *"In school . . . sense of myself."* Shewey, Don, "Madonna: The Saint, the Slut, the Sensation," *The Advocate*, May 7 and 21, 1991.

26 *"Look at women . . . tragic."* Taraborrelli, op cit, p. 29.

26 *"He was my . . . everything,"* Worrell, op cit.

26 *"I knew . . . told me."* Ibid.

26 *"I feel . . . a warrior,"* Bego, Mark, *Madonna: Blonde Ambition* (Cooper Square Press, New York, 2000), p. 45.

28 *"It was a punk . . . attention,"* Morton, Andrew, *Madonna* (Michael O'Mara, London, 2001), p. 60.

28 *"brilliant . . . thin."* Taraborrelli, op cit, p. 31.

28 *"I'm sure . . . anorexic."* Morton, op cit.

29 *"a force . . . human."* From *Naked Ambition*. UK Channel 4, December 2000.

29 *"I played . . . dancing."* *Naked Ambition,* op cit.

29 *"She embarked . . . friend."* Taraborrelli, op cit, p. 31.

30 *"was to modern . . . art."* Gale.com/free_resources/whm/bio/graham_m.htm, 2005.

30 *"the hidden language of the soul."* Quotationspage.com/quotes/martha graham, 2005.

30 *"It was not . . . 180 degrees."* Jowitt, Deborah, *Time and the Dancing Image* (University of California Press, Berkeley and Los Angeles, 1988), p. 173.

31 *"I don't believe . . . people."* From UK LWT *South Bank Show* documentary *The Alvin Ailey American Dance Theater,* 1987.

31 *"In the nightclub . . . free,"* Garfield, Simon, "Looks Good on the Dance Floor," *Observer Music Monthly*, November 2005.

31 *"The dance floor . . . a magical place."* Eccleston, Danny, "Power Is an Aphrodisiac," Q magazine, June 1998.

32 *"didn't get good advice."* Morton, op cit, p. 64.

32 *"Stop . . . me!"* Taraborrelli, op cit, p. 35.

3. THE ARROGANCE AND THE NERVE!

34 *"I'm pissed off . . . from Viv."* Reddington, Helen, *The Lost Women of Rock Music: Women Musicians of the Punk Era* (Ashgate Press, London, 2007), p. 144.

34 *"We'd be dressed . . . coming or going."* O'Brien, Lucy, *She Bop II: The Definitive History of Women in Rock, Pop & Soul* (Continuum, London & New York, 2002), p. 146.

36 *"I got her a job . . . meal she was getting."* From *Naked Ambition,* UK Channel 4, December 2000.

37 *"The other way . . . compromising."* From *Madonna: The Unauthorized Biography*, M.I.A. Video, 1993.

38 *"I have been raped . . . glamorize."* Morton, Andrew, *Madonna* (Michael O'Mora, London, 2001) p. 69

38 *"It was a very heavy . . . story."* Morton, op cit, p. 69

39 *"sensual . . . made of light."* *Naked Ambition*, op cit.

39 *"I'm a beats . . . in my place."* From *The Truth About Madonna's Men*, UK Channel 5, September 2005.

42 *"You're all naked . . . no talent."* Taraborrelli, J. Randy, *Madonna: An Intimate Biography* (Sidgwick & Jackson, London, 2001) p. 54.

42 *"She had a set . . . working together."* *Naked Ambition*, op cit.

42 *"Some people . . . about you."* Ibid.

45 *"My role models . . . courage."* St. Michael, Mick, *Madonna "Talking"* (Omnibus Press, London, 2004), p. 40.

45 *"An aggressive . . . groundbreaker."* Gaar, Gillian G., *She's a Rebel: The History of Women in Rock & Roll* (Blandford Press, London, 1993), p. 107.

45 *"I was hugely influenced . . . reference."* Che, Cathay, *Deborah Harry: Platinum Blonde* (Andre Deutsch, London, 1999), from summary on the flap.

45 *"That made a huge . . . clicked there."* *Naked Ambition*, op cit.

4. JAM HOT

54 *"I saw her . . . 'straight.'"* From *Naked Ambition*, UK Channel 4, December 2000.

54 *"She seemed . . . know yet."* Ibid.

56 *"You can dance . . . excitement."* Garfield, Simon, "Looks Good on the Dance Floor," *Observer Music Monthly*, November 2005.

57 *"We had no money . . . programmers."* From *The Truth About Madonna's Men*, UK Channel 5, September 2005.

57 *"I think . . . that much."* From *Madonna: The Unauthorized Biography*. M.I.A. Video, 1993.

60 *"I don't think . . . life."* Artquotes.net/masters/basquiat-quotes.htm, 2006.

60 *SAMO . . . PLAYING ART.* Ibid.

60 *"Jean was . . . arranged marriage."* Hoban, Phoebe, *Basquiat: A Quick Killing in Art* (Viking Penguin, New York, 2004), p. 163.

60 *"Madonna turned . . . everywhere."* Ibid.

61 *"never . . . emotionless."* Ibid, p. 165.

62 *"I told her . . . coupla grand."* Sutcliffe, Phil, "Lucky Star," *At Home and in Bed with Madonna*, Q Special Edition, 2003, p. 13.

62 "*Rica . . . let's do it.*" Hoban, op cit, p. 160.

63 "*Reggie . . . like them.*" Hoskyns, Barney, "Cheek to Cheat," *NME*, November 5, 1983.

63 "*commercial song . . . refrain.*" Tatit, Luiz, "Analysing Popular Songs," from Hesmondhalgh, David and Negus, Keith, eds., *Popular Music Studies* (Arnold, London, 2002), pp. 33–49.

63 "*a search . . . melody.*" Ibid.

65 "*Most of my friends . . . like that.*" Bouncefm.com, 2006.

65 "*The music . . . cool!*" Ibid.

66 "*The vibe . . . heartbreak.*" Shapiro, Peter, *Turn the Beat Around: The Secret History of Disco* (Faber & Faber, London, 2005), p. 266.

66 "*It was quite common . . . record.*" Bouncefm.com, op cit.

66 "*So she decided . . . singing a pop song.*" Sutcliffe, op cit.

66 "*I now know . . . category.*" Hoskyns, op cit.

67 "*Maripol . . . happen,*" O'Brien, Glenn, in the Introduction to *Maripolarama: Polaroids by Maripol* (powerHouse Books, New York, 2005).

5. SICK AND PERVERTED

71 "*Not everyone . . . bringing it back.*" Johnson, Howard, "Do You Remember the First Time?" Q Special Edition, 2003, p. 24.

72 "*I told her . . . artist.*" Ibid.

72 "*She was convinced . . . nuts?*" Ibid, p. 25.

73 "*Sick and perverted . . . people.*" Zollo, Paul, *Songwriters on Songwriting* (Da Capo Press, Cincinnati, 2003), p. 622.

73 "*Losing your . . . to it.*" Johnson, op cit.

76 "*The thing . . . one-take stuff.*" Ibid.

77 "*We spent . . . relationship.*" From *The Truth About Madonna's Men,* UK Channel 5, September 2005.

78 "*Music is . . . target.*" St. Michael, Mick, *Madonna "Talking"* (Omnibus Press, London, 2004) p. 36.

78 "*It was no . . . that governed.*" Eliot, Marc, *Rockonomics: The Money Behind the Music* (Omnibus Press, London, 1990), p. 188.

78 "*The superstar . . . you can have.*" Ibid, p. 193.

79 "*out of anger . . . I wasn't!*" O'Brien, Lucy, *She Bop II: The Definitive History of Women in Rock, Pop & Soul* (Continuum, London and New York, 2002) p. 228.

80 "*You can't live . . . sell myself.*" Ibid, p. 229.

80 "*seemed kind of . . . It's silly.*" Ibid, p. 230.

6. HOW I STOPPED WORRYING AND LEARNED TO LOVE MADONNA

86 *"Madonna . . . shoplifts."* Hackett, Pat, *The Andy Warhol Diaries* (Warner Books, New York and Boston, 1989), p. 632.

86 *"Madonna . . . they agreed."* Metropolitan.com/producer.html, 2005.

88 *"I thought . . . rock video."* Matthew-Walker, Robert, *Madonna: The Biography* (Pan, London, 1989), p. 81.

89 *"I like to . . . good on me."* Ibid, p. 93.

90 *"If they're happy . . . X rating."* Ibid, p. 91.

7. MAKEUP IN THAT GREAT HOLLYWOOD WAY

93 *"We were out . . . stuntman to do."* Matthew-Walker Robert, *Madonna: The Biography* (Pan, London, 1989), p.95.

95 *"The only thing . . . to say anything."* Ibid, p. 97.

96 *"She was . . . at the time."* Imdb.com/name/nm0000576/publicity, 2006.

97 *"I remember the sun . . . my power."* Deevoy, Adrian, "I'm a Tormented Person," Q magazine, June 1991.

98 *"It turned into . . . believed it."* Matthew-Walker, op cit, p. 105.

98 *"the perfect mixture . . . new Hollywood look."* Hackett, Pat, *The Andy Warhol Diaries* (Warner Books, New York and Boston, 1989), p. 670.

99 *"someone . . . really act."* Matthew-Walker, op cit, p. 109.

99 *"had no knowledge . . . his head."* St. Michael, Mick, *Madonna "Talking"* (Omnibus Press, London, 2004) p. 59.

100 *"I kept saying . . . anything now."* Ibid, p. 59.

100 *"He has given . . . movie."* Ibid, p. 58.

100 *"famous pop star . . . LSD."* Wise, Damon, "The Player," Q Special Edition, 2003, p. 39.

100 *"a phony . . . abysmal."* Walker, John, ed., *Halliwell's Film & Video Guide 2003* (HarperCollins, London, 2003), p. 752.

100 *"I was the only . . . great."* Hackett, op cit, p. 762.

100 *"As a friend . . . watch it,"* St. Michael, op cit, p. 59.

102 *"friendly-ass corny shit."* Morton, Andrew, *Madonna* (Michael O'Mara, London, 2001) p.165

102 *"In popular music . . . machine."* Adorno, Theodor W. "On Popular Music," from Frith, Simon and Goodwin, Andrew, *On Record: Rock, Pop, & the Written Word* (Routledge, London, 1990), p. 303.

104 *"beauty . . . people."* Andersen, Christopher, *Madonna Unauthorized* (Michael Joseph, London, 1991), p. 152.

104 *"It's only Anglos . . . helps!"* O'Brien, Lucy, *She Bop II: The Definitive History of Women in Rock, Pop & Soul* (Continuum, London & New York, 2002) p.373.

104 *"She was . . . love songs,"* St. Michael, op cit, p. 43.

104 *"a message . . . wrong way."* Ibid, p. 34.

107 *"She was . . . goddess-like,"* Madonnatribe.com/idol/jeri.htm, 2006.

107 *"I asked Madonna . . . hot right now."* Hackett, op cit, p. 616.

107 *"Gee . . . a year ago."* Ibid, p. 649.

107 *"Madonna . . . just perfectly."* Ibid, p. 675.

108 *"ease . . . realm of conduct."* Koestenbaum, Wayne, *Andy Warhol* (Phoenix, London, 2001), p. 188.

108 *"Profoundly . . . silkscreens."* Ibid, p. 131.

8. ME IN THE PICTURE

111 *"I was really excited . . . comedy."* St. Michael, Mick, *Madonna "Talking"* (Omnibus Press, London, 2004) p. 59.

112 *"I had a lot . . . vulnerability she feels."* Matthew-Walker, Robert, *Madonna: The Biography* (Pan, London, 1989) pp. 124–25.

112 *"All Warner's . . . better."* St. Michael, op cit, p. 60.

114 *"When she . . . doesn't require that."* Kelly, Richard T., *Sean Penn: His Life and Times* (Cannongate, New York, 2004), p. 183.

114 *"There are people . . . fields,"* St. Michael, op cit, p. 60.

118 *"In a funny . . . from here."* Eccleston, Danny, "True Blue," Q Special Edition, p. 35.

119 *"It was internal . . . spirit."* Lahr, John, "Citizen Penn," *Observer Magazine,* June 4, 2006.

119 *"Trying to . . . shit."* Ibid.

119 *"She never . . . function."* Ibid.

119 *"It's hard . . . interesting."* Ibid.

120 *"They were . . . bums!"* Leigh, Wendy, "I'm Just Attracted to Bums," NoW *Sunday* magazine, August 9, 1987.

120 *"Sean . . . husband."* Kelly, op cit, p. 189.

120 *"In grabbing . . . jackpot,"* From *The Truth About Madonna's Men,* UK Channel 5, September, 2005.

121 *"It's like going to bed with a nine-year-old."* Ibid.

121 *"I'm the only . . . lips."* From *The Arsenio Hall Show,* Fox Broadcasting, 1990.

121 *"She's one . . . ballsy girl,"* Shewey, Don, "Madonna: The Saint, The Slut, The Sensation," *The Advocate,* May 7 and 21, 1991.

121 *"She is . . . death to her."* Morton, Andrew, *Madonna* (Michael O'Mara, London, 2001) p.159.

122 *"She developed . . . haircut."* Lahr, op cit.

9. THE SIN IS WITHIN YOU

123 *"I didn't try . . . I felt."* Zollo, Paul, *Songwriters on Songwriting* (Da Capo Press, Cincinnati, 2003), p.616.

124 *"She was . . . divorce album."* Kinnersley, Simon, "The Real Madonna: 'I Just Call Her Daisy,'" *Mail on Sunday*, March 1989.

127 *"I don't think . . . in her own way."* From *Naked Ambition*, UK Channel 4, December 2000.

127 *"Sometimes . . . painful religion."* Zehme, Bill, '"Madonna: The *Rolling Stone* Interview,"' *Rolling Stone*, March 23, 1989.

128 *"I really wanted . . . choir."* Zollo, op cit, p. 620.

129 *"It's me dealing . . . in life."* Ibid, p. 621.

130 *"this really . . . out of it."* Ibid.

130 *"Maybe I wasn't . . . us."* Taraborrelli, J.Randy, *Madonna: An Intimate Biography,* (Sidgwick & Jackson, London, 2001), p. 356.

131 *"It's very much . . . can't end."* Zehme, op cit.

132 *"[We] didn't really . . . over the line."* Ibid.

133 *"confession . . . to God."* O'Toole, James M., ed, *Habits of Devotion: Catholic Religious Practice in Twentieth-Century America* (Cornell University Press, Ithaca and London, 2004), p. 85.

133 *"For sins . . . prayer."* Ibid, p. 157.

133 *"The sexual impulse . . . Original Sin."* McBrien, Richard P., *Catholicism.* 3rd ed. (Geoffrey Chapman, London, 1994), p.560.

134 *"You have to . . . people you're with."* Zollo, op cit, p. 620.

134 *"The 'Like a Prayer' . . . on me."* "Madonna Speaks!!!," *Smash Hits*, June 28–July 11, 1989.

136 *"I had to dye . . . serious."* Ibid.

137 *"Breathless Mahoney . . . villainy."* St. Michael, Mick, *Madonna "Talking"* (Omnibus Press, London, 2004), p.60.

137 *"Madonna . . . why they're colossal."* Nisbet, Jenny, "Stars and Hypes," *Sunday Express* magazine, August 1986.

137 *"It would have . . . did then."* St. Michael, op cit, p. 56.

10. GIVING GOOD FACE

140 *"That level of production . . . rocked."* Madonnatribe.com/idol/carlton .htm, 2006.

141   *". . . In the guise . . . closeness occurs."* Deevoy, Adrian, "I'm a Tormented Person," Q magazine, June 1991.

141   *"She's always . . . few people can."* From *Truth or Dare* documentary, 1991.

145   *"Justify . . . thievery."* Jimdero.com/News2001/NewsAug26Madonna.htm.

147   *"break every rule . . . performance arts."* Doyle, Tom, "The Greatest Show on Earth," Q Special Edition, 2003, p. 48.

147   *"a landscape . . . one."* Buys, Sara, "Rebel Without a Pause," *Harper's Bazaar*, October 2006.

147   *"My clothes . . . vulnerability."* Doyle, op cit.

147   *"Cone bras . . . went for it."* From *The Truth About Madonna's Men*. UK Channel 5, September 2005.

148   *"Madonna . . . healthy for a woman."* Menzies, Janet, "Body of a Bombshell," *Daily Express*, April 30, 1991.

151   *"that believes . . . own judgments." Truth or Dare.*

152   *"I'll film you . . . worn off."* O'Brien, Lucy, "Is *That* the Real Me?" *Select*, May 1991.

153   *"I was completely . . . all-encompassing."* Ibid.

153   *"I'm revealing . . . very revealing."* Rickey, C., "Madonna on Madonna," *Philadelphia Inquirer*, May 16, 1991.

153   *"I always . . . the eyes."* Doyle, op cit.

153   *"She often . . . reprisal."* Fisher, Carrie, "True Confessions: Part Two," *Rolling Stone,* June 27, 1991.

154   *"Why was I . . . a little awkward." Truth or Dare.*

155   *"What was really weird . . . Mars."* Deevoy, op cit.

156   *"[That] drove me . . . privacy that I have."* Jonkers, Gert, interview on Buttmagazine.com/?p=182, 2006.

157   *"I didn't stand . . . shit."* O'Brien, op cit.

158   *"In Truth or Dare . . . patriarchal lines."* hooks, bell, *Black Looks: Race and Representation* (Turnaround, London, 1992), p. 162.

158   *"So why did . . . at the center."* Ibid, pp.163–64.

159   *"She's a real . . . bathroom."* O'Brien, op cit.

159   *"A clever . . . self-portrait,"* Maslin, Janet, "No One Ever Called Her Shy," *New York Times*, May 10, 1991.

159   *"raw . . . entertaining."* Walker, Robert, *Madonna: The Biography* (Pan, London, 1989) p.876.

160   *"I thought . . . going to hurt." Truth or Dare.*

11. FALLEN ANGEL

161   *"It started . . . think tank."* O'Brien, Lucy, *She Bop II : The Definitive History of Women in Pop, Rock & Soul* (Continuum, London and New York, 2002), p. 224.

161 *"I want a real . . . harem."* St. Michael, op cit, p. 39.

162 *"'The Body' . . . Topic."* Kent, Sarah, "Virgin on the Ridiculous," *Time Out,* October 21–28, 1992.

162 *"This is essentially . . . bad behavior."* Neil, Andrew, "Laid Bare: Unmasking Madonna," *Sunday Times Magazine,* October 18, 1992.

162 *"speaks verbosely . . . silence."* Foucault, Michel, *The History of Sexuality,* Volume 1 (Penguin, London, 1990), p. 8.

163 *"In all my work . . . . afraid."* Neil, op cit.

163 *"Sexuality . . . power."* Foucault, op cit, p. 107.

165 *"All of my sexual . . . watches."* Shewey, Don, "Madonna: the Saint, the Slut, the Sensation," *The Advocate,* May 7 and 21, 1991.

165 *"When she comes . . . righteous!"* Madonna, *Sex* (Martin Secker & Warburg, London, 1992).

165 *"Because . . . kisser."* *The Truth About Madonna's Men,* UK Channel 5, September 2005.

165 *"I'm not . . . a woman."* Neil, Andrew, "I'm on a Mission: Part 2" *Sunday Times Magazine,* October 25, 1992.

166 *"the pure . . . not real."* Grace, Della, panel contribution to "Unwrapping Sex," discussion on Madonna's *Sex* at the ICA, London, March 30, 1993.

166 *"Madonna . . . for yuppies."* Baker, Russell, "Those Vile Few," *New York Times,* October 24, 1992.

166 *"[She's] the first . . . for celebrities."* O'Brien, Lucy, *She Bop II: The Definitive History of Women in Rock, Pop & Soul* (Continuum, London and New York, 2002), p.270.

167 *"I look . . . pass it."* Morton, Andrew, *Madonna* (Michael O'Mara, London, 2001) p.185.

167 *"spoiled rich . . . best friend"* Owen, Frank, *Clubland (The Fabulous Rise and Murderous Fall of Club Culture)* (Broadway Books, New York, 2003), p.115.

167 *"There was . . . would've happened,"* *The Truth About Madonna's Men,* op cit.

167 *"I believe . . . community than Madonna."* Carolin, Louise, "Madonna—Icon or Vampire?" *Diva* magazine, August 2006.

167 *"I think . . . those qualities."* Czyzselska, Jane, "Jenny Shimizu & Rebecca Loos: What's the Story?" *Diva* magazine, November 2005.

168 *"I met Madonna . . . confident woman."* Ibid.

168 *"The lesbian . . . show."* Carolin, op cit.

168 *"There is . . . act of love."* Madonna, op cit.

169 *"Placed . . . martyrdom."* Cirlot, J. E., *A Dictionary of Symbols* (Routledge, London and New York, 1988), pp. 68–69.

169 *"The definition . . . hurt you."* Neil, op cit.

169 *"a kind of evil . . . dream world."* Ibid.

169 *"Generally . . . digging it."* Madonna, op cit.

170 *"I didn't . . . At all."* *The Truth About Madonna's Men,* op cit.

170 *"It was fun . . . turn you off!"* Ibid.

171 *"She can . . . pause."* Warner, Marina, "Body politic," *Observer,* October 18, 1992.

172 *"Here at last . . . parted ways."* Isherwood, Charles, *Wonder Bread and Ecstasy: The Life and Death of Joey Stefano* (Alyson Books, Los Angeles and New York, 1996), pp.135–36.

173 *"If she doesn't . . . psychological harm."* Neil, op cit.

173 *"I felt great . . . change it."* "Madonna Speaks!!!" *Smash Hits,* June 28–July 11, 1989.

175 *"I have an iron will . . . not exercising!"* Hirschberg, Lynn, "The Misfit," *Vanity Fair,* April 1991.

183 *"What was problematic . . . book."* Aizlewood, John, "Bedtime Stories," Q Special Edition, 2003, p. 73.

185 *"It was devastating . . . cunt."* Morton, Andrew, *Madonna* (Michael O'Mara, London, 2001) p. 152.

185 *"Madonna . . . as a child even."* Kelly, Richard T., *Sean Penn: His Life and Times,* (Cannongate, New York, 2004), p.180.

187 *"The female groupie . . . right job."* Fonarow, Wendy, *Empire of Dirt: The Aesthetics and Rituals of British Indie Music* (Wesleyan University Press, Middletown, Connecticut, 2006), p. 210.

187 *"I'm not upper-middle class . . . bag lady."* O'Brien, op cit, p. 171.

187 *"Madonna's interest . . . victim."* Brite, Poppy Z., *Courtney Love: The Real Story* (Simon & Schuster, New York, 1997), p. 135.

188 *"Who's got . . . pissed at me?"* From interview after MTV Video Music Awards, October 1995.

188 *"such a miserable . . . slag off."* St. Michael, Mick, *Madonna "Talking"* (Omnibus Press, London, 2004) p. 105.

188 *"They slag me . . . independence from you."* Garratt, Sheryl, "Je ne regrette rien," *Face,* October 1994.

188 *"This figure . . . psyche,"* Izod, John, "Madonna as Trickster," from Lloyd, Fran, ed., *Deconstructing Madonna* (B. T. Batsford Ltd., London, 1993) p. 59.

189 *"I've so infiltrated . . . than off."* Turner, Kay, ed., *I Dream of Madonna* (Thames & Hudson, London, 1993), p. 11.

189 *"She was interested . . . attention."* Ibid, p. 83.

189 *"an unofficial . . . dialogue."* Ibid, p. 20.

191 *"celebrating . . . idea of them."* Izod, op cit, p. 55.

12. I ONLY SHOOT WHAT I NEED

194 *"I divide . . . terrifying people."* Morton, Andrew, *Madonna* (Michael O'Mara, London 2001) p.183.

197 *"I think that . . . in my opinion."* Jonkers, op cit.

199 *"I wanted . . . 'Madonna record.'"* Maverick/Sire Records press release, October 1994.

200 *"It's about God . . . pedestal."* Ibid.

202 *"My lullabies . . . people of color."* Harris, Julius, "Lullabies That Wake You Up," *Interview*, September 1993.

203 *"I had written . . . drunk in a bar or something."* Aston, Martin, *Björk: Björkgraphy* (Simon & Schuster, London, 1996), p. 262.

205 *"lush soul . . . whimper."* O'Dair, Barbara, album review, *Rolling Stone*, October 15, 1994.

205 *"the girl . . . featheriness."* Snow, Mat, album review, Q magazine, October 1994.

211 *"Basketball players . . . closely."* Rodman, Dennis, *Bad as I Wanna Be* (Dell, New York, 1996), p. 234.

211 *"made-up dialogue . . . life,"* Madonna, "Madonna's Private Diaries," *Vanity Fair*, November 1996.

211 *"I went . . . dumped."* Interview with author for Q magazine, November 1996.

212 *"a nerdy . . . innocent."* Thompson, Douglas, *Madonna: Queen of the World* (John Blake, London, 2001), p.234.

213 *"it was . . . across the page."* Morton, op cit, p.204.

13. BITS AND ZEROES AND ONES

221 *"There is . . . calculating."* St. Michael, Mick, *Madonna "Talking"* (Omnibus Press, London 2004), p. 110.

222 *"Lourdes . . . never did."* Eccleston, Danny, "Power Is an Aphrodisiac," Q magazine, June 1998.

222 *"Catholics . . . Russia."* Kane, Paula M. "Marian Devotion Since 1940: Continuity or Casualty," from O'Tode, James, ed., *Habits of Devotion, Catholic Religious Practice in Twentieth-Century America* (Cornell University Press, Ithaca and London, 2004). pp.89–129.

226 *"weirdly, disruptively . . . social."* Brewster, Bill and Broughton, Frank, *Last Night a DJ Saved My Life (The History of the Disc Jockey)* (Headline, London, 2006).

227 *"I love . . . good match."* French, Paul, "Weird Science," Q Special Edition, 2003, p. 107.

227 *"sound great . . . listening to it."* Eccleston, op cit.

228 *"She's much . . . do her."* French, op cit.

228 *"It was hard . . . completely."* Ibid.

229 *"Water . . . songwriting."* Eccleston, op cit.

229 *"The Church . . . Easter spirit."* McBrien, Richard P., *Catholicism,* 3rd ed. (Geoffrey Chapma, London, 1994) p. 815.

230 *"'Ray of Light' . . . record."* Hogwood, Ben, "Head in a Cellcloud," Music omh.com, March 2006.

230 *"[Lola] doesn't . . . perspective."* Eccleston, op cit.

232 *"She stepped . . . spooky."* Ibid.

233 *"I walked into . . . exactly what she is."* Ibid.

235 *"There were . . . found one."* Gannon, Louise, "Madonna: 'I've Been so Lonely for Much of My Life,'" *Grazia,* June 27, 2005.

235 *"You know . . . my body!"* Sawyer, Miranda, "The Future Sound of London," *Face,* August 2000.

236 *"Guy says . . . he was."* Thompson, Douglas, *Madonna: Queen of the World* (John Blake, London, 2001). p.260.

237 *"I was very . . . .socks off a bit."* Steuer, Joseph, "This Director Shoots from The Hip," *Interview,* February 2001.

238 *"a work ethic . . . learn."* Furnish, David, "Guy About Town," *Interview,* March 1999.

239 *"Each new scene . . . different."* Emimusicpublishing.com, 2006.

239 *"With Taxi Girl . . . the culture."* McDonnell, Evelyn, "For This Avant-gardist, Music Is More Than a Rock Star Cliché," *Interview,* February 2001.

239 *"music is prophecy . . . visible."* Attali, Jacques, *Noise: The Political Economy of Music* (University of Minnesota Press, Minneapolis and London, 1985), p. 11.

239 *"The challenge . . . musician."* McDonnell, op cit.

240 *"I feel like . . . energy."* Sawyer, op cit.

241 *"It's not experimental . . . underground music."* McDonnell, op cit.

241 *"They're all . . . amazing."* Sawyer, op cit.

241 *"It's a love song . . . uncomfortable."* Ibid.

244 *"If I had known . . . idealizes."* Madonna, "Madonna's Private Diaries," *Vanity Fair,* November, 1996.

246 *"He was small . . . much stronger."* Thompson, op cit, p.270.

247 *"Madonna . . . in love for real."* Taraborrelli, J. Randy, *Madonna: An Intimate Biography* (Sidgwick & Jackson, London, 2001) p.351.

14. HARD-WORKING AND HARD-LAUGHING

249 *"I have to stay current . . . Aguilera."* Taraborelli, J. Randy, *Madonna: An Intimate Biography* (Sidgwick & Jackson, London, 2001), p. 345.

252 *"My God, just look at you."* Ibid., p.377.

252 *"I'm finally going . . . nervous."* O'Brien, Lucy, "The Second Coming," Q Special Edition, 2003, p. 122.

253 *"I wasn't expecting . . . different."* Ibid.

254 *"After finishing . . . useful."* Ibid.

255 *"Her music . . . intriguing."* Madonnatribe.com/idol/jamie_one .htm.2006.

255 *"I grew up . . . God's theater."* DrownedMadonna.com/modules .php?name=bruce_rodgers, 2006.

256 *"I thought, . . . still hurts."* O'Brien, op cit, p. 125.

257 *"He is very demanding . . . had."* Madonnatribe.com/idol/jull.htm, 2006.

258 *"A big part . . . climax of the show."* O'Brien, op cit.

261 *"commemorative event . . . difficulty."* Madonnatribe.com/idol/jull.htm, 2006.

263 *"Celebrity is bestial . . . cut off by lions."* (2006 W.H. Smith Diary, quote for September 17).

263 *"There is an erotic . . . manufactured."* T. Eagleton: "The Love That Speaks Its Name in Hello!" *Times Higher*, December 9, 2005.

263 *"the allure . . . I was."* Rees, Paul, "Listen Very Carefully, I Will Say This Only Once," Q magazine, May 2003.

264 *"Madonna . . . at base camp."* Everett, Rupert, *Red Carpets and Other Banana Skins* (Little, Brown, London, 2006). p. 242.

264 *"I sit his ass . . . in years."* Kelly, Richard T., *Sean Penn: His Life and Times* (Cannongate, New York, 2004). p.190.

266 *"I'm saying . . . than me?"* Rees, op cit.

266 *"The music . . . like that."* Ibid.

270 *"It is an antiwar . . . against all of them."* Ibid.

271 *"The entire country . . . Why?"* Sweeting, Adam, "How the Chicks Survived Their Scrap with Bush," *Daily Telegraph*, June 15, 2006.

271 *"I'd rather . . . Toby Keith."* Tryangiel, J. "In the Line of Fire," *Time*, May 29, 2006.

272 *"very intellectual . . . George Bush."* Garfield, Simon, "Looks Good on the Dance Floor," *Observer Music Monthly*, November, 2005.

272 *"There is an atmosphere . . . doing it."* Davies, H., "Sir Elton Attacks New 'Era of Censorship' in America," *Daily Telegraph*, July 17, 2004.

15. MOMMY POP STAR

274 *"I kissed Britney . . . to her."* Peterson, Todd, "Madonna to Daughter: I'm Not Gay," *People*, April 18, 2007.

276 *"Madonna . . . the users."* Madonnatribe.com/idol/jamie_one.htm, 2006.

278 *"Religion breeds . . . one."* From *I'm Going to Tell You a Secret* documentary, 2005.

278 *"It was Madonna's idea . . . well."* DrownedMadonna.com/modules.php? name=lorne_cousin, 2006.

279 *"Here's the weird . . . awe."* Segal, David, "Prime Madonna," *Washington Post,* June 15, 2004.

280 *"I'm not interested . . . do it."* Ginsberg, M., "Madonna: the Saga Continues," W magazine, March 2003.

281 *"Madonna's . . . religion."* Ibid.

282 *"I can enjoy fashion . . . not about that."* Ibid.

285 *"I insisted . . . anyone can."* Shakespeare, Jocasta, "Hollywood and Divine," *Observer Magazine,* August 27, 2006.

285 *"It's challenging . . . appeals to Guy."* Dougary, Ginny, "The American Rose," *Times Magazine,* September 13, 2003.

286 *"Men and women . . . light."* Ruth Nahmias, speaker at the Kabbalah Center, London, January 2006.

287 *"Intent on . . . purification."* Lancaster, Brian L., *The Essence of Kabbalah* (Eagle Editions, Royston, Herts., 2006), p. 167.

287 *"I thought . . . book author."* Dougary, op cit.

287 *"The women . . . crap."* Ibid.

288 *"First they . . . likeable indeed."* Madonna, *The English Roses* (Puffin, London, 2003), p. 42.

289 *"The music . . . candies."* Barthes, Roland, "On Popular Music," *Image Music Text* (Fontana Press, New York, 1977), p. 448.

16. AMERICAN WIFE

292 *"Speaking . . . golden age,"* Bowles, Hamish, "Like a Duchess," *U.S. Vogue,* August 2005.

292 *"Guy . . . animals."* Ibid.

292 *"We did a couple . . . slightly macabre."* Thompson, Douglas, *Madonna: Queen of The World* (John Blake, London, 2001), p. 264.

293 *"You can choose . . . world."* Ibid.

294 *"that heavy . . . blood."* Gill, A. A., "A. A. Gill Is the Deer Hunter," GQ, January 2003.

294 *"Madonna . . . aristocratic lifestyle,"* Albiez, Sean, "The Day the Music Died Laughing: Madonna and Country," from Santiago, Fouz-Hernandez, and Jarman Ivens, *Freya Madonna's Drowned Worlds: New*

Approaches to Her Cultural Transformations, 1983–2003 (Ashgate, London, 2004), p. 130.

297 *"I never thought . . . turned out."* Laskas, Jeanne Marie, "The Once and Future Madonna," *Ladies' Home Journal,* July 2005.

297 *"Its generous . . . tax haven."* Meek, James, "Super Rich," *Guardian*, April 17, 2006.

297 *"I consider . . . surrogate mothers!"* St. Michael, Mick, *Madonna "Talking"* (Omnibus Press, London, 2004). p.123

298 *"written from . . . subconscious."* O'Brien, Lucy, *She Bop II: The Definitive History of Women in Rock, Pop & Soul* (Continuum, London and New York, 2002), p.467

298 *"I saw . . . went mainstream."* Ibid.

299 *"I cannot . . . away like that."* St. Michael, op cit, p. 121.

300 *"It's one thing . . . too."* Dougary, Ginny, "The American Rose," *Times Magazine*, September 13, 2003.

300 *"They look . . . for me!"* Shakespeare, Jocasta, "Hollywood and Divine," *Observer Magazine*, August 27, 2006.

304 *"Madonna's voice . . . lucid."* Newton, V., and Kennedy, S., "Madonna with Ze Big Bruises," *Sun*, August 17, 2005.

304 *"It was the most . . . experience."* Strauss, Neil, "How Madonna Got Her Groove Back," *Rolling Stone*, December 1, 2005.

304 *"Marriage is hard . . . restaurants."* Laskas, op. cit.

17. ABBA ON DRUGS

307 *"My apartment consists . . . kettle."* Robinson, Peter, "She's More of a 'Padder' . . ." popjustice.com/index.php?option=com_content&task=viewid=188&itemid=9, October 25, 2005.

307 *"I couldn't . . . any frills."* Garfield, Simon, "Looks Good on the Dance Floor," *Observer Music Monthly,* November 2005.

307 *"What we're . . . you've got? and singing over it."* Herlihy, Gavin, "Driving Ms. Ravey," *Mixmag*, December 2005.

307 *"If there are . . . molecular structure."* Garfield, op cit.

308 *"'Hung Up' is . . . the good minute."* G. Greig, "All Loved Up," *Tatler*, December 2005.

308 *"I had to send . . . they didn't."* Todd, Matthew, "Confessions of an Icon," *Attitude*, November 2005.

309 *"I love London . . . socket."* Ibid.

310 *"It suggests . . . generation."* Hastings, Chris, "Madonna Uses Secret Nightclub 'Focus Groups' to Pick Songs for New Album," *Daily Telegraph*, August 28, 2005.

311 *"With her last . . . rest."* Paoletta, Michael, "Dancing Queen," *Billboard*, November 12, 2005.

311 *"It's all about . . . We're good."* Ibid.

311 *"I'm a businesswoman . . . now."* Ibid.

312 *"Madonna . . . disco ball."* From *The Confessions Tour* DVD, 2007.

312 *"When I shot . . . strong again."* Bailey, Sarah, "Madonna's Secrets," *Harper's Bazaar*, March 2006.

313 *"In the simpler . . . endless."* Maine, Margot, *Father Hunger: Fathers, Daughters and the Pursuit of Thinness* (Gurze Books, Carlsbad, California, 2004), Introduction.

314 *"Even with . . . can't solve."* Simpson, Richard, "Even with Muscles Like These . . ." *Daily Mail*, June 26, 2006.

314 *"When I . . . respect that."* Gannon, Louise, "I've Been So Lonely for Much of My Life," *Grazia*, June 27, 2005.

314 *"She complains . . . like her."* "Madonna: Marriage 'Close to Breaking Point,'" *Grazia*, February 5, 2007.

316 *"picked so much . . . Bay City, Michigan."* Flett, Kathryn, "A Box of Madges," *Observer*, December 4, 2005.

323 *"She's . . . the cage,"* Wark, Kirsty, "In Deep with Madonna," *Sunday Times*, November 5, 2006.

18. COMING FROM GOD

326 *"I was going . . . thought again."* Interview with Jo Wiley for BBC *Live 8* broadcast, July 2, 2005.

327 *"one has . . . didn't know."* Dougary, Ginny, "The American Rose," *Times Magazine*, September 13, 2003.

328 *"He feels . . . interests her."* Harris, Ed, "Is Guy out in Cold . . . ?" *Evening Standard*, February 3, 2005.

328 *"[It's] based . . . three months."* "Guy Ritchie: The Director of *Revolver* Interviewed," Futuremovies.co.uk/filmmaking.asp?ID=139, 2006.

329 *"I had no idea . . . making it."* Interview with Kuki de Salvertes, Totem fashion.com/NouvoSite/reportages/Reportages.htm, 2007.

330 *"In Africa, babies . . . popular."* Swinford, Steven, "Madonna & Child," *Sunday Times*, October 15, 2006.

330 *"was coming from God."* Ibid.

331 *"They told me . . . . grow up healthy."* Ibid.

331 *"The rich . . . the system."* Frith, Maxine, and Thompson, Christopher, "Madonna Polarises Opinion as David Flies Out," *Independent*, October 17, 2006.

331 *"Where possible . . . the child."* Stimson, Ella, "Madonna and Child: Saintly—or Sinning?" *Thelondonpaper,* October 12, 2006.

332 *"People have . . . whole process."* Widdup, Ellen & Bentham, Martin, "Madonna 'Bad Example to Parents,'" *Evening Standard,* October 19, 2006.

332 *"We must be . . . boost for the country."* Frith and Thompson, op cit.

332 *"Madonna was . . . emotional about it."* Taraborrelli, Randy J. "The Story Behind Why Madonna Has Adopted One-Year-Old David," *Hello!* October 24, 2006.

333 *"How dare . . . love and wealth."* Low, Valentine, "Sorry David but This Is Life in Madge's Circus." *Evening Standard,* October 17, 2006.

334 *"I'm a detail-oriented . . . for that."* Interview with Kirsty Wark, BBC *Newsnight,* October 2006.

335 *"I saw . . . devastate me."* Taraborrelli, op cit.

336 *"I don't usually . . . vacation!"* Interview on *Entertainment News,* BBC Radio 1, January 2007.

337 *"Guy is really . . . nicer to her."* "Madonna: Marriage 'Close to Breaking Point,'" *Grazia,* February 5, 2007.

338 *"People underestimated . . . planet."* Taraborrelli, op cit.

339 *"like what . . . public patronage."* Andrew Ross quoted in Robertson, Pamela, *Guilty Pleasures: Feminist Camp from Mae West to Madonna* (Duke University Press, Durham and London, 1996), p. 130.

339 *"When she . . . hypnotic."* From Martha Graham documentary BBC *Omnibus,* 1992.

SELECTED BIBLIOGRAPHY

Bego, Mark. *Madonna: Blonde Ambition*. New York: Cooper Square Press, 2000.

Berg, Yehuda. *The 72 Names of GOD: Technology for the Soul*. New York & Los Angeles: Kabbalah Center International, 2003.

Bordo, Susan. *Unbearable Weight: Feminism, Western Culture, and the Body*. Berkeley and Los Angeles, University of California Press, 2004.

Brewster, Bill, and Broughton, Frank. *Last Night a DJ Saved My Life (The History of the Disc Jockey)*. London: Headline, 2006.

Bowlby, John. *Attachment and Loss*, Volume 3, *Loss*. London: Pimlico, 1998.

Che, Cathay. *Deborah Harry: Platinum Blonde*. London: Andre Deutsch, 1999.

Eichenbaum, Luise, and Orbach, Susie. *Understanding Women*. London: Pelican Books, 1985.

Everett, Rupert. *Red Carpets and Other Banana Skins*. London: Little, Brown, 2006.

Frith, Simon, and Goodwin, Andrew. *On Record: Rock, Pop, & The Written Word*. London: Routledge, 1990.

Fonarow, Wendy. *Empire of Dirt: The Aesthetics and Rituals of British Indie Music*. Middletown, Connecticut: Wesleyan University Press, 2006.

Foucault, Michel. *The History of Sexuality*, Volume 1. London: Penguin, 1990.

Frank, Lisa, and Smith, Paul. *Madonnarama: Essays on Sex and Popular Culture*. Pittsburgh and San Francisco: Cleis Press, 1993.

Guilbert, Georges-Claude. *Madonna as Postmodern Myth*. Jefferson, North Carolina: McFarland & Co., 2002.

Hackett, Pat, ed. *The Andy Warhol Diaries*. New York and Boston: Warner Books, 1989.

Hoban, Phoebe. *Basquiat: A Quick Killing in Art.* New York: Viking Penguin, 2004.

hooks, bell. *Black Looks: Race and Representation.* London: Turnaround, 1992.

Jowitt, Deborah. *Time and the Dancing Image.* Berkeley and Los Angeles: University of California Press, 1988.

Kelly, Richard T.. *Sean Penn: His Life and Times.* New York: Cannongate, 2004.

Koestenbaum, Wayne. *Andy Warhol.* London: Phoenix, 2001.

Lancaster, Brian L. *The Essence of Kabbalah.* Royston, Hertsfordshire, England: Eagle Editions, 2006.

Lloyd, Fran, ed. *Deconstructing Madonna.* London: BT Batsford Ltd., 1993.

Maripolarama: Polaroids by Maripol. New York: powerHouse Books, 2005.

Maine, Margot. *Father Hunger: Fathers, Daughters and the Pursuit of Thinness.* Carlsbad, California: Gurze Books, 2004.

McBrien, Richard P. *Catholicism,* 3rd ed. London: Geoffrey Chapman, 1994.

Morton, Andrew. *Madonna.* London: Michael O'Mara, 2001.

O'Toole, James, ed. *Habits of Devotion: Catholic Religious Practice in Twentieth-century America.* Ithaca and London: Cornell University Press, 2004.

O'Brien, Lucy. *She Bop I & II.* London and New York: Penguin, 1995 and Continuum, 2002.

Paglia, Camille. *Sex, Art, and American Culture.* London and New York: Viking, 1992.

Reddington, Helen. *The Lost Women of Rock Music: Women Musicians of the Punk Era.* London: Ashgate Press, 2007.

Robertson, Pamela. *Guilty Pleasures: Feminist Camp from Mae West to Madonna.* Durham, North Carolina, and London: Duke University Press, 1996.

Santiago, Fouz-Hernandez, and Ivens, Jarman. *Madonna's Drowned Worlds: New Approaches to Her Cultural Transformations, 1983–2003.* London: Ashgate, 2004.

Shapiro, Peter. *Turn the Beat Around: The Secret History of Disco.* London: Faber & Faber, 2005.

Swichtenberg, Cathy. *The Madonna Connection: Representational Politics, Subcultural Identities, and Cultural Theory.* Boulder, Colorado: Westview Press, 1993.

Taraborrelli, J. Randy. *Madonna: An Intimate Biography.* London: Sidgwick & Jackson, 2001.

Taylor, Marvin J., ed. *The Downtown Book: The New York Art Scene 1974–1984.* Princeton & Oxford: Princeton University Press, 2006.

Thompson, Douglas. *Madonna: Queen of the World.* London: John Blake, 2001.

Turner, Kay, ed. *I Dream of Madonna.* London: Thames & Hudson, 1993.

Zollo, Paul. *Songwriters on Songwriting.* Cincinnati: Da Capo Press, 2003.

DISCOGRAPHY

Singles 7" (UK and US; on vinyl, cassette, and CD)

*from 1982–1992, all issued on the Sire label (except where indicated)

1982
"Everybody" (3.19 Remix)/ (4.42 Dub)

1983
"Holiday" (Edit)/ "I Know It"
"Holiday"/"Think of Me"

1984
"Borderline"/"Think of Me"
"Borderline"/"Holiday" (U.S.: back-to-back hits)
"Borderline" (Edit)/"Physical Attraction"
"Lucky Star" (Edit)/"I Know It" (LP)
"Borderline" (Edit)/"Physical Attraction" and "Holiday" (Edit)/"Think
    of Me"
"Like a Virgin"/"Stay"
"Like a Virgin"/"Lucky Star" (U.S.: back-to-back hits)

1985
"Material Girl"/"Pretender"
"Crazy for You"/"No More Words" (Geffen label; B-side by Berlin)
"Crazy for You"/"Gambler" (U.S.: back-to-back hits)

"Crazy for You"/"I'll Fall in Love Again" (B-side by Sammy Hagen)
"Angel" (Remix)/ (Edit)
"Angel"/"Material Girl" (U.S.: back-to-back hits)
"Angel" (Fade)/"Burning Up" (Remix)
"Dress You Up"/"Shoo-Bee-Doo"
"Dress You Up"/"I Know It"
"Into the Groove" (U.S.: back-to-back hits)
"Into the Groove" /"Shoo-Bee-Doo"
"Gambler"/"Nature of the Beach" (B-side by Black n' Blue)

1986
"Papa Don't Preach" (LP)/"Pretender"
"Everybody"/"Papa Don't Preach" (U.S.: back-to-back hits)
"Papa Don't Preach" (LP)/"Ain't No Big Deal"
"True Blue"/"Ain't No Big Deal"
"True Blue" (Remix)/"Holiday" (Edit)
"Open Your Heart"/"White Heat"
"Open Your Heart"/"Lucky Star"
"Holiday"/"True Blue"
"Live to Tell" (Edit)/(Instr.)
"Live to Tell"/"True Blue" (U.S.: back-to-back hits)

1987
"La Isla Bonita" (LP)/(Instr. remix)
"La Isla Bonita"/"Open Your Heart" (U.S.: back-to-back hits)
"Who's That Girl"/"White Heat"
"Causing a Commotion"/"Jimmy Jimmy"
"Causing a Commotion"/"Who's That Girl" (U.S.: back-to-back hits)
"The Look of Love"/"I Know It"

1989
"Like a Prayer" (7-inch)/"Act of Contrition"
"Like a Prayer" (7-inch)/"Oh Father" (Edit) (U.S.: back-to-back hits)
"Express Yourself" (7-inch remix)/"The Look of Love" (LP)
"Cherish" (7-inch)/"Supernatural"
"Cherish" (Fade)/"Express Yourself" (7-inch remix) (U.S.: back-to-back hits)
"Oh Father"/"Pray for Spanish Eyes" (LP)
"Dear Jessie"/"Till Death Do Us Part"
"Like a Prayer" (7-inch)/(7-inch Fade)
"Keep It Together" (Single remix)/(Instr.)

1990
"Vogue" (Single)/"Bette Davis Dub"
"Vogue" (Single)/"Keep It Together" (Single remix)
"Vogue"/"Keep It Together" (U.S.: back-to-back hits)
"Hanky Panky" (LP)/"More" (LP)
"Justify My Love"/"Express Yourself" (Shep's 'Spressin' Himself Re-Remix)
"Justify My Love"/ (U.S.: back-to-back hits)

1991
"Rescue Me" (Single)/ (Alt. Single Mix)
"Rescue Me" (7-inch mix)/"Spotlight" (LP)
"Crazy for You" (Remix)/"Keep It Together" (7-inch remix)
"This Used to Be My Playground" (Single)/(Long)
"This Used to Be My Playground" (Single)/"Hanky Panky" (U.S.: back-to-back hits)

1992

*ALL SINGLES ISSUED FROM 1992 TO 2005 ON MAVERICK/SIRE LABEL
"Erotica" (LP)/(Instr.)
"Deeper and Deeper" (LP)/(Instr.)
"I'll Remember" (LP)/"Secret Garden" (LP)

1993
"Bad Girl" (Edit)/"Fever"
"Bad Girl" (Edit)/"Erotica" (William Orbit Dub)
"Rain" (Radio Remix)/"Waiting" (LP)
"Rain" (Remix)/"Open Your Heart" (LP)
"Fever" (LP)/(Remix)

1994
"I'll Remember" (LP)/"Secret Garden" (LP)
"Secret" (LP)/(Instr.)
"Secret"/"Let Down Your Guard" (Rough Mix Edit)
"Take a Bow" (LP)/(In Da Soul Mix)
"Take a Bow" (LP)/(Inst.)
"Bedtime Story" (Album Edit)/(Junior's Single Mix)

1995
"Bedtime Story" (LP)/"Survival" (LP)
"Human Nature" (Radio)/"Sanctuary" (LP)
"You'll See" (LP)/(Instr.)
"You'll See" (LP)/"Live to Tell" (Live from the Who's That Girl Tour)

1996

"Love Don't Live Here Anymore" (Soulpower Radio Remix)/(Album Remix)

"One More Chance"/"Veras" (Spanish version of "You'll See")

"You Must Love Me" (LP)/"Rainbow High" (LP)

"Don't Cry for Me Argentina"/"Santa Evita"

1998

"Frozen" (LP)/ "Shanti/Astangi" (LP)

"Ray of Light" (LP)/"Has to Be" (non-album track) (Won 1999 Grammy for Best Dance Recording, and was nominated for Record of the Year, also CD single)

"The Power of Goodbye"/"Mer Girl"

"The Power of Goodbye"/"Little Star"

1999

"Nothing Really Matters"/"To Have and Not to Hold" (LP)

2000

"Music" (LP)/"Cyber-Raga" (non-album track with Talvin Singh)

"Drowned World"/"Substitute for Love"

2001

"Don't Tell Me" (LP)/(Thunderpuss 2001 Hand in the Air Radio Edit)

"What It Feels Like for a Girl"/"Don't Tell Me"

2002

"Die Another Day" (Radio Edit)/ (LP)

"Die Another Day" (Radio Edit)/ (Dirty Vegas Main Mix)

2003

"American Life" (Radio Edit)/"Die Another Day" (Calderone & Quayle Afterlife Mix)

"American Life" (Radio Edit)/"Die Another Day" (Richard Humpty Vission Radio Edit)

2006

"Sorry" (Radio Version)/"Let It Will Be" (Paper Faces Vocal Edit)

Singles 12" (U.K. and U.S.; on vinyl, cassette, and CD maxi-singles)

1982
"Everybody"; "Everybody" (Instr.)
"Everybody" (Dub)

1983
"Burning Up"; "Physical Attraction"
"Lucky Star" (Full Length); "I Know It"
"Holiday" (Full Length); "Think of Me"

1984
"Borderline" (New Mix); "Lucky Star" (New Mix)
"Borderline" (U.S. Remix); (Dub Remix); "Physical Attraction"
"Like a Virgin" (Ext. Dance Remix); "Stay"
"Material Girl" (Ext. Dance Remix); "Pretender"

1985
"Angel" (Ext. Dance Mix); "Into the Groove" (Single)
"Angel" (Ext. Dance Mix); "Burning Up" (Mix)
"Dress You Up" (12-inch Formal Mix); (Casual Instr. Mix); "Shoo-Bee-
    Doo" (LP)
"Dress You Up" (12-inch Formal Mix); (Casual Instr. Mix); "I Know It"
"Gambler" (Ext. Dance Mix); (Instr.); "Nature of the Beach" (U.K.,
    "Nature of the Beach" by Black n' Blue)
"Crazy for You"
"Into the Groove"; "Everybody"; "Shoo-Bee-Doo"

1986
"Cosmic Climb" (Ext. Dance Mix); (Ext.); "We Are the Gods" (subtitled
    "The Early Years")
"Live to Tell" (LP); (Edit); (Instr.)
"Open Your Heart" (Ext.); (Dub); "White Heat"
"Open Your Heart" (Ext.); (Dub); "Lucky Star"
"Papa Don't Preach" (Ext. Remix); "Pretender"
"Papa Don't Preach" (Ext. Remix); "Pretender" ; "Ain't No Big Deal";
    "Papa Don't Preach" (LP)
"True Blue" (Color Mix); (Instr.); "Ain't No Big Deal"; "True Blue"
    (Remix/Edit)
"True Blue" (Ext. Dance); "Holiday" (Full Length)

1987
"La Isla Bonita" (Ext. Remix); (Ext. Instr.)
"Causing a Commotion" (Silver Screen Mix); (Dub); (Movie House Mix);
   "Jimmy Jimmy"
"Causing a Commotion" (Silver Screen Mix); (Movie House Mix); "Jimmy
   Jimmy" (Fade)
"The Look of Love"; "Love Don't Live Here Anymore"; "I Know It"
"Who's That Girl" (Ext.); (Dub); "White Heat" (LP)
"Who's That Girl" (Ext.); "White Heat" (LP)

1988
"Cosmic Climb"; "We Are the Gods"; "Wild Dancing" (Wild Dance Mix)
   (subtitled "The Early Years")
"Cherish" (Ext.); (7-inch); "Supernatural"

1989
"Dear Jessie" (LP); "Till Death Do Us Part" (LP); "Holiday" (12-inch)
"Express Yourself" (Non-Stop Express Mix); (Stop & Go Dubs)
"Express Yourself" (Non-Stop Express Mix); (Stop & Go Dubs); (Local
   Mix); "The Look of Love" (LP)
 "Keep It Together" (12-inch Remix); (Dub); (12-inch Ext. Mix); (12-inch
   Mix); (Bonus Beats); (Instr.)
"Like a Prayer" (12-inch Dance Mix); (12-inch Ext. Remix);
   (Churchapella); (12-inch Club); (7-inch Remix/Edit); "Act of
   Contrition"
"Like a Prayer" (12-inch Dance Mix); (Churchapella); (7-inch Remix/Edit)

1990
"Hanky Panky" (Bare Bottoms 12-inch Mix); (Bare Bones Single Mix);
   "More" (LP)
The Holiday Collection: "Holiday" (LP); "True Blue" (LP); "Who's That Girl"
   (LP); "Causing a Commotion" (Silver Screen Single Mix) (U.K. mini-
   LP)
"Justify My Love" (Orbit 12-inch Mix); (Hip Hop Mix); (The Beast
   Within Mix); "Express Yourself" (1990 Remix—Long)
"Justify My Love" (Orbit 12-inch Mix); (LP); "Express Yourself" (1990
   Edit)
"Justify My Love 2" (Hip Hop Mix); (Q-Sound Mix); (The Beast Within
   Mix)
"Vogue" (12-inch); (Bette Davis Dub); (Strike-a-Pose Dub)
"Vogue" (12-inch); "Keep It Together" (12-inch Remix)
"Vogue" (12-inch), (Strike-a-Pose Dub)

1991

"Rescue Me" (Titanic Vocal); (Lifeboat Vocal); (Houseboat Vocal); (S.O.S Mix)

"Rescue Me" (Titanic Vocal); (Lifeboat Vocal); (Houseboat Vocal)

"Rescue Me 1" (7-inch mix); (Titanic Vocal); (Demanding Dub)

"Rescue Me 2" (Lifeboat Vocal); (Houseboat Vocal)

"Crazy for You" (Remix); "Keep It Together" (Special Remix); "Into the Groove" (Shep Pettibone Remix)

"Get Down"; "Get Down" (Ext. Mix) (subtitled "The Early Years")

1992

"Erotica" (Kenlou B-Boy Mix); (Jeep Beats); (Madonna's in My Jeep Mix); (WO 12-inch); (Underground Club Mix); (Bass Hit Dub)

"Erotica" (LP); (Instr.); (Radio Edit)

"Erotica" (Orbit Mix); (Kenlou B-Boy Mix); (Underground Club Mix); (Orbit Dub); (Madonna's in My Jeep Mix)

"Deeper and Deeper" (Shep's Classic 12-inch); (Shep's Deep Makeover Mix); (Shep's Deep Beats); (David's Deeper Dub); (Shep's Deeper Dub)

"Deeper and Deeper" (Shep's Classic 12-inch); (Shep's Deep Makeover Mix); (David's Klub Mix); (David's Love Dub); (Shep's Deeper Dub)

"Deeper and Deeper" (LP); (Shep's Deep Makeover Mix); (David's Klub Mix); (Shep's Classic 12-inch); (Shep's Fierce Deeper Dub); (David's Love Dub); (Shep's Deep Beats)

Michael Jackson: "In the Closet"; (Cm) (Tum) (Tmd) (K 12-inch) (Mixes Behind Door 1, Madonna as Mystery Girl)

Michael Jackson: "In the Closet"; (Tum) (Fsm) (Tmof) (Tud) (Mixes Behind Door 2, Madonna as Mystery Girl)

1993

"Bad Girl" (Ext. Mix); "Fever" (Ext. 12-inch Mix); (Shep's Remedy Dub); (Murk Boys" Miami Mix); (Murk Boys' Deep South Mix); (Oscar G's Dope Dub)

"Bad Girl" (Ext. Mix); (Edit); "Fever" (Ext. 12-inch Mix); (Hot Sweat 12-inch) ; (Murk Boys' Miami Mix); (Murk Boys Deep South Mix)

"Bad Girl" (LP); "Erotica" (William Orbit 12-inch); (William Orbit Dub); (Madonna's in My Jeep Mix)

Erotica: "Bad Girl" (Ext. Mix); "Erotica" (Kenlou B-Boy Instr.); "Erotica" (Underground Tribute); "Erotica" (Wo Dub); "Erotica" (House Instr.); "Erotica" (Bass Hit Dub)

Keep It Together (Remixes); "Cherish" (Ext.); (Includes 7 mixes of the title track: 12-inch Remix, Dub, 12-inch Ext. Mix, 12-inch Mix, Bonus Beats, Instr., and Original Version)

"Rain" (Radio Remix); (LP); "Up Down Suite" (Non-LP track); "Waiting" (Remix)

"Rain" (Radio Remix); "Up Down Suite" (Non-LP track); "Waiting" (Remix)

Remixed *Prayer* EP: "Like a Prayer" (12-inch Dance Mix); (12-inch Extended Mix); (Churchapella); (12-inch Club); (7-inch Remix); "Express Yourself" (Non-Stop Express Mix); (Stop & Go); (Local Mix)

"This Used to Be My Playground" (Single); (instr.); (Long)

"Fever" (Hot Sweat 12-inch Mix); (Ext. 12-inch Mix); (Shep's Remedy Dub); (Murk Boys' Miami Mix); (Murk Boys' Deep South Mix); (Oscar G's Dope Dub)

1994

"I'll Remember" (Guerilla Beach Mix); (LP); (Guerilla Groove Mix); (Orbit Alternative Mix)

"I'll Remember" (Guerilla Beach Mix); (Orbit Mix); "Why It's So Hard" (Live from the Girlie Show Tour)

"Secret" (Junior's Sound Factory Mix); (Junior's Sound Factory Dub); (Junior's Luscious Club Mix); (Junior's Luscious Club Dub); (Allstar Mix). CD maxi-single includes "Secret" (Edit), (Junior's Luscious Single Mix), and (Some Bizarre Mix), but omits (Junior's Sound Factory and Luscious Club Dub)

"Secret" (Junior's Luscious Single Mix); (Junior's Extended Luscious Club Mix); (Junior's Luscious Dub); (Junior's Sound Factory Mix); (Junior's Sound Factory Dub)

"Secret" (LP Edit); "Let Down Your Guard" (Rough Mix Edit); "Secret" (Instr.); (LP)

"Take a Bow" (InDaSoul Mix); (LP); (Silky Soul Mix); (InDaSoul Instr.); (Instr.)

"Take a Bow" (Edit); (LP);(Instr.)

"Bedtime Story" (Junior's Sound Factory Mix); (Junior's Sound Factory Dub); (Orbital Mix); (Junior's Wet Dream Mix); (Junior's Wet Dream Dub)

"Bedtime Story" (LP Edit); (Junior's Wet Dream Mix); (Junior's Dreamy Drum Dub); (Junior's Sound Factory Mix); (Junior's Single Mix)

1995

"Oh Father"; "Live to Tell" (Live Edit from the Ciao Italia Tour); "Why's It So Hard" (Live from the Girlie Show Tour)

"Bedtime Story" (Junior's Sound Factory Mix); (Junior's Sound Factory Dub); (Orbital Mix); (Junior's Wet Dream Mix)

"Bedtime Story": (1) "Bedtime Story" (Junior's Single Mix); "Secret" (Some Bizarre Mix); (All-Star Mix); (Some Bizarre Single Mix); (2) "Bedtime Story" (LP); (Junior's Wet Dream Mix); (Junior's Dreamy Drum Dub); (Orbital Mix); (Junior's Sound Factory Mix) (Limited edition U.K. double CD)

Into the Groove: "Into the Groove"; "Everybody"; "Shoo-Bee-Doo"

"Like a Virgin" (Ext. Dub); "Stay"

"Live to Tell" (LP); (Edit); (Instr.)

"Lucky Star" (U.S. Remix); "I Know It"

"Material Girl" (Jellybean); "Pretender"

Open Your Heart: "Open Your Heart" (Ext.); "Open Your Heart" (Dub); "White Heat" (LP)

Papa Don't Preach: "Papa Don't Preach"; "Ain't No Big Deal"; "Papa Don't Preach" (LP)

"Who's That Girl" (Ext.); "White Heat" (LP)

"You'll See" (LP); (Instr.); (Spanish); "Live to Tell" (Live from the Who's That Girl Tour)

"You'll See" (Edit); "Rain" (LP); "You'll See" (Instr.)

"Human Nature" (Runway Club Mix); (Master with Nine Sample); (I'm Not Your Bitch Mix)

"Human Nature" 1 (LP); "Bedtime Story" (Junior's Sound Factory Mix); (Orbital Mix)

"Human Nature" 2 (Radio Edit); (Human Club Mix); (Chorus Door Slam with Nine Sample); (I'm Not Your Bitch Mix)

1996

"One More Chance" (LP); "You'll See" (Spanish); (Spanglish)

Wild Dancing: "Wild Dancing" (Original); (Dance Mix) (Madonna sings backup vocals)

"You'll See" (LP); (Instr.); (Spanish); "Live to Tell" (Live from the Who's That Girl Tour)

"Love Don't Live Here Anymore" (Soulpower Radio Remix Edit); (LP Remix Edit); (Soulpower Radio Remix); (LP Remix)

"Another Suitcase in Another Hall"; "Don't Cry for Me Argentina" (Miami Mix Edit); "You Must Love Me"; "Hello and Goodbye"

"You Must Love Me" (Video); "Rainbow High" (LP); "You Must Love Me"/"I'd Be Surprisingly Good For You" (Orchestra) (Warner U.K. CD maxi-single)

"Don't Cry for Me Argentina" (Miami Mix, Alt. Ending); (Miami Spanglish Mix); (Miami Mix Edit); (Miami Dub Mix); (Miami Mix Instr.); (Miami Spanglish Mix Edit)

"Don't Cry for Me Argentina"; "Santa Evita"; "Latin Chant"

1997
"Don't Cry for Me Argentina" (Miami Mix Edit); (Miami Spanglish Edit);
(Miami Mix); (LP)
Rescue Me (Alternate Mix); "Justify My Love" (Q-Sound Mix); (Orbit
12-inch Mix); (Hip Hop Mix); "Express Yourself"; "Justify My Love"
(The Beast Within Mix); "Rescue Me" (Single Mix); (Titanic Mix);
(Houseboat Vocal); (Lifeboat Vocal); (S.O.S. Mix)

1998
"Ray of Light" (LP); (Sasha UltraViolet Mix); (William Orbit Liquid
Mix); (Victor Calderone Club Mix)
"Ray of Light" (12-inch single)
"The Power of Goodbye"; "Mer Girl"
"The Power of Goodbye" (Remix EP); (LP); (Dallas's Low End Mix);
(Luke Slater's Super Luper Mix); (Luke Slater's Filtered Mix); (Fabian's
Good God Mix)
"Frozen" (LP); (Stereo MCs Mix); (Extended Club Mix); (Meltdown
Mix–Long)
"Frozen" (Extended Club Mix); (Stereo MCs Mix); (Meltdown Mix—
Long). U.K. maxi-single had bonus tracks (LP) and (Widescreen Mix)
"Ray of Light" (LP); (Sasha Ultra Violet Mix); (William Orbit Liquid
Mix); (Victor Calderone Club Mix)

1999
"Nothing Really Matters" (LP); (Club 69 Vocal Club Mix); (Club 69
Future Mix); (Club 69 Phunk Mix); (Club 69 Speed Mix); (Kruder &
Dorfmeister Mix); (Vikram Radio Mix); (Club 69 Future Mix); (Club
69 Radio Mix)
"Nothing Really Matters" (LP); (Club 69 Radio Mix); (Club 69 Vocal
Club Mix); (Club 69 Phunk Mix); (Vikram Radio Dub); (Kruder &
Dorfmeister Mix) (U.S. limited edition)
"Beautiful Stranger" (LP); (CC Mix); (CR Mix) (From the soundtrack of
Austin Powers 2: The Spy Who Shagged Me)

2000
"Music" (HQ2 Club Mix); (Groove Amada 12-inch Mix); (Calderone
Anthem Mix); (LP); (Deep Dish Dot Com Mix); (Young Collective
Club Remix)
"Music" (HQ2 Club Mix); (Calderone Anthem Mix); (Deep Dish Dot
Com Mix); (Groove Amada Club Mix); (Young Collective Club Remix);
(HQ2 Radio Mix); (Calderone Radio Edit); (Deep Dish Dot Com
Radio Edit); (Groove Amada 12-inch Mix)

"Music" (Deep Dish Dot Com Radio Edit); (LP); (Groove Amada Club Mix); (Gab 12-inch Mix)

"American Pie" (LP); (Vision Radio Mix); (Calderone Filter Dub Mix); (Vission Visits Madonna). One of Madonna's two contributions to *The Next Best Thing Original Soundtrack.*

"American Pie Part 1" (LP); (Calderone Filter Dub Mix); (Calderone Vocal Dub Mix) (UK maxi-single)

"American Pie Part 2" (LP); (Richard Vision Radio Mix); (Vission Visits Madonna); (U.K. maxi-single)

"American Pie Part 3" (Calderone Vocal Dub Mix); (Calderone Extended Vocal); (Vission Visits Madonna); (Vission Radio Mix) (LP) (U.K. maxi-single)

"American Pie Remixes" (Richard Hampty Version); (Richard Hampty Version Radio Mix); (Victor Calderone Vocal Mix); (Victor Calderone Vocal Club); (Victor Calderone Extended Vocal Club Mix); (LP); (Japanese maxi-single)

2001

"Don't Tell Me" (Timo Maas Mix); (Tracy Young Club Mix); (Vission Remix); (Thunderpuss 2001 Hands in the Air Anthem); (Victor Calderone Sensory Mix); (Vission Radio Mix); (Thunderpuss 2001 Hands in the Air Radio)

"Don't Tell Me" (Thunderpuss 2001 Hands in the Air Anthem); (Timo Maas Mix); (Victor Calderone Sensory Mix); (Tracy Young Club Mix); (Thunderpuss 2001 Tribe-a-Pella)

"Don't Tell Me" Part 1 (Radio Edit); (Cyber-Raga); (Thunderpuss Club Mix) (U.K. CD maxi-single exclusive)

"Don't Tell Me" Part 2 (LP); (Vission Remix); (Thunderpuss Radio Mix)

"Don't Tell Me" Part 3 (Radio Edit); (Cyber-Raga); (Thunderpuss Club Mix); (Vission Remix)

"Don't Tell Me" (Remixes) (Timo Maas Remix); (Thunderpuss Mix); (Victor Calderone Mix); (Richard Humpty Vission Mix)

"What It Feels Like for a Girl" (Paul Oakenfold Perfecto Mix); (Richard Vission Velvet Masta Mix); (Calderone & Quayle Dark Side Mix); (Tracy Young Club Mix); (Above & Beyond 12-inch Club Mix); (Tracy Young Cool Out Radio Mix); (Richard Vission Velvet Masta Edit); (Above & Beyond Club Radio Edit); (Spanish)

"What It Feels Like for a Girl" (LP); (Calderone & Quayle Dark Side Mix); (Above & Beyond Club Mix); (Paul Oakenfold Perfecto Mix); (Richard Vission Velvet Masta Mix); (U.K. limited edition)

2002

"Die Another Day" (Dirty Vegas Main Mix); (Thunderpuss Club Mix):
(Thee RetroLectro Mix); (Deepsky Remix); (Dirty Vegas Dub)
"Die Another Day" (Radio Edit); (Dirty Vegas Main Mix); (Thee
RetroLectro Mix); (Thunderpuss Club Mix); (Deepsky Remix);
(Brother Brown's Bond-Age Club)
"Die Another Day" (Radio Edit); (Dirty Vegas Main Mix); (Deepsky Edit)
"Die Another Day" (Radio Edit); (Thunderpuss Club Mix); (Thee
RetroLectro Mix)

2003

"American Life" (Radio Edit); (Oakenfold Downtempo Remix); (Felix Da
Housecat's Devin Dazzle Club Mix)
"American Life" (Radio Edit); (Missy Elliott American Dream Mix);
(Peter Rauhofer's American Anthem Part 1)
"American Life" (Missy Elliott American Dream Mix); (Oakenfold
Downtempo Remix); (Felix Da Housecat's Devin Dazzle Club Mix);
(Peter Rauhofer's American Anthem Part 1); (Peter Rauhofer's
American Anthem Part 2); "Die Another Day" (Richard Humpty
Vission Electrofried Mix)
"American Life" (Missy Elliott American Dream Mix) ; (Oakenfold
Downtempo Remix); (Felix Da Housecat's Devin Dazzle Club Mix);
(Peter Rauhofer's American Anthem Part 1); (Peter Rauhofer's
American Anthem Part 2); "Die Another Day" (Richard Humpty
Vission Electrofried Mix)
"American Life" (Edit With Rap); "Die Another Day" (Calderone &
Quayle Afterlife Mix); "American Life" (Missy Elliott American Dream
Mix); (Oakenfold Downtempo Remix); (Peter Rauhofer's American
Anthem Part 1); (Felix Da Housecat's Devin Dazzle Club Mix); "Die
Another Day" (Calderone & Quayle Afterlife Mix); "American Life"
(Peter Rauhofer's American Anthem Part 2)
"American Life" (Missy Elliott American Dream Mix); (Oakenfold
Downtempo Remix); (Peter Rauhofer's American Anthem Part 1);
(Felix Da Housecat's Devin Dazzle Club Mix); "Die Another Day"
(Calderone & Quayle Afterlife Mix); "American Life" (Peter Rauhofer's
American Anthem Part 2)
"Hollywood" 1 (The Micronauts Remix); (Oakenfold Full Remix);
(Calderone & Quayle Glam Mix)
"Hollywood" 2 (Jacques Lu Cont's Thin White Duck Mix); (Oakenfold
12″ Dub); (Deepsky's Home Sweet Home Vocal Remix)

"Hollywood" 1 (The Micronauts Remix); "Hollywood" (Oakenfold Full Remix); (Calderone & Quayle Glam Mix)

"Hollywood" 2 (Jacques Lu Cont's Thin White Duck Mix); (Oakenfold 12″ Dub); (Deepsky's Home Sweet Home Vocal Remix)

"Hollywood" (Radio Edit); (Jacques Lu Cont's Thin White Duck Mix); (The Micronauts Remix); (Oakenfold Full Remix); (Deepsky's Home Sweet Home Vocal Remix); (Calderone & Quayle Glam Mix)

"Hollywood" (Radio Edit); (Jacques Lu Cont's Thin White Duck Mix); (The Micronauts Remix)

"Hollywood" (Radio Edit); (Oakenfold Full Remix); (Deepsky's Home Sweet Home Vocal Remix)

"Hollywood" (Radio Edit); (Jacques Lu Cont's Thin White Duck Mix); (Oakenfold Full Remix)

"Nothing Fails" (Peter Rauhofer's Classic House Mix) ; (Nevins Big Room Rock Mix): (Tracy Young's Underground Mix); (Nevins Global Dub); (Jackie's in Love in the Club Mix) ; (Peter Rauhofer's Private Life Mix Part 1); (Above & Beyond 12″ Mix);(Mount Sims Italo Kiss Mix)

"Nothing Fails" 1 (Peter Rauhofer's Classic House Mix) ; (Nevins Big Room Rock Mix); (Tracy Young's Underground Mix); (Jackie's in Love in the Club Mix)

"Nothing Fails" 2 (Nevins Global Dub); (Mount Sims Italo Kiss Mix); (Mount Sims Old School Mix); (Tracy Young's Underground Dub)

"Nothing Fails" (Peter Rauhofer's Classic House Mix); (Nevins Big Room Rock Mix); (Tracy Young's Underground Mix) ; (Nevins Global Dub); (Jackie's in Love in the Club Mix); (Peter Rauhofer's Private Life Mix Part 1); (Above & Beyond 12″ Mix); (Mount Sims Italo Kiss Mix)

"Love Profusion" (LP); (Ralphi Rosario House Vocal Mix); (Above & Beyond 12″ Mix)

"Love Profusion" (Blow-Up Mix); (The Passengerz Club Profusion); (Ralphi Rosario House Vocal) (Extended); (Craig J.'s Good Vibe Mix); (Ralphi Rosario Big Room Vox) (Extended); (Ralphi Rosario Big Room Dub); (Peter Rauhofer's Lost in Space Mix)

"Love Profusion" (Passengerz Club Mix); (Above & Beyond 12″ Mix)

"Love Profusion" 1 (The Passengerz Club Profusion); (Blow-Up Mix); (Ralphi Rosario House Vocal) (Extended); (Ralphi Rosario Big Room Dub) 8:57

"Love Profusion" 2 (The Passengerz Dub Profusion); (Craig J.'s "'Good Vibe'" Mix); (Ralphi Rosario Big Room Vox) (Extended)

"Love Profusion" (LP); "Nothing Fails" (Radio Edit); "Love Profusion" (Passengerz Club Mix)

(Hereafter all releases on Warner Bros. label)

2005
"Hung Up" (Radio Version) 3. (SDP Extended Vocal); (Tracy Young's Get Up and Dance Groove Edit); (Bill Hamel Remix); (Chus & Ceballos Remix); (SDP Extended Dub)
"Hung Up" (LP); (SDP Extended Vocal); (Bill Hamel Remix); (SDP Extended Dub); (Chus & Ceballos Remix); (Tracy Young's Get Up and Dance Groove)
"Hung Up" (Radio Version); (Tracy Young Get Up and Groove Edit)
"Hung Up" (Radio Version); (Tracy Young Get Up and Groove Edit); (SPD Extended Vocal)
"Hung Up" (SPD Extended Dub); (SPD Extended Vocal); (Tracy Young's Get Up and Dance Groove Mix)

2006
"Sorry" (Single Edit); (Man with Guitar Mix); (PSB Maxi-Mix); (Paul Oakenfold Remix); (Green Velvet Remix)
"Sorry" (Radio Version); "Let It Will Be" (Paper Faces Vocal Edit)
"Sorry" (Album Version); (PSB Maxi-Mix); (Paul Oakenfold Remix); (Green Velvet Remix)
"Sorry" (Single Edit); (Man with Guitar Edit); (PSB Maxi-Mix); (Paul Oakenfold Remix); (Green Velvet Remix) "Let It Will Be" (Paper Faces Vocal Edit)
"Sorry" 1 (Album Version); (Man with Guitar Mix); (PSB Maxi-Mix)
"Sorry" 2 (Paul Oakenfold Remix); (Green Velvet Remix); "Let It Will Be" (Paper Faces Mix)
"Sorry" 1 (Album Version); (Man with Guitar Mix); (PSB Maxi-Mix)
"Sorry" 2 (Paul Oakenfold Remix); (Green Velvet Remix); "Let It Will Be" (Paper Faces Mix)
"Sorry" (Single Edit); (Man with Guitar Edit); (PSB Maxi-Mix); (Paul Oakenfold Remix); (Green Velvet Remix); "Let It Will Be" (Paper Faces Vocal Edit)
"Sorry" (Single Edit); "Let It Will Be" (Paper Faces Mix); (Man with Guitar Mix)
Confessions Remixed: "Hung Up" (SDP's Extended Vocal); "Hung Up" (SDP's Extended Dub); "Sorry" (Man with Guitar Mix); "Get Together" (Jacques Lu Cont Mix); " I Love New York" (Thin White Duke Mix); "Let It Will Be" (Paper Faces Mix)
"Get Together" (Album Version); (Jacques Lu Cont Remix); (Danny Howells & Dick Trevor Kinky Funk Mix); (Tiefschwarz Remix); (James Holden Remix); (Thin White Duke Remix)

"Get Together" (Radio Edit); (Jacques Lu Cont Mix)

"Get Together" (Radio Edit); (Jacques Lu Cont Remix); (Tiefschwarz Remix)

"Get Together" 1 (LP); (Jacques Lu Cont Remix); (Danny Howells & Dick Trevor Kinky Funk Mix)

"Get Together" 2 (Tiefschwarz Remix); (James Holden Remix; "I Love New York" (Thin White Duke Remix)

"Get Together" (Radio Edit); (Jacques Lu Cont Vocal Edit)

"Get Together" (LP); (Jacques Lu Cont Remix); (Danny Howells & Dick Trevor Kinky Funk Mix); (Tiefschwarz Remix); (James Holden Remix)

"Get Together" (LP); (Jacques Lu Cont Remix); (Danny Howells & Dick Trevor Kinky Funk Mix); (Tiefschwarz Remix); (James Holden Remix) "I Love New York" (Thin White Duke Remix)

"Jump" (Single Edit);(Junior Sanchez's Misshapes Mix)

"History" (Unreleased B Side)

"Jump" (LP); (Extended LP Version)

"Jump" (Jacques Lu Cont Mix); (Extended Album Version);

"History" (Unreleased B Side)

"Jump" (Radio Edit);(Jacques Lu Cont Mix) ;(Axwell Remix); (Junior Sanchez's Misshapes Mix); (Extended LP Version); "History" (Non-album track)

"Jump" 1 (Jacques Lu Cont Mix); (LP); (Extended LP Version); (Axwell Remix

"Jump" 2 (Junior Sanchez's Misshapes Mix); "History" (Unreleased B Side); (Radio Edit)

Albums

(VINYL, CASSETTE AND CD)

1983

Madonna: "Lucky Star" "Borderline" "Burning Up," "I Know It," "Holiday," "Think of Me," "Physical Attraction," "Everybody" (Remastered with bonus tracks, 2001)

1984

Like a Virgin: "Material Girl," "Angel," "Like a Virgin," "Over and Over," "Love Don't Live Here Anymore," "Dress You Up," "Shoo-Bee-Doo," "Pretender," "Stay" (UK version included "Into the Groove') (Remastered with bonus tracks, 2001)

Revenge of the Killer B's: "Ain't No Big Deal" (Warner Bros., one Madonna track)

1985
Vision Quest (Soundtrack): "Crazy for You," "Gambler" (Geffen, two
Madonna tracks)

1986
True Blue: "Papa Don't Preach," "Open Your Heart," "White Heat," "Live
to Tell," "Where's the Party," "True Blue," "La Isla Bonita," "Jimmy
Jimmy," "Love Makes the World Go Round" (Remastered with bonus
tracks, 2001)

1987
Who's That Girl (Soundtrack): "Who's That Girl," "Causing a Commotion,"
"The Look of Love," "24 Hours" (Duncan Faure), "Step by Step" (Club
Nouveau), "Turn It Up" (Michael Davidson), "Best Thing Ever" Scritti
Politti), "Can't Stop," "El Coco Loco" (Coati Mundi) *(Madonna chose
soundtrack and perfomed four songs. The rest are by other artists)*
You Can Dance. "Spotlight," "Holiday," "Everybody," "Physical Attraction,"
"Over and Over," "Into the Groove," "Where's the Party" (Cassette and
8-track included bonus dubs of "Spotlight," "Holiday," "Over and Over
and "Into the Groove." CD released without "Spotlight," but included
the dub versions, plus "Where's the Party")
A Very Special Christmas: "Santa Baby" (A&M, one Madonna track)

1989
Like a Prayer: "Like a Prayer," "Express Yourself," "Love Song," "Till Death
Do Us Part," "Promise to Try," "Cherish," "Dear Jessie," "Oh Father,"
"Keep It Together," "Spanish Eyes," "Act of Contrition"
The Early Years: "Wild Dancing (Ext.), "Time to Dance" (Ext.), "On the
Street," "We Are the Gods," "Cosmic Climb," "Time to Dance," "Cosmic
Climb" (Ext.), "On the Street" (Ext.), "Wild Dancing," "Time to Dance"
(Instr.) (U.K. release)
Best of & Rest of Madonna Vol. 1 (UK CD, five tracks from *The Early Years*, plus
interview)
Best of & the Rest of Madonna Vol. 2 (UK CD, ten tracks from *The Early Years*)

1990
The Immaculate Collection: "Holiday," "Lucky Star," "Borderline," "Like a
Virgin," "Material Girl," "Crazy for You," "Into the Groove," "Live to
Tell," "Papa Don't Preach," "Open Your Heart," "La Isla Bonita," "Like
a Prayer," "Express Yourself," "Cherish," "Vogue," "Justify My Love,"
"Rescue Me" (Also released as *The Royal Box* with either cassette or CD

of the album, plus *The Immaculate Collection* video, eight postcards, and a poster).

I'm Breathless: Songs from and Inspired by the Film *Dick Tracy:* "He's a Man," "Sooner or Later," "Hanky Panky," "I'm Going Bananas," "Cry Baby," "Something to Remember," "Back in Business," "More," "What Can You Lose," "Now I'm Following You, Part I," "Now I'm Following You, Part II," "Vogue"

1991

The Immaculate Conversation (U.K. interview) (cassette album only)

Dangerous, by Michael Jackson: "In the Closet" (one track with Madonna as Mystery Girl)

1992

Erotica: "Erotica," "Deeper and Deeper," "Where Life Begins," "Bad Girl," "Waiting," "Thief of Hearts," "Words," "Rain," "Why's It So Hard," "In This Life," "Did You Do It?," "Secret Garden" (Two versions released, the *Clean Version* without "Did You Do It?')

Barcelona Gold: "This Used to Be My Playground" (one Madonna track)

1994

With Honors (Soundtrack): "I'll Remember" (Maverick, one Madonna track)

Just Say Roe: "Goodbye to Innocence" (Sire, one Madonna track)

1995

Bedtime Stories: "Survival," "Secret," "I'd Rather Be Your Lover," "Don't Stop," "Inside of Me," "Human Nature," "Forbidden Love," "Love Tried to Welcome Me," "Sanctuary," "Bedtime Story," "Take a Bow"

Something to Remember: "I Want You," "I'll Remember," "Take a Bow," "You'll See," "Crazy for You," "This Used to Be My Playground," "Live to Tell," "Love Don't Live Here Anymore," "Something to Remember," "Forbidden Love," "One More Chance," "Rain," "Oh Father," "I Want You" (Orchestral)

Inner City Blues: The Music of Marvin Gaye: "I Want You" (Motown, one Madonna track)

1996

Evita—Highlights: "Requiem for Evita," "Oh What a Circus," "On This Night of a Thousand Stars," "Eva and Magaldi/ Eva Beware of the City," "Buenos Aires," "Another Suitcase in Another Hall," "Goodnight and Thank You," "I'd Be Surprisingly Good for You," "Peron's Latest Flame," "A New Argentina," "Don't Cry for Me Argentina," "High

Flying, Adored," "Rainbow High," "And the Money Kept Rolling (In and Out)," "She Is a Diamond," "Waltz for Eva and Che," "You Must Love Me," "Eva's Final Broadcast," "Lament"

1997
Carnival (Rainforest Foundation Concert): "Freedom" (Victor, one Madonna track)

1998
Ray of Light: "Drowned World/Substitute for Love," "Swim," "Ray of Light," "Candy Perfume Girl," "Skin," "Nothing Really Matters," "Sky Fits Heaven," "Shanti/Ashtangi," "Frozen," "The Power of Goodbye," "To Have and Not To Hold," "Little Star," "Mer Girl" (Won 1999 Grammy Award for Best Pop Album.)

1999
Austin Powers 2: The Spy Who Shagged Me: "Beautiful Stranger" (Soundtrack, one Madonna track. She plays Seductress on the video only.)

2000
Music: "Music," "Impressive Instant," "Runaway Lover," "I Deserve It," "Amazing," "Nobody's Perfect," "Don't Tell Me," "What It Feels Like for a Girl," "Paradise (Not for Me)," "Gone" (Won 2001 Grammy Award for Best Recording Package. CD has bonus track "American Pie.")

2001
The Early Years: Give It to Me: "Give It to Me," "Shake," "Get Down," "Time to Dance," "Wild Dancing," "Let's Go Dancing," "We Are the Gods," "Cosmic Climb," "On the Street," "Oh My!"

GHV2 (Greatest Hits Volume Two): "Deeper and Deeper," "Erotica," "Human Nature," "Secret," "Don't Cry for Me Argentina," "Bedtime Story," "The Power of Goodbye," "Beautiful Stranger," "Frozen," "Take a Bow," "Ray of Light," "Don't Tell Me," "What It Feels Like for a Girl," "Drowned World (Substitute for Love)," "Music"

2003
American Life: "American Life," "Hollywood," "I'm So Stupid," "Love Profusion," "Nobody Knows Me," "Nothing Fails," "Intervention," "X-Static Process," "Mother and Father," "Die Another Day" (From the MGM Motion Picture *Die Another Day*), "Easy Ride"

Remixed and Revisited EP: "Nothing Fails" (Nevins Mix), "Love Profusion"

(Headcleaner Rock Mix), "Nobody Knows Me" (Mount Sims Old School Mix), "American Life" (Headcleaner Rock Mix), "Like a Virgin/Hollywood Medley" feat. Christina Aguilera, Britney Spears, and Missy Elliott (2003 MTV VMA Performance), "Into the Hollywood Groove" feat. Missy Elliott (The Passenger Mix), "Your Honesty" (Unreleased Song)
(Hereafter all releases on Warner Bros. label)

2005
Confessions On a Dance Floor: "Hung Up," "Get Together," "Sorry," "Future Lovers," "I Love New York," "Let It Will Be," "Forbidden Love," "Jump," "How High, "Isaac," "Push," "Like It Or Not"

Music Videos

1982 "Everybody" (director (dir.) Ed Steinberg)
1983 "Burning Up" (dir. Steve Barron)
1984 "Borderline" (dir. Mary Lambert)
1984 "Holiday" No. 1 (unknown director, low budget. Not released)
1984 "Lucky Star" No. 1 (dir. Arthur Pierson)
1984 "Like a Virgin" (dir. Mary Lambert)
1985 "Like a Virgin" (MTV Video Music Awards)
1984 "Lucky Star" No. 2 (dir. Arthur Pierson, extended version)
1985 "Material Girl" (dir. Mary Lambert)
1985 "Crazy for You" (dir. Harold Becker)
1985 "Into the Groove" (dir. Susan Seidelman, from *You Can Dance,* made with clips from *Desperately Seeking Susan*)
1985 "Dress You Up" No. 1 (dir. Danny Kleinman, from *Like a Virgin*)
1985 "Dress You Up" No. 2 (dir. Danny Kleinman, extended version from *Like a Virgin*)
1985 "Gambler" No. 1 (dir. Harold Becker)
1985 "Gambler" (*The Virgin Tour Live*)
1985 "Like a Virgin" (*The Virgin Tour Live*)
1985 Over and Over (*The Virgin Tour Live*)
1986 "Live to Tell" (dir. James Foley, includes clips from *At Close Range*)
1986 "Papa Don't Preach" (dir. James Foley)
1986 "True Blue" (dir. James Foley)
1986 "Open Your Heart" (dir. Jean-Baptiste Mondino)
1987 "La Isla Bonita" (dir. Mary Lambert)
1987 "The Look of Love" (dir. James Foley, made with clips from *Who's That Girl?*)
1987 "Causing a Commotion" (MTV Video Music Awards)

1988 "Into the Groove" (*Ciao Italia—Live,* promo for the commercial video)

1989 "Like a Prayer" (dir. Mary Lambert)

1989 "Make a Wish" (Pepsi commercial, broadcast March 2)

1989 "Express Yourself" (MTV Video Music Awards)

1989 "Cherish" (dir. Herb Ritts)

1989 "Express Yourself" (dir. David Fincher)

1989 "Oh Father" (dir. David Fincher)

1989 "Dear Jessie" (unknown director, animations only, released outside USA)

1989 "Papa Don't Preach" (Warner, laser disc only)

1990 "Vogue" (dir. David Fincher)

1990 "Vogue" (MTV Video Music Awards)

1990 "Vote!" (commercial for "Rock the Vote" campaign, broadcast October 22 to November 6)

1990 "Justify My Love" (dir. Jean-Baptiste Mondino. Sold as first-ever video single)

1991 "Like a Virgin" (dir. Alek Keshishian, made with clips from *Truth or Dare*)

1991 "Holiday" No. 2 (dir. Alek Keshishian, made with clips from *Truth or Dare*)

1992 "This Used to Be My Playground" (dir. Alek Keshishian, including clips from *A League of Their Own*)

1992 "Erotica" (dir. Fabien Baron)

1992 "Deeper and Deeper" (dir. Bobby Woods)

1993 "Bad Girl" (dir. David Fincher)

1993 "Fever" (dir. Stephan Sednaoui)

1993 "Rain" (dir. Mark Romanek)

1993 "Bye Bye Baby" (*Live From the Girlie Show Tour,* Australia only)

1994 "I'll Remember" (dir. Alek Keshishian, including clips from *With Honors*)

1994 "Secret" (dir. Melodie McDaniel)

1994 "Take a Bow" (dir. Michael Haussman)

1995 "Bedtime Story" (dir. Mark Romanek)

1995 "Human Nature" (dir. Jean-Baptiste Mondino)

1995 "I Want You" (dir. Earle Sebastian, from *Inner City Blues: the Music of Marvin Gaye*)

1996 "Love Don't Live Here Anymore" (dir. Jean-Baptiste Mondino)

1996 "You Must Love Me" (dir. Alan Parker, including clips from *Evita*)

1996 "Don't Cry for Me Argentina" (dir. Alan Parker, including clips from *Evita*)

1997 "Another Suitcase in Another Hall" (dir. Alan Parker, including clips from *Evita*, not released in USA)

1997 "Buenos Aires" (including clips from *Evita*)

1998 "Frozen" (dir. Chris Cunningham)

1998 "Ray of Light" (dir. Jonas Akerlund, won 1999 Grammy Award for Best Short Form Music Video)

1998 "Drowned World/Substitute For Love" (dir. Walter Stern, not released in USA)

1998 "The Power of Goodbye" (dir. Matthew Rolston)

1999 "Nothing Really Mattters" (dir. Johan Renck)

1999 "Beautiful Stranger" (dir. Brett Ratner, including clips from *Austin Powers 2: The Spy Who Shagged Me*)

2000 "American Pie" (dir. Philip Stolzol, including clips from *The Next Best Thing*)

2000 "Music" (dir. Jonas Akerlund)

2000 "Don't Tell Me" (dir. Jean-Baptiste Mondino, also released in the U.S. as enhanced CD single in January 2001)

2001 "What It Feels Like for a Girl" (dir. Guy Ritchie. Video banned for excessive violence)

2001 "Paradise" (dir. Dago Gonzalez, filmed exclusively for the Drowned World Tour)

2001 "GHV2 Megamix" (dir. various, promo for *GHV2* album)

2001 "Holiday Live" (dir. Hamish Hamilton, live from Drowned World Tour)

2002 "Die Another Day" (dir. Traktor, including clips from *Die Another Day*)

2003 "American Life" (dir. Jonas Akerlund)

2003 "Hollywood" (dir. Jean-Baptiste Mondino, remix video by Dustin Robertson)

2003 "Me Against the Music" (dir. Paul Hunter. Britney Spears, featuring Madonna)

2004 "Love Profusion" (dir. Luc Besson)

2005 "Hung Up" (dir. Johan Renck)

2006 "Sorry" (dir. Jamie King)

2006 "Get Together" (dir. Logan, animation company)

2006 "Jump" (dir. Jonas Akerlund)

World Tours

1985 *The Virgin Tour* (tour director: Brad Jeffries, musical director [MD]: Patrick Leonard)

1987 *Who's That Girl? World Tour* (tour director: Jeffrey Hornaday, MD: Patrick Leonard, choreography: Shabba Doo)

1990 *Blond Ambition World Tour* (tour director: Madonna, MD: Jai Winding, choreography: Vincent Patterson)

1993 *The Girlie Show World Tour* (artistic director: Christopher Ciccone, MD: Jai Winding, choreography: Alex Magno, Keith Young)

2001 *Drowned World Tour* (tour director: Jamie King, MD: Stuart Price, choreography: Jamie King, Alex Magno)

2004 *Re-Invention World Tour* (tour director: Jamie King, MD: Stuart Price, choreography: Jamie King, Talauega Brothers, Liz Imperio)

2006 *Confessions World Tour* (tour director: Jamie King, MD: Stuart Price, choreography: Jamie King)

Films

1972 (untitled) short Super-8 film project starring Madonna, Carol Belanger, and a fried egg (dir. Wyn Cooper)

1980 *A Certain Sacrifice* (dir. Stephen Jon Lewicki, 60 mins. Madonna plays Bruna)

1983 *Vision Quest* aka *Crazy for You* (dir. Harold Becker, 105 mins. Plays cameo)

1985 *Desperately Seeking Susan* (dir. Susan Seidelman, 104 mins. Plays Susan)

1986 *Shanghai Surprise* (dir. Jim Goddard, 90 mins. Plays Gloria Tatlock)

1987 *Who's That Girl?* (dir. James Foley, 92 mins. Plays Nikki Finn)

1988 *Bloodhounds of Broadway* (dir. Howard Brookner, 93 mins. Plays Hortense)

1990 *Dick Tracy* (dir. Warren Beatty, 103 mins. Plays Breathless Mahoney)

1991 *Truth or Dare*/(outside USA) *In Bed with Madonna* (dir. Alek Keshishian, 119 mins)

1992 *A League of Their Own* (dir. Penny Marshall, 128 mins. Plays Mae "All-the-Way-Mae" Mordabito)

1992 *Shadows and Fog* (dir. Woody Allen, 86 mins. Plays Marie, the Strongman's wife)

1993 *Body of Evidence* (dir. Ulrich Edel, 101 mins. Plays Rebecca Carlson)

1993 *Dangerous Game* (dir. Abel Ferrara, 108 mins. Plays Sarah Jennings)

1995 *Blue in the Face* (dir. Paul Auster; Wayne Wang, 89 mins. Plays a Singing Telegram)

1995 *Four Rooms* (dir. Allison Anders; Alexandre Rockwell, 98 mins. Plays Elspeth in *The Missing Ingredient*)

1996 *Evita* (dir. Alan Parker, 134 mins. Plays Eva Peron)

1996 *Girl 6* (dir. Spike Lee, 108 mins. Plays Boss No. 3)

2000 *The Next Best Thing* (dir. John Sclesinger, 108 mins. Plays Abbie Reynolds)

2002 *Swept Away* (dir. Guy Ritchie, 86 mins. Plays Amber Leighton)

2002 *Die Another Day* (dir. Lee Tamahori, 133 mins. Plays Vanity, the fencing instructor)

2005 *I'm Going to Tell You a Secret* (dir. Jonas Akerlund)

2007 *Arthur and the Invisibles* (dir. Luc Besson, 103 mins. Voice of Princess Selenia)

Tour Films and Video Collections

1984 *Madonna* (dir. Steve Baron; Mary Lambert, video, 17 mins)

1985 *The Virgin Tour—Live* (dir. Danny Kleinman, 50 mins)

1987 *Who's that Girl—Live in Japan* (dir. Mitchell Sinoway, 92 mins)

1988 *Ciao Italia—Live from Italy* (dir. Egbert van Hees, 100 mins)

1990 *Blond Ambition World Tour Live* (dir. David Mallet, 112 mins)

1990 *Blond Ambition—Japan Tour 90* (dir. Mark Aldo Miceli, 105 mins)

1990 *The Immaculate Collection* (dir. various, 60 mins)

1993 *The Girlie Show—Live Down Under* (dir. Mark Aldo Miceli, 118 mins)

1999 *Madonna: The Video Collection 93–99* (dir. various, 67 mins)

2001 *Drowned World Tour 2001* (dir. Hamish Hamilton, 105 mins)

2007 *The Confessions Tour—Live from London* (CD and DVD) (dir. Jonas Akerlund, 121 mins)

Theater

1987 *Goose and Tom-Tom* by David Rabe. Lincoln Center Theater workshop. Played Lorrai.

1988 *Speed-the-Plow* by David Mamet. Produced by the Lincoln Center Theatre at the Royale Theater, Broadway. Played Karen.

2002 *Up For Grabs* by David Williamson, Wyndam's Theatre, London. Played Loren.

Books

1992 *Sex* (Warner Books/Calloway)

1994 *The Girlie Show* (Calloway)

1996 *The Making of Evita*, by Alan Parker, with foreword by Madonna (HarperCollins)

2003 *X-STaTIC Pro=CeSS* (Photographs by Steven Klein, limited edition art book, handbound and printed in Italy)

2004 *Nobody Knows Me* (rare photographs commented on by "an Icon and her angels," publication for one month only via the official website madonna.com)

2003 *The English Roses* (Illustrations [Illus.] Jeffrey Fulvimari. Puffin)

2003 *Mr Peabody's Apples* (Illus. Loren Long. Puffin)

2004 *Yakov and the Seven Thieves* (Illus. Gennady Spirin. Puffin)

2004 *The Adventures of Abdi* (Illus. Andrej Dugin. Puffin)

2005 *Lotsa De Casha* (Illus. Rui Paes. Puffin)

2006 *The English Roses—Too Good to Be True* (Illus. Stacy Peterson. Puffin)

Index

INDEX 389